Palgrave Studies in Chinese Management

Aim of the series

Palgrave Studies in Chinese Management series is a showcase for in-depth research into Chinese management providing systematic knowledge on the fast growing Chinese economy and enterprises from the management perspective. Research efforts such as this are already forging ahead and have led to the creation of a scholarly community: the International Association for Chinese Management Research (IACMR). The series draws on the research and knowledge being created by this international community, seeking to address an audience of academics and practitioners interested in Chinese management. The series provides a platform for Chinese management researchers to exchange ideas and research; it will enable collaboration between management researchers in and outside of China; and push forward the development of management research in and about China. The purpose of this book series is not only to provide information on doing business in China, but also to create systematic knowledge on Chinese management, both on Chinese management of theory and on Chinese theory of management. It will cover reflective thoughts, theoretical contribution and empirical evidence becoming a reference point for systematic knowledge on Chinese management.

More information about this series at
http://www.springer.com/series/14646

Anne S. Tsui • Yingying Zhang • Xiao-Ping Chen

Leadership of Chinese Private Enterprises

Insights and Interviews

Anne S. Tsui
University of Notre Dame
Notre Dame, Indiana, USA
Peking University and Fudan University
China

Yingying Zhang
CUNEF
Madrid, Spain

Xiao-Ping Chen
University of Washington
Seattle, Washington, USA

Palgrave Studies in Chinese Management
ISBN 978-1-137-40233-2   ISBN 978-1-137-40235-6   (eBook)
DOI 10.1057/978-1-137-40235-6

Library of Congress Control Number: 2016947433

Cover illustration: © Xiao-Ping Chen

Printed on acid-free paper

This Palgrave Macmillan imprint is published by Springer Nature
The registered company is Macmillan Publishers Ltd.
The registered company address is: The Campus, 4 Crinan Street, London, N1 9XW, United Kingdom

To Amelia, my daughter, a young woman of compassion and joy
— Anne S. Tsui
To Meier, my grandma, a spiritual leader of the whole family
— Yingying Zhang
To Yang, my soulmate, and to Rebecca and Erica, my life inspirations
— Xiao-Ping Chen

Preface

Curiosity regarding the causes of China's economic miracle between 1980 and 2014 and predictions about China's economic future have remained strong. It is not only because China is now the largest economy in the world, but also because it has been experiencing tremendous fluctuations in recent years. A close examination of the Chinese economy indicates that its strength comes from its private sector, which contributes more than 60% to the GDP and provides 70% of employment. In a country that has adopted the ideology of socialism and conducts economic reform in the name of socialism, the rise of such a strong private economy was once unimaginable and is still unbelievable to many, including the Chinese people themselves.

Many efforts have been made to account for such a remarkable economic achievement, especially on tracing the developmental journey of the private sector, relative to that of the state and foreign sectors. However, much less systematic knowledge is available about the people who founded and led the successful private firms. In this book, we advocate Chandler's (1978) view and suggest that it is the 'visible hands' of Chinese entrepreneurs that have replaced the 'invisible hand' of market forces; that is, the success of the private sector in China is not a result of the forces of the 'free market'—because the market was neither truly free nor fair to private entrepreneurs. We also agree with Nee and Opper's (2012) judgement that the China economic miracle was caused by 'capitalism from below' rather than by 'top down design' or governmental vision and guidance. A brief review of the evolution of Chinese private business indicates that entrepreneurs have suffered from disrespect, hardship and unfair policies from the government. But they have worked hard, struggled and stuck together, co-operated with one another, built networks for financial and social support, and created norms that were able to go under the radar and sustain their businesses. Only after their success, and with their substantial contribution to the economy, were they afforded legitimacy and reluctantly admitted as an integral part of the Chinese economy. Therefore, during the entire process, 'the entrepreneur was the central agent who drives the institutional innovations that give rise to the private enterprise economy' (Nee and Opper 2012: 106).

The narratives and data presented in this book provide a micro-level, vividly detailed picture of these 'central agents' who were China's first generation of company founders, and whose life journeys corresponded to some degree to the rough steps taken by the Chinese economy itself in its climb to the top of the world economy. We have identified 13 founder/entrepreneurs in four different industries and who are widely recognized as their industry's leaders. They include three in the financial services industry: Xinjun Liang, co-founder of the Fosun Group, Dongsheng Chen, founder of Taikang Life, and Weihua Ma, former CEO of China Merchants Bank; four in the information technology and e-commerce industry: Jiren Liu, founder of NeuSoft, Chuanzhi Liu, founder of Lenovo, Fansheng Guo, founder of HC360, and Jack Ma, co-founder of Alibaba; three in the real estate industry: Lun Feng, co-founder of Vantone, Shi Wang, founder of Vanke, and Shengzhe Nie, founder of Tecsun; and three in the consumer goods and retail industry: Qinghou Zong, founder of Wahaha, Ning Li, founder of Li-Ning Sports, and Jianguo Wang, founder of Five Star Holdings and Kidswant. Their stories are told in the entrepreneurs' own words and style. Each story is different and is fascinating in its own way. Through in-depth narrative analyses, we have identified distinguishing personal characteristics of these leaders, their management thoughts and leadership practices. We further have discovered some themes that are common across industries, some that are shared only by certain industries, and even some unique to individual companies. These leadership attributes and practices might set them apart from less successful entrepreneurs. We offer a concentric model of private firm leadership integrating the themes derived from the narratives of the 13 exemplary leaders.

At the core of this concentric model is *reflective thinking*, an ability to step back and engage in critical thinking by analysing and making judgements about what has happened and what has been learned. In a business environment full of legal, political, social and market uncertainty, an ability constantly to reflect, learn and adjust is of crucial importance for creativity and innovation, and essential for survival. Then there are the four **D**s: Determination—perseverance and commitment; Discipline—consistency and principle; Duality-focus—focus on balancing the short and long term, modernity and traditionality, self and other interests; and Divinity belief—belief in the role of both human agency and divine power. These attributes allowed the entrepreneurs to develop strategies balancing the interests of multiple stakeholders (customers, employees, suppliers, society), to focus on both short-term returns and the long-term development of the firm, to lead with modern methods guided by traditional cultural philosophies, and to maintain humility and integrity while acting with determination, boldness and discipline. The four Ds manifest themselves in eight management principles that guide the entrepreneurs' actual leadership practices: (1) holding on to moral and ethical principles and (2) engaging in humanistic management; focusing on both (3) market development and (4) business sustainability; (5) pursing innovation and (6) constant transformation; building (7) organizational capability and (8) a dual system that consists of structure and culture, accountability and flexibility, and empowerment and control.

The story of these central agents is told in 16 chapters. Chapter 1 provides a brief historical overview of the evolution process of private business in China after the People's Republic of China (PRC) was established in 1949. Chapter 2 provides an analysis of the studies about private firm (CEO) leadership by chief executive officers (CEOs) gleaned from published academic papers since 2000. Chapters 3 to 15 offer the original interview texts with each of the 13 entrepreneur CEOs, complemented by descriptions of their backgrounds and our summary comments. Finally, in Chap. 16 we offer our analysis of the 13 interviews and present the concentric model of Chinese private firm leadership. We hope this framework will offer a unique insight into the distinctive characteristics of Chinese private firms' business leadership that has contributed to the overall economic growth of China since 1980. We also hope that this book will shed light on the future of Chinese economic development in general as well as on Chinese management.

The book is intended for those who wish to understand the growth of the Chinese economy and the role of private entrepreneurship in this growth. We hope the book could provide a resource for business students studying the Chinese private economy and Chinese leadership. We also invite scholars interested in China to further explore and solve the puzzle of the rising dominance of the private sector despite the unfavourable institutional environment that continues to be a major source of uncertainty for private enterprises. Critics might take issue with the one-sided focus of our study, and suggest that we are painting a rosy picture of the private sector and its leaders. We acknowledge that the private sector is largely, though not solely, responsible for damage to the physical environment and for fuelling increasing income inequality in China. The rich are becoming immensely richer and the poor are holding steady, but the quality of life of the middle class is declining because wages are not keeping up with the rising cost of living in China. A change to the economic development model in 2016, as President Xi stated to clarify the drop in gross domestic product (GDP) growth, is intended to correct the course of the Chinese economic phenomenon. Changing from a sole focus on economic development to a more balanced social economic development with innovation and at this turning point in both the Chinese economy and in management, synthesizing the wisdom of the exemplary leaders is a necessity for the leaders of the next generation. As we can see from the interviews and analysis in this book, the exemplary leaders have been linking firm performance with societal needs and responding to collective well-being, rather than treating enterprises solely as money-making machines. China remains a massive, complex and extremely intricate intellectual puzzle that offers an interesting and important opportunity for research and analysis by social scientists. We hope our book is the aperitif to an intellectual feast.

Anne S. Tsui
Yingying Zhang
Xiao-Ping Chen

Acknowledgements

Many people have contributed to the idea and the execution of the project that resulted in this book. We must first thank the 13 leaders who contributed their time and were unreserved in sharing their stories with the interviewers. Second, we thank the interviewers, who were well prepared and conducted the interviews in a professional, thoughtful and skilful manner. We thank the Guanghua Leadership Institute at Peking University, Beijing, for providing the funding for this project. We thank Eve Yan Li for her assistance in co-ordinating the interviews, and editing both the Chinese and English versions of the interview texts in the first round. We thank Zhang Chen, who assisted in translating some interview texts. The early versions of these interviews were shared with members of the International Association for Chinese Management Research (IACMR) through the online Chinese Management Insight platform. We thank IACMR for supporting us in polishing the interviews for this book. We also thank Xuhong Li, Athena Du and Tian Mu for the data collection for Chap. 1; and Wenjie Ma, Tian Mu and Amy Xia, who assisted with the content analysis in Chap. 16. We are grateful to Professors Chao Chen, John Child and Victor Nee for giving us valuable feedback on the chapter contents, and offering important suggestions to improve our ideas. We thank Liz Barlow and Maddi Holder of Palgrave for their guidance during the preparation of the book and their understanding when we had to postpone the delivery date. We acknowledge the financial support of research grants from the Guanghua Leadership Institute at Peking University and the Chinese Natural Science Foundation (grant # 71032001). Finally, we thank our families for their support and patience throughout the years of this project. To everyone involved, we express our deepest gratitude.

Table of Contents

List of Figures

List of Tables

Part I

Entrepreneurship in the Turbulent
Sea of Chinese Economic Reform

1

Chinese Private Enterprises: Evolution and Challenges for Leadership

According to the IMF World Economic Outlook database, in 2014 China became the largest economy in the world, with a gross domestic product (GDP) of US$18.088 trillion (16.6 % of the world total), based on purchasing power parity (PPP) valuation, surpassing the USA (US$17.348 trillion; 15.9 % of the world total) (IMF 2015). It is an average GDP (PPP) per capita of $13,224, a growth of 42,764 % from 1980, the beginning of its economic reform period, when GDP (PPP) was US$309 per capita (IMF 2015). The estimated calculation of IMF data put China in the top position in 2015 in terms of PPP.

This rate of economic growth is truly remarkable. China's ability to sustain a consistent growth in GDP of approximately 10 % per annum since the mid-1990s is considered an economic miracle (BBC News China 2012) that has impressed economic experts while earning the

We would like to express our gratitude to Athena Du, Xuhong Li and Mu Tian for their assistance in statistics data collection.

The data listed in the chapter needs to be compared cautiously if they are from different sources. Different definitions are used in the data collection processes by different statistics groups.

© The Author(s) 2017
A.S. Tsui et al., *Leadership of Chinese Private Enterprises*, Palgrave Studies in Chinese Management, DOI 10.1057/978-1-137-40235-6_1

envy of political leaders around the world. However, recently economic development has slowed and GDP growth for China in 2016 is estimated at less than 7 %. China has attracted a great deal of both scholarly and public attention for a long time (Coase and Wang 2012; Huang 2008; Lardy 2014; Nee and Opper 2012; Tsui et al. 2004; Tsui et al. 2006). Researchers and practitioners alike have demonstrated a strong interest in understanding how China has been able to gain this international economic leadership in such a short period of time. Even though the recent slowdown of Chinese GDP growth is a worry to many people, it is considered by some as a change in the economic development model of China from manufacturing and export to domestic consumption, therefore yielding better-quality GDP growth (Wong 2016). Some have also speculated the end of this 'miracle' (e.g. Powell 2014), but the question of how this 'dragon' (Economist 2001; Guthrie 1999; Zeng and Williamson 2003) has managed to achieve this incredible feat since the 1980s, defying all economic logic and prediction, is still fascinating and worthy of being explored.

The most fascinating part of China's economic growth is that it is a story of two paths (Coase and Wang 2012; Lardy 2014; Huang 2008). The first is a path of top-down, centrally managed capitalism (Lin 2011), which gave disproportional advantage to state-owned and foreign-owned firms. The second is a path of bottom-up, decentralised grass-roots capitalism (Nee and Opper 2012) and this path accounts for the phenomenal success of private entrepreneurship. A capitalism with Chinese characteristics grew out of socialism, and the Chinese government carried out market reforms in the name of socialism (Coase and Wang 2012). At the beginning of the economic reform, the government approached private entrepreneurs as a way of solving unemployment issues and of addressing poor economic performance, but with no policy in place to support its development. Compared to the state-owned and foreign firms, private firms actually faced a hostile environment on multiple fronts because they were not provided with formal channels to access bank loans or a policy to support their development (Ahlstrom and Bruton 2001; Tsui et al. 2006; S.E.A. 2014). However, against all odds, possibly through a combination of the ingenuity of the entrepreneurs and a tremendously hungry market where almost everything produced was gobbled up, both domestically and globally, private entrepreneurship gained an unstoppable momentum. By the mid-1990s, some 15 years after embarking on economic reform, it became clear that the private sector was the major engine of economic growth for China. Then the government began to recognise the potential value of the private sector to the overall economic growth of China. By the early 2000s, with China's entry to the World Trade Organization, Chinese private firms also began to 'go out,' in part an escape to the more friendly business terrains outside China (Boisot and Meyer 2008). Through the ups and downs of three-and-a-half decades of economic transformation, step by step the private economy and privately-owned firms have gained legal and social legitimacy (Ahlstrom and Bruton 2001) and are playing an important role in the economic success of both the emerging economy of China and its globalisation (Coase and Wang 2012; Lardy 2014).

In this introductory chapter we describe the evolution of Chinese private enterprises in the Chinese economic development and transformation, and the principal challenges that such enterprises have faced in their developmental journey. In explaining the growth of modern industrial enterprises in the USA in the early 1900s, Chandler (1978) concluded that, in many sectors of the economy, the visible hand of management replaced the invisible hand of market forces. A similar developmental journey has occurred in China: 'No nation has had sustainable economic growth absent sustainable firms and managers guiding those firms' (Tsui et al. 2004: 133). The success of the private sector is not caused by the forces of the 'free market'—because the market was not truly free or fair to private entrepreneurs, as we shall show later. It is the 'visible hands' of the Chinese entrepreneurs who have contributed to the development of a vibrant private economy through their hard work, co-operation and competition, network building, business norm shaping and constant innovation. During this process, 'the entrepreneur is the central agent who drives the institutional innovations that give rise to the private enterprise economy' (Nee and Opper 2012: 106).

This book is devoted to understanding the success of private firms through a study of their leaders—those entrepreneurs who decided to 'jump into the sea' (*xiahai* 下海) because of their perception and confidence that their success would be greater by manoeuvring in the hostile situation of the open, turbulent sea rather than by being stuck in an equally, if not more, difficult political landscape (i.e. working in state-owned enterprises or government agencies), where individual competence is less important for career success than social relationships or political behaviours. We provide insight into the leadership of private firms through published scholarly research that has studied the leaders—some of them founders of entrepreneurial firms—and through in-depth original interviews with 13 extremely successful private entrepreneurs. We aim to understand the background, perspectives and leadership behaviours of those who founded and led these firms to success. The question guiding our analysis is this: What are the most distinctive features of these leaders who have managed and led the firms from inception to success? We have identified four distinct characteristics (4 **D**s): **D**etermination (perseverance, commitment); **D**iscipline (consistency, principle); **D**uality focus (focus on balancing short and long terms, modernity—traditionality, self—other interests), and a **D**ivinity belief (belief in the role of both human agency and a divine force, *tianrenheyi* 天人和一). These characteristics allow entrepreneurs to settle on strategies that balance the interests of multiple stakeholders (customers, employees, suppliers, society), to focus on both short-term returns and the long-term development of the firm, to lead with modern methods guided by traditional cultural philosophies, and to maintain humility and integrity while acting with determination, boldness and discipline. We derived these four Ds from a preliminary analysis of published research on Chinese private firm CEOs and further confirmed and expanded them through an in-depth analysis of the interview data obtained from the 13 exemplary Chinese private firm entrepreneurs.

Private Enterprises: Particularity in the Recent History of Modern China

While private enterprise is an almost taken-for-granted term in the market economy in the West, there are at least two related terms in the corresponding Chinese context: privately-run enterprises (*si ying qi ye*私营企业) and civilian-run enterprises (*min ying qi ye*民营企业). These terms are used almost interchangeably in the Chinese context, though differences exist. At the beginning of the economic reform period, private business was a sensitive term perceived to be connected to capitalism, in that words such as 'private' and 'capitalism' were contrary to the core ideology of Communism (which does not allow for private ownership of any property). To avoid potential conflict because of its political sensitivity, the term 'civilian-run enterprises' was introduced, differentiating them from state-run enterprises which were the dominant type of business enterprise in the planned economy at the beginning of the economic reform period. Clearly, private business is not a recent invention; it has existed in China for centuries and certainly was prevalent before the founding of the People's Republic of China (PRC) in Mainland China in 1949. 'National bourgeoisie capital' (*minzuziben* 民族资本), the term used to refer to these private businesses before 1949, was estimated to be about a third of the national economy with net assets of about 2.1 billion yuan[1] (currency value in 1952) (Sun 1989: 726). However, the domestic productivity of the private firms was essentially destroyed after a long period of war in China before the PRC was formed. One of the principal tasks at the beginning of the PRC was economic development with governmental encouragement to develop a civilian-run economy, given its importance in domestic economic recovery (Feng and He 2012; Wu 2009). By the end of 1949, private enterprises composed 48.7 % of the total GDP, with more than 123,000 private enterprises and 1.64 million employees (Cong and Zhang 1999).

During this existential period of transition, most of the private businesses were run by self-employed entrepreneurs, literally called Individual Industrial and Commercial Business Units (*getigongshanghu* 个体工商户, also commonly abbreviated as Individual Business *getihu* 个体户; see also Liu 2003). According to Feng and He (2012) and S.E.A. and Horizon (2014), the registered number of these self-employed businesses reached 5.4 million according to 1952 national statistical data, though that year was also a pivotal point for the decline of private business. The economic model of the PRC (hereafter we shall use the word 'China' to

---

[1] Yuan (CNY) is the currency of the PRC, also called renminbi (RMB). By the mid-market rate of 1USD = 6.16 CNY, 1 EUR = 7.57 CNY; www.xe.com, accessed 8 December 2014.

refer to the PRC) soon altered after 1952, when the central government took over control of the economy, and its principal ideology was to create a government-driven economic model. Influenced by the Russian economic system, China initiated a path to a unitary public ownership economic system with a centrally planned economy involving three reforms: transformation of private business to state and private-state joint ventures; socialistic reform of agriculture and craft industries; and the socialistic reform of capitalistic industry and commerce. This was essentially a process of nationalising all private assets.

A unitary public ownership economic system and planned public administration was largely completed around 1956. By 1965, private business only existed in sectors such as retailing, food and social services, with a reduction of registered numbers of businesses to 479,000 enterprises, only 9 % of the number registered in 1952. This decline continued, with only 178,000 private businesses surviving by 1978, just before the economic reform—the opening of the economy to non-state firms. Private business had a tense period under the centralised economic model from 1952 to 1978, a period of long-suffering transformation. Even at the beginning of the economic reform, the private economy and private firms were seemingly taboo topics until they were legitimised by the central government in several official documents in the ensuing years (Feng and He 2012; S.E.A. and Horizon 2014). During the transition, the preferred term for private business was civilian-run enterprises, a business mode that is neither state-run nor foreign-related. In this book, we use the term 'private,' because readers from outside China are more familiar with the term 'private' than the term 'civilian' in this context.

As economic reform progressed, three types of firms emerged in China, with each type having several subcategories. The state economy consisted of enterprises of both government-owned (state-owned enterprises—SOEs) and urban collectives, and the ownership of these firms is the government at central, provincial, city and township levels. The collectives are generally smaller units. Both SOEs and collectives belonged to the 'public sector.' The second type, the foreign economy, are foreign-owned enterprises (FOEs), which consist of investments in China by companies from Hong Kong, Macau and Taiwan, and all other nations such as the USA, Japan and European countries as another group. Though Hong Kong and Macau are part of the PRC, because of their historically different economic and political systems, they are categorised as FOEs in the national statistics. It is especially so for Hong Kong, which has played an important role in bridging Chinese mainland enterprises with enterprises of other nations. This is also called the 'foreign sector' in China. Private economy, the third type, consists of four subcategories: private firms—privately owned enterprises (POEs) (with eight or more employees), either listed on the stock markets, or unlisted; individual businesses (with seven employees or fewer); and township and village enterprises. Many of the private firms in the early years of the reforms were disguised as township and village enterprises (sometimes referred to as 'red hats' (Chen 2007a)); the number of these firms has been declining, and are now slowly disappearing in today's China. The term 'private sector' is used to refer to all four types of firms in the private economy.

The non-state sector includes the private sector and foreign sector firms. The government releases irregular aggregate data on the GDP of the private sector as a whole (all four types of firms combined). Before 1989, it was less than 10 %. In 2005, they represented around 50 %, and by 2012, a figure of more than 60 % was reported (People's Daily 2013). By the end of 2013, the number of POEs (including both private firms and individual businesses) had reached about 94 % of the total number of firms (National Bureau of Statistics of China 1995—2014). Their registered capital was about 41 % of the total for China (State Administration for Industry and Commerce (SAIC) statistics 2013).

In this chapter, we focus on the private firms—POEs (both listed and non-listed) as systematic data are not always available for the individual businesses (firms with seven employees or fewer). While we are interested in the absolute level of contribution to the economy as a whole, we are particularly interested in the historical growth of the private sector relative to the decline of the state sector. As we shall show below, the private firms (listed and non-listed POEs) in absolute terms are only a partial reflection of the real private economy in China.

Private Firms' Contribution to China's Economic Development

As a result of China's transition from being a planned economy to a quasi (i.e. centrally managed) market economy, private firms developed rapidly after they were officially approved in 1988 (Garnaut et al. 2012). Table 1.1 shows the historical development of private firms—POEs (excluding individual businesses and township and village enterprises) in China since 1989 in terms of key government statistics, including the number of firms, the contribution to GDP in Chinese yuan (RMB), the number of employees, and listing in China's stock exchanges.

The data in Table 1.1 demonstrate unambiguously the growth and prosperity of this private economic sector. Figure 1.1 exhibits the annual growth rate of firm numbers, employment, GDP and registered capital from 1990 to 2013 based on data in Table 1.1. It shows a peak of more than a 200 % growth rate in 1993 for registered capital and more than 150 % in 1994 for GDP. After that, there is a steady growth of double digits in the range of 10 % to 40 %. As an illustration of the impressive growth, there were 91,000 registered private firms in 1989; and the number reached 12,539,000 at the end of 2013, an increase of 138 times. By the end of January 2015, this number had reached 15,764,000, with an increase of more than 173 times since 1989 (China Industry and Commerce News 2015).

This growth pattern is even more impressive when compared to that of the other two major forms of enterprises: the state-owned and the foreign-owned firms. Table 1.2 shows the number of firms in the state, private and foreign sectors in the period 1990 to 2013. Figure 1.2 compares these numbers graphically. Before 1993, numbers of both private and foreign firms were negligible compared to state-owned companies. The number of private firms (POEs) surpassed the number of state firms (SOEs) in 2000. In 2011, the number of foreign firms (FOEs) surpassed the number of state firms. The steep growth slope of the private firms since 1998 is truly impressive.

Table 1.1 Key statistics about Chinese private firms (1989–2013)

Year	Firm number (10,000s)	GDP (100 million RMB)	Employment (10,000s)	Registered capital (1000 Trillion RMB)	No.# listed on Chinese stock exchanges
1989	9.1	97	164	0.0084	–
1990	9.8	122	170	0.0095	0
1991	10.8	147	184	0.0123	1
1992	14	205	232	0.0221	4
1993	23.8	422	373	0.0681	31
1994	43.2	1140	648	0.1448	56
1995	65.5	2295	956	0.2622	60
1996	81.9	3227	1171	0.3752	96
1997	96.1	3923	1349	0.514	128
1998	120.1	5853	1709	0.7189	152
1999	150.9	7686	2022	1.0287	172
2000	176.2	10740	2406	1.3308	206
2001	202.9	12317	2714	1.8212	221
2002	243.5	15338	3409	2.4756	243
2003	300.6	20083	3526	3.5	285
2004	365.1	22950	5017	4.7936	343
2005	430.1	27434	5824	6.1331	356
2006	498.1	31855	6586	7.6029	420
2007	551.3	36730	7253	9.3873	502
2008	657.4	39965	7904	11.7356	568
2009	740.2	47414	8607	14.65	655
2010	845.5	55750	9418	19.2054	991
2011	967.7	68785	10354	25.788	1274
2012	1085.7	n.a.	11296	31.1	1427
2013	1253.9	n.a.	12522	39.31	1436

Source: Own elaboration based on data from China Bureau of Industry and Commerce, National Bureau of Statistics of China, Database of IFind and Wind
Notes: GDP data for private firms in 2012 and 2013 are not available; The data of the number of listed private firms (POEs) on Chinese stock exchanges is from the Wind database (for 1990–2009) and IFind (for 2010–2013). The number of listed POEs exceeded the number of listed SOEs in 2010.

Figures 1.3, 1.4, 1.5, and 1.6 compare the assets, revenue from principal business, profits and returns on sales of above-designated-size (large-scale) industrial private firms—POEs; state firms—SOEs; and foreign firms—FOEs from 2000 to 2013, respectively. (The criteria for above-designated-size is an annual revenue from the principal economic

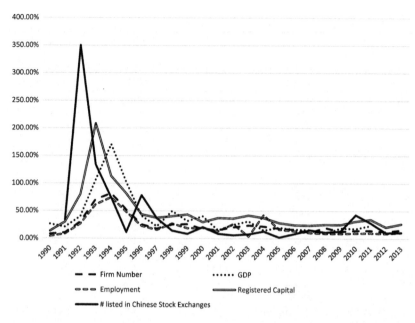

Fig. 1.1 Private firms' growth rate (1990–2013). *Source:* Based on data in Table 1.1

activity of more than 5 million yuan between 1998 and 2010; and more than 20 million yuan after 2011). We can observe a significant growth of numbers of private firms—POEs in all these indices, in comparison with state firms—SOEs, and with foreign firms—FOEs, in most cases. Foreign firms seem to enjoy a stable pattern of higher profits relative to private firms and state firms. Since 2007, the above-designated-size private firms had more revenue and profits than the corresponding state firms and large-scale private firms; and since 2008 more in terms of assets. The private firms are therefore increasing, as demonstrated in Fig. 1.6 in terms of profitability (return on sales—ROS), in their competitiveness, not only compared to state firms, but also comparably competitive to foreign firms that have been considered as lions with advanced technology and modern management.

Undoubtedly, the growth of private enterprises has contributed significantly to the different aspects of economic development in China. Since

Table 1.2 Number of firms with different ownership types (1990–2013, in 10,000s)

Year	SOEs	Collectives	POEs	Individual businesses	FOEs
1990	115.15	338.19	9.8	1328.31	2.54
1991	125.37	348.00	10.8	1416.84	3.72
1992	154.72	415.94	14	1533.91	8.43
1993	195.17	515.65	23.8	1766.87	16.75
1994	216.63	545.68	43.2	2186.60	20.61
1995	221.86	533.77	65.5	2528.50	23.36
1996	216.33	501.34	81.9	2703.70	24.04
1997	207.83	447.05	96.1	2850.90	23.57
1998	183.63	373.64	120.1	3120.20	22.78
1999	164.99	317.25	150.9	3160.06	21.24
2000	149.22	262.71	176.2	2571.40	25.92
2001	131.78	220.85	202.9	2433.00	28.50
2002	117.25	188.59	243.5	2377.50	25.92
2003	104.97	162.55	300.6	2353.19	28.50
2004	91.60	139.37	365.1	2350.49	31.65
2005	79.45	120.70	430.1	2463.89	35.30
2006	71.69	109.42	498.1	2595.61	37.67
2007	63.74	96.35	551.3	2741.53	40.64
2008	56.88	85.67	657.4	2917.33	43.49
2009	49.82	75.61	740.2	3197.37	43.43
2010	45.78	64.79	845.5	3452.89	44.52
2011	42.21	59.12	967.7	3756.47	44.65
2012	39.50	53.67	1085.70	4059.27	44.06
2013	36.40	48.08	1253.90	4436.30	44.60

Sources: National Bureau of Statistics of China website; China statistical yearbook 1995–2014

employment is a big concern for China because of its large population, the contribution to employment eventually also translates into the social stability of society. The private firms have created more jobs than state firms since 2006. Table 1.3 and Fig. 1.7 compare employment by different types of private, state-owned and foreign-owned firms. As shown, there is a steady decline in the employment figures in state firms—SOEs and collectives, but a sharp increase in private firms—POEs and individual businesses. The employment number in POEs exceeded that of the SOEs in 2006, and the employment number of individual businesses exceeded that of the SOEs in 2009. By the end of 2013, the POEs employed twice

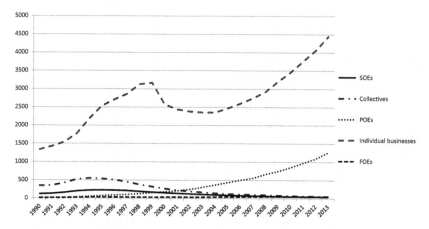

Fig. 1.2 Comparative number of firms with five types of ownership (1990–2013). *Source*: Based on data in Table 1.2

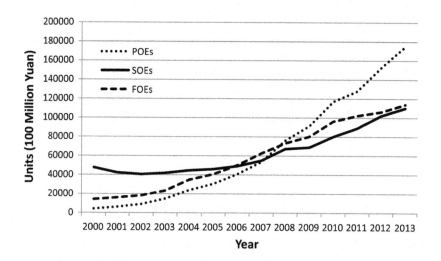

Fig. 1.3 Comparative assets of enterprises (2000–2013). *Source*: Own elaboration based on data from National Bureau of Statistics of China. *Notes*: SOEs: State Owned Enterprises; POEs: Private Owned Enterprises; FOEs: Foreign Owned Enterprises; Data only include industrial enterprises with above designated size. The definition is all enterprises with annual revenue from principal economic activity of more than 5 million yuan between 1998 and 2010. The scale criteria increased to more than 20 million yuan after 2011.

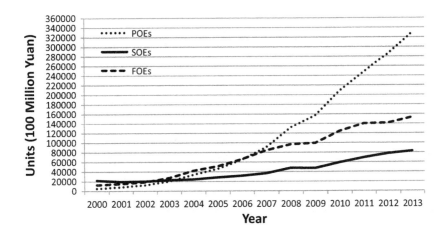

Fig. 1.4 Comparative revenue from principal business (2000–2013). *Source*: Own elaboration based on data from National Bureau of Statistics of China. *Notes*: SOEs: State Owned Enterprises; POEs: Private Owned Enterprises; FOEs: Foreign Owned Enterprises; Data only include industrial enterprises with above designated size. The definition is all enterprises with annual revenue from principal economic activity of more than 5 million yuan between 1998 and 2010. The scale criteria increased to more than 20 million yuan after 2011.

as many workers as did the SOEs. The POEs and individual businesses combined employed 68.8 % of the total labour force, with SOEs and collectives employing 21.8 % and FOEs employing 9.3 %. It is not surprising that the government began to consider the private sector as a strategic player for the future economic growth and social stability of China.

Figure 1.8 shows the number of firms listed on the two Chinese stock exchanges from 1990 to 2013. As shown, the listing of private firms (POEs) grew at a much faster rate than the state firms, a ratio of nearly three to one. By the end of 2011, the number of POEs listed on the two stock exchanges has surpassed that of the SOEs. Given this trend, it is reasonable to extrapolate that the private sector, especially entrepreneurial and family firms, in a similar way to that of other developed economies, will in the future be the major contributor to job creation and the further economic development of China.

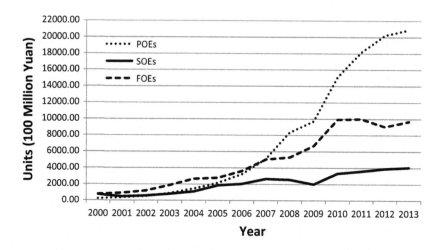

Fig. 1.5 Comparative profits of enterprises (2000–2013). *Source*: Own elaboration based on data from National Bureau of Statistics of China. *Notes*: SOEs: State Owned Enterprises; POEs: Private Owned Enterprises; FOEs: Foreign Owned Enterprises. Data only include industrial enterprises with above designated size. The definition is all enterprises with annual revenue from principal economic activity more than 5 million yuan between 1998 and 2010. The scale criteria increased to more than 20 million yuan after 2011.

The Evolutionary Stages of China's Private Enterprises Since 1978

Despite their impressive growth performance, the POEs' path to success has not been a smooth one; in fact, it has been rocky and sometimes turbulent. Private firms faced multiple challenges in the process of establishing legitimacy within a complex and often hostile institutional environment (Ahlstrom and Bruton 2001). Even today, while the private economy is formally recognised by the central government, many restrictions still apply to private firms, creating a less-than-fair competitive environment for them (Yang and Hu 2011; Feng and He 2012). These restrictions include limitations in entering certain industries, and difficulties in accessing financial products, credits and loans (Li 2006; Tsai 2007). Overall, the status of private firms has risen monumentally

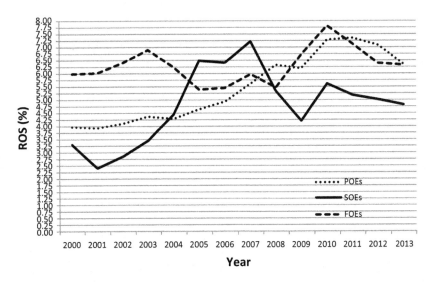

Fig. 1.6 Comparative profitability (Return on Sales—ROS) of enterprises (2000–2013). *Source*: Own elaboration based on data from National Bureau of Statistics of China. *Notes*: SOEs: State Owned Enterprises; POEs: Private Owned Enterprises; FOEs: Foreign Owned Enterprises. Data only include industrial enterprises with above designated size. The definition is all enterprises with annual revenue from principal economic activity of more than 5 million yuan between 1998 and 2010. The scale criteria increased to more than 20 million yuan after 2011.

in comparison to their position before the economic reforms in 1978, when the government considered private business to be the source of evil behaviour (Diao and Zhang 2007; Liu 2003). Below we provide details regarding the evolution of POEs in their different phases after 1978, drawing on works by Feng and He (2012), S.E.A. and Horizon (2014), and Wang (2012a).

1978–1991: A Phase of Emergence

After the Third Plenary Session of the Eleventh Central Committee of the Communist Party in 1978, China entered a period of general economic opening and transformation, and this period saw the emergence of China's

Table 1.3 Employment in firms with different ownership types (1989–2013, in 10,000s)

	State sector		Private sector		Foreign firms	
Year	SOEs	Collectives	POEs	Individual businesses	Other countries	Hong Kong, Macau and Taiwan	Total
1989	10109	3502	164				
1990	10346	3549	170	2093	61	5	66
1991	10664	3628	184	2258	96	69	165
1992	10889	3621	232	2468	138	84	222
1993	10920	3393	373	2939	133	155	288
1994	10890	3285	648	3776	191	208	399
1995	11261	3147	956	4614	241	272	513
1996	11244	3016	1171	5017	275	265	540
1997	11044	2817	1349	5442	300	281	581
1998	9058	1900	1709	6114	293	294	587
1999	8572	1712	2022	6241	306	306	612
2000	8102	1499	2407	5070	332	310	642
2001	7640	1291	2714	4760	345	326	671
2002	7163	1122	3410	4743	391	367	758
2003	6876	1000	4299	4637	454	409	863
2004	6710	897	5017	4587	563	470	1033
2005	6488	810	5824	4901	688	557	1245
2006	6431	764	6586	5160	796	611	1407
2007	6424	718	7253	5496	903	680	1583
2008	6447	662	7904	5776	943	679	1622
2009	6420	618	8607	6585	978	721	1699
2010	6516	597	9418	7008	1053	770	1823
2011	6704	603	10354	7945	1217	932	2149
2012	6839	589	11296	8628	1246	969	2215
2013	6365	566	12522	9336	1566	1397	2963

Source: National Bureau of Statistics of China website.

private enterprises (Coase and Wang 2012; Feng and He 2012; Lardy 2014). It is a period of private enterprise recovery because private firms had essentially disappeared from the economic landscape between 1952 and 1978. The reform that stimulated the birth, growth and development of private entrepreneurship began in the rural areas with agricultural reform.

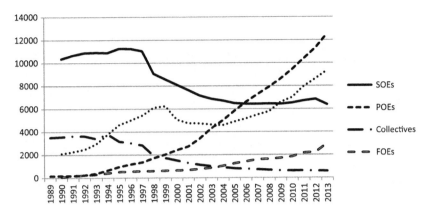

Fig. 1.7 Comparative employment (number of employees) of five types of enterprises (1989–2013). *Notes*: Based on data from Table 1.3. FOE includes Hong Kong/Taiwan/Macau and other nations.

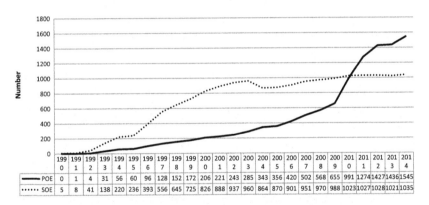

Fig. 1.8 Number of enterprises listed on Chinese stock exchanges. *Source*: Database of IFind (for 2010–2014) and Wind (for 1990–2009). We thank Xuhong Li of Fudan University for the provision of the data.

The southern province of Anhui played a pioneering role from 1978 in China's agricultural reforms. China's former paramount leader, Deng Xiaoping, said in the spring of 1992, 'China's reform began in rural areas and China's rural reform started from Anhui Province' (Xinhua Net 2007). In 1978, 18 peasants in Xiaogang village of Anhui's Fengyang county took a criminal risk (it was illegal to do so at that time), and secretly signed a land contract with the local government that ushered in the rural reforms to China's contracted household responsibility system (*bao chan dao hu* 包产到户) (CCCPC Party Literature Research Office 2009; Shui and Veeck 2012). By the end of 1979, the Xiaogang village had turned from consisting of families with fleeing-hunger to an annual income of more than 400 yuan per capita, with grain output equal to a five-year sum between 1966 and 1970 (Deng et al. 2005). Though the first 10,000-yuan family was reported in 1980 by *The People's Daily* in Lanzhou, Gansu province (CCCPC Party Literature Research Office 2009), it was Anhui province that was regarded as the birthplace of national agricultural reform.

With the success of the Anhui experiment, the Communist Party of China (CPC) Central Committee approved in 1982 as in 'National Rural Work Meeting Minutes' and established a household contract responsibility system (*jiating lianchan chengbao zerenzhi* 家庭联产承包责任制), which specified a production responsibility system under a socialist collective economy. The household contract responsibility system broke down the previous egalitarian practice of 'everybody eats from the same big pot.' Under the new responsibility contract, people could work hard to earn income with various sources such as farming, business or other employed work. Farmers could retain the income from selling the excess of their produce after meeting their contracted quota. It was the first time after a long period of economic depression that the Chinese people could dream of becoming rich. Many rural households could, and did, achieve an annual income of over 10,000 yuan, and this type of household (ten-thousand-yuan households—*wanyuanhu* 万元户) widely represented the pride of being rich and established a model for others to follow (Kelliher 1992; S.E.A. and Horizon 2014).

At the same time, in 1979, China was suffering the pressure of a high level of urban unemployment, since a huge number of educated young people returned to the cities after the end of the Cultural Revolution in 1976, adding to the existing numbers of unemployed urban residents. Different sources have documented unemployment statistics as between 5 and 12 million people, which was some 5 % to 11 % of the non-agricultural labour force. However, this figure ignored the urban young, who were still legally consigned to agricultural jobs in the countryside (Whyte 1984). Urban unemployment could have potentially serious consequences for economic, political and social development (Ge 2011); therefore the CPC Central Committee and the State Council promulgated several official regulations in 1981, allowing individual entrepreneurs to employ up to seven people (two assistants and, if with special technology, up to five apprentices) for their businesses (Feng and He 2012; Zhang et al. 2011). This restriction on the numbers employed to seven is differentiated from the definition of private firms, which could employ eight or more people in regulations issued in 1988 (Feng and He 2012). The release of labour from rural areas looking for job opportunities in urban areas; in addition to the unemployed youth in the city, provided space and the need to be brave and creative in becoming an entrepreneur to survive a harsh economic situation at the beginning of the Chinese economic opening and development. Individual business (*getihu* 个体户) was the main way to carry out entrepreneurial activities. Along with township and village ownership, the individual businesses built the foundation for the development of Chinese private enterprises or POEs (*siyingqiye*私营企业), especially the industrial and manufacturing production centres in the economic zones such as the Yangtze River Delta Area and the Pearl River Delta Area.

The legitimisation process of POEs in the economy took place gradually during this period, with the recognition of private enterprise as a legal entity to complement economic activities in the socialistic ownership system (Hsu 1991; Lardy 2014; Liu 2003; S.E.A. and Horizon 2014). In this phase of emergence, the number of registered private (civilian-run) enterprises increased by 7.4 times (ibid.). However, doubts still remained regarding the economic, social and political direction of China's economic reform. Therefore a move towards a capitalistic character of private ownership was taken with caution at the policy level. Meanwhile, the boom of private businesses also brought certain social conflicts and environmental problems such as water and air pollution because of widespread industrialisation, and labour exploitation to keep costs low (Stevens et al. 2013).

1992–2001: A Phase of Rapid Growth

While a rapid development of the private economy occurred during the phase of emergence, the real growth of private enterprises, which was responsible for leading China to today's co-existence of a capitalistic market economy and a single-party political system, did not appear until 1992. It is commonly believed that the speech by Deng Xiaoping during his tour of south China in 1992 had the most profound impact on the Chinese market economy and modern economic development. Deng's 1992 speech set a clear tone about the direction of economic development in China: the critical issue of the Chinese economic revolution was the terminology of 'capitalism' or 'socialism.' While China needed to be cautious about the 'rightist' move (Coase and Wang 2012), the principal obstacle was the 'leftist' (Deng 1994; Parker 1992). The speech clarified many questions and doubts regarding how to develop the Chinese economy on the basis of its political and social foundations. It left the legacy of Deng's pragmatic 'cat' theory: it does not matter whether a cat is white or black; as long as it catches mice, it is a good cat (Bregolat 2014; Feng and He 2012).

This change in the direction of economic development swung the private economy upwards. The Fourteenth National Congress of the Communist Party of China held in 1992 set explicit objectives for the reform of a socialistic market economic system, in which the private economy held a complementary position, and different ownership enterprises could establish joint ventures. This clarification of the legal position for private enterprises provided the foundation for their rapid development. In the same year, the provisional regulations for limited liability companies (LLCs) and joint-stock (limited) companies were issued to establish the modern corporate ownership structure in China (S.E.A. and Horizon 2014; Zhou and Xia 2008). This initiative opened up a new era for Chinese private enterprises as many more people jumped into 'the sea of business' (*xiahai* 下海) from previously stable jobs in the public sector, to become founders and leaders of many of today's leading private enterprises. According to surveys conducted by the All China Federation of Industry and Commerce (ACFIC) (2007), 22.1 % of entrepreneurs who initiated a business in 1992 previously held positions as officers in the public system; and the principal motive for *xiahai* was the perceived obstacles to displaying their talents when in their government jobs. Some of the first-generation private firm executives interviewed for this book were previously government bureaucrats who decided to become private entrepreneurs, with greater risks but also greater opportunities.

Some observers consider that private enterprises did most of their initial capital accumulation through opportunistic trading and labour exploitation during the period of emergence. However, the rise of technological firms such as Lenovo and Huawei (Zhang and Zhou 2015) changed the image of private firms as being only labour-intensive factories. A decision of the CPC Central Committee and the State Council in 1995 on strengthening scientific and technological advances pointed out, 'civilian-run enterprises are a vital strength of the national high and new technology industry. We need to continue guiding and encouraging their healthy development' (Feng and He 2012: 10). In addition, the 15th National Congress of the CPC's report in 1997 noted that, 'China's individual, private and other non-public economy is an important part of the socialist market economy' (Feng and He 2012: 10). This simple statement was significant for the private firms because it meant that they were no longer a complementary form of the Chinese economy but were now recognised as one of its core components. By the end of 1997, the number of registered private firms was almost 10 times that of 1991, while GDP increased by 27 times and employee numbers grew by more than seven times. Extending to 2002, the end of this period of rapid development, the growth rate is most astonishing. The number of registered firms increased by 22 times, GDP growth was 104 times greater, and employment 18 times higher. These figures do not even include the similarly dramatic growth of individual businesses.

S.E.A. and Horizon (2014) suggest three principal reasons for the rapid growth of POEs. The first is the sustained overall rapid economic development of the country; the second is the developmental changes in the economic structure; and the third is the reform of public and collective enterprises. Xu et al. (2014) also observed a similar economic transition from SOEs through collectively owned enterprises to POEs.

The steady decline in state-owned firms is a strategic policy at the central government level. The number of national or central SOEs declined from 84,000 in 1978—the start of the economic reforms—to 52,000 in 2013 (Tao 2014), while the registered number of other ownership types (e.g. POE, FOE) increased significantly. The number of provincial and municipal public firms has remained stable over the years (Wang and Fan 2010). The strategic changes in the state-owned enterprises have transformed many small and medium-sized SOEs into private LLC or joint-stock (limited) companies owned by previous managers or employees. The modernisation of the corporate law and financial systems provides further flexibility for private enterprises to operate and compete in a dynamic market economy. By 2001, the leaders of private firms were recognised by the CPC for their efforts in contributing to China's economic development, considering them to be 'workers' (to differentiate them from their previous consideration as 'capitalists' who exploit workers), and 'contributors to the socialist mission with Chinese characteristics' (S.E.A. and Horizon 2014: 24).

2002–2011: A Phase of Integration

The years from 2002 to 2011 witnessed a relatively stable period of development (Feng and He 2012). This was a phase of integration, in which Chinese private enterprises consolidated their standing in the market and integrated their positions within society. This integration has also been reflected in the internationalisation of private enterprises consistent with the 'go-out' policy advocated by the Chinese government (Liu 2003).

A study by the Chinese Academy of Social Sciences in 2002 classified private entrepreneurs as the top three of ten major occupational strata in Chinese society (Bregolat 2014: 102; Lu 2002): (1) state and public (government) officials; (2) managerial personnel; (3) private enterprise owners; (4) professionals; (5) office workers; (6) small self-employed individuals; (7) employees in commerce and services; (8) industrial workers; (9) agricultural labourers; and (10) urban and rural unemployed and semi-employed. This official classification legitimised the entrepreneurs' social standing and gave them the possibility of joining the Communist party, and potentially to get involved in political activities. Increasing numbers of private entrepreneurs became representatives and delegates at the national congress and participated actively in social, economic and political decision-making. Between 1995 and 2012, the proportion of CEOs or chairpersons of listed privately owned firms who had appointments on the People's Congress (PC) or the People's Political Consultative Conference (PPCC), two important political entities that influence policies from town to national levels, increased from 22 % in 1995 to 40 % in 2012 (Li and Liang 2015). In 2013, 71 % (356) of the 500 richest Chinese business people ranked by *Forbes* held political appointments on the PC or the PPCC.

The progress and legitimisation of the private economy in this integration and optimisation period were further consolidated by a constitutional modification in 2004 which specified that a 'citizen's legal private assets are protected by laws.' Legal protection of private assets may be taken for granted in the West, but until this time it was not constitutionally recognised in China. Even with this modification, the Chinese constitution still gives priority in protecting public assets over private ones.

In 2005, the State Council promulgated Opinions on Encouraging, Supporting and Guiding the Development of Individually-Run Business and Other Forms of Non-Public Owned Economy (popularly referred to as the '36 Articles of Non-Public Economy'). This is the first official policy document by the Chinese central government specifying support for the private economy with actions 'to eliminate system obstacles which affect the development of non-public economy, to establish equal market core position' (Feng and He 2012: 12). This framework includes seven aspects of the non-public economy: 'opening up market access, enlarging financial and taxation support, consummating social services, safeguarding the legitimate interests of entities and their staffs, guiding the upgrade of quality, improving government's regulation, and strengthening guidance and policy harmonization' (Huang 2011: 248). It was the first time private civilian capital was allowed to enter traditional monopolistic sectors such as mining, electricity, telecommunications, airlines, petroleum, banks, security and insurance; as well as the participation of private capital in the restructuration of SOEs (Chen et al. 2013; Feng and He 2012; People Daily 2005). To repair a common image of labour exploitation in private enterprises, it also demands that private enterprises establish labour unions and ensure the legal rights of employees (Wang 2008).

The significant contribution of the private economy to the 10 % GPD growth of China also carries a large cost to society in terms of social and environmental issues. This period saw the increasing discrepancy between the poor and the rich, the inequality in wealth distribution in different regions, serious problems of environmental pollution, and food and drug safety issues. The new Chinese Labour Contract Law in January 2008 was intended to introduce a healthier employment relationship and better employee rights. However, the global financial crisis in the summer and autumn of 2008 worsened economic and financial conditions, and private enterprises were confronted by serious economic problems, especially for those that were heavily dependent on export business (Qian and Chang 2008; Wang and Gong 2009).

In spite of the rhetorical support of private enterprises, SOEs still enjoyed the favouritism and protectionism of the Chinese government. The problems that private enterprises encountered led to several incidents of asset acquisition by SOEs (presumably with government approval, or even encouragement) in 2009. This includes the acquisition of the well-known Chinese dairy company MengNiu (蒙牛) by COFCO (China National Cereals, Oils and Foodstuffs Corporation); the civilian-run YingLian Airlines (鹰联航空) by SOE SiChuan Airline Co.; the private NingBo Steel (宁波钢铁) by SOE Bao Steel; and the profitable private firm Rizhao Steel and Iron Co. by the loss-making SOE Shandong Steel and Iron Group (Chen et al. 2013; Chen and Wallace 2014; Eaton 2013; Feng and He 2012).

The opening of traditional monopolistic industries to private enterprises has not provided more and better space, as originally perceived or intended, for the development of Chinese private enterprises. Instead, private firms have encountered tremendous obstacles in the process of entering these strictly regulated industries (Huang 2011). To stimulate further economic development by integrating the private economy, in 2010, the State Council issued '36 New Articles of Non-Public Economy.' This new regulation emphasises opening more fields for private investments such as infrastructure, social and public services, financial services, national defence, and technological industries (gov.cn 2012). It attempts to encourage private enterprises to strengthen their self-initiated innovation and upgrading of their capabilities by developing better investment environments, improving investment-related services, and providing guidance and regulation of private investment (Feng and He 2012). The turning point during this period was the change of the overall development direction of Chinese society as a whole. Instead of focusing solely on economic development,integrating economic development into addressing social and environmental issues became the principal objective. In this directional change at the national level, the private economy was considered to be an integral part to help reach a new equilibrium.

2012–Present: A Phase of Adjustment

This phase saw the beginning of slower economic growth in comparison to previous periods that had attained an average of a two-digit GDP increase. Since the second trimester of 2012, GDP growth has dropped to less than 8 %, and the trend appears to be continuing (Economist 2015), with 6.9 % estimated for 2015 and beyond. High market competition along with increasing labour costs have caused a large number of manufacturers (almost all of them private entrepreneurs) in the eastern regions to lose their competitiveness. Many have had to declare bankruptcy or to close their businesses. However, the slowdown in economic growth is not entirely unexpected. A double-digit increase in growth is simply not sustainable because, as the economic base increases, the space for market development decreases and competition intensifies. Current President Xi JinPing is not concerned with high GDP growth alone, but also focuses on whether the economy is on track for needed reforms and macroeconomic rebalancing (Wong 2016). While in previous years entrepreneurship benefited from an unsaturated market, to succeed in a competitive field now requires innovation, good management and good governance—all within the control of the 'visible hands' of management (Chandler 1978).

Many scholars have recognised that future economic growth will need to come from technological development and innovation (Bregolat 2014; Zhang and Zhou 2015). This means that firms, private or otherwise, will have to invest more of their resources in research and development (R&D). The national priority to develop better social well-being and environmental protection means that the central government will work even harder to integrate private enterprises in this sustainable and harmonious development process. This demand for investment in innovation and contributions to social development may cut into private firms' profitability, which has been on the rise since the 1990s. From Fig. 1.6 we can see that foreign firms (FOEs) had higher profitability (measured by return on sales—ROS) since 1998 but were overtaken by state firms (SOEs) during the period 2005 to 2007, and then by private firms (POEs) in 2008 and again between 2011 and 2013. POEs have surpassed SOEs since 2008 in profitability level, and it seems that this trend will continue. However, it is unclear how long this upward trend in profitability for private firms will last as market volatility continues, and as the private firms take on an increasingly important role as major innovators and technological leaders, as well as making significant contributions to the building of a harmonious society.

Wealth and Wealth Inequality Associated with the Private Economy

We asserted earlier that the growth of the private sector may in part be the outcome of the capable 'visible hands' of management (Chandler 1978). Viewing the evolution of the private sector in the Chinese economy, one thing stands out; i.e. private entrepreneurs have contributed significantly to the development of the Chinese economy with their extraordinary leadership and sophisticated management practices. In this book we have identified a number of these entrepreneurs who have navigated their firms through the turbulent and hostile sea and built highly successful organisations. The visible and capable hands of the good leaders and managers have contributed to this growth and development and, it is hoped, to the sustainability of the private economy in modern China.

Private firms have now gained a central position in the economy, contributing to more than 60 % of GDP on an annual basis since 2009 (WTO 2010). Domestically, many well-known businesses are privately owned and operate across a variety of industries, such as computer and internet technologies (Huawei, Lenovo), banking (Ming Sheng, China Merchants), consumer goods (Haier, Wahaha), and construction and real estate (Vanke, Vantone), among many others. Globally, seven of the 85 Chinese firms listed in 2013's *Fortune* Global 500 were private (Zhang 2013). In 1997 the first Chinese private-firm leader appeared on the *Forbes* World's Billionaires List. The number rose to 115 in 2011, 122 in 2013, and 242 in 2014 (Wang 2012; Forbes 2014). It is especially remarkable because only 35 years ago (in 1978), all employed Chinese citizens, regardless of position, rank, place of employment or nature of work, received an identical salary of about 40 RMB per month or 480 RMB (or US$60 in 1978 currency) per year. The official data from the National Bureau of Statistics of China indicate that the annual per capita disposable income of urban households was 343 RMB in 1978; but this income reached 26,955 RMB in 2013, a 7858 % increase. The average annual salary was 5,439 RMB in 1995 in urban areas, and increased to 51,483 RMB in 2013 (and 90,908 RMB in Shanghai).

This overall improvement, ironically, has been accompanied by an increasing degree of wealth inequality. The Gini index (an index measuring inequality in individual or household income) in 1980 for China was 0.29 (World Bank 2015), and in 2012 it was 0.47 (Economist 2012). Kaiman (2014) reported that China had a Gini of 0.73 in 2012, based on an article in the *China Daily*, China's official mouthpiece. A Gini index greater than 0.40 is considered to be very large and indicates a risk of social unrest. A 2013 Reuters report mentioned that China had 2.7 million US dollar millionaires and 251 billionaires, but 13 % of Chinese people lived on less than US$1.25 per day (Yao and Wang 2013). By law, SOE managers do not receive market-competitive salaries, and their true income is unknowable (as a result of many expenses-type subsidies and under-the-table payments) (Liu 2015). However, it is clear that most of the 251 billionaires are self-made private entrepreneurs, contributing greatly not only to the increasing wealth of China as a whole but also to the increasing wealth inequality in the nation. Given that China remains a country with a socialist ideology, it is not surprising that government and citizens alike would expect these successful entrepreneurs to contribute to social development, including the restoration of a higher level of wealth equality among the Chinese people. In other words, the Chinese private sector will be the primary engine for technological and managerial innovation, including developing environmentally sustainable products and processes. This sector will also be a major source of contributions towards the social sustainability of the country, by undertaking leadership in good management and generosity to the less fortunate through philanthropy.

Contribution of the Private Sector to Society beyond GDP

As their wealth has accumulated, leaders of private businesses have begun to pay attention to issues outside their business, such as environmental and social challenges. With permission from the government, many foundations have been established to address these issues, such as alleviating suffering caused by natural disasters (e.g. 2008 and 2011 earthquakes) or structural poverty.

There has been a noticeable increase in charitable giving and philanthropy by private entrepreneurs since the 1990s. As can be seen from Fig. 1.9, the annual donations to charity by private firms has been on an upswing since 1997 (Yang 2014). Donations up to 2009 included primarily the Guangcai Program, a charity foundation established in 1994 by 10 private entrepreneurs (China Society for Promotion of the Guangcai Program 2016). It aims to eliminate poverty in mid-western and other poor, isolated regions within China. In 2007, the donation data showed a spike because it included contributions to all other charities not reported in previous years beyond the Guangcai Program. Including the other public charities, the total was nearly 38.6 billion RMB in 2010. The number dropped to 28.1 billion RMB in 2011 and 27.5 billion RMB in 2012, but was back to 34.5 billion RMB in 2013. Figure 1.9 also provides donation data from FOEs between 2007 and 2012. We provide this data for comparison to show that private firms (POEs) are contributing more than FOEs to charitable causes in China.

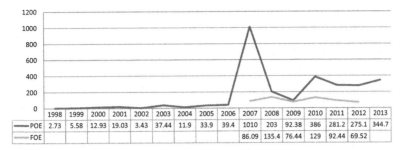

	1998	1999	2000	2001	2002	2003	2004	2005	2006	2007	2008	2009	2010	2011	2012	2013
POE	2.73	5.58	12.93	19.03	3.43	37.44	11.9	33.9	39.4	1010	203	92.38	386	281.2	275.1	344.7
FOE										86.09	135.4	76.44	129	92.44	69.52	

Fig. 1.9 Philanthropic giving by private firms each year (1998–2013, in 100 million RMB). *Notes:* Annual donation data from 'The blue book of charity in China.' Annual donations between 1997 and 2006 represent primarily donations to the Guangcai Program. The 2007 data point represents annual donations to Guangcai Program and cumulative amounts of donations to other public charities from previous years that were not reported, which accounts for the rise in the 2007 donation figure. The 2008–2013 data points represent annual donations to the Guangcai Program and annual donations to other public charities. 2007–2012 donations by FOEs are from Yang (2014).

Donation data of SOEs are difficult to obtain and, even if they are available, are not meaningful since they are the result of government policies rather than leadership action.

One of the most noticeable programmes in the contribution of private entrepreneurs to the public good is the Alashan Society of Entrepreneurs & Ecology (SEE) (see http://see.sina.com.cn/en/), founded in 2004 by 80 entrepreneurs. Its mission is to improve and recover the ecological environment in Alashan, Inner Mongolia, the origin of more than 80 % of sandstorms in northern China. SEE is committed to addressing increasingly serious environmental problems such as air pollution, water pollution, disappearance of grazing, or desertification. The overall mission of SEE is to encourage Chinese entrepreneurs to take more ecological and social responsibility and intends to develop a sustainable model for other entrepreneurs to follow. SEE has been very successful in pursuing its mission and has gained wide support from society.

At the end of 2008, the Alashan SEE started the SEE Foundation, to provide financial support to grass-roots environmental groups, in order to find a sustainable way to help solve environmental problems. Since its founding, the SEE Foundation has established programmes such as the 'Green Leadership Partner Plan,' the 'Chinese Youth Environmental Action Plan,' and the 'SEE—TNC Ecological Award' to finance environmental protection programmes and organisations, and to provide skills training for young leaders of these organisations. Between 2009 and 2014, the SEE Foundation supported more than 200 programmes (for details, see http://www.see.org.cn/foundation/NewsDetail.aspx?id=1544). In the 2014 Hurun Ranking of Philanthropy of Asia, Jack Ma, founder and chair of Alibaba, topped the list by giving RMB14.5 billion (US$2.35bn) to charity (Hurun Report 2014). He established the Alibaba Foundation to tackle environmental issues.

The Guangcai Program, Alashan SEE and the Alibaba Foundation are examples of private foundations in China. The creation of private foundations is new in China but is increasing rapidly (Feng 2013). The public foundations are established, funded and managed by the government, the first being the Chinese Children and Youth Foundation in 1981. In June 2004, China issued Regulations on the Administration of Foundations, proviving a framework to encourage the private sector to contribute to charity. Since 2005, private foundations have been on the rise. Figure 1.10 shows the number of private and public foundations between 2005 and 2013. The number of private foundations surpassed the number of public

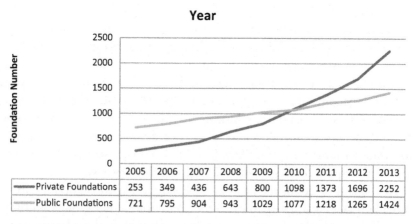

Fig. 1.10   Number of private and public foundations (2005–2013). *Source:* Own elaboration based on Feng (2013).

foundations in 2010, and there were 58 % more private than public foundations in 2013. The trend appears to be continuing.

Contribution to Good Management

One may attribute this significant growth and prosperity of the private economy to different institutional factors such as some of the above-mentioned policies and regulations promulgated by the central government. No doubt the business environment for the private sector is becoming friendlier now than in the past. However, it is clear that these favourable policies and conditions follow rather lead the development of the private sector (Nee and Opper 2012). How did these private firms navigate in this inhospitable environment and become successful? The founders of some of these private enterprises were able to manoeuvre an extremely difficult and delicate situation in the process of legitimising their businesses and competing for resources with SOEs and FOEs (which received relatively very favourable treatments) under unfair conditions. Nee and Opper's (2012) book detailed individual entrepreneurs' stories and how, as a group, the entrepreneurs in the Yangtze Delta area worked together to create reliable networks to help each other both physically and financially to work 'under the radar,' through trial and error, navigating the system and finally legitimising their existence. In recent years, more favourable and fairer policies were introduced to support the private firms, although the industrial regulatory authorities and state-owned or state-related factories and merchants did not give up their privileged positions voluntarily (Chen and Wallace 2014; Huang 2011). In a recent study (S.E.A. and Horizon 2014), entrepreneurs in private firms still expressed major dissatisfactions in many areas: volatile policies and regulations, an incomplete legal system for personal and capital security, and a social environment inhospitable to the development of private enterprises.

Under conditions of resource constraint and a lack of legal protection, we suggest that agency plays a particularly important role in accounting for the success of private enterprises. This agency perspective points to the entrepreneurs' skills and creativity in acquiring and managing their resources, and their courage and wisdom in decision-making. Clearly, many private firms have failed, but those that have succeeded could be a source of learning for others. Studies in mature economies suggest that the ups and downs of corporations are the result of corporate leaders' vision and guidance in corporate capability building to predict, adapt and confront market volatility. We expect a similar, if not a stronger, case to be made that it was the leaders/entrepreneurs who made the private economy in China. Therefore, the focus of this book is about leadership in Chinese private firms, focusing on the leaders of successful firms. By analysing published papers on Chinese business leadership, especially of private firms, and, as already discussed above, by studying the management philosophies and practices of 13 exemplary Chinese entrepreneurs/founder/leaders, we hope to identify the leadership attributes and patterns that contribute to the growth and development of the private sector in China, and of the entire Chinese economy at large.

The Structure of the Book

This book attempts to gain an in-depth understanding of the leadership of private firms, with special attention to the leaders, based on an analysis of published studies and of first-hand interviews with the founders or CEOs of 13 highly successful private firms. Chapter 2 provides an analysis of the ideas about private firm (CEO) leadership gleaned from published papers since 2000.

Given the general lack of knowledge on this subject, we consider it appropriate and even advantageous to offer a dedicated space to the voices of top leaders and founders of successful Chinese private enterprises on their management philosophy, best practices, critical decisions and principal learning experiences. Chapters 3–15 offer the original interview texts with each of the 13 entrepreneur CEOs. Readers will be able to appreciate the CEOs' ideas in their own words. We offer in the final chapter, Chap. 16, our analysis of the thirteen interviews, and present a model of leadership attributes and patterns that summarises the thoughts and beliefs of these leaders, their management philosophies about the role of business for employees, customers and society in general, and their unique management practices. We hope this framework will offer insights on the unique characteristics of Chinese private firms' business leadership that has contributed to the overall economic growth of China since the 1980s.

Reference

ACFIC (All China Federation of Industry and Commerce) (Ed.) (2007) *The Large-scale survey on private enterprises in China* (1993–2006). Beijing: ACFIC Press. 中华全国工商业联合会(编, 2007, 中国私营企业大型调查(1993–2006), 北京:中华工商联合出版社.

Ahlstrom, D., & Bruton, G. D. (2001). Learning from successful local private firms in China: Establishing legitimacy. *Academy of Management Executive, 15*(4), 72–83.

BBC News China (2012) *China's economic miracle*. Retrieved March 13, 2015, from http://www.bbc.com/news/world-asia-china-20069627

Boisot, M., & Meyer, M. (2008). Which way through the open door? Reflections on the internationalization of Chinese firms. *Management and Organization Review, 4*(3), 349–365.

Bregolat, E. (2014). *The second Chinese revolution*. London: Palgrave Macmillan.

Cao, H. (2001). Guangcai program: Hope and happiness (in Chinese). In H. Zhang (Ed.), *The blue book of private enterprises in China no. 2 (2000)* (pp. 115–121). Beijing: Social Sciences Documentation Publishing House.

CCCPC Party Literature Research Office. (2009). *China 1978–2008*. Changsha: HuNan People Press. 中共中央文献研究室 (2009) 中国 1978–2008. 长沙: 湖南人民出版社.

Chandler, A. D. (1978). *The visible hand: The managerial revolution in American business*. Cambridge, MA: Harvard University Press.

Chen, S. (2013). Are Chinese small and medium enterprises victims of institutional pitfalls? In G. Wang, and Y. Zheng (Eds), *China: Development and governance* 237–245. Singapore: World Scientific Publishing.

Chen, W. (2007a). Does the colour of the cat matter? The red hat strategy in China's private enterprises. *Management and Organization Review, 3*(1), 55–80.

Chen, Y. (2007b). The development report of the private economy in China (in Chinese). In M. Huang (Ed.), *The blue book of private economy in China No. 4 (2006–2007)* (pp. 3–45). Beijing: Social Sciences Documentation Publishing House.

Chen, S. and Wallace, J. (2014) State advancing: China's State-owned enterprises after the global financial crisis, Working paper. Retrieved March 1, 2015, from http://www.jeremywallace.org/work-in-progress.html

China Industry and Commerce News (2015) *The report on national market's main development.* Retrieved March 2, 2015, from http://www.cicn.com.cn/content/2015-02/13/content_151232.htm. 中国工商报 (2015) 2015年1月全国市场主体发展报告.

China Society for Promotion of the Guangcai Program. (2016). Retrieved February 7, 2016, from http://www.cspgp.org.cn/publicfiles/business/htmlfiles/cspgp/english/index.html.

Coase, R., & Wang, N. (2012). *How China became capitalist.* New York: Palgrave Macmillan.

Cong, S. and Zhang, X. (1999). *Economy development history of new China.* Shanghai: Shanghai Finance and Economy University Press. 从树海,张行 (1999,新中国经济发展史, 上海:上海财经大学出版.

Deng, S., Li, M., Wu, X. and Su, J. (eds) (2005). *Transit time* (1970–1979) (China detailed events in history). JiLin: JiLin AudioVisual Publishing House. 邓书杰, 李梅, 吴晓莉, 苏继红 (编者) (2005) 转机时刻(1970-1979)(中国历史大事详解). 吉林:吉林音像出版社.

Deng, X.-P. (1994). *Selected works of Deng Xiaoping* (Vol. 3). Beijing: Foreign Language Press.

Diao, S. and Zhang, F. (2007). Deng Xiaoping's historical contribution to protect China's private property. *Journal of Normal College of Qingdao University*, 24(03): 11–18. 刁世存, 张丰国 (2007) 邓小平对中国私产保护的历史贡献. 青岛大学师范学院学报, 2007年9月第24卷第3期: 11–18 页.

Eaton, S. (2013). Political economy of the advancing state: The case of China's Airlines reform. *The China Journal, 69*(January), 64–86.

The Economist (2001). Special: Enter the dragon. (10 March): 23–25. Retrieved March 13, 2015, from http://www.economist.com/node/526368

The Economist (2012). Inequality: Gini out of the bottle. Retrieved March 15, 2015, from http://www.economist.com/news/china/21570749-gini-out-bottle

The Economist (2015). Why China's economy is slowing. Retrieved March 13, 2015, from http://www.economist.com/blogs/economist-explains/2015/03/economist-explains-8

Feng, X. (2013). China's Charitable Foundations: Development and policy-related issues. Stanford Center for International Development, Working paper No. 485.

Feng, X. and He, G. (2012). *A report on the survival environment of Chinese private enterprises.* Beijing: China Economic Publishing House. 冯兴元,何广文 (2012) 中国民营企业生存环境报告,北京:中国经济出版社.

Forbes (2014). China rich list. Retrieved March 13, 2013. from http://www.forbes.com/china-billionaires/list/#tab:overall

Garnaut, R., Song, L., Yao, Y. and Wang, X. (2012). *Private enterprise in China.* Australian National University, Canberra ePress.

Ge, W. (2011). China's urban unemployment challenge. *International Journal of Business and Social Science, 2*(4), 16–31.

gov.cn (2012). *Implementing regulations on encouraging and guiding healthy development of private investment,* 24 July 2012. 中央政府门户网站 (2012, 鼓励引导民间投资健康发展实施细则出台, 2012 年7月 24 日. Retrieved April 10, 2015, from http://www.gov.cn/gzdt/2012-07/24/content_2176326.htm

Guthrie, D. (1999). *Dragon in a Three-Piece Suit: The emergence of capitalism in China.* Princeton, NJ: Princeton University Press.

Hsu, R. C. (1991). *Economic theories in China, 1979–1988.* Cambridge: Cambridge University Press.

Huang, Y. (2008). *Capitalism with Chinese characteristics: Entrepreneurship and the state, Vol. 1.* Cambridge: Cambridge University Press.

Huang, Y. (2011). Coordination of international competition policies—An anatomy based on Chinese reality. In A. Guzman (Ed.), *Cooperation, comity and competition policy* (pp. 229–264). New York: Oxford University Press.

Hurun Report (2014). Hurun 2014 Philanthropy List. Retrieved March 15, 2015, from http://www.hurun.net/CN/ArticleShow.aspx?nid=5581

IMF (International Monetary Fund) (2015). World Economic Outlook Database October 2015. Retrieved January 19, 2016, from http://www.imf.org/external/pubs/ft/weo/2015/02/weodata/index.aspx

Kaiman, J. (2014). China gets richer but more unequal. *The Guardian,* 28 July 2014. Retrieved February 18, 2016, from http://www.theguardian.com/world/2014/jul/28/china-more-unequal-richer

Kelliher, D. (1992). *Peasant power in China: The era of rural reform, 1979–1989.* New Haven, CT/London: Yale University Press.

Lardy, N. R. (2014). *Markets over Mao: The rise of private business in China.* Washington, DC: Peterson Institute for International Economics.

Li, X. and Liang, X. (2015). A Confucian social model of political appointments among Chinese private entrepreneurs. *Academy of Management Journal*, 58(2): 592–617.

Li, Y. (2006). Four hurdles hindering the development of non-public sectors, people net. Retrieved March 3, 2015, from http://theory.people.com.cn/GB/49154/49155/5141829.html. 厉以宁 (2006) 四道坎阻碍非公有制经济发展,人民网.

Lin, N. (2011). Capitalism in China: A centrally managed capitalism (CMC) and its future. *Management and Organization Review*, 7(1), 63–96.

Liu, J. (2015). SOE salary reform sets an example. *China Daily USA*. Retrieved March 18, 2015, from http://usa.chinadaily.com.cn/epaper/2015-01/05/content_19240882.htm

Liu, Y. (2003). Development of private entrepreneurship in China: Process, problems and countermeasures, in *Entrepreneurship in Asia: Playbook for prosperity* (CD publication by the Maureen and Mike Mansfield foundation program). Retrieved December 20, 2014, from http://www.mansfieldfdn.org/backup/programs/program_pdfs/ent_china.pdf

Lu, X. (Ed.) (2002). *The study report of contemporary Chinese Social Class*. Beijing: Social Science Academic Press. 陆学艺 (主编)(2002) 当代中国社会阶层研究报告, 北京: 社会科学文献出版社.

National Bureau of Statistics of China. (n.d.). *China statistical yearbook, 1995–2014*. Beijing: China Statistics Press.

Nee, V., & Opper, S. (2012). *Capitalism from below: Market and institutional change in China*. Cambridge, MA: Harvard University Press.

Parker, J. K. (1992). China's reform economists make comeback, support Deng, *UPI Archives*, 16 March 1992. Retrieved February 18, 2016, from http://www.upi.com/Archives/1992/03/16/Chinas-reform-economists-make-comeback-support-Deng/9107700722000/

People's Daily (2005). Rules on non-public economy's entry into mineral resource area to release. Retrieved December 12, 2014, from http://en.people.cn/200510/13/eng20051013_214198.html

People's Daily (2013). Civil-run Economy weights more than 60% in GDP, retrieved December 20, 2014, from http://paper.people.com.cn/rmrb/html/2013-02/03/nw.D110000renmrb_20130203_8-01.htm

Powell, B. (2014). Is this the end of China's economic miracle? *Newsweek*. Retrieved March 13, 2015, from http://www.newsweek.com/2014/12/05/china-after-gold-rush-286757.html

Qian, J. W. and Chang, J. (2008). The financial crisis influence the export of small-medium sized enterprises. *Modern Bankers*, (12). 钱杰王, 常杰(2008) 金融危机影响中小企业出口, 当代金融家, (12).

S.E.A. and Horizon (eds) (2014). *2014 development indicators of Chinese Civilian-run Enterprises*. Shanghai: Shanghai Academy of Social Science Press. 上海新沪商联合会,零点研究咨询集团 (2014), 2014 中国民营企业发展指数,上海:上海社会科学院出版社.

Shui, W., & Veeck, G. (2012). China's grain production under bottom-up and top-down patterns of agricultural reforms: a typical case study in Anhui province. *Journal of Geography and Geology*, 4(2), 22–35.

Stevens, R. J. L., Moustapha, M. M., Evelyn, P., & Stevenson, R. J. (2013). Analysis of the emerging China Green Era and its influence on small and medium-sized enterprises development: Review and perspectives. *Journal of Sustainable Development*, 6(4), 86–105.

Sun, J. (1989). *Chinese Economic Histroy-Modern Times* (1840–1949). Beijing: China Renmin University Press. 孙健 (1989), 中国经济史–近代部分 (1840–1949), 北京:中国人民大学出版社.

Tao, Y. (2014). First public information on SOEs: Less than 1 % of enterprises own 30 % of total assets. Sina Finance. Retrieved March 1, 2015, from http:// finance.sina.com.cn/china/20140731/002619866660.shtml. 陶娅洁(2014), 国企家底首次公开:企业户数不到1 %资产总额占30 %, 新浪财经.

Tsai, K. S. (2007). *Capitalism without democracy: The private sector in contemporary China*. Ithaca, NY: Cornell University Press.

Tsui, A. S., Bian, Y., & Cheng, L. (2006). *China's domestic private firms: Multidisciplinary perspectives on management and performance*. New York: M. E. Sharpe.

Tsui, A. S., Schoonhoven, C. B., Meyer, M. W., Lau, C. M., & Milkovich, G. T. (2004). Organization and management in the midst of societal transformation: The People's Republic of China. *Organization Science, 15*(2), 133–145.

Wang, A. S. and Gong, P. (2009). The Influence of financial crisis on the export enterprise and countermeasures. *Shanghai Enterprise*, (08): 18–20. 王安顺, 龚萍 (2009)金融危机对出口企业的影响及应对策略, 上海企业, 2009 年第08期. 18–20页.

Wang, J. and Fan, Z. (2010). *Income tax reform and the stability of state-owned enterprise's accounting information*. Retrieved 4, March, 2015, from http:// www.sinoss.net/qikan/uploadfile/2010/1130/11120.pdf. 王静静, 范宗辉 (2010)所得税改制与国有企业会计信息稳健性

Wang, Q. (Ed.) (2012a). *Report on economic operation of China's private enterprises*. Beijing: China Economic Publishing House. 王强 (主编)(2012,中国民营企业经济运行报告,北京:中国经济出版社.

Wang, Y. (2012b). *The Forbes World's Billionaires 2012*. Retrieved March 8, 2012, from http://wiki.mbalib.com/wiki/2012. (in Chinese).

Wang, Z. (2008). *The private sector and China's market development*. Oxford: Chandos Publishing.

Whyte, M. K. (1984). *Urban life in contemporary China*. Chicago, IL: University of Chicago Press.

Wong, J. (2016). China's economy 2016: How 'scary' is its sustained slowdown? *Straits Times*, 9 January 9. Retrieved January 19, 2016, from http://www. straitstimes.com/opinion/chinas-economy-2016-how-scary-is-its-sustained-slowdown

World Bank. (2015). Gini index (World Bank estimates). Retrieved March 15, 2015, from http://data.worldbank.org/indicator/SI.POV.GINI?page=6

WTO (World Trade Organization) (2010). Economic environment: China. Retrieved March 18, 2015, from www.wto.org/english/tratop_e/tpr_e/s230-01_e.doc

Wu, L. (2009). Sixty years of Chinese contemporary private enterprises' development. The institute of contemporary China studies. Retrieved March 2, 2015, from http://www.iccs.cn/contents/496/8806.html. 武力 (2009) 中国当代私营经济发展六十年. 当代中国研究所.

Xinhua Net (2007). Why did China's rural reform begin and succeed in Anhui province? *xinhua.org*, 6 December 2007. 新华网 (2007). 中国的农村改革因何始于安徽,成于安徽. Retrieved April 21, 2015, from http://news. china.com/zh_cn/news100/11038989/20071206/14528849.html

Xu, D., Lu, J. W., & Gu, Q. (2014). Organizational forms and multi-population dynamics: Economic transition in China. *Administrative Science Quarterly*, 59(3), 517–547.

Yang, T. (Ed.) (2014). *Philanthropic blue book: China's philanthropic development report (2014)*. Beijing: Social Sciences Academic Press (China). 杨团 (主编)(2014)慈善蓝皮书:中国慈善发展报告(2014),北京:社会科学文献出版社.

Yang, X., and Hu, J. (2011). Private enterprises' achievements, challenges, and solutions during the period of 'eleventh five-year'. *Study and Exploration*, 6, 137–141. 杨新铭, 胡家勇 (2011) '十一五'期间民营经济发展成就, 面临问题与解决途径,学习与探索, 6期. 137–141页.

Yao, K. and Wang, A. (2013). China lets Gini out of the bottle: wide wealth gap. *Reuters*. Retrieved March 13, 2015, from http://www.reuters.com/

article/2013/01/18/us-china-economy-income-gap-idUSBRE
90H06L20130118
Zeng, M. and Williamson, P. J. (2003). Hidden Dragon. *Harvard Business Review*, 81 (10) (October): 92–9137.
Zhang, J. (2013). *Fortune the global 500 companies.* Retrieved July 5, 2005, from http://economy.enorth.com.cn/system/2005/07/05/001060964.shtml (in Chinese).
Zhang, Y., & Zhou, Y. (2015). *The source of innovation in China: Highly innovation systems.* Basingstoke, UK: Palgrave Macmillan.
Zhang, Y., Ren, B., Du, G., & J., Y. (2011). Dancing with change: An co-evolutionary perspective for private entrepreneurship during China's institutional transitions. In C. Usui (Ed.), *Comparative entrepreneurship initiatives: Studies in China, Japan and the USA.* Basingstoke, UK: Palgrave Macmillan.
Zheng, J. (1993). Actively promoting the healthy development of individual-private economy. *Hu Bei Social Science*, (10): 19–20. 郑金良 (1993)积极推动个体私营经济健康发展, 湖北社会科学, (10): 19–20.
Zhou, T. and Xia, X. (2008). The history of Chinese state-owned enterprises' reform. C.f. D. T. Zhou, and R. H. Ouyang (Eds.), (2008) *Blue book of development and reform: China 30 years of reform and opening-up (1978–2008).* Beijing: Social Sciences Academic Press. 周天勇,夏徐迁(2008)我国国有企业改革的历程。引自邹东涛, 欧阳日辉 (2008)中国经济发展和体制改革报告:中国改革开放30年(1978–2008发展和改革蓝皮书),北京:社会科学文献出版社.

2

Leadership Insights from Published Studies on Chinese Top Executives

In Chap. 1, we suggested that the growth of the economy in China as a whole is a story of both top-down centrally managed capitalism (Lin 2011) and bottom-up grass-roots capitalism (Nee and Opper 2012). The former focused on the reform of state-owned enterprises and the attraction of foreign investment, while the latter allowed for the creation of a private economy without much policy guidance or support. Private individuals overcame extremely disadvantageous initial conditions and developed robust enterprises that became the major engine of growth for China. Nee and Opper (2012), through their five-year study of over 700 entrepreneurs in the Yangzi River Delta region, provided convincing evidence and a persuasive argument that this economic miracle is the result of the actions and ambitions of entrepreneurs. Since they could not rely on formal institutions, private entrepreneurs had to develop their own informal lending systems and networks of suppliers and distributors. They contributed a large proportion of the national GDP and provided employment as the state sector's contributions to both declined steadily over the years. Formal institutional changes that legitimised the private

© The Author(s) 2017   **43**
A.S. Tsui et al., *Leadership of Chinese Private Enterprises*, Palgrave Studies in Chinese Management, DOI 10.1057/978-1-137-40235-6_2

firms' existence and supported their further development came after their initial success. Private entrepreneurs, the 'capitalists' who were despised, scorned and viewed with suspicion in the early years of the reforms, are now legitimate members of Chinese society. Even though the sea is still turbulent and the entrepreneurs are still complaining about the difficult business environment and continued unfair treatment by the government relative to state-sector firms, their economic success is undeniable, earning social acceptance as well as raising expectations by both government and citizens of their role in contributing to a balanced economic and social development of China. Even though the future is uncertain, we can conclude from the solid results that this resounding success can be credited to the 'leadership' or agency of the entrepreneurs and founders of these private enterprises. This conclusion is consistent with the 'visible hand' theory of the growth and development of industrial enterprises (Chandler 1978) in the West as well as the strategic choice theory of business and organisation management (Child 1972).

Who are these 'visible hands'? How do they lead? This chapter is devoted to a discussion of this question by reviewing and analysing studies of executive leaders, especially chief executive officers (CEOs) from China. Even though there are many books that provide accounts of the success of private entrepreneurs, the focus of these works is often on the institutional environment and the role of social capital (e.g. Krug 2004; Nee and Opper 2012). They rarely focus on leaders' behaviours and management approaches (including their philosophical foundations), and do not offer a conceptual analysis of the leadership practices of these leaders. Using the published studies of top leaders in Chinese firms, in this chapter we aim to develop a preliminary understanding of the key behaviours and characteristics of the top leaders of Chinese firms, with a keen eye on those who founded and managed the private enterprises.

The Literature

Chen and Lee (2008) offer an informative discussion of Chinese business leadership focusing on the influence of traditional Chinese philosophies and Western management practices. Despite the impressive rise of

China as an economic power in the world, their observation, based on their review of the literature, is that 'the twenty-first-century leadership in China is not well understood by the outside world' (Chen and Lee 2008: 3). Their book focuses on leadership at all levels, not just on the top leaders of private firms. Our review of the literature suggests that knowledge about top executives is even more scarce in the Western literature. For example, Jia et al. (2012) carried out a comprehensive review of research papers that reported studies using Chinese samples, and identified 259 articles published in six leading English-language management and organisation journals between 1981 and 2010. Among these articles, only a few focused on the top leaders of Chinese firms. Most of the leadership studies analysed the top executives' social networks, especially their connections to government officials, through their own direct past associations or indirect contacts. This is part of the body of literature on *guanxi* networks in the Chinese context (Chen et al. 2013). For example, entrepreneurs use these *guanxi* networks in resource acquisition as a substitute for incomplete formal institutions (Xin and Pearce 1996). Their social capital, especially the strong ties between entrepreneurs and venture capitalists, led to the venture capitalists' favourable investment decisions (Batjargal and Liu 2004). The entrepreneurs' political networking had a positive effect on new venture performance (Li and Zhang 2007). Nee and Opper (2012) found that the entrepreneurs in their study used *guanxi* (or social) networks for control, collaboration and mutual support.

Only a handful of studies focused on CEOs' human capital as reflected in their personal attributes. One study focused on CEO hubris (Li and Tang 2010) and found it to be related to risky investments in a sample of 2790 CEOs of diverse manufacturing firms in China. The results are consistent with the literature in the West that CEO hubris, or overconfidence, has negative or variable firm consequences (e.g. Hiller and Hambrick 2005). The authors used an indirect measure of hubris by comparing the CEOs' subjective performance evaluation of their firms over the previous six months compared to the objective return on sales (ROS) total during the same period. In two studies of Chinese firm CEOs, personal values and personality were the focal interests. One is Fu et al.'s (2010) study that measured CEOs' leadership behaviour and personal values, and investigated how they influenced middle managers' organisational commitment and turnover intentions. The other is Ou et al.'s (2014) study of CEOs' personal attribute of humility and its influence on top management team (TMT) integration, the CEOs' empowering leadership, and middle managers' responses. In general, research on Chinese CEOs or top management team leadership is scanty.

We must admit that it is not an easy task to study CEOs, because understanding their thought processes and behaviours requires original data from them. These data are not readily available from archival sources. CEOs are extremely busy people, and hence are not easy to contact. To gain their co-operation to complete a survey or be interviewed is particularly difficult. Hence using indirect measures of personal attributes, such as the method used by Li and Tang (2010), is a practical alternative. This difficulty may explain the low number of studies on CEO attributes or leadership. In this chapter, we focus on published studies that have carried out a direct measurement of CEOs' personal attributes and behaviours to gain an understanding of their leadership attributes. We do not claim to have carried out an exhaustive literature review, since we focus only on the relatively large sample studies published in a few leading scholarly journals and relevant Chinese leadership books. We aim to develop some preliminary ideas on top leadership characteristics from analysing these large-sample studies and then to use in-depth interview data (which we report in Chaps. 3 to 15) to further explore and develop insights into private firm's top leadership. In the final chapter (Chap. 16), we present the results of a thorough content analysis of the interview data of the 13 exemplary founder/CEOs of Chinese private firms who took part in our survey.

Below, we first provide a summary of the major focus and findings of each study, in chronological order of publication date. Then we describe an integration of the findings and derive four attributes that seem to define the very top leaders of Chinese firms, especially those who founded and led successful private enterprises.

Large-Sample Empirical Studies of Chinese CEO Leadership

In general, empirical research on China since the mid-1980s has concentrated on explaining the transformation of state-owned enterprises (SOEs), the influence of traditional and modern culture on individuals, multinationals in China, and human resource management issues (Tsui et al. 2004). Only a handful of studies have focused on private firms—less than 10 % of the several hundred studies reviewed by Li and Tsui (2002) and Tsui et al. (2004). Jia et al. (2012) found the majority of the 259 articles using Chinese samples offered a very low degree of understanding of China, because most studies analyse problems, use theories and adopt concepts that are popular in the Western literature. Not surprisingly, there is limited knowledge about Chinese management, especially executive leadership. Even when a journal calls specifically for the analysis of business leadership in the Chinese context, the results are disappointing. The guest editors of a special issue of *Management and Organization Review* conclude, 'While we praise the theoretical contributions these papers make, there continues to be a disconnection between the … papers and the Chinese context' (Zhang et al. 2014: 210). Those scholars who accept the premise of visible hands and strategic choice would agree that the leadership of private firms might be an important key to understanding the success of these organisations in turbulent times.

Our search of the literature resulted in eight empirical studies that focused explicitly on the CEO, the top leader of the firm. However, not all CEOs are leaders of private firms. Many are from a mix of private and state firms, with a few foreign firms. Each of these eight studies involves a sample size of at least 30 or more CEOs. Some studies involve lower-level employees (e.g. top or middle managers) describing their CEOs. A few studies report differences in the leadership style or approach in the different types of firms, including SOEs (state-owned enterprises), POEs (privately owned enterprises), and FOEs (foreign-owned enterprises). Only two studies focus exclusively on the CEOs of private firms (i.e. Li and Liang 2015; Ou et al. 2014). We analysed these articles for the CEOs' backgrounds, and their leadership behaviour, values, personality and thought processes whenever available. As far as we could, we identified differences in the leadership characteristics in POEs relative to those in SOEs and FOEs. Table 2.1 summarises the profiles of the CEO samples, the major findings of the eight studies, and the findings relevant for executive leadership of POEs.

In a study entitled 'Let a Thousand Flowers Bloom: Variety of leadership styles among Chinese CEOs', Tsui et al. (2004) reported their observations on the variety of leadership styles found in two samples of top executives. They discussed three main forces that might have influenced the behaviours of firms' leaders: Confucian values; communist ideologies; and modern culture associated with economic reforms. These three forces have co-evolved with the emergence of private entrepreneurial firms, the entry of foreign-invested companies, and the reformation of state-owned enterprises. The changing institutional environment combined with younger employees endorsing values and expectations different from those of their older counterparts suggest a context receptive to a variety of leadership practices and behaviours. It was a period of experimentation and learning. Leaders, like their firms, were learning as they progressed. The authors used focus-group interviews and two large-sample surveys (one with 446 managers and another with 1000 managers describing their companies' CEOs), and were able to identify six distinct leadership behaviours. They are (1) being creative and taking risks; (2) relating and communicating; (3) articulating vision; (4) showing benevolence; (5) monitoring operations; and (6) being authoritative. The authors then conducted a profile analysis (using a clustering procedure) and found the six behaviours actually represented four different leadership styles. They labelled these as *advanced leadership* (exhibiting high levels on all five leadership behaviours and a lower level on being authoritative); *progressing leadership* (medium level on the six behaviours); *authoritative leadership* (high on authoritative behaviour but lower on other five behaviours); and *invisible leadership* (low on all six behaviours). These four styles were replicated in the second sample. Further analysis revealed that most of the advanced leaders are CEOs in the POEs in both samples, and there were no invisible leaders in POEs. These findings suggest a dynamic and active leadership style in the owner-entrepreneurial firms. The invisible leadership style may have its roots in Daoism, emphasising that the 'superior leader gets things done with little motion' (Tsui et al. 2004: 17).

Table 2.1 Basic demographics of the CEO samples and major findings in the eight empirical studies

Study	No. of CEOs studied/ownership	CEO average age	CEO educational level	Overall findings	Findings relevant to POEs and implications
1. Variety of leadership styles (Tsui, et al. 2004)	Study 1: 450 Study 2: 130 (1000 middle managers) A mixture of POEs, SOEs, and FOEs	Not reported	Not reported	– Six behaviors: Articulating vision, monitoring operations, being creative and risk-taking, relating and communicating, showing benevolence, being authoritative–Four leadership types: Advanced (a high level on all except low on authoritative); Progressive (average level on all except authoritative); Authoritative (high on this only); Invisible (low on all)	– Most of the Advanced leaders are CEOs in the POEs, compared to SOEs and FOEs. – No Invisible leaders in POEs – POEs leaders are active leaders, dealing with a variety of leadership functions

(continued)

Table 2.1 (continued)

Study	No. of CEOs studied/ownership	CEO average age	CEO educational level	Overall findings	Findings relevant to POEs and implications
2. Leadership behaviour and firm culture (Tsui et al. 2006)	Study 1: Sample 1—542 Sample 2—152 Study 2: 6 CEOs Around 30 % POEs, 45 % SOEs and 25 % POEs.	Not reported	Not reported	Study 1 (2 samples, survey): – More companies with coupling than decoupling of leader behavior and organisational culture. Study 2 (6 firms, interview): – Two types of CEO leadership behavior: performance builders (focus on short-term financial) and institution builders (focus on long-term sustainable development)	Study 1 – Sample 1: 59 % of POEs with strong leadership and strong culture (relative to 26 % for SOEs and 53 % for FOEs) – Sample 2: 53 % of POEs with strong leadership and strong culture (relative to 33 % for SOEs and 41 % for FOEs) – POEs leaders' influence on their firm's organisational culture seems evident

3. Chinese traditions and Western influences on business leadership in China (Zhang et al. 2008)	35 CEOs: 26 % SOEs 74 % POEs	42.3	16.7 years	– Seven management philosophical notions: Sincerity is essential, Pursuit of excellence, Social responsibility, Harmony is precious, The Golden Mean, Specialisation, and Scientific management. – Four major influences: Life experiences, books and literature, role models, business education – Chinese traditions influence philosophy on managing people and Western theories on managing tasks	– Most findings are relevant to POEs given that they make up 74 % of the sample – Many examples of private firm entrepreneurs' experiences and perspectives

(continued)

Table 2.1 (continued)

Study	No. of CEOs studied/ownership	CEO average age	CEO educational level	Overall findings	Findings relevant to POEs and implications
4. Leader behaviour and personal values (Fu et al. 2010)	42 19 % POEs 33 % SOEs 22 % FOEs Rest unknown	50	83 % BA/BSc	– Congruence between transformational behaviour and self-transcendence values associated with strong middle manager commitment – Commitment highest when the transformational CEO also has a high level of self-transcendence and a low level of self-enhancement values	– No specific results reported for different ownership types – POEs tend to be younger and smaller, relative to SOEs – CEO influence on middle managers may be stronger in POEs because of the smaller size relative to SOEs

5. Leader behaviour, employees' attitudes and firm performance (Wang et al. 2011)	125	Ownership types not reported	44	6 years beyond high school	– Relationship-focused leadership behaviours (relating and communicating, showing benevolent, non-authoritative) relate to firm performance through positive middle manager attitudes, but not directly – Task-focused leadership behaviours (articulating a vision, being creative and risk-taking, monitoring operations) influence firm performance directly	– CEOs show more benevolence and engage in more monitoring of operations in small rather than in large firms – Since POEs tend to be smaller firms, we can infer that CEOs of POEs may tend to show more benevolence and hands-on leadership (monitoring operations)

(continued)

Table 2.1 (continued)

Study	No. of CEOs studied/ownership	CEO average age	CEO educational level	Overall findings	Findings relevant to POEs and implications
6. Humble CEOs, TMT and middle managers (Ou et al. 2014)	63 100 % POEs	42	97 % had Bachelor or higher degree	– Humility has both behavioural and cognitive/motivational dimensions. The former is about acknowledging weaknesses and appreciating others. The latter is about a belief in low self-focus and self-transcendent pursuit – Humble CEOs engage in empowering leadership – Empowering leadership facilitates top management team integration – TMT integration produces an empowering organisational climate – Empowering climate facilitates positive middle managers' job performance, commitment and work engagement	– The average humility level of the CEOs is higher when based on their conversations with the researchers than when described by their subordinates (top managers), suggesting that the CEOs might be able to present a more positive image to acquaintances than to those with whom they have frequent interactions – CEOs in private firms may have a greater influence on middle managers because of more frequent interaction in the smaller POEs or FOEs than in the larger SOEs

7. CEO and top manager leadership (Song et al. 2014)	40	Ownership type not reported	Not reported	Not reported	– Three types of CEO leadership behaviour: caring (extended care to employees' families), task-focus (attention to operations future firm development), and authoritative (concentrating decision power) – Middle manager performance is high when the CEO shows a high level of caring regardless of level of supervisory support – Supervisory support can compensate for a low level of caring by the CEO to boost middle manager performance – A high task-focus or a high authoritative CEO can stimulate high middle manager performance only when there is strong supervisory support	– Caring CEOs also tend to have a high task-focus – Authoritative CEOs tend to have a low caring and low task-focus – Caring and task-focus capture the relationship and performance focus of CEOs in other studies (e.g. Wang et al. 2011). – This dual focus on both task and people, along with a low level of authoritativeness (high humility) may be characteristic of effective leadership of private firms

(continued)

Table 2.1 (continued)

Study	No. of CEOs studied/ownership	CEO average age	CEO educational level	Overall findings	Findings relevant to POEs and implications
8. CEO pro-social orientation and political appointments (Li and Liang 2015)	Study 1: 166 Study 2: 1323 100 % POEs	Study 1: 42 Study 2: 50	Study 1: BA/BSc Study 2: BA/BSc	– Successful entrepreneurs' desire to seek political appointment declines substantially when they have a high level of pro-self motive or a low level of pro-social motive – Entrepreneurs' desire to seek political appointment is high when they have a high level of pro-self motive along with low business success – Entrepreneurs' desire to seek political appointment is high when they have a high degree of pro-social motive, regardless of the degree of business success – Hypotheses supported using political appointments of chairmen of listed private firms	– Confucian teaching emphasises caring for society after one has attained personal success – Study shows that only those with a pro-social motive would advance to this stage of contribution to the greater good – This pro-social motive seems to capture the idea of self-transcendence and humility identified in other studies (e.g. Fu et al. 2010; Ou et al. 2014).

There has been a long history of debate about the role of leadership for organisational culture. Schein (1985, 1992) is a strong proponent of the functional perspective of leadership. Leaders, especially founders, define the core values of the organisation and shape the organisation's culture, or commonly accepted beliefs and values guiding decision-making throughout the organisation. Other scholars, building on attribution theory (Calder 1977; Meindl et al. 1985; Pfeffer 1977, 1981), argue that leaders play a symbolic role in explaining, justifying and providing meaning to decisions and outcomes of the organisation. Therefore followers attribute both positive and negative outcomes to the leader. A third, contingency perspective, points to the potential limits of the leader's ability to change or shape an organisation's culture, suggesting conditions when leadership behaviour and organisational culture may be decoupled. Employing the contingency perspective, Tsui et al. (2006) aim to understand when and why decoupling between CEO leadership behaviour and organisational culture may occur. The authors reasoned that, in China, CEOs in state-owned and foreign-owned companies would have more constraints on their discretion than would CEOs in the privately owned firms. In other words, POE leaders have more discretion; therefore their behaviour should have a more direct connection with the culture of the firm. The authors conducted two large-sample survey studies using middle managers to describe their CEOs' leadership behaviour and organisational culture (sample 1 has 542 firms, with one respondent per firm; and sample 2 has 152 firms with an average of seven respondents per firm). This study also included an interview study of six firms. In general, the authors found support for their predictions.

Specifically, the occurrence of decoupling between leadership behaviour and organisational culture is more likely in state-owned and foreign-owned firms than in privately owned firms. Conversely, coupling is more likely in private firms than in state or foreign firms. The interview study further revealed that CEOs can emphasise either performance enhancement or institution building in shaping their organisation's culture. The former focuses on maximising the firm's short-term financial performance, while the latter articulates values and puts in place systems and processes important for the organisation's long-term development. The authors also found that the CEOs who emphasise short-term performance tend to be younger professional managers with MBA degrees. Those who emphasise the long-term development of the firm tend to be older, with less formal education, and more mild-mannered. They remind us of the Taoist (the word Dao is used in mainland China) or Confucian sage who led with a high level of vision and a long-term perspective for the organisation.

Fu et al. (2010) began with the premise that effective CEOs tend to engage in transformational leadership, characterised by vision, intellectual stimulation, high expectations and role modelling. This leadership approach motivates followers to go beyond their own self-interest and to act for the good of the collective. Through transforming followers' attention from the self to the collective, these leaders raise their followers' commitment to the organisation. However, transformational leadership implies an underlying value of self-transcendence by the leader him/herself; i.e. caring for others' well-being is more important than caring for one's own interests. The authors point out that not all transformational leaders have self-transcendent values, however; some leaders favour a high level of self-enhancement. They theorise that CEOs' values may either enhance or attenuate the effect of the leaders' transformational behaviours on followers. Self-enhancement values—focusing on the leaders' own happiness—would attenuate the effect, whereas self-transcendent values—focusing on happiness of others—would accentuate the effect of CEOs' transformational behaviours on the followers' commitment. The sample consisted of 177 top managers, 605 middle managers, and the CEOs of 42 firms. About 20 % of the 42 CEOs were owners of private firms, around 33 % were from state-owned firms, and 22 % from foreign firms. The CEOs' tenure was longer in private firms, and their firms were younger than the other two types. Interestingly, the authors did not find any difference in transformational behaviour or personal values among CEOs of different types of firms, except that younger CEOs tended to have a higher level of self-enhancement values than did older CEOs.

The results show that middle managers expressed the highest level of commitment to the organisation when the CEOs' transformational behaviour is paired with a high level of self-transcendence value but a low level of self-enhancement. Meanwhile, their commitment is lowest when the CEOs' transformational behaviour accompanies a high level of self-enhancement and a low level of self-transcendence values. Further interviews with the CEOs provided insight into the nature of self-transcendence. The leaders with self-enhancement values expressed their life goals to be the pursuit of happiness in life, career success, honouring ancestors, and self-fulfillment. The leaders with self-transcendence values expressed life goals of attaining social justice, integrity, true love, giving back to society, contributing to the development of society, and bringing happiness and opportunities for the success of others.

These findings are consistent with the general notion that morality in leaders is important in all cultures (House et al. 2004; Parsons and Shils 1951), and that one should practise what one preaches. While the authors did not conduct separate analyses of leadership behaviour and personal values in the private firms, nor compare them to those in other types of firms, there is no reason to expect that self-transcendence values, and congruence between internal values and external behaviour, would not be equally important for the leadership of private firms.

The importance of moral character also appears in an interview study by Zhang et al. (2008). They interviewed 35 CEOs, nine from SOEs (26 % of the sample) and 26 from POEs (74 %). Through content analysis of the 35 interviews, with each lasting 60 to 150 minutes, the authors identified seven management notions (a term similar in meaning to philosophy): sincerity, pursuit of excellence, social responsibility, harmony is precious, the Golden Mean, specialisation, and scientific management.

The most frequently mentioned notion is *sincerity* (by 66 % of the interviewees). It means honesty and honouring promises made. It includes honesty, trustworthiness and self-discipline. A private-firm CEO reported that being honest allowed him to be credible and gain support from others who trusted him. The second most frequently mentioned notion is *pursuit of excellence*, by 60 % of the interviewees. This means providing customers with the best products and services. It also means achieving the best performance and sustain continuous development. Several private-firm leaders said they were dedicated to building a 'centennial enterprise.' Others aspired to change the perception that there was no 'excellent brand in China' (Zhang et al. 2008: 245). Social responsibility was mentioned by 46 % of the interviewees. It refers to a firm being beneficial for both its stakeholders and society as a whole. It is the duty of business leaders to develop the nation and bring stability to the country, in addition to providing jobs and offering valuable products and services. The company should take care of its employees, shareholders and other stakeholders, and to share profits with all of them. An entrepreneur from a private company said, 'I do not consider my firm as a money-making machine but as a carrier which can push the society forward' (Zhang et al. 2008: 247).

Harmony is precious was mentioned by 37 % of the interviewees. It refers to maintaining harmony both inside and outside the company, and includes being kind and co-operative. The interviewees gave examples of not laying off employees during restructuring, or even when company performance was not satisfactory. Some leaders even developed harmonious relationships with their customers, believing that harmony can bring wealth.

Each of the next three notions received a mention by 31 % of the interviewees. The Confucian idea of the *Golden Mean* means maintaining balance and everything in moderation, as expressed by one leader as 'going beyond is as bad as falling short' (Zhang et al. 2008: 250). Being flexible, maintaining stability and maintaining steady development are the essence of taking the middle way. *Specialisation* refers to professionalisation, competence and being principled. *Scientific management* includes standardisation, institutionalisation and transparency. It involves developing rules, regulations and standards to replace personal relationships in task assignment and management.

The interviews further revealed that both Chinese culture and Western management theories influenced their thinking. The former were responsible for the notions of harmony, Golden Mean, and social responsibility while the latter might have influenced the notions of specialisation and scientific management. Sincerity might have the influence of both Chinese tradition and Western thought. About half of the leaders also said that traditional Chinese thoughts inspired them to develop strategies, while Western management theory influenced them in identifying tactics. As a group, they placed a great emphasis on learning. The learning came from more formal executive programmes in management schools as well as from reflecting on observation, reading and conversing. One executive kept a diary of all his learning and his notebook contained more than 500 million words. This interview study provided valuable insights that could not be obtained from survey studies.

Wang et al. (2011), using a structured survey format, explored the links between CEO leadership behaviours (the same six behaviours reported in the Tsui et al. 2004 study), employee (middle manager) attitudes (organisational commitment, perceived support from the supervisor, perceived fairness in outcome distribution and the fairness of process in managerial decision-making), and firm performance (evaluated subjectively). The authors grouped the six leadership behaviours into task-focused (articulating a vision, being creative and taking risks, and monitoring operations) and relationship-focused (relating and communicating, showing benevolence, and being authoritative). They hypothesised that relationship-focused leadership behaviour would influence firm performance by creating positive employee attitudes, while the task-focused leadership behaviour would influence the firm's performance directly. The hypotheses were tested on a matched sample of 739 middle managers and their supervisors (top managers) in 125 firms. Results support the hypotheses.

This study did not report information on the ownership type of the firms surveyed. As leaders of small entrepreneurial firms in the emerging economic context of China, the founder/CEO may need to attend to both task and people issues. Even though attention to tasks, necessary for survival in a highly inhospitable and uncertain environment, may be overwhelming, the emphasis on relationships as grounded in Confucian culture is likely to be equally salient in the minds of the Chinese business leaders.

Ou et al. (2014) focused on private firms and examined the concept of humility among the private-firm CEOs. They traced the process through which CEO humility may influence the degree of integration among members of the top management team (TMT) and further influence positive responses from the middle manager in terms of work engagement, commitment to the firm, and job performance. By using three different samples, the authors developed a measure of humility comprising six components: (1) self-awareness; (2) openness to feedback; (3) appreciation of others; (4) low self-focus; (5) self-transcendent pursuit; and (6) transcendent self-concept. While the existing literature has focused on behavioural manifestations (e.g. Owens 2009), i.e. the first three of the six dimensions, this study expanded the humility idea for the top leader of the firm by adding three cognitive and motivational dimensions that emphasise low self-focus and high transcendent self-concept, the fourth to the sixth dimensions in Ou et al.'s (2014) measurement. The authors hypothesised that humble CEOs (those high on all six dimensions relative to others who are average on all, or those high on some but low on others, as well as those who are low on all dimensions) would engage in empowering leadership behaviours (those that enhance the meaningfulness of work, fostering participative decision-making, expressing confidence in followers, and providing autonomy). These empowering behaviours would in turn encourage the TMT members to engage in collaborative behaviours, joint decision-making, open information sharing, and developing and supporting a shared vision. Such a highly integrated TMT would then lead with a similar orientation and convey similar expectations to the middle managers. The middle managers would then in turn receive consistent messages from their leaders (the top managers) and would perceive that the organisation emphasises information sharing, autonomy and self-management, all behavioural norms consistent with empowering organisational climates. The end result of this process that begins with CEO humility is the elicitation of positive responses from middle managers.

To test this hypothesis, the authors gathered survey data from 328 TMT members and 645 middle managers in 63 private companies in China at two different times three months apart. The survey results provide support for the hypothesis. The authors also conducted interviews with 51 CEOs, who provided additional insights into the meaning of humility and the differences between those with high and low humility. Specifically, high and low humility differed most on transcendent self-concept. Those who have high humility expressed openness to feedback, appreciation of others, willingness to acknowledge their weaknesses, and belief that mankind exists within the constraints of a larger force. As one humble CEO said when interviewed, 'I believe that man proposes and nature disposes' (Ou et al. 2014: 57).

The authors did not explain these findings as being unique to Chinese culture, as some Western scholars (e.g. Collins 2001) have also observed humility among CEOs of some very successful American organisations. On the other hand, successful leaders in the Western culture, especially those at the helm, are often described as dynamic, outgoing, flamboyant, and with an extreme air of confidence. The image of humbleness, especially the acknowledgement of weaknesses and one's smallness within a large universe, does not seem to fit the stereotype of a successful CEO. The confirmation of the humility effect in this study might mean that it may be an important personality trait for executive leaders in the Chinese context. After all, humility is a core idea in Daoism.

The study by Song et al. (2014) also focused on how CEOs transmit their influence on middle managers through their top managers. This study analyses the leadership of both the CEO and the top managers, and how each relates to the performance of the middle managers. The authors reasoned that middle managers (at two levels below the CEO) would be influenced by the leadership styles of both the CEO and the middle managers' immediate supervisor (the top manager as the team leader). These supervisors may play a buffering role in softening the strong leadership style of the CEO. When the CEO has a highly caring leadership style (with an emphasis on well-being concern being extended to the employees' families), middle managers would perform well without the need for a high level of support from their immediate supervisors. When the CEO has a task-focused style (emphasis on efficiency, operational control, innovation, experimentation, long-term development of the firm) or an authoritative style (emphasis on concentration of power, unilateral decision-making), middle managers would benefit from the supportiveness of their immediate supervisors. In other words, middle managers are subject to the influence of both the CEO as a distant leader and the top manager as their immediate supervisor.

The sample consisted of 608 middle managers and 140 of the direct supervisors (top managers) in 40 companies. The top managers described the leadership style of the CEO, and the middle managers described the supportive behaviour of the top managers. Results show that the middle managers' performance is lowest when there is a non-caring or authoritative CEO plus a non-supportive supervisor. Middle manager performance is high when a highly authoritative or a highly task-focused CEO is paired with a supportive supervisor. The most important finding of this study is that neither CEO leadership style nor the supportiveness of the immediate supervisor has a direct effect on middle manager performance. It is the combination of the two that can enhance or depress the middle managers' performance. Supportive supervisors are important in the absence of a caring CEO, and in the presence of an authoritative and strong performance-oriented CEO.

This study offers insight into the nature and influence of CEO leadership in the context of the work environment of middle managers. This insight is especially important for understanding the executive leadership of private enterprises, which tend to be smaller and with fewer hierarchies. The CEOs tend to focus on both strategies and operations, and on both task and people issues, a form of dual-focus or paradoxical leadership behaviour described by Zhang et al. (2015). These CEOs would have frequent contact with the middle managers who serve as the key implementers of strategic and operational decisions. The findings of this study also imply that, in order to motivate middle managers to achieve high performance, CEOs need to show all three leadership behaviours: extended care for employees, an authoritative manner, and performance-focused with visionary, strategic and operational control. However, the effect of the latter two would be realised only in the presence of a supportive immediate supervisor.

As discussed in Chap. 1, in recent years, increasing numbers of successful private-firm entrepreneurs hold (part-time) representational appointments in political councils such as the People's Congress (PC) or People's Political Consultative Conference (PPCC), at both the national and provincial levels. However, past research has suggested that the main purpose of entrepreneurs making political connections is to obtain resources that could not otherwise be obtained to maintain their business. When they become successful, there is a decreasing need to rely on political connections (Luo et al. 2012). From records of private firms publicly listed on the two stock exchanges in China, Li and Liang (2015) observed that many successful entrepreneurs are actually members of political committees such as the PC or PPCC. Intrigued by this observation, the authors sought to understand the complex motivations of successful entrepreneurs for joining political councils. They proposed a Confucian social model of role transition to explain the pursuit and attainment of political appointments by successful private entrepreneurs. According to Confucian teaching, a great man progresses through life in four stages, and each stage involves specific roles and responsibilities. The first stage is to cultivate self (develop self-discipline); the second is to regulate a family (develop harmony); the third is to order national life (develop a successful career); and the last is to bring world peace (contribute to progress in society). This is a prescriptive model in that not all people would go through all four stages, especially the final stage. Li and Liang (2015) considered two types of motives that distinguish those who would advance to the fourth stage and accept its role from those who would not: a pro-self and a pro-social motive for seeking political connections. The former focuses on bringing benefits to themselves (and their firms), while the latter focuses on achieving benefits for society as a whole (industry, community, nation). They hypothesised that successful entrepreneurs would be less likely to seek or attain political appointments when they had a high level of pro-self motive, but more likely when they have a high level of pro-social motive. In other words, only those entrepreneurs with a high level of pro-social motive would advance to the fourth stage and become a sage.

The authors conducted a cross-sectional survey of 166 private-firm CEOs/chairpersons and a longitudinal archival study of 1323 Chinese publicly listed private firms using publicly available data from 2006 to 2012. The findings support the hypotheses, offering insights into how Confucian cultural values may explain the dynamics between business success and political appointments of private entrepreneurs in China.

In summary, the eight studies provide some insights into the leadership behaviours and attributes of Chinese CEOs, though not all are from the private sector. Two of the eight studies have 100 % private entrepreneurs (Li and Liang 2015; Ou et al. 2014); and three studies have 74 % (Zhang et al. 2008), 30 % (Tsui et al. 2006) and 19 % (Fu et al. 2010), respectively. Three studies (Song et al. 2014; Tsui et al. 2004; Wang et al. 2011) did not report a breakdown of ownership type in the samples. The eight studies involved a total of about 3068 CEOs. The five studies that reported ownership type involve a total of 2323 CEOs. Among them, there were 1793 private entrepreneurs (77 % of 2323). Based on these numbers, we assumed that the findings would describe private-firm leadership to some extent. However, the descriptions of Chinese leadership were also influenced by the theories and methods used. Many of the eight studies were hypothesis testing, guided by Western theories. Four studies explicitly explored the 'indigenous' nature of Chinese leadership (Li and Liang 2015; Tsui et al. 2004; Tsui et al. 2006; Zhang et al. 2008). One study drew on Confucianism to develop an indigenous hypothesis (e.g. Li and Liang 2015), and another discussed the deep influence of Confucianism on the management thoughts of modern entrepreneurs (Zhang et al. 2008). One study discovered the influence of Daoism reflected in the 'invisible leadership' approach (Tsui et al. 2004).

A glaring omission from the studies of top leaders is the idea of paternalistic leadership, which was found to be highly descriptive of Chinese entrepreneurs in overseas Chinese family businesses, mainly in Southeast Asia, Hong Kong and Taiwan (Farh and Cheng 2000; Redding 1990; Westwood 1997). Paternalistic leadership combines strong authoritarianism with fatherly benevolence and moral integrity. Some recent empirical studies on Chinese paternalistic leadership (Chen et al. 2015; Wu et al. 2012) found authoritarianism to be negative while benevolence and morality were positively related to a variety of employee outcomes. The studies used TMT and other lower-level supervisors. However, two studies in our review (Song et al. 2014; Tsui et al. 2004), using CEO samples, confirmed the presence of authoritative behaviour and its negative effects on followers.

The studies we reviewed focused primarily on the leaders' behaviours, personality and values. Most studies identified multiple leadership behaviours (e.g. Tsui et al. 2004; Tsui et al. 2006; Wang et al. 2011), multiple styles (Tsui et al. 2004), or multiple management philosophies (Zhang et al. 2008). These findings are consistent with the proposal by Chen and Lee (2008) that the pluralistic challenges of the Chinese context 'call for the multiple and divergent perspectives and approaches' that are revealed in their book. Therefore they recommend an eclectic and holistic approach to the study and practice of leadership. We support their view by contributing to the holistic understanding of Chinese private-firm leadership by identifying important personal attributes.

Our observation and synthesis of the published work, and the context in which the private entrepreneurs had to operate, led to the identification of four personal attributes that might be particularly descriptive of private-firm leaders. During economic reform, both state and private firms underwent dramatic changes. However, as we explained in Chap. 1, government policies still favour state firms. Many state enterprises are still very bureaucratic (Schlevogt 2002; Weihrich 1990), and the government may have a direct interest in appointing more bureaucratic CEOs (Bryson et al. 2012), even though there are exceptions. What we discovered and propose may also describe some state-firm leaders, but in general we focus our synthesis with a keen eye on the private-firm leaders who had to overcome extraordinarily challenging conditions.

Identifying Personal Attributes of Private-Firm Leaders

Combining what we learned from the eight survey studies, and information about the developmental path of the private-sector entrepreneurs, we inductively derived several unique personal characteristics. First, these leaders appear to be able to deal with two opposing forces or contradictory requirements simultaneously. They may pay attention to both people and task issues (Song et al. 2014; Wang et al. 2011); short-term performance and long-term development (Tsui et al. 2006); and self-interest and collective needs (Fu et al. 2010; Li and Liang 2015; Ou et al. 2014; Song et al. 2014). This *dual focus* reflects the Chinese contemporary setting, which has a deep traditional culture of primarily Confucianism and secondarily Daoism. Confucianism emphasises social roles, the importance of family and relationships, and the authority and responsibility of those at higher levels in society (Li and Liang 2015), along with modern values of professionalism, efficiency, control and creativity (Song et al. 2014; Tsui et al. 2004). This dual -focus also reflects the paradoxical or dialectic thinking that is deeply rooted in both Confucianism and Daoism (Ma and Tsui 2015). Zhang et al. (2015), in a study of lower-level supervisors, observed that Chinese leaders often face contradictory demands and frequently behave in a seemingly paradoxical manner. The authors proposed a multidimensional concept of paradoxical leadership with five dimensions: combining self-centeredness with other-centeredness; maintaining both distance and closeness with subordinates; treating subordinates uniformly while allowing individuality; enforcing work requirements while allowing flexibility; and maintaining decision control while allowing autonomy. Using five samples, they developed a valid measure for this construct. With a different sample of 76 first-level supervisors and 516 subordinates from six firms, they tested the hypothesis that relates paradoxical leadership to a set of antecedents and consequences. They found that supervisors' holistic thinking and integrative complexity cognition relate positively to paradoxical leader behaviours, which in turn are associated with subordinate proficiency, adaptivity and proactivity. In other words, effective leaders maintain a dual focus when they deal with contradictory and seemingly incompatible people, tasks, and firm and environmental issues. The survey studies do not provide direct evidence, but are suggestive of such characteristics among successful Chinese leaders, especially the private entrepreneurs, since they operate in a highly complex, dynamic and uncertain institutional environment that is a blend of both traditionality and modernity.

Several studies point to the leader's orientation towards the common good over and beyond the success and survival of their enterprises. Ou et al. (2014) described humble CEOs who have a self-transcendent concept; they believe in the existence of something greater than the self in the universe. Not everything is within their control: man proposes and heaven disposes. Along the same lines, they recognise and acknowledge that they are not omnipotent, having both strengths and limitations, just as others do. So they appreciate the strength of others as much as they recognise their own weaknesses. Li and Liang (2015) describe the CEOs who accept the Confucian teaching of caring for society after they have completed their own self-development, and have attained success in their businesses and careers. These CEOs are similar to those with a high level of humility who have a self-transcendent concept. They consider giving back to society and making the world a better place to be a duty after they have achieved their personal success. This reflects their gratitude towards the invisible force and identifies their success as being a gift rather than an entitlement. Similarly, about half of the CEOs in the Zhang et al. study (Zhang et al. 2008: 246) considered it their duty 'to reciprocate contributions by employees and society' and 'sharing can bring more happiness than keeping all for oneself.' To them, a company should be a good citizen in society. In the Fu et al. (2010) study, the CEOs were asked about the most important things in life for them. Those with a high level of self-transcendence values responded with these statements: 'have a high level of integrity, social justice, and true love', 'take care of people and give back to society', and 'be good to society and be good to myself' (Fu et al. 2010: 246). These executives seem to understand and accept the golden rule, important in all religions, 'One should treat others as one would like others to treat oneself.' Similarly, they seem to accept implicitly the second Commandment in the Christian religion: 'love your neighbour as yourself' by expressing a desire to take care of society and self at the same time. Similar ideas can be found in Daoism. The word 'Dao' (道)refers to a mystery that cannot be expressed explicitly. Essentially, it means 'true, authentic, unchangeable laws ruling all things' (Ma and Tsui 2015). These are not human laws, but laws from an unnameable divine force. All people, including leaders, must follow the Dao's guidance. As summarised in Ma and Tsui (2015: 15):

The leader must follow the Dao, do good to all, pursue whatever the people want, avoid competition with followers, be pure and innocent as babies, refuse to pursue material goods, high salaries, praise, reputation, or fame. If leaders are humble and sincerely listen to others' ideas, their followers will tend to listen to the leaders. In this sense, strong and effective leaders embrace self-transcendence and self-sacrifice rather than self-enhancement (Fu et al. 2010; Li and Liang 2015).

Given the underlying assumption of the existence of a larger force that is looking after humanity and one's duty to show gratitude for one's fortune, we call this characteristic a *divinity belief.*

One trait is evident based on our discussion in Chap. 1, rather than coming from any of the eight published studies. Private entrepreneurs operate in an extremely inhospitable institutional environment. To succeed in this very difficult terrain, entrepreneurs must have *determination.* Entrepreneurship in the early years of Chinese economic reform was not for the fainthearted. It takes courage, perseverance, patience and an indestructible attitude to manoeuvre around the immensely difficult institutional setting. Overall, determination is probably the primary defining characteristic of the entrepreneurs who were able to overcome seemingly insurmountable obstacles in their entrepreneurial journey.

In addition to the three characteristics described above, we also derive a fourth based on our integrative analysis of the situational constraints and the enormity of the success achieved by the private-firm leaders in the 35 years of reform in China. We suggest that the leaders must have a high degree of *discipline* to accomplish such apparently impossible feats. Discipline refers to a form of self-control and control of others through establishing and following a set of rules or order. Because the institutional environment and the market are undisciplined, in that there are no transparent and consistently enforced rules, so the private-firm leaders must be disciplined to avoid swaying in the wind like a weak tree. They must develop a set of rules to guide the people in their firms and to ensure predictable behaviours. This disciplined approach to leadership is also necessary to ensure reliability and dependability in their interactions with suppliers and customers, or even government officials. Tsui et al. (2004) discovered that private firms (POEs) have more advanced leaders who demonstrate a high level of performance on five of the six leadership behaviours. These authors also found that such leaders pay attention to developing and institutionalising systems and processes for the development of an organisational culture aimed at a sustainable future (Tsui et al. 2006). Leaders who have discipline make sure that their actions are consistent with their beliefs or internal values, as the study of Fu et al. (2010) has shown. Their task-focus includes control over the business conditions of the organisations, the close monitoring of operations, strict requirements for quality and efficiency, the clear communication of a vision for the future of the firm, and paying attention to the long-term planning of the company (Song et al. 2014). Three of the seven philosophical notions discovered by Zhang et al. (2008) relate to this idea of discipline: specialisation, scientific management and pursuit of excellence. All in all, through discipline, the leaders provide the structure, rules and standards to guide their own decisions and the actions of their employees. These companies usually have a rigorous orientation and socialisation process during which new employees are taught the company's rules and are tested on them. Their employment continues only when they have shown a clear understanding and strong commitment to the disciplined way of doing their work. Such companies are strong on standardisation and formalisation, measurement, control, systematic evaluation, and a high level of professionalisation.

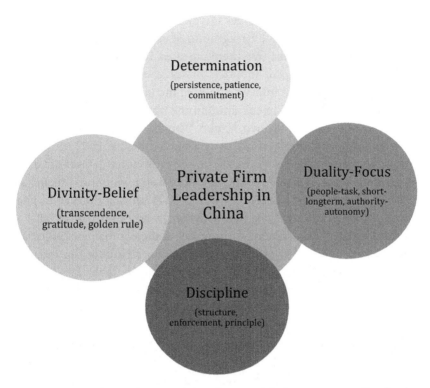

Fig. 2.1 Four defining characteristics of successful Chinese private firm leaders

Figure 2.1 is a graphical portrayal of the four defining characteristics of successful Chinese leaders, especially of the private-firm entrepreneurs.

Seeking In-depth Understanding of Leadership—From the CEOs' Own Words

Based on a limited number of large-sample survey studies, and integrating our analysis of the development of private firms within China's institutional environment (which was extremely difficult in the early years and remains challenging today), we have derived four key characteristics of these entrepreneurs. These ideas are tentative, and further insights and verification are necessary. Large surveys cannot provide an in-depth understanding of the unique background of each leader and cannot delve into their inner thoughts. We therefore used in-depth, semi-structured interviews with a group of founders of successful private firms to gain this understanding. Our interview sample included 13 firms in different industries, founded at different times in the phases of Chinese economic reform: six of them (i.e. Lenovo, Vanke, Wahaha, China Merchants Bank, Li-Ning Company and Neusoft) were founded before 1992, during the first phase of emergence (see Chap. 1 for the evolutionary stages of China's private enterprises); six (i.e. Fosun, HC360, Tecsun, Vantone, Taikang and Alibaba) were founded between 1992 and 2001, during the second phase of rapid growth; and only one (i.e. Kidswant) was founded after 2001, in the third phase of adjustment. A summary of the companies studied and their leaders, along with other key information regarding the interview date, interviewers and core themes can be found in Table 2.2. How the exemplary entrepreneurs and leaders were identified, and the qualifications of the interviewers are detailed in Appendix 2.1. Information on the interview protocol and process is shown in Appendix 2.2.

As in many other under-explored management topics, qualitative methodology appears advantageous to explore phenomena that are ambiguous in nature. With the above four leadership attributes as a starting point, we use a qualitative exploration approach to analyse the words and thought patterns of the natives—the Chinese private firm founders/entrepreneurs/leaders. Since the four attributes were derived inductively by synthesising studies conducted in China and the context surrounding these leaders, we were not influenced pre-conceptually by pre-existing leadership frameworks and existing (Western) literature (Tsui 2006; Yin 2013). This is especially appropriate when the studied phenomenon calls for 'inside-out' analysis (Tsui 2006). We engaged in an inductive analysis of the interview data in two ways. The first was an 'attribute content analysis' guided by the preliminary set of four traits. The second is a 'thematic content analysis' which employed an open and data-driven coding procedure based on the subdivision of industrial enterprises (Boyatzis 1998). The detailed description of the two content analyses is presented in the Appendix of Chap. 16.

Table 2.2 The thirteen companies and their leaders in the interview study

Industry	Company name	Interviewer	Interviewee	Position	Core theme
Banking, insurance and financial investments	Fosun Group	Xiao-Ping Chen	Xinjun Liang	Vice Chairman and CEO	Building a company with teamwork and co-operation, diversity and unity
	Taikang Life Insurance Co. Ltd.	Xiao-Ping Chen and Eve Li Yan	Dongsheng Chen	Chairman and CEO	Learning about wars when fighting in wars
	China Merchants Bank	Xiao-Ping Chen	Weihua Ma	Former President and Chairman	Changing with your need, changing with the situation: How was China Merchants Bank transformed?
Information technology and e-commerce	Neusoft	Jianjun Zhang and Anne Tsui	Jiren Liu	Founder, Chairman and CEO	If you do business for money, you might not be able to make money
	The Lenovo Group	Xiao-Ping Chen and Weiying Zhang	Chuanzhi Liu	Chairman	Building Lenovo into a family business without kinship
	HC360.com	Lynda Jiwen Song and Anne Tsui	Fansheng Guo	Founder and Chairman	Let employees work for themselves

(continued)

Table 2.2 (continued)

Industry	Company name	Interviewer	Interviewee	Position	Core theme
Construction and real estate	Beijing Vantone Holding Corp.	Xiao-Ping Chen	Lun Feng	Founder and Chairman	Morality and integrity keep a company out of trouble
	Vanke Group	Xiao-Ping Chen	Shi Wang and Liang Yu	Chairman and CEO	Managing with simplicity, transparency, system and responsibility
	Tecsun (Suzhou) Homes Co.	Qing Qu and Pingping Fu	Shengzhe Nie	Founder and Director	Provide the best product, treat employees well, and work for the public good
Consumer goods and retailing	Li-Ning Company	Jianjun Zhang and Anne Tsui	Ning Li	Founder and Chairman	My dream relies on the team to realise
	Wahaha Group	Anne Tsui and Katherine Xin	Qinghou Zong	Founder, Chairman and CEO	Chinese companies need strong and open-minded leaders
	Five-Star/Kidswant Holdings	Xiao-Ping Chen	Jianguo Wang	Chairman and President	Applying internet thinking in building strong relationships with customers

In the next thirteen chapters, we present the text of the interviews with each leader as showed in Table 2.2, following a standard format. We use a semi-structured interview format. This provided a standard set of information while allowing for differences to emerge for different leaders. We have retained the original words of the leaders as much as possible, subject to minor editorial clarification and polishing. In the final chapter (Chap. 16), we present the results of the attribute and thematic content analyses and offer a revised and expanded model of private leadership at both the individual and organisational level.

Appendix 2.1

Identifying Exemplary Entrepreneurs/Leaders and the Qualifications of the Interviewers.

Exemplary leaders are referred to as those who have not only achieved high performance and successful business outcomes with their enterprises, but also are highly active in Chinese society and who have been recognised for their social impact beyond the economic contribution of their enterprises. We therefore used several criteria in selecting interviewees. The first criterion is that the company must have demonstrated a strong financial performance and be well respected by peers and the general public. Second, the founder/CEO has demonstrated strong leadership, strong social responsibility, and is often considered to be a role model for other business leaders. Based on these criteria, we developed a list of qualified leaders and succeeded in gaining an agreement to be interviewed from 13 entrepreneurs/leaders. All of them are founders of their enterprises. We interviewed the 13 leaders between 2011 and 2014.

Not only did the selection of interviewees need to be filtered judiciously, but also the qualifications of those who participated in the interview process as interlocutors and interviewers was highly demanding. Stening and Zhang (2007) note that a researcher's cultural background may potentially bias the study; therefore, the participation of local researchers is desirable (Tsui et al. 2007) to fully capture insights and follow the flow of communication and knowledge exchange. Given the knowledge intensity of each interviewee in his area of expertise, interviewers engaged in a thorough preparation with careful thought given to the development of specific company questions, and familiarity with the background of both the company and the leader/interviewee. To manage the interview process tactfully and fully explore the leaders' insights in a short interview time, only experienced and well-prepared researchers were engaged in conducting the interviews. In this way, culturally sensitive researchers could contribute to the conversation with their local knowledge, both cultural and contextual, to enhance the knowledge exploration process in the interviews. Eight management scholars familiar with the Chinese background as well as fluency in the Chinese language conducted these interviews. They include Professors Xiao-Ping Chen (University of Washington), Pingping Fu (Chinese University of Hong Kong), Qing Qu (Tsinghua University), Jiwen Song (Renmin University of China), Anne Tsui (Arizona State University), Katherine Xin (China European International Business School), Jianjun Zhang (Peking University), and Weiying Zhang (Peking University).

Appendix 2.2

The Interview Protocol and Interview Process.

The purposes of the interview can be broadly divided into three areas. First, similar to the Zhang et al. (2008) study, we wanted to learn about the interviewees' management philosophy and the significant life experiences that had shaped that philosophy. Beyond this, we wanted to find out about any significant events they had encountered during the process of building the business. Third, we wanted to learn about the best leadership and management practices that led their companies to success, and the most important advice they would give to future entrepreneurs.

We prepared an interview guide, including an introduction to the purpose of the interview, a statement of confidentiality, and a list of questions to be discussed. We used six standard questions with all the interviewees. These are:

1. How would you describe your management philosophy, management perspective, and management style?
2. What were the significant life experiences that shaped your management philosophy, perspective and style?
3. What were the main challenges you encountered during your role change from founder to CEO to Chairman of the company?
4. When do you handle problems by yourself? When do you let others make decisions?
5. During the many years of running this company, you must have encountered many situations that involve conflict between maintaining interpersonal harmony and making a rational choice for the business. How did you make the decisions you chose, and why?
6. What is the most important piece of advice you would give to future entrepreneurs and CEOs?

For each company, we added a few additional questions specific to the leader and the company. These questions were intended to capture the company's or the leader's unique historical background, unique management practices, and other extraordinary elements. Sample questions include:

- (To Jack Ma) You are one of the founders who emphasises the building of a corporate culture. In your mind, what is an ideal culture for Alibaba? How did you initiate and maintain such culture? Please provide a few examples.
- (To Weihua Ma) The slogan of China Merchants Bank is 'Change with your need', emphasising your care for customers. In today's internet era, what is most needed by customers? What can banks do to build a loyal customer group?
- (To Dongsheng Chen) You once said, 'The first imitator is the innovator in China.' When you started Taikang Life, which were the companies you imitated? After more than a decade of development, compared to these companies, how would you evaluate the similarity between Taikang Life and these model companies?
- (To Shi Wang) You have said that Vanke values 'simplicity instead of complexity; transparency instead of opaqueness; standardisation

instead of particularism; and responsibility instead of abuse of power.' Please describe how these values are implemented in the daily management practices of your company.

We sent the questions to the interviewees about a week ahead of the scheduled interview. The interviews were carried out in a variety of settings: some were in the interviewee's office, some were in hotel conference rooms, and in two cases it was via a telephone. A confidentiality statement was supplied at the beginning of the interviews to encourage candid and open discussion. We also sought permission to audiotape the interviews, and no interviewee declined. All interviews were conducted in the local language, Chinese, and each interview took around two hours or more. We followed a semi-structured format during the interview process but without strictly following the order to allow for flexibility, to enhance the connection with the interviewees, and to ensure fluid communication during the process. We made sure that all the questions had been discussed before the interview ended. As can be seen from the interview texts in Chaps. 3 to 15, the specific questions asked in each interview varied somewhat. This was as a result of the open-ended and dynamic nature of each case.

Further, to avoid self-serving bias, and in particular to ensure that what the respondents said during their interviews was translated into actual practice within their firms, we also triangulated their statements in several ways. We asked the interviewees to provide critical events or specific examples on the statements. We collected second-hand company information and stories, and verified with the interviewees the events that had occurred. Finally, after the interviews, we checked public information sources if we had any doubts about the authenticity of information provided by the interviewees. Since these are all well-known companies, there is a good deal of public information available about them.

We transcribed the audiotaped interviews and sent copies of the final versions of the interview transcripts to the interviewees for review. We obtained additional company or CEOs' biographical information as well as photographs at this point, and contacted the interviewees if any further clarification was needed. We sought the interviewees' approval of the final versions of the transcripts to ensure the accuracy of the transcription and any necessary revision of their statements. We shared these interviews with members of the International Association for Chinese Management Research (IACMR), a scholarly association dedicated to the advancement of Chinese management research among global scholars. The final report of these interviews was published in both English and Chinese in Chinese Management Insights (CMI), an online bilingual magazine of the IACMR. The interviews presented in Chaps. 3 to 15 of this book are further edited versions of the CMI reports, with additional information on the backgrounds of both companies and leaders.

References

Batjargal, B., & Liu, B. (2004). Entrepreneurs' access to private equity in China: The role of social capital. *Organization Science, 15*(2), 159–171.

Boyatzis, R. E. (1998). *Thematic analysis and code development: Transforming qualitative information*. Thousand Oaks, CA: Sage.

Bryson, A., Forth, J. and Zhou, M. (2012). What do we know about China's CEO's? Evidence from across the whole economy. NIESR Discussion Paper No. 397. 25 August, National Institute of Economic and Social Research. Retrieved February 16, 2012, from http://www.niesr.ac.uk/sites/default/files/publications/dp397.pdf

Calder, B. J. (1977). An attribution theory of leadership. In B. M. Staw & G. R. Salancik (Eds.), *New direction in organizational behavior* (pp. 179–204). Chicago, IL: St. Clair.

Chandler, A. D. (1978). *The visible hand: The managerial revolution in American business*. Cambridge, MA: Harvard University Press.

Chen, C.-C., & Lee, Y.-T. (Eds.) (2008). *Leadership and management in China: Philosophies, theories, and practices*. New York: Cambridge University Press.

Chen, C. C., Chen, X.-P., & Huang, S. (2013). Chinese *Guanxi*: An integrative review and new directions for future research. *Management and Organization Review, 9*, 167–207.

Chen, L., Yang, B., & Jing, R. (2015). Paternalistic leadership, team conflict, and TMT decision effectiveness: Interactions in the Chinese context. *Management and Organization Review, 11*(4), 739–762.

Child, J. (1972). Organizational structure, environment and performance: The role of strategic choice. *Sociology, 6*(1), 1–22.

Collins, J. C. (2001). *Good to great: Why some companies make the leap... and others don't*. New York: Jim Collins.

Farh, J. L., & Cheng, B. S. (2000). A cultural analysis of paternalistic leadership in Chinese organizations. In A. S. Tsui, E. Weldon, & J. T. Li (Eds.), *Management and organizations in the Chinese context* (pp. 84–127). Basingstoke, UK: Palgrave Macmillan.

Fu, P. P., Tsui, A. S., Liu, J., & Li, L. (2010). Pursuit of whose happiness? Executive leaders' transformational behaviors and personal values. *Administrative Science Quarterly, 55*(2), 222–254.

Hiller, N., & Hambrick, D. (2005). Conceptualizing executive hubris: The role of (hyper-) core self-evaluations in strategic decision-making. *Strategic Management Journal, 26*, 297–319.

House, R., Hanges, P., Javidan, M., Dorfman, P., & Gupta, P. (Eds.) (2004). *Culture, leadership and organizations: The Globe study of 62 societies*. Thousand Oaks, CA: Sage.

Jia, L., You, S., & Du, Y. (2012). Chinese context and theoretical contributions to management and organization research: A three-decade review. *Management and Organization Review, 8*(1), 173–209.

Krug, B. (2004). *China's rational entrepreneurs: The development of the new private sector*. New York: Routledge.

Li, H. Y., & Zhang, Y. (2007). The role of managers' political networking and functional experience in new venture performance: Evidence from China's transition economy. *Strategic Management Journal, 28*(8), 791–804.

Li, J., & Tsui, A. S. (2002). A citation analysis of management and organization research in the Chinese context: 1984–1999. *Asia Pacific Journal of Management, 19*(1), 87–107.

Li, J., & Tang, Y. I. (2010). CEO hubris and firm risk taking in China: The moderating role of managerial discretion. *Academy of Management Journal, 53*(1), 45–68.

Li, X., & Liang, X. (2015). A Confucian social model of political appointments among Chinese private entrepreneurs. *Academy of Management Journal, 58*(2), 592–617.

Lin, N. (2011). Capitalism in China: A Centrally Managed Capitalism (CMC) and its future. *Management and Organization Review, 7*, 63–96.

Luo, Y., Huang, Y., & Wang, S. L. (2012). *Guanxi* and organizational performance: A meta-analysis. *Management and Organization Review, 8*, 139–172.

Ma, L., & Tsui, A. S. (2015). Traditional Chinese philosophy and contemporary leadership. *Leadership Quarterly, 26*(1), 13–24.

Meindl, J. R., Ehrlich, S. B., & Dukerich, J. M. (1985). The romance of leadership. *Administrative Science Quarterly, 30*, 78–102.

Nee, V., & Opper, S. (2012). *Capitalism from below: Market and institutional change in China.* Cambridge, MA: Harvard University Press.

Ou, A. Y., Tsui, A. S., Kinicki, A. J., Waldman, D. A., Xiao, Z., & Song, L. J. (2014). Humble chief executive officers' connections to top management team integration and middle managers' responses. *Administrative Science Quarterly, 59*(1): 34–72.

Owens, B. (2009). Humility in organizational leadership. (Unpublished doctoral dissertation). University of Washington, Seattle, WA.

Parsons, T., & Shils, E. A. (1951). *Toward a general theory of action: Theoretical foundation for the social sciences.* Cambridge, MA: Harvard University Press.

Pfeffer, J. (1977). The ambiguity of leadership. *Academy of Management Review, 2*, 104–112.

Pfeffer, J. (1981). Management as symbolic action: The creation and maintenance of organizational paradigms. *Research in Organizational Behavior, 3*, 1–52.

Redding, S. G. (1990). *The spirit of Chinese capitalism.* New York: Walter de Gruyter.

Schein, E. H. (1985). *Organizational culture and leadership.* San Francisco: Jossey-Bass.

Schein, E. H. (1992). *Organizational culture and leadership: A dynamic view* (2nd ed.). San Francisco: Jossey-Bass.

Schlevogt, K.-A. (2002). *The art of Chinese management: Theory, evidence, and applications.* New York: Oxford University Press.

Song, L. J., Zhang, X., & Wu, J. B. (2014). A multilevel analysis of middle manager performance: The role of CEO and top manager leadership. *Management and Organization Review, 10*(2), 275–297.

Tsui, A. S., Schoonhove, C. B., Meyer, M. W., Lau, C. M., & Milkovich, G. T. (2004a). Organization and management in the midst of societal transformation: The People's Republic of China. *Organization Science, 15*(2), 133–144.

Tsui, A. S., Wang, H. U. I., Xin, K., Zhang, L., & Fu, P. P. (2004b). 'Let a thousand flowers bloom': Variation of leadership styles among Chinese CEOs. *Organizational Dynamics, 33*(1), 5–20.

Tsui, A. S. (2006). Editorial: Contextualization in Chinese management research. *Management and Organization Review, 2*(1), 1–13.

Tsui, A. S., Zhang, Z. X., Wang, H., Xin, K. R., & Wu, J. B. (2006). Unpacking the relationship between CEO leadership behavior and organizational culture. *The Leadership Quarterly, 17*(2), 113–137.

Wang, H., Tsui, A. S., & Xin, K. R. (2011). CEO leadership behaviors, organizational performance, and employees' attitudes. *The Leadership Quarterly, 22*(1), 92–105.

Weihrich, H. (1990). Management practices in the United States, Japan, and the People's Republic of China. *Industrial Management, 32*, 3–7.

Westwood, R. (1997). Harmony and patriarchy: The cultural basis for 'paternalistic leadership' among the overseas Chinese. *Organization Studies, 18*, 445–480.

Wu, M., Huang, X., & Li, C. (2012). Perceived interactional justice and trust-in-supervisor as mediators for paternalistic leadership. *Management and Organization Review, 8*(1), 97–121.

Xin, K. R., & Pearce, J. L. (1996). *Guanxi:* Connections as substitutes for formal institutional support. *Academy of Management Journal, 39*(6), 1641–1658.

Yin, R.K. (2013). *Case study research: Design and methods* (3rd ed). Thousand Oaks, CA: Sage Publishing.

Zhang, Y., Waldman, D., Han, Y., & Li, X. (2015). Paradoxical leader behavior in people management: Antecedents and consequences. *Academy of Management Journal.* doi:10.5465/amj.2012.0995.

Zhang, Z. X., Chen, C. C., Liu, L. A., & Liu, X. F. (2008). Chinese tradition and Western theories: Influences on business leadership in China. In C. C. Chen & Y. T. Lee (Eds.), *Leadership and management in China: Philosophy, theories and practices.* New York: Cambridge University Press.

Zhang, Z. X., Chen, Z. X., Chen, Y. R., & Ang, S. (2014). Business leadership in the Chinese context: Trends, findings, and implications. *Management and Organization Review, 10*, 199–221.

Part II

Leaders in Financial Services Industry

3

Building a Company with Teamwork and Co-operation, Diversity and Unity
Interview with Fosun Group Vice Chairman and CEO Xinjun Liang

The interview was conducted by: Xiao-Ping Chen, University of Washington.

Fosun Group[1]

Founded in 1992, the Fosun Group is a classic story of success following China's reform and opening-up. Moreover, the Fosun Group is becoming a representative model for Chinese home and global investments by actively implementing an investment model 'Combining China's Growth Momentum with Global Resources.' In recent years, Fosun has put great effort into internationalisation and global investments. The most recent investments include the 2015 acquisition of the French Club Méditerranée SA (Club Med) and a strategic alliance with British tour operator, the Thomas Cook Group.

Listed on the main board of the Hong Kong Stock Exchange since 16 July 2007, Fosun's development model comprises four growth engines: insurance, industrial operations, investments and asset management. The company has

---

[1] This section is based on information from the company website (Fosun 2015a), Fosun Group (Fosun 2014), 2014 Annual Report (Fosun 2015b), and IACMR's *Chinese Management Insights* publication on Fosun in June 2013.

© The Author(s) 2017   **85**
A.S. Tsui et al., *Leadership of Chinese Private Enterprises*, Palgrave Studies in Chinese Management, DOI 10.1057/978-1-137-40235-6_3

transformed itself into an insurance-oriented investment group, with a view to implementing its philosophy of value investment effectively. These efforts have established Fosun as 'a premium investment group with a focus on China's growth momentum.' Currently, Fosun invests mainly in sectors that would benefit significantly from the growth in China's domestic demand, such as consumption and consumption upgrade, financial services, resources and energy, and manufacturing upgrade, with a view to participating in China's rapid economic development.

Fosun's investment philosophy is to maintain a strong base in China and invest in the country's fundamental growth. It taps proactively into investment opportunities arising from China's economic transformation, with a focus on domestic demand as well as on China's urbanisation and industrialisation. Fosun also seeks to capitalise on structural changes in the global economy, implementing its unique investment model of 'combining China's growth momentum with global resources' and reinforcing its position as China's global expert constantly creating value for society and shareholders alike.

In practice, Fosun unremittingly identifies and captures investment opportunities while benefiting from China's growth, improving management, enhancing investor value, and establishing a multichannel financing system to access quality capital. With the value chain based on these three core competencies and a group of entrepreneurs endorsing its corporate culture, Fosun has laid a solid foundation for continuous and rapid growth.

Twenty-year-old Fosun, in gratitude for the support the company has received, shares the fruitful results of its economic development with its staff, partners, communities and society in general. Meanwhile, Fosun also works actively to improve China's business and natural environments to support the rejuvenation of the Chinese economy and culture. In 2014, Fosun International Limited (listed on the Hong Kong Stock Exchange) earned a revenue of 61.74 billion RMB with an after-tax profit of 9.59 billion RMB, extending its markets to the USA, the UK, Japan, Israel, Italy, France, Greece and Malaysia. 'Going overseas' and seeking all kinds of investment opportunities has become the keyword of Fosun for its internationalisation strategy. For example, it purchased a 20 % stake in the American insurer Ironshore Inc. in August 201, for

464 million USD, expanding its insurance business into the European and American markets. Two months later, Fosun International bought One Chase Manhattan Plaza for 725 million RMB from J.P. Morgan Chase & Co.

In July 2014, Fosun International Ltd. completed this batch of investments by taking a 20 % stake in the famous Spanish ham- and wine-producing Osborne Group, and taking a seat on the board of directors of the Osborne Group. In the same month, Fidelidade, an affiliated and indirect holding company of Fosun, bought a 23.16 % share of the equity stake of Tom Tailor, a German clothing company, through which it gained access to the German consumer market.

A few months later, in October 2014, Fosun International announced the purchase of a 51 % equity stake in the hospital operator Espirito Santo Saude SGPS SA from Rioforte Investments SA for 244 million EUR. And one month later, Transcendent Resources, a Fosun International's wholly owned affiliated company, completed the acquisition of a 92.6 % stake in Rock Oil Co. Ltd., a leading Australian upstream oil and gas company.

Vice Chairman and CEO: Xinjun Liang[2]

Born in 1968 in Taizhou, Zhejiang province, in the People's Republic of China (PRC), Xinjun Liang co-founded the Fosun Group with Guangchang Guo and others in 1992, after a short period of teaching at Fudan University, Shanghai. He was ranked 5th, with an estimated wealth of 1.6 billion USD in the Hurun Report's Midas China Rich List 2015.

Mr. Xinjun Liang, vice chairman and CEO of the Fosun Group and a long-time expert in China's economic reform and development, is often invited to speak at various economic forums. He is a member of the Eleventh Shanghai Committee of Chinese People's Political Consultative Conference, vice chairman of the China Youth Entrepreneurs Association, chairman of the Taizhou Chamber of Commerce in Shanghai, and execu-

---

[2] This section is based on IACMR's *Chinese Management Insights'* publication on Fosun in June 2013 with permission, complemented by public information from maigoo.com (Maigoo 2015) and Hurun Midas Rich List 2015 (Hurun 2015).

tive chairman of the Shanghai Fudan University Alumni Association. He graduated from Fudan University with a BSc degree in genetic engineering in 1991, and from Cheung Kong Graduate School of Business in Beijing with an EMBA in 2007.

Some of his many honours include the Innovation Award of Shanghai Science & Technology Entrepreneurs, Outstanding Entrepreneur of China's Science & Technology Private Enterprise, Innovation Management Award for Young Entrepreneurs in China, and Top 10 Outstanding Youth of Shanghai. As an active speaker at various kinds of economic forums and summits, Xinjun Liang was named the 'Young Business Leader' by the World Economic Forum and appeared on the cover of the *Institutional Investor*.

Building a Company with Teamwork and Co-operation

Interviewer Chen: Could you please describe your management style, and what is most distinctive about it?

Xinjun Liang (hereafter referred to as Liang): Teamwork and co-operation are fundamental to our present success. Team management is Fosun's most striking difference from other companies in terms of management style. The four founders make up the first team. They enjoy a certain influence, prestige and recognition. Other teams work directly for the founders, including our medicines team, real estate team, insurance team and investment team. Teamwork is in Fosun's genes and can be traced back to the four founders who started the business: Guangchang Guo, Xinjun Liang, Qunbin Wang and Fan Wei.

Three of us were classmates at Fudan University. Guangchang Guo was not; he was a little older. But we did not start a business just because we were classmates. We became business partners through our relationship with Guangchang. To some degree, a crucial reason for Fosun's success lies in the selection of its shareholders. Many people are careful when selecting top management teams and independent board directors, but not when choosing shareholders. When relationships among shareholders go wrong, the company goes wrong too. We have supported each other for many years because we got the right people on the founding team. This team spirit has influenced many of our decisions, and contributed to our outstanding co-operation.

We four share some common characteristics. First, we are all good learners, so nobody falls behind. Second, we all care relatively little about money and do not make a fuss about it. Third, we toleratce each other, despite our different personalities and work styles, which indicates unity and yet diversity. Our different styles are important because, as a team, we can cope with a variety of situations. Lastly, we divide our responsibilities quite fairly and all take our responsibilities seriously.

Interviewer Chen: How does this co-operative spirit or style extend beyond the founding team?

Liang: We co-operate even with those who seem to be our direct competitors. Take foreign capital, for example. We collaborated with Prudential of the United States, starting from fund co-operation, to a jointly funded insurance company, and to investment co-operation. We also work well with top-tier companies such as Carlyle and Forbes. Additionally, we also co-operate with private companies. The largest is Jianlong Iron and Steel, with which we have a long-standing co-operation. Sinopharm Group is the largest state-owned company with whom we co-operate. We also co-operate with former state-owned, but now restructured companies, such as Shanghai Dahua. Other state-owned companies, such as Nanjing Iron and Steel, Zhaoyuan Gold, Shanghai Yuyuan and Hainan Mining, are either the absolute first in quality in their local provinces or cities, or they are the largest state-owned companies in their industry. This also includes foreign-funded companies, such as Club Med and the Greek company Folli Follie, which makes and distributes jewellery, watches and fashion accessories. In summary, our success depends most crucially on our spirit and culture of co-operation.

Interviewer Chen: What contributes to the good co-operation among the founders?

Liang: We four founders co-operate well because we are all high in both EQ (emotional quotient [emotional intelligence]) and IQ (intelligence quotient). But EQ and IQ are not enough. We follow a few basic principles. First is an awareness of our own ability. Once we are aware where our ability is limited, we know we must co-operate with others because we need them.

Second, we each manage our own needs and refrain from greed. We each ask for a little less compensation, interest or rights, and feel more pleased with emotional rewards. Third, we care about others' interests so that no substantial conflict will stand between us. By following these principles, co-operation will naturally be pleasant. Of course, the core of these principles lies in value creation. If co-operation eventually fails to create value, both parties must part company. So I think an important reason for our good co-operative spirit is the relatively high EQ of the founders.

Self-challenging and Outcome-Responsible Entrepreneurship

Liang: The other point that makes our company distinctive is our entrepreneurial spirit, which I define as, first, the courage to face any results and outcomes. That is, I enjoy whatever successes may come, but also accept responsibility for whatever failure I face. Some people may brag about their accomplishments, but if they have failed to actually achieve, they are not qualified to preach. Only those who rank among the top players have the right to brag about their success. In my employee conferences, I often explain that I listen to opinions, but if an employee has done well, I will listen more willingly. What can you tell me if you cannot do it well yourself? The second aspect of entrepreneurship is the ability to set high goals, to be self-motivated and self-driven. Many ask: why are you working so hard? They truly do not understand that I do not want much, and I do not have much personal wealth. Some can win millions of RMB by playing card games, but I do not like card games, I cannot play, and I do not have the time. I do not run after money. The answer is my strong self-motivation, my need for a challenge, and my strong passion for work.

This entrepreneurial spirit is true of all of the employees in our company, not merely the four of us. If you visit Fosun, you will see that we are a big team of individuals with strengths in both learning and entrepreneurship. We are all outcome-responsible, self-motivated, and always serious about following processes and regulations properly.

A third aspect of entrepreneurship is to know how to duplicate success. If I like your pattern of operations, I will ask whether you can copy it at a low cost. Even if the pattern is good, if it cannot be copied at low cost, it cannot be scaled up. Only duplicable things make sense. In fact, the logic is the same: if one does well in one thing, we should ask further: can he repeat such success easily? If not, the success is only good luck.

So you must turn any success into regulations and processes. As we often say, you fail if your outcome is poor, but even if the outcome is good, you only score 60 points (out of 100). If you can also promote outcome realisation by appropriately co-ordinating process, regulation and teams, you can reach 90 points. So the third aspect of entrepreneurship is to create outcomes and processes that are easy to replicate.

The fourth aspect is the attitude toward successors. For example, if a person has created value for the company for three years, but did it alone, such a person cannot be employed for long. He might lead small teams, but never large ones. He can serve as a manager for a one-off crisis, but could not be assigned to key posts. Of course, he should be given reasonable compensation, but he should never be a manager. We like those who cultivate or provide fresh blood to our managerial teams. If a leader of a small team has the ability not only to work with members to outperform large teams, but also to develop his/her members to take leadership roles in the company, such a team leader is far more important than the manager who only handles a one-off crisis.

One more aspect is the attitude toward change. There are macro controls (from the government) and unexpected changes in the real estate industry. They will keep coming in the future and will come more frequently in the next few years. You must learn to accept them and adapt to them, whether you like them or not. Eventually, you learn to use them to your own advantage. Rather than being born optimistic, people can make themselves optimistic through training and self-regulation. I think that is also an important aspect of entrepreneurship.

Gathering the Power of Growth

Liang: In my opinion, Fosun's core management philosophy is 'gathering the power of growth,' that is, we choose to collaborate with or invest in partners that have growth power or positive energy. In addition, we develop a reasonable reward allocation mechanism intended to attract these partners with growth potential to work with us, so we can leverage their strength to grow our company.

We try to avoid creating everything from scratch. Instead, we learn to employ and integrate social resources. So both our core business concept and our core values should be about gathering growing power. We are reconsidering our vision. Previously it was 'the ability to grow into a world-leading investment group in realms benefiting from China's growth impetus.' Now, we should rethink our vision. I think we are actually helping two kinds of people: (1) dreamers who will achieve success through our investment group; and (2) insecure individuals who will feel psychologically secure about the future after they join us.

Interviewer Chen: What are the greatest challenges you see for diversified companies such as Fosun that invest in many industries, and how do you rise to these challenges?

Liang: I must clarify first that we are not a diversified company. Many diversified companies rise and fall because of their singular funding source. They finance industries freely and gather enormous capital in the short term, and thus appear to be successful. However, the singular source of funds eventually kills them, because when an industry fails to be competitive, the company must fund this business from its own financial resources. This is the first issue. The second issue with diversified companies lies in their unbalanced cash flow; that is, there is a lack of attention to cash flow. When I gained my EMBA in 2004, I did research showing that a company with an annual net profit of over 100 million RMB made investments amounting to over 10 billion RMB. So, where did the money come from? There should always be a reasonable leverage. Leverage can be used in a given year, but if you must use it every year, how can you survive? So, unbalanced cash flow is an obvious cause for the collapse. The third issue is improper liability composition. Such an imbalance occurs because most of their liabilities are short-term debts. If you can negotiate a 30-year debt, the issue of a high debt rate will be solved. The fourth issue, to my mind, is overly high leverage. Of course, these issues are interrelated, but they are not the same. So, as you can see, some may succeed in an industrial operation, may be far-sighted in terms of financial layout, and are logically expected to grow into a great company. But from the perspective of tactics, they have been wrong in all four aspects.

We are aware that we are definitely positioned as an investment group, though investment groups have been unpopular in China in recent years, and you cannot get loans there as an investment group. Loans are clearly to be used as 'capital flow for business operations', or for investment in nationally approved projects. Financing a project is the precondition for a loan, so as an investment group, we do not qualify for loans. That's why we did not correct others when they said we were a diversified company. But since we were publicly listed in 2007, our reliance on external funds has been eased, and we can just be what we are and call ourselves an investment group. An investment group comes with many properties, or DNAs. We have them all.

DNAs of Investors: Forward-Looking, Optimised Operation, Caring for Each Other's Core Interests, and Risk Control

Liang: First, we are keenly sensitive to the macroeconomic environment. We can foresee changes over the next five or ten years and can clearly see possible upcoming changes in the next one to two years. Of course, sometimes we may be wrong, but our history proves that is rare. We consider future changes in depth, even if we are not familiar with some realms. For example, if I talk about real estate tonight, I will mention the internet from time to time. We are not internet experts, but we must understand it so that the internet experts will trust our judgement. As an investment company, keenness and confidence are essential because Chinese government intervention has enabled the great economic leap over the past three decades. The leap shortened many industry cycles artificially.

Being forward-looking and insightful is important to an investment company. After the 2008 financial crisis, we noticed rapidly shrinking local domestic demand and falling exports. We also noticed that those taking domestic demand as the market encountered difficulties. However, some sectors based on domestic demand, such as luxury goods and high-end services, were still much sought after in China. So we proposed that the Chinese impetus should be based on global resources: we should buy foreign brands and introduce them into China. First you must look ahead; second you must carefully research and verify. After verification, you must still turn it into feasible business patterns. So I think as an investment company, we have our own strength: being forward-looking.

The second property of an investment company is optimising operations. We have dealt with industrial and commercial businesses from the beginning, so we know about issues and difficulties when optimising operations. When we invest, if an Internal Rate of Return (IRR) of 30% is taken as full score 100, you may get that 100 if you play well; but, it may take a long time. If you make a correct decision, you may probably secure an IRR of 18%; if you want to achieve an IRR of 25%, you must rely on optimized operation; and if you want to reach an IRR of 30%, then you must have good sales capability. So our familiarity with optimised operations makes us better than others in terms of profitability and investment performance. We take a long time to optimise operations. There are innumerable such examples, and I can provide numerous details of current or past cases.

Interviewer Chen: Do you mean that you help those companies receiving investment by you to optimise their operations?

Liang: Right. Investment companies have limited liability, so you can only propose some conditions at board meetings and supervisors' meetings. You cannot take over the invested company to run its business. Meanwhile, you must check out two things: first, does the company have well-established systems for its operation? If yes, then it should be able to run smoothly without missing the most important issues. Second, you must clarify their needs; that is, identify the company's weakest points. You must combine a well-established system with individualised tools to assist the company's optimisation. We can help them with many details. Apart from that, co-operation also counts. When we have co-operated with foreign companies, we have not encountered any cross-cultural issues. We know such issues could arise: first, existing shareholders may be unhappy when someone else suddenly becomes the biggest shareholder. Second, some management team members may fear being replaced by Chinese managers. Third, labour unions or local governments may have concerns. I think it is easy to cope with such issues. You must discover meticulously their core interests and then, on the precondition of not impairing your own core interest, promise them what is in their interest, and moreover, get them to help you to achieve your aims.

For example, the existing shareholders' core interest is control. In this case, I can allow them to maintain control even when I am the largest shareholder. I do not need to control anything. I only want to ensure that they negotiate with me when they are laying out strategies for China. This eliminates their concerns. Regarding the management team, we choose to invest in companies with reliable management teams, so, we reassure them and, moreover, let them become shareholders so they can share the additional wealth created. In this way, they will feel that they are treated even better than the existing shareholders and will accept you imme-diately. Employees and consumers want products made in the original country. So we announce that factories and assembly lines will all remain local; what's more, after China's sales volume rises, job opportunities will also increase.

This logic is likewise applicable to state-owned companies taking part in a joint investment. You should take care of their core interest: what do shareholders, teams, labour unions, and retired workers want? So long as what they want does not conflict with your core interest, give them what they need; and tell them what you want in a definite way. I think that achieves pleasant co-operation. For overseas companies, I want growth in China; for state-owned companies, I want them to secure a place among the top 20 % of companies in the industry, but I will let them take time to do so. For example, if you are dealing in mining, I will give you specific targets and tell you to 'secure a place among the top 20 % of companies in this industry.' First, consider the overall cost rate. Take mining for gold, for example: if there are 2000 tons of gold in the world, you should make clear how many are sold at less than 100, 120, 150 and 250 RMB per ton, respectively. I require you to be 'among the top 20 % compa-nies.' If you cannot achieve this immediately, give me a roadmap with a time horizon. Second, I require you to be 'among the top 20 %' in reserve costs while increasing your reserve. First is production costs; second is reserve costs. Third, when gold prices go up, you should produce more. With these targets reached, your compensation will be boosted. We also require safety; that is, zero accidents. I have the right to veto a bonus in case of any accident. You do not get a bonus just because of no accidents; that is the minimum requirement. We communicate our requirements explicitly. We absolutely never talk about increasing shareholder value; that is nonsense. You should definitely understand and explain what shareholder value means, or they will focus merely on the share price. I do not care about the share price because I am a value controller. Share value varies based on market judgement, but when your value is growing, the share price is certain to go up in the long term.

Besides, we are keenly aware that it is very important in the investment realm to control risks, and the most difficult is control over the growing risks of a big industry. Some investors keep investing in a declining industry because they could not see the risks. To develop a good sense of risk control, one must have a deep understanding of different industries and the broad picture of globalisation. The second risk control approach is to build a routine daily report system. For example, I grade all the projects in my charge as red, yellow and green in terms of adding value. Among these grades, details are provided specific to each land plot, each real estate project, each investment project, and each fund. In this way, when we invest in this project, we can predict the target for its growth over the following three years. If the growth is less than 15 %, investment is reduced and the project graded as red. We have an administrative mechanism for those graded as red: our director, supervisor, or members of board of directors may intervene. Without such a system, your risks are out of control. Risk control is crucial.

Three Transitions of Fosun: From Investment to Asset and to Insurance Management

Liang: I have considered in depth the profit patterns of investment companies. We often evaluate which companies deserve investment. In fact, few people think about what constitutes a good investment company. I personally think a good investment company is the same as a good production company. First, can the company obtain a steady, continuous and cheap supply of raw materials? Materials refer to money and projects.

How to find cheap money? How to find cheap projects? Does the company use sustainable and duplicable methods? Second, with raw materials at hand, can they produce efficiently? As far as we are concerned, high-efficiency production corresponds to business progress. Can this company grow rapidly to become great in its industry? Third, are highly efficient and premium-priced sales possible? This is consistent with the logic for sales with brand names. Fourth, can those with these core technologies and core resources at hand join the company and stay for a long time? If these questions can be answered in the affirmative, the company will grow to become a great investment over time.

As I said earlier, Fosun is not a diversified company. So what kind of company is it? I have worked in the company for 21 years since graduating from college. From the first to the 18th year, we were an investment company, investing with our own money.

We started with 38,000 RMB. When we reached the 17th year, the total assets amounted to roughly 140 billion RMB. Of course, the debt rate was about 50 % to 60 %. Starting from the 18th year, from 2011/12, we became an asset management company. Why? Because our cash flow output conflicted with the size of our investment demand, and the conflict was quite striking. We had to choose: should we increase the debt rate to make investments? Slow our investments? Or find another way out? We chose to find another way out: namely, asset management.

We expect to continue for over a decade on the road of asset management. After embarking on asset management, you find that with so many parties depositing money, if your ROI is less than 20 %, you cannot raise any new funds. So in retrospect, such money is in fact very costly. So you must find ways to find cheap money. In my opinion, regarding the cheapest money possible, the successful pattern is the one combining its float. First, the money does not belong to you as a general partner; it belongs to the limited partner. Second, specific to such a float, it takes away the limited partner's gains; in fact, such gains go to the insurance company in your control. So our future hope is to change Fosun gradually into an asset management group or an investment group centred around insurance. That is our three transitions during our development. In our first 20 years, we started from nowhere to grow into one of China's largest investment groups. In the next 10 years, our plan is to grow into one of the world's or China's biggest asset management groups, and in the following 20 years, we plan to grow into the world's, or China's, largest insurance company, including its operating pattern. So I think it is better to look 20 years ahead.

Four Challenges in Globalisation

Interviewer Chen: What assumption and consideration has Fosun made about globalisation? What is its view on talent globalisation?

Liang: There are four investment considerations when it comes to globalisation. First is value investment; second is the Chinese impetus, where it is hoped that the increase in the invested company's future sales will come from or benefit China; third is inflation, which I think is quite severe; and fourth is the internet. Value investment lies mainly in value discovery, promotion of value addition, and value realisation. Regarding value discovery, specifically speaking, you must invest in an industry when it is doing badly, and sell at its peak. From the macro perspective, you must find the change in the global division of work: in the great tide of global division of work, you should buy when China is at low tide and sell when China is at high tide. Currently, Europe is at low tide.

During the process of globalisation, we found that it was cheap to invest overseas. Without competent rivals, we found we were the only buyer. Moreover, this globalisation process is favourable to our investment strategy and is consistent with our future long-term strategic direction. Of course, we can also see difficulties. First, without access to information, we are in the dark about where to find transaction opportunities. Cheap buys are available, but you cannot rush to them because, first, without transaction information, you do not know where you can get them; and second, even if you know about them, you do not know whether they are comparable. Therefore, it is difficult for us to access information, and even if we have access, it is hard to judge global risks and value; it is easy to judge those in China, but hard to assess those elsewhere. We are also worried about challenges to our corporate culture.

How did we solve these issues? First, we found a consultant, Mr. Snow, an older man who brought us current merger and acquisition information. Therefore we were a presence in cases of large global mergers and acquisitions involving China, such as AIA of Guangdong, Prada and NSK. Generally, we were the only buyer bidding for them. In addition to finding a consultant, we co-invested and established a global strategy partnership with the investment company, The Carlyle Group, which allowed us to share global investment information. They helped us to make many important strategic value judgements, and we helped them to predict the growth of their investment targets in China.

The third step is to build a team of our own, step by step. Starting from the 2008 financial crisis, a considerable amount of talent was introduced from Europe and the United States. After working with Fosun for a number of years, they entirely understand our investment values and have grown to become independent actors in certain aspects. After fully blending with us, they like our style. I think that, regarding globalisation and talent comparison, the price for talent in China is rising too fast. In terms of global talent recruitment, the gap in demand is comparatively small.

Talent Is Having an Entrepreneurial Spirit and not Following Routines

Interviewer Chen: I notice that you define talent quite differently from other companies. You want creative, hard-edged and vibrant recruits. Do HR managers challenge you on those standards? If so, how do you tackle that problem?

Liang: In studying courses about innovative or modest leaders, I have noticed that they share similar characteristics. When you are making decisions, first you must decide whether the person is right rather than whether the pattern is right. If the person is wrong, the decision itself may have been wrong. That is to say, it is dangerous if you choose the wrong person to tell you that something is right. Second, you must consider the right person for success. So, in my view, human resources are the most crucial factor. Of course, in evaluating talent, efficiency is the most important. People of high calibre are able to work highly efficiently and can capture a leading position in the industry. Ability shows potential;

performance is in the record. However, people of high calibre often have sharp tempers. Those who always follow routines are useless, even if you have a lot of them. So I think it is necessary to be tolerant. If your system cannot tolerate that individual, it is you who are wrong, not that individual. As I said, we need those with an entrepreneurial spirit. Those who are routine-oriented cannot mix well with our team. They will sooner or later become so upset that they leave the company.

Corporate Culture Combining Yin and Yang, Looseness and Tightness, and Tension and Relaxation

Interviewer Chen: What about your Tai Chi culture? Can you describe briefly the core values exhibited in Tai Chi culture?

Liang: The most important thing in Tai Chi is tolerance of yin and yang. If you think yang is right, you must clearly know that yin causes yang. Never try to eliminate conflicts or rivals. You must discover the co-existence of their interests.

Second, the motions of Tai Chi constitute dynamic peace. What is dynamic peace? When your body is in motion, if the left part of your body is relaxed, there must be a point in your left body that would be very tense. Along the same lines, if the right side of your body is very tense, there must be a point in your right side is very relaxed. Only in this way can you understand the essence of Tai Chi. Otherwise, you are not practising Tai Chi; you are doing Shaolin Boxing. Such a combination of looseness and tightness is very interesting. For example, if you are strict and demanding when handling a work task or a person, you must be very considerate at the same time; or, while being very loving, you must also be very realistic. For example, when you are engaged in charity work, you should also control it with measurement, key performance indicators (KPIs), and the red/green lamp mechanism. It's not just giving out money. Sometimes we find it hard to control the balance; we may be too loose or too tight. So Tai Chi should always combine both tension and relaxation in equal degrees. Using such a Tai Chi pattern for thinking will bring new perspectives to many things. Whatever it may be, we should not go to extremes or overdo things. It is the same for external publicity. When a private company tries to be a star, it is the start of their downfall. When you are not a star, 99 % of the public ignores you. They might say you are good, but they will not say you are bad. The degree of fame should be well-controlled. If you were once an expert but now want to be a star, people will judge you based on the criteria for a star rather than those for an expert. Being a star is not directly related to running a successful business, so one should be careful about whether or not to become a star.

Making such a choice will influence the whole philosophy of your company. I think it is not necessary to be a star. In the realm of investment, if people say a company is worth their respect, that is enough. Never let people idolise you; if you do you are ruined. We are strongly against being stars.

A Straightforward Way to Manage Conflict

Interviewer Chen: Have you ever faced conflicts between your personal feelings and rational business judgement? How did you solve such conflicts?

Liang: Whenever I am in such a conflict, I think of the word straightforward. I have no particular skill in conflict management; rather, I try to communicate what I am truly thinking. I often tell members of my teams to just ask their hearts when they do not know what to do. Just tell others what you want to do. Even when it is hard to express what is in your heart, you should try to say it anyway. The results are always good if you speak the truth. I'd like to share two stories about speaking the truth when dealing with conflict. One is about recruiting a new office manager with a high level of compensation; the other is about dismissing a high-ranking employee. Both were tough to deal with.

We once had an office manager who had been working well for us for a long time. His annual pay was 500,000 RMB. But later, as the company's business expanded, he could not do all the work. So I decided to recruit a new office manager. At that time, the annual pay for those qualified for such a job had exceeded 1 million RMB. So I recruited a new office manager with an annual salary of 1.5 million RMB. When the incumbent office manager learned about that, he was very upset, of course, and asked for a meeting. How would I explain my decision?

The next day he came to my office and I said 'though I have recruited a new office manager, that does not mean I don't trust you. In fact, I trust you more because we have worked together for so many years. If we must cut staff, I may choose to dismiss him rather than loyal people like you who have followed me for so long. On the other hand, when our company is in crisis, I believe this newcomer will be the one to quit, and, as for you, you will stay even without pay. So you should continue to trust me.' Those were my heartfelt words. That's how I treat those who work with me for so many years. Having heard that, he wept and was no longer dissatisfied. Later I also took some compensation measures. I gave him a subsidy to be deposited in his future pension based on his working years in my company.

The other case that impacted me particularly deeply is the first time I had to dismiss an employee of quite a high rank. I followed my principles of persuading people. I wanted to care for his core interest, not to let him focus on his losses but instead to focus on his gains. If he still resisted, I would go the other way and explain what he would lose if he failed to comply. And if I wanted him to give up something, I would explain what he would get for what he gave up. There are two sides to everything. I do not lie, but I may not tell the whole truth.

Interviewer Chen: Then how did you communicate with him?

Liang: I said, 'It is obvious to all that you have done well in our company. But in our company, many do as well as you. You can't take full advantage of your strengths here, but you will excel if you work for other companies.' He thought for a while, took what I said to be reasonable, and quickly left.

So you can see, our thinking is often restricted. If you want to raise funds, others will count what gains they will get if they invest and whether such gains will be sufficient. They calculate their risks. If you tell them that if they do not make the investment, within the coming 5 to 10 years they will have lost their opportunity to invest in a great company. This is more than just a transaction. Thus an alternative reasoning makes them change their mind and become eager to invest.

In my opinion, when you are trading, you should not say you win and he loses, or he wins and you lose. I think each side wants something different. It is possible to achieve a win—win situation. Who gets more and who gets less is not the question. You get more in that part and I get more in this part; so both sides are satisfied.

Interviewer Chen: This is consistent with your Tai Chi philosophy. Finally, could you please briefly give us a few concluding remarks regarding starting and managing a business?

Liang: Specific to entrepreneurs and business start-ups, I think the most important factor for success is to align your long-term personal needs with your followers' needs, society's expectations, and the world's common goals. After the alignment, your heart will no longer experience tension. In my view, that is of utmost importance. If your pursuit of business harms your community, the interests of those around you, the system you are in, or your social interests, your business will definitely fail, as well it should.

As for management, I think it is more efficient to gather or integrate than to invent from scratch. Inventors are often admired and hailed as heroes. Those who gather or integrate may not be heroes, but they will become giants of outcomes. Inventing something new consumes energy, whereas gathering or integrating saves social resources: you can integrate and synthesise existing resources to generate new, bigger, and more powerful resources.

Commentary

As a rising star in the global capital market, Fosun has developed an innovative business model by taking advantage of global resources rooted in the Chinese market and Chinese culture. The success of international acquisition and the strategic alliances of Fosun since around 2005 suggests the successful integration of Chinese private multinationals in a global context. It is an excellent example of how a Chinese company leverages the best of Chinese culture (yin—yang philosophy, modesty-not-stardom, loose—tight control), entrepreneurial mindset (courage, drive, boldness, replicable success, successor development), and Western business practices (teamwork, direct communication, optimisation, win—win problem solving, risk control).

As one of the pioneer Chinese enterprises who lead the global integration of resources and capability, Fosun represents a new model for Chinese multinationals to follow in the global scenario. Business model innovation is more than technology to generate new value in an industry, and often functions in the following dimensions: value proposition, target market, value chain, revenue chain, value network or ecosystem, and competitive strategy (Chesbrough 2007). The innovative business model and strategic management of Fosun also provides insights for the potential integration of what Barney and Zhang (2009) debate for the theory of Chinese management and Chinese theory of management. Rooted in Chinese culture, traditions and market, Fosun integrates Western management conceptualisations holistically as an inseparable part of global leverage.

References

Barnet, J. B., & Zhang, S. (2009). The future of Chinese management research: A theory of Chinese management versus a Chinese theory of management. *Management and Organization Review, 5*(1), 15–28.

Chesbrough, H. (2007). Business model innovation: It's not just about technology anymore. *Strategy & Leadership, 35*(6), 12–17.

Fosun (2014). Fosun Annual Report 2013. Retrieved July 25, 2015, from http://www.fosun.com/site/site-adv/upload/1397554884639.pdf

Fosun (2015a) News release. Retrieved July 25, 2015, from http://www.fosun.com/en/news/news.html

Fosun (2015b) Fosun Annual Report 2014. Retrieved July 25, 2015, from http://www.fosun.com/site/site-adv/upload/1429582061044.pdf

Hurun (2015) Hurun Midas rich list 2015. Retrieved July 25, 2015, from http://www.hurun.net/EN/ArticleShow.aspx?nid=9595

Maigoo (2015) Introduction of CEO Fosun International Ltd: Xinjun Liang. 梁信军-复星国际有限公司首席执行官介绍,精英名人堂. Retrieved July 25, 2015, from http://mingren.maigoo.com/853.html

4

Learning About Wars When Fighting in Wars

Interview with Taikang Life Insurance Chairman and CEO Dongsheng Chen

The interview was conducted by: Xiao-Ping Chen, University of Washington, and Eve Li Yan, Peking University.

Taikang Life Insurance Co. Ltd[1]

Founded on 22 August 1996 after obtaining approval from the People's Bank of China, Taikang Life Insurance Co. Ltd (hereafter Taikang) is one of largest insurance companies in China, offering services ranging from life insurance to asset management.

In its efforts to build an insurance company of an international standard, Taikang first succeeded in attracting foreign capital investment and established its internationalised corporate management structure in the year 2000. Since then, the company has developed greatly at a rapid pace taking advantage of the increasing speed of development of the Chinese economy, the reform of the insurance and pension system in China, and

---

[1] This section is based on information and news from the company's website (Taikang 2015a), and other professional social media (Taikang 2015b), and IACMR's *Chinese Management Insights'* publication on Taikang in September 2012.

© The Author(s) 2017
A.S. Tsui et al., *Leadership of Chinese Private Enterprises*, Palgrave Studies in Chinese Management, DOI 10.1057/978-1-137-40235-6_4

increasing demand for an alternative in the market to the previous state provision. With the business established in the industry sector of pensions and insurance, Taikang's asset management business also matured. In 2006 and 2007, Taikang split the business into two different subsidiaries: Taikang Asset Management Co. Ltd and Taikang Pension and Insurance Co. Ltd. The principal business of Taikang Asset Management is to invest and generate returns on capital, which concentrates substantially on the domestic capital market, generating returns in a leading position in the following years.

In 2009, Taikang's business extended to the health care industry, becoming the first insurance company to obtain the Chinese government's approval to invest in nursing provision. Meanwhile, the company's pension business achieved major business breakthroughs in 2010, with more than 10 billion RMB of net company assets, and CBN Financial Value Ranking rated Taikang as the most competitive pension company. At the end of 2010, Taikang had total assets of about 300 billion RMB, with net assets of about 13.4 billon RMB. The solvency ratios of Taikang was more than 170 %, with an annual profit of more than 2 billon RMB, from a premium revenue of about 86.8 billion RMB. In 2009/10, Taikang was ranked in the top 100 in the list of China's Top 500 Enterprises.

Taikang's expansion strategy continued successfully. Its chairman and CEO, Dongsheng Chen, and the company's top management team formulated the growth strategy with 'specialisation, standardisation, and internationalisation,' guided by the principles of 'operating with robustness and developing with compliance.' Innovation has also been an important priority in the business, creating many new products and approaches in the insurance industry. In 2011, Taikang Life had end-of-year total assets totalling 350 billion RMB and net company assets totaling 12.5 billion RMB. By the end of 2013, Taikang Pension and Insurance had completed the strategic layout of a retirement community in four cities: Beijing, Shanghai, Guangzhou and Sanya. By 2014, the company's total assets were close to 530 billion RMB and net assets over 32.9 billion RMB, with adequate solvency and net profits close to 6.8 billion RMB. Its managed assets exceeded 700 billion RMB. Taikang has 35 branch companies, with over 4200 institutions across the country at all levels. It has served nearly 29.78 million personal customers and around 250,000 effective institutional clients. By 30 June 2014, it had provided insurance services to a total of 11 million customer claims with the cumulative amount of 13 billion RMB.

In May 2015, Taikang announced its intention to list publicly on the Hong Kong Stock Exchange for an initial public offering (IPO) of about 3 billion USD. In the second half of 2015, Taikang made several changes of principal shareholders to adapt and prepare themselves for this process (Liu 2015), aiming for an IPO in 2016 (Tencent Finance 2015). The most recent strategic actions have been the creation of Taikang's Online Wealth Insurance Company and the opening of the first Taikang hospital in November 2015.

Founder, Chairman and CEO, Dongsheng Chen[2]

The successful growth and expansion of Taikang has been carried out under the leadership of its Chairman and CEO, Dongsheng Chen. Born in Tianmen, Hubei province in 1957, Dongsheng Chen also founded China Guardian Auctions Co. Ltd, and is founder and honorary chairman of ZJS Express Co. Ltd. Of the three companies, Taikang was founded most recently, but is the most well-known of the three in China, and the company of which Chen is the most proud, considering it best demonstrates his strategic insights into business development and model building.

After earning a PhD in economics from Wuhan University, Dongsheng Chen worked in the International Trade Research Center of the Ministry of Foreign Trade and Economic Co-operation from 1983 to 1988. In the following five years, he was associate editor of the journal *Management World*. In 1993, he founded his first business, China Guardian Auctions, and in 1996 he founded Taikang. Since then he has been immersed in the business world, with constantly evolving entrepreneurial projects.

---

[2] This section is based on IACMR's *Chinese Management Insights'* publication on Taikang in September 2012 with permission, complemented by public information from worldofceos.com (worldofceos, 2015).

Taikang and Dongsheng Cheng have donated to different social causes and activities, for natural disasters, education or other issues, with a total of more than 200 million RMB by 30 June 2014. He is also a part-time professor at several universities. For his contribution to business and society, he is honoured to be listed among the Most Respected Entrepreneurs in China, the Most Insightful Entrepreneurs in China, and the Most Influential Chinese Business Leaders, among other honours.

Modelling After the Best

Interviewers Chen and Yan: Would you please describe your management style?

Dongsheng Chen (hereafter referred to as Chen): To put my management style simply and plainly, I am idealistic and want to build a great enterprise. I value specialisation, standardisation, marketisation and internationalisation. My mottoes are 'To innovate is to imitate first' and 'Learn from the West', Western countries have been running market economies for hundreds of years, and those businesses have paid a great price to develop market patterns and rules. Their historical experience has given them coherent logic. We may be unable to understand this totally yet, but we can learn from the West's experiences.

Basically our management style can be summarised in five words: steady, professional, amiable, innovative and honest. Life insurance operates in the financial sector and is client-oriented. Clients trust you to use their money to build their future, so being steady is the most important aspect. Being professional is the minimum standard we expect of ourselves. We try to be amiable with our customers and to listen to them carefully. Robustness in terms of steadiness and professionalism does not conflict with innovation; rather, the two can be unified. Lastly, honesty is absolutely essential for financial firms.

Interviewers Chen and Yan: Your motto is 'To innovate is to imitate first', but some executives argue that China's special conditions mean that copying will not work.

Chen: To imitate is to model those who do the best work. In the process of modelling, we can omit practices that do not work, and keep those that succeed. That's the simple way I run my business, by imitating the best.

I was the associate editor of *Management World* for five years, and that experience gave me some important insights. The most important things for an entrepreneur who starts up a business are innovation, sharing and fairness. You cannot retain talent if you cannot lead your enterprise to be innovative. You cannot retain excellent teams if you lack mechanisms for ensuring fairness and sharing. Therefore, I have always advocated innovation, sharing and fairness as the three 'must-dos' for entrepreneurs.

During the early stages of Taikang Life, we were like a piece of blank paper. We had to learn about how other companies developed their infrastructure and divided the labour. Our model companies included those in Hong Kong, Taiwan, Europe, North America and Japan. We learned how to build sales teams and sales systems, how to establish actuaries and dividends systems, and then how to establish an investment system. Sales and basic operation came first, then products and actuaries, then investment. We also studied the back-end functions, such as finance, human resources, administration and meetings. We sent many people to study in related specializations, and hired many professionals to train us.

I would say we had no single specific company as our model; but we learned from everyone's best parts. For example, our sales system has learned much from Taiwan's Cathay Life Insurance's sales system, which they adopted from Japan.

Compared with big international firms, Taikang certainly has a long way to go to reach maturity despite many years having passed since the company's foundation. As a company with 15 years of rapid growth, we still lag behind leading firms in maturity and technical competency, though our overall framework is fairly well established. We are now strong enough to compete with large firms for talent, the most important prerequisite for building a great company. I am very satisfied that Taikang has managed to retain a core group of talented young and middle-aged employees.

Interviewers Chen and Yan: What life experience has profoundly influenced your management style?

Chen: I learn by doing. As Mao Zedong said, 'I learn about wars when I'm fighting in wars', which means exploring and reflecting while practising. For example, I am very interested in American business history and American entrepreneurs. I have been encouraged, inspired and influenced in both a macro and an abstract way through reading many biographies of entrepreneurs. But primarily I explore and reflect on my original thoughts and style. For example, I alone developed my ideas about organisational culture and the positioning of the CEO and CFO (chief financial officer).

Passing on Honesty and Amiability in the Corporate Culture

Interviewers Chen and Yan: Is it possible to pass on your beliefs and values across all levels so that every employee will indeed perform honestly and amiably?

Chen: Under rapid development, we often hire people from other companies in the same industry, but these new employees may know nothing about Taikang, so they just perform based on their past experience and their own imaginations, which may deviate greatly from our expectations. We realised then that newly hired employees from other companies should first be based at our headquarters. Being close to the boss, they learn about Taikang and its culture. Later, when they are assigned elsewhere, they will represent the Taikang culture and values. It's really difficult to pass on the culture in a company with such rapid growth. When branches implement corporate decisions, variance still exists among managers in terms of knowledge and professionalism.

For professional training, we require consistency within the company, but also leave some room for branches to be flexible. China is a big country with huge regional, cultural and climatic differences, so we must allow a balance between consistency and flexibility. We need to pass on our core company cultural values, but we must respect special features in different markets. There are no exact numbers to keeping such a balance. Mainly it is about the 'soft' side of business: management style and management culture. We are consistent within Taikang in terms of the requirements for management, the products sold, and employee training. However, management styles, employee requirements, organisational climates and organisational cultures still vary greatly.

In the early stages of a rapidly growing company, sales and business people usually play important roles and contribute significantly. As a company becomes more complex and mature, though, general managers will become more important. As when new empires are established, military generals are usually the first forces, and then the civil officers run the empire. When a company is developing very quickly, sales and business people expand the territory, but when the company reaches a certain scale, general managers begin to play a critical role. Managers who have worked for a long time at the headquarters are usually capable overall, and when they are sent to work in branches they do better in passing on our culture. Currently, we rarely hire managers externally; instead, we promote our own people to manager level. At one time we introduced many outsiders, but now we rely more on internal development. We also seldom hire salespeople from other firms. We have already passed that stage. It costs a lot to 'steal' people from other companies, and the outcomes are often disappointing.

Formulating Strategy, Managing Risks and Building Teams

Interviewers Chen and Yan: What do you think is the biggest risk in the life insurance sector?

Chen: All commercial activities involve some exaggeration, so the biggest risk is misleading people. For example, in medical care, exaggerating and misleading people can be lethal. We cannot talk only about the positive side of insurance without also revealing the negative aspects. This is why I stressed the importance of honesty. We cannot build an honest society overnight. Honesty will only prevail under sufficient competition. Insufficient competition in the early stages of the market economy allows dishonesty to be profitable. When we have sufficient competition, dishonest companies will be revealed, and honesty will prevail. Many do not understand this point, so we commonly see exaggeration and deceit in the early stages of market development. I am not saying that dishonest practices should go unpunished. I am suggesting that we should understand why they exist. In addition to misleading people and being dishonest, I see three more threats to life insurance firms: investment failures, actuarial pricing errors, and poor security in the information system.

We do have risk-control procedures to deal with complaints and cheating within the company. When our public relations department spots a problem, we inform the operations department, which immediately contacts customers. Many problems arise from information asymmetry, or from customers not knowing enough about insurance. For example, our insurance plans do not cover carcinoma in situ, but customers may mistakenly believe that all types of cancer are covered. Therefore the major solution is for customers to understand insurance plans thoroughly. Sometimes our own defects cause problems, which we solve basically with fast-response procedures and guidelines for contacting clients within certain time frames. Necessary procedures involve people from different departments, such as branding, operations and other operational lines. This industry has grown quite big, and one customer may face 25 sales-persons. We realise that it's common and usual for such problems to occur, and each phase of the value chain is interrelated. Our final goal is to solve problems.

In China, competition in the life insurance industry is very fierce. The entrance costs to this market remain high, and market centralisation is also relatively high, with the top seven life insurance companies having 85 % of the market share. It's difficult for small companies to do well and to grow, given the established reputation and power of the large companies. However, this competition is in a primitive stage, since firms are very homogenous. They have no market segmentation, and lack exploration and a deep understanding of clients. The lack of market segmentation results from a lack of in-depth understanding of the market. Consequently, we are still in the early stages of homogeneous and vicious competition, and have not yet entered the advanced stages of competing on segmentation and specialisation.

Primitive competition involves significant malicious attempts to steal talented staff from competitors. In addition, homogeneous competition does not focus on specialisation and segmentation, so small companies have little chance to succeed. When Taikang first started the business, it was the era of 'department stores' in this industry, and now it should be moving into the era of 'specialised stores.' The biggest problem is that many still want to run department stores rather than specialised stores.

Interviewers Chen and Yan: As the first CEO in China's insurance industry, you are a scholarly entrepreneur with outstanding personal charisma. Do you know an established management approach that can help Taikang's salespeople also to stand out from their competitors?

Chen: This is difficult, as the market allows little discretion. I was personally involved in the training from the first to the 34th sales training programme, but it became impossible to continue when the insurance market began to grow so rapidly. The corporate culture becomes diluted. I often reflect that if we had built our teams gradually and then sent them out, we would have become a great company. But the market has the final say. If time allows, I go to training classes and speak to new employees. Otherwise, they watch a video of my speech.

Forces that Subvert the Market: Products, Channels and Markets

Interviewers Chen and Yan: How do your current ideals differ from your original ideals when you started your new venture?

Chen: People should not understand idealism too generally and broadly. For me, idealism requires having an entrepreneurial spirit, having great goals, and trying to realise the value of human beings. Our current goal is specialisation; our business model is 'from cradle to heaven.' We hope to change the way that Chinese people live through life insurance and nursing communities, making them an integral part of Chinese life. We strive to achieve and fight for this specific ideal, not just to have a good job.

Interviewers Chen and Yan: What is Taikang's greatest challenge in seeking further rapid growth?

Chen: We cannot have rapid growth for as long as we want it. The opportunities come from the market. In the past, we had the opportunity to set up more facilities and expand our territory, which ensured ten years of rapid growth. Another opportunity was the emergence of 'ban-cassurance'—selling insurance through banks—which gave us another five years of rapid growth. Now the banking market is experiencing major adjustments, and the traditional market is in a relatively reasonable stage of expansion. So probably pensions and Medicare are new opportunities to grow, and we are building nursing communities and exploring these.

High-growth is from market subversion, opening up a new blue ocean, and enjoying the prosperity for a while. But all products have certain life cycle when opening up new revenue channels. They reach their peak, stay on top for a while, but will not last forever. Generally speaking, I have discerned three forces that can subvert the market: products, channels and markets. Great products, such as those from Apple, can reshape the market. Sometimes new channels emerge, such as the 'bancassurance' I just mentioned. As for markets in China, the middle class is rising, and insurance should have room for rapid growth. But having the will alone does not determine growth, and we must seek forces that can rock the market. The pension industry and the medical industry provide opportunities for new growth, but we need breakthrough innovations. We believe the business of nursing communities for older citizens is such a breakthrough that will enjoy further development.

The Greatness of Your Ambition Determines How Far You Can Go; The Size of Your Framework Determines the Size of Your Market

Interviewers Chen and Yan: You have a very acute business sense. Can you share some tips regarding how to develop that sense?

Chen: I often tell my employees that we must consider framework and structure first. The extent of your ambition determines how far you can go, and the size of your framework determines how large your market can be and how far your vision can go. Framework is strategy, structure and system. You must understand your business deeply, and must aim high and look at the world from a historical perspective. How can you reach that high level and at the same time have a historical perspective? You must have a broad mind, and possess deep knowledge as well as framework thinking. This is the methodology: gathering an in-depth understanding of the field you are entering. This could be carried out on three levels: being familiar with your enterprises; very familiar with the industry; and with the whole world, particularly with the national economy and politics. These three levels build foresight, which is essential in building frameworks. Another benefit of having your own framework is that it will immunise you from rivals throughout your lifetime. When you lack your own framework, structure, strategy and system, many competitive market actions will shake your resolve. If the enterprise lacks a clear and steadfast strategy, it will miss good opportunities.

My advantage is that I understand the decreed fate (*Zhitianming* 知天命). I am already over fifty years old, with my life experience spanning half a century. My historic experiences have coalesced to form an integral framework in my mind. I witnessed China's change from a command economy to today's market economy, and then I witnessed the integration of the Chinese economy into the world economy, e-economy and so on. These experiences give me a foundation for making good judgements.

Even if we have a grand framework, the market still changes dynamically, so the truth lies at the very basic level of the organisation. When we first entered this market, life insurance was still a simple business, with only personal and corporate business, then later, banks emerged as a new channel for selling insurance. Since around 2005, revenues from sales in banks have accounted for about 50 % of all premium revenues, and more recently, telephone sales have also increased, making up about 5 % to 10 % of premium revenues.

At present the insurance industry has three major trends. The first is that China's middle classes are beginning to manage their wealth so that there are profound changes in insurance products. It is not a matter of whether wealth management products are good or bad, but a market trend. It also explains why insurance products with wealth management sell well. Without this new era of wealth management, we would not have this high average premium level per person, and the insurance industry would not have reached the large size it has today. The second trend is 'urban-rural integration', as rural residents are richer now. Our business penetrates into rural counties and towns, with the whole insurance market becoming a binary-focus market integrating urban and rural areas. The third trend is the rise of bank assurance sales and the emergence of multiple sales channels, such as phone and online sales.

Taikang has developed businesses through all these channels. We are relatively weak on personal sales, ranking fifth. We ranked third on bank sales, second on phone sales, and first on online sales of life insurance. Our corporate business and pension businesses rank third or fourth. Those are our positions in the various market segments.

The truth lies at very heart of the organisation. It means that I did not devise these changes and new channels, but people working at elementary levels did so. For example, bank assurance sales have changed greatly in China. At first we imitated practices in Western countries to promote wealth-management products. Later, the development of bank assurance in China led to the emergence of new products in the domestic market, such as the product that allows you to pay premiums for five or ten years in advance all at once.

I often talk about the combination of enterprise, industry and country. Only a thorough understanding of the world and the nation can expand your vision. 'Standing sky high to look through one century's history' is much more than just fancy talk. Strategy is indeed what I am good at. I worked in a macroeconomic department for a long time, so have developed such ways of thinking. Past experience can have a strong influence on future direction.

Mao Zedong's revolution started from scratch. It went from small to big, weak to strong, and it finally succeeded. When problems are encountered in practice, reflect and resolve them. Mao's writings have been greatly influential because the same logic also applies to business. To resolve problems every day is a process of summarising, learning and inducting, to develop one's own system of thought and approaches. This is what Taikang does. At various times, we encountered different problems, so our thoughts and ideas also changed. Basically, all thoughts and ideas serve the purpose of solving present problems.

Serving the Collective Good and Being Sincere Can Be a Powerful Influence

Interviewers Chen and Yan: In your many years of running businesses, you must have encountered some conflicts between interpersonal emotions and business rationality. Could you describe one or two such incidents? In retrospect, how should you have handled such conflicts?

Chen: We once hired headhunting firms to look for professional talent. However, one should not expect too much, because the real world is never perfect. It is most important to allow people to fully realise their potential. Many leaders notice only their subordinates' shortcomings and thus always complain about the lack of talent, but everyone has merit. Enabling people to use their talents fully is easier said than done, however. A leader's core responsibility is to use people's expertise and talents, and that will solve the problems you mentioned. For example, I can tell an employee, 'You are not competent enough to be in charge of these things, but you can use your talent to do other things.' I can be totally frank and sincere. I was once concerned about 'face issues', but now I can criticise people to their faces, as long as it is for the collective good. Serving the collective good and being sincere can be a powerful influence. You can handle problems well if you avoid being secretive, and if your words and thoughts are consistent. You must tell people what you sincerely think. Managers should be sincere and collective-oriented.

Interviewers Chen and Yan: When appointing mid-level and top-level managers, do you prefer people who match your values and styles, or do you prefer people who are more experienced in business?

Chen: Just as in an orchestra, you can afford to have only one person who is an idealist. You need people with experience and expertise to get things done. An enterprise is like a person: it has characteristics, ideals and ambitions, and these are determined by top management. The founders of the first generation are often mysterious and legendary, with many stories being told of their personal characteristics. Just like the old saying 'birds of a feather flock together', people who dislike your style and culture will leave or not come to you in the first place, and people who think they have found a good fit will stay. So it's a process of natural selection.

However, it's always essential to have people who can get things done and have strong professional expertise. It will not work if all the team members are dreamers! Idealism cannot live without solid work on the ground. Do not mistake me for a pure dreamer; I am essentially a doer, a man of action. Guardian Auctions executive Wang Yannan interpreted my style well: 'You have great ambitions and ideals. But what makes you stand out is that you have kept your feet on the ground: you do things; you act to accomplish goals one by one. So you have succeeded.'

Interviewers Chen and Yan: Could you please summarise your advice in one or two sentences?

Chen: I advise learning through practice: learn about war when fighting war, and learn about business when doing business. I also advise having clear goals and focusing on them fully. Time will work it out if you do the right things. Taikang focuses firmly on life insurance with the clear goal of becoming a specialist life insurance firm. It would be a bad idea to wander off the road and try all kinds of other businesses, such as banking or property insurance. You cannot do everything in the world. Be patient, and your effort will pay off eventually.

Commentary

The insurance market in China is highly competitive in spite of an apparently monopolistic situation as a result of relatively homogeneous and standard products. Only through innovative and competitive strategy can one be differentiated from the others and stand out in the market. Taikang Life Insurance has built a strong reputation among its customers, commits to managing risk and corporate culture, and proposes new and innovative products and services to fulfil emerging market demands.

For Dongsheng Chen, to innovate is to imitate first. This is not a simple imitation but modelling the best. That is, the knowledge conversion process from others, like explicit and tacit knowledge, is spiral and transcendental (Nonaka 1991; Nonaka and Takeuchi 1995). As part of innovative imitation (Levitt 1966), through learning first from diverse experiences in the West and other Great China regions, Taikang's own models have been built through the fusion of different pieces of knowledge to create something new. This is also termed 'learning by doing' (Christensen 1997; Tsang 2002) or 'learning through reflection on doing' (Felicia 2011: 1003), a principal characteristic of doing business in the emerging markets in China, where initially no clear rules were present and no specific business model was to serve as a benchmark in a market with ambiguous norms and transitional institutional environments (Peng 2003). Chen's depth of industry knowledge along a broad global perspective added to historic sensitivity have contributed to Taikang's framework, which emphases both consistency and control balanced by flexibility and innovation.

References

Christensen, C. M. (1997). Making strategy: Learning by doing. *Harvard Business Review* (November–December), 141–156.

Felicia, P. (2011). *Handbook of research on improving learning and motivation.* Hershey, PA: IGI Global.

Levitt, T. (1966). Innovative imitation. *Harvard Business Review* (September–October), 63–70.

Liu, A. (2015). Taikang Life Insurance goes for IPO and 'eliminates barriers': Five changes of shareholder structure in three months. 21 Jingji.com, 13 October. Retrieved December 7, 2015ś, from http://epaper.21jingji.com/html/2015-10/13/content_21326.htm

Nonaka, I. (1991). The knowledge creating company. *Harvard Business Review, 69*(6) (November–December), 96–104.

Nonaka, I., & Takeuchi, H. (1995). *The knowledge creating company: How Japanese companies create the dynamics of innovation.* New York: Oxford University Press.

Peng, M. W. (2003). Institutional transitions and strategic choices. *Academy of Management Review, 28*(2), 275–296.

Taikang (2015a). Taikang Life website. Retrieved March 26, 2015, and December 7, 2015, from http://www.taikang.com/about/news/media/index.shtml

Taikang (2015b). Taikang Life website. Retrieved March 26, 2015, from https://www.linkedin.com/company/taikang-life-insurance?trk=top_nav_home

Tencent Finance (2015). News says Taikang Life aims to go for A+H IPO to capitalize 20 billion RMB. Retrieved December 7, 2015, from http://finance.qq.com/a/20140908/003994.htm

Tsang, E. W. K. (2002). Acquiring knowledge by foreign partners from international joint ventures in a transition economy: Learning-by-doing and learning myopia. *Strategic Management Journal, 23*(9), 835–854.

Worldofceos.com (2015). Dongsheng Chen. Retrieved March 26, 2015, from http://www.worldofceos.com/dossiers/dongsheng-chen

5

Changing with Your Needs, Changing with the Situation

Interview with China Merchants Bank Former President Weihua Ma

The interview was conducted by: Xiao-Ping Chen, University of Washington.

China Merchants Bank[1]

In 1987, as China's first commercial bank founded by an enterprise and a pilot bank in the efforts of the Chinese government to drive financial reform, China Merchants Bank (CMB) was established at the forefront of China's reform and opening-up campaign, in Shenzhen Special Economic Zone. In 2002, CMB was listed on the Shanghai Stock Exchange; and in 2006, the bank was listed on the Hong Kong Stock Exchange.

Since its establishment, CMB has adhered to its business service concept of 'changing for you,' with constant innovation in products and services. As a consequence, CMB developed from a small bank with a capital of only 100 million yuan, one branch and some 30 employees to become China's sixth-largest commercial bank in 2014 with net assets

---

[1] This section is based on information and news from the company website (CMB 2015a), and 2014 Annual Report (CMB 2015b), and IACMR's *Chinese Management Insights'* publication on China Merchants Bank in December 2013.

© The Author(s) 2017
A.S. Tsui et al., *Leadership of Chinese Private Enterprises*, Palgrave Studies in Chinese Management, DOI 10.1057/978-1-137-40235-6_5

of 360 billion yuan, a net profit of 55.9 billion yuan (an annual increase of 8.06 %), over 1200 branches and more than 70,000 employees. CMB is currently listed among the global top 100 banks. Over time it has developed into the most influential commercial bank brand in China as a result of its continuous financial innovation, quality customer service, prudent management and strong business performance.

Since 2009, CMB has gained a great deal of recognition: it was rated by the Boston Consulting Group as the bank with the best return on net assets in the world; it won the titles of the Best Commercial Bank of China, the Best Retail Bank in China, the Best Private Bank in China, China's Best Custody Specialist from the British *Financial Times*, *Euromoney* and *The Asset*. The Bank was shortlisted as a World-Class Chinese Brand and ranked No. 1 in the P/B (price to book ratio) list of the world's top 50 banks, with the highest market value by the British *Financial Times*. It was also listed at No. 56 among the world's Top 1000 Banks by *The Banker*. Most recently, in 2014, CMB was ranked number 350 in the Global Fortune 500 Enterprises, and its brand was ranked at No. 14 in the most valuable Chinese brands by BrandZ with a value of 6.7 billion USD.

As of 2014, CMB had 125 branches and 1297 sub-branches, 2 branch-level specialised institutions (a credit card centre and an enterprise credit centre), 2330 self-service banks and one wholly-owned subsidiary (CMB Financial Leasing). In the overseas market, CMB has two wholly-owned subsidiaries—Wing Lung Bank Ltd. and CMB International Capital Corporation Limited—and one branch in Hong Kong, a branch and a rep-office in New York, branches in Singapore and Luxembourg, and rep-offices in Taipei and London. Its opening of a New York branch during the worldwide financial crisis in 2008 was called a spring breeze in the Wall Street's winter.

Founder and Former President Weihua Ma[2]

Dr. Weihua Ma, PhD in Economics, is the former executive director, president and CEO of China Merchants Bank, a position he held until he retired in May 2013. He was previously the chairman of the Wing Lung Bank,

---

[2] This section is based on IACMR's Chinese *Management Insights'* publication on China Merchants Bank in December 2013 with permission, complemented with public information from China Entrepreneur Club (China Entrepreneur Club 2013).

and chairman of the board of directors for CIGNA & CMC Life Insurance Company Ltd. and China Merchants Fund Management Co. Ltd.

Dr. Ma was a deputy to the 10th National People's Congress (NPC) and a member of the 11th National Committee of the Chinese People's Political Consultative Conference (CPPCC). He is currently a member of the 12th National Committee of the CPPCC. In addition, he is vice chairman of China Chamber of International Commerce, the executive deputy chairman of China Enterprise Directors Association, the executive director of China Society for Finance, and the president of Shenzhen Soft Science Development Foundation. Dr. Ma is an adjunct professor at Peking University and Tsinghua University, both in Beijing. Before China Merchants Bank, Dr. Ma was deputy director and later deputy secretary general of the Economic Planning Committee of Liao Ning Province, director of the Party Office in CPC Liao Ning Committee and CPC An Hui Committee, deputy director of the General Office of People's Bank of China (PBOC), deputy director of the Finance and Planning Office of PBOC, as well as governor of PBOC Hainan Branch and chief of State Administration of Foreign Exchange (SAFE) Hainan Branch.

Dr. Ma is the chairman of the China Business Initiative of Columbia University, a member of the Emerging Markets Advisory Council of the Institute of International Finance, a member of the global council of the International Finance Forum, a member of the Advisory Council of the City of London, a member of the Advisory Board of the New York Financial Consulting Committee, and a member of the VISA Asia-Pacific senior advisory committee.

Dr. Ma has received numerous awards and wide recognition. He was named 'China Economic Person of the Year 2001' by China Central Television (CCTV);one of the 'Rising Stars of Banking' by *The Banker* in 2005; and 'China Business Leader of the Decade 1999–2009' by CCTV in 2009. In 2010, he received the 'Gold Award of Yuan Baohua Enterprise Management.' In 2011, Dr. Ma was awarded 'Outstanding Contributor to the Civil Society', 'Shenzhen 30 Years Excellent Quality Leadership Achievement Award' and 'Shenzhen 30 Years Industry Leading Character' by People's Daily Online. He was awarded 'Asia's Best CEO,' 'Asia's Banking Industry Leader, 'Asia's Best Banking President' and 'Asia's Excellent CEO' by *Institutional Investor* in 2007, 2008, 2009 and 2011, respectively. He was also awarded 'Retail Banker of the Year 2008' and 'The Asian Banker Talent and Leadership Development Award' by *The Asian Banker*, and 'Asia's Best CEO in 2009' by *Finance Asia*. In 2012, Dr. Ma was included in the Excellence 50 List of China's Listed Companies, released by *Harvard Business Review*; awarded 'China's Overseas Investment Annual Figure' by CCTV; and ranked in fourth place in 'China Influence List' released by the *Wall Street Journal*. He was also named 'Ernst & Young Entrepreneur of the Year 2012 China Awards.'

Changing with Your Needs, Changing with the Situation

Interviewer Chen: Mr. Ma, since you became the president of China Merchants Bank (CMB) in 1999, you have taken many measures to transform it from a small local bank into a joint-equity commercial bank alongside the five state-owned traditional banks. What measures did you find were most effective? How were they devised and implemented?

Weihua Ma (referred to Ma hereafter): This is a big question. Let me begin with how I became the president of CMB in 1999. Before that, I was in Hainan for seven years—six years as president of Hainan People's Bank and one year studying at the Central Party School. After my time in Hainan, I became interested in running a commercial bank. When I was an officer at the Central Bank, I was involved in currency policy and financial regulation, but never led a commercial bank, and I wanted to try it. Coincidentally, at that time the president of CMB was about to retire and was looking for a successor. He approached me just as I was searching for such an opportunity.

The Two 'Welcome Presents' from CMB

Ma: I started my job on 2 January 1999. Unexpectedly, something big happened in the first week. The Central Bank was giving up its offshore business because it was in great difficulties after the Asian financial crisis.

CMB had the largest share of offshore business at that time, accounting for about 50 % of the bank's total revenue (slightly over 100 billion RMB). The offshore business mainly included equity investments and loans, which became non-performing assets after the Asian financial crisis. That's why the Central Bank decided to stop its offshore business. As CMB had the most offshore business, I was faced with an extremely serious challenge. If information about the offshore business ending was leaked, overseas depositors would withdraw their money, but they would not be able to do so because it had been loaned out, and we had no US dollar reserves. Even if the Central Bank was willing support us, it could provide support only with RMB, so you can see the situation was dangerous: if a bank cannot pay its debts, it will be forced to close down.

Interviewer Chen: How did you handle that?

Ma: I consulted with the president and vice president of the Central Bank and explained the seriousness of the situation to them, and asked them to keep it a secret—to be 'intense internally but appearing relaxed externally.' I recall that all the official documents of that time were handwritten. I had arrived just one week before this, but I knew clearly that it was most important to assure that liquidity was not a problem; we could not afford a payment crisis or the bank would go out of business. So we took some action. First, we tried to attract foreign exchange deposits through floating interest rates. Second, we restricted foreign exchange loans. We loaned our RMB to other banks, and they loaned us foreign exchange. We did this for six months, and our foreign exchange investment reached over 600 million USD in June. Only then did I relax. That was my first welcome present.

Interviewer Chen: That was a close call! What was the second?

Ma: The second challenge was also very severe: the run on our Shenyang branch. It was rare to have runs on banks in China. What triggered it? One reason was that people did not trust joint-equity commercial banks. The second was a rumour that the previous president had disappeared along with the bank's money. In fact, the president had retired according to normal procedures, but outsiders did not know this.

It was the first run on a bank in China. The director of our Shenyang branch went to the branch to explain the situation, attempting to increase confidence by his presence. But people did not believe him. A RMB run bank is a liquidity risk. I was relatively experienced in this respect as I had spent six years in Hainan dealing with liquidity. I told the director that he could borrow money from the Central Bank, and we would also make some internal position adjustments. We asked the local government to help calm people. We told the branch director not to panic but to keep a stiff upper lip. He would tell people that no matter how much they wanted to withdraw from the bank, they would have it, but they would lose the interest as the current interest rate would apply only to term deposits. We told the director that, if people were still worried, he could deliver cash to their homes. Moreover, we piled up our counters with cash to give people confidence. We did this for nine days, and the run stopped. We rode out the crisis with our confidence—whatever amount people wanted, they got it.

Banks base their existence on credibility. You cannot afford people losing faith in you. Thee two incidents described occurred within my first three months as president of CMB, so I call them CMB's 'welcome presents' for me. What did I learn from dealing with them? Well, I realised that a bank's liquidity is actually superficial, like flu symptoms of a runny nose and tears, and that's nothing to worry about. However, when the internal immune system is compromised, one's health will suffer. For this reason, I started focusing on the quality of the bank's assets, and realised the importance of risk management.

At the time, CMB's non-performing asset ratio was at two digits. At my first CMB board meeting, I saw that our profit objective was 2 billion RMB. I decided to cut this by a third. Why? Shareholders had been pursuing yearly returns, and no provision had been made for the previous eleven years. I felt that the risk was too high, so I lowered the profit target, and made a provision equal to the sum of the previous eleven years. Some directors were unhappy with me, as reduced profits meant worse performance than previous years.

In the second half of the year after I joined CMB, we took two critical actions. One was risk management. At the end of the year, we established 10 iron rules called 'The Ten Nos' that includes managing risks with an iron fist, increasing provisions and writing off bad debts. The second action was to formulate a five-year plan that featured three steps: internet banking, capital marketisation, and international growth. The logic was that, if we did not plan for the future, we would be bound to find ourselves in trouble occasionally.

CMB's Three Strategies: Internet Banking, Capital Marketisation, and International Growth

Ma: If you look at the macro environment at that time, it was immediately after the Asian financial crisis, and China's economy was sluggish. However, IT e-commerce emerged. While Alibaba was still very small, many already knew about the four major portal websites—for example, Sina.com. Back then we had only nine branches with a relatively advanced IT system. The nine branches adopted a uniform model of planning, design and management, based on which we developed the 'One Card' solution. Customers could deposit or withdraw money at any of the nine branches by using this card. We embarked on internet banking in 1999.

My view on the internet was inspired by Bill Gates of Microsoft. He said that if traditional banks did not change in today's world, they would become extinct dinosaurs by the twenty-first century. He really gave me food for thought. Banks have two major functions: they are intermediaries for financing and platforms for payment. Each IT revolution will bring a further revolution in a bank's payment function, like evolving from riding horses to driving cars, to using telegrams, telephones and then the internet. That's why we believed that banks should seize the internet opportunity as a catalyst for transforming the entire banking industry. I was lecturing at many schools at that time. In Washington, I talked about e-commerce and the transformation of traditional banks. I told audiences that e-commerce's impacts on banking were not limited to one product or one service. Rather, it would trigger a revolution in the entire process, organisation, framework and even concepts.

Interviewer Chen: The way you interpreted the internet's impact on banking was really forward-looking.

Ma: CMB rode the wave of the internet at the beginning of the twenty-first century. Someone designed a 72-hour survival test, giving participants a card to use to get money. The final successful contestant managed to buy soybean milk with CMB's card. This attracted a good deal of attention in China. The media commented that CMB's internet success outweighed its profits that year. Thus CMB had its first success in China's internet banking. Then, in the second half of 1999, we launched an online personal banking system, including an online store, and online payment with five major functions. Other banks had those too, but they were not as comprehensive in terms of functions. CMB was the first to establish a relatively comprehensive online system. After that we started developing CMB's retail business using the One Card and One Network solution as two propellers, followed by constant innovations such as wealth management, credit cards and private banking. CMB's private banking originated from the internet in this way.

Our strategy was to be a bit earlier, a bit faster and a bit better than others. You have to be a couple of years earlier than others in developing new services so that when they start to explore the idea, you have already achieved a certain scale, established the brand, and laid down a solid foundation.

Interviewer Chen: Recently I noticed that you have been talking about the impact of social media on banking. Can you share your opinion?

Ma: We are ahead of others in this respect too, and consider it to be another aspect of our internet banking. Last year we began mobile payments. I feel that the internet and social media have unlimited possibilities. Even if internet finance comes into the picture in the future, banks will still have their own space. We now divide internet banking into three types: the first is the networking of traditional business—that is, carrying out traditional business via the internet; the second is internet companies conducting financial business, such as Jack Ma's AliFinance; and the third is pure internet financial business, such as social media. But no matter what, banks will not disappear in the foreseeable future. We proposed that banks need to have the internet thinking process and gene, as the internet is now more than just a means of communication: it is a lifestyle and conveys values.

Our second strategy was capital marketisation. When CMB started, it had only one shareholder—China Merchants Group, operating out of three rooms and with some 30+ employees. After the Asian financial crisis, the Basel Committee (the international body for banking supervision) constantly emphasised the capital adequacy ratio. Consequently, CMB undertook several financing activities. It was internal financing at the beginning, not public issuance of stock. We did not prepare to go public and follow the path of the capital market until 2002. It was not an easy process; banks encountered very complicated conditions in going public at that time.

CMB Going Public Was a Process of Rebirth

Interviewer Chen: So CMB made an initial public offering (IPO) in China?

Ma: Yes, in A shares.[3] At the time, CMB had to write off non-performing assets. As the Ministry of Finance could not give us money to do that, we could rely only on shareholders' earnings. It was a tough process. We finally went public in 2002. Then we did it again with H shares in 2006 in Hong Kong.[4] We led in the number of circulating shares and market value. We were also the first to adopt international standards.

We thought that the purpose of going public was not just to reach the capital adequacy ratio (CAR); it was more of a process of rebirth for us. After a company goes public, it is subject to regulations and adopts generally accepted accounting standards. Its provision and financial practices will be standardised. It is also a process of management upgrade and internationalisation, and international standards must be adopted across the board. At the same time, the process of making an IPO is of brand communication. Therefore going public was of great significance to CMB.

---

[3] A shares are securities of Chinese incorporated companies that trade on either the Shanghai or Shenzhen stock exchanges, quoted only in yuan (CNY). They can be traded only by PRC residents or under the Qualified Foreign Institutional Investor (QFII) and Renminbi Foreign Institutional investor (RQFII) schemes. B shares can be quoted in US dollars and Hong Kong dollars, and can be traded by non-residents of the PRC and retail investors of the PRC.

[4] H shares are securities of Chinese incorporated companies nominated by the Central Government for listing and trading on the Stock Exchange of Hong Kong, quoted and traded in Hong Kong dollars, without restrictions on the trader (FTSE 2014).

Two years after the A shares were listed, we started to issue convertible bonds. The market had a downturn, and funds banded together against our issuance of convertible bonds because in China's market, additional stock issuance normally depresses stock prices. This was CMB's convertible bond incident, in which we learned how to communicate with investors. Two years later, our H shares were listed. Listing of H shares required us to have 30 % of overseas shareholders. The bank became more international. After such experiences in the capital market, CMB improved its management substantially. This is what we call capital marketisation.

CMB's third strategy was international growth. Actually, not long after the bank was established at the beginning of the present century, we formulated a strategy for growth both inside and outside China. We set up a representative office and then a branch in Hong Kong. We were among the earliest to set up a branch there. Later, we opened a New York branch, earlier than both the Industrial & Commercial Banks of China and the China Construction Bank. Before us, the Bank of China and the Communications Bank were the only two Chinese banks in New York.

The process involved a long story. From establishing the representative office at the beginning to making it a branch later, we dealt with Wall Street and the Federal Reserve for eight years. I wrote a book entitled *On Wall Street* to record the process. We set up the New York branch in 2008, amid the US financial crisis. I remember New York's mayor, Michael Bloomberg, saying: 'We are closing but you are opening' at the opening ceremony in New York, which was quite an event. More than 500 people attended the ceremony, including Henry Kissinger and some big shots from Wall Street. One reason we attracted so much attention was that during the process I had made friends with people from different countries in the banking industry. Starting from our branch in New York, we later opened our representative offices in London and Taiwan, and we are now planning to open a branch in Singapore. These are all part of our international growth efforts. In fact, so far international growth has just been our future goal rather than a major business activity.

Of course, international growth has another meaning. It means that we are not only developing our business overseas to establish an international network but also upgrading our management to match international standards, because even if we do not do business overseas, we are still faced with international competition inside China. Fundamentally, if a bank does not adopt international practices and standards, it will not be successful even if it does business only in China.

Two Transformations of CMB

Ma: We just talked about the three strategies. During the implementation process, CMB has gone through two transformations, so we have a special term to describe it: 'three steps and two turns.' The first transformation occurred in 2004. At that time, all the banks in China wanted to expand, to do wholesale business, to earn more interest income, and to spread their income. That was when we started our management training programme. Up to now we have conducted more than 20 training sessions, with four being held each year. Two or three times each year we invite famous international and domestic experts to be our trainers. The training covers many areas, such as predicting world development trends, macroeconomics, risk management and new capital agreements. We also invite fashion experts such as the chief editor of *Bazaar* to share with our management team information about the latest trends in design and fashion to enhance our wealth management and private banking.

Back then, the problem of homogenisation was pervasive in the banking industry. We derived the concept of disintermediation and interest rate adjustment according to the market situation. We felt that for us to grow, we could not just follow others blindly. Therefore, we worked on our first transformation to focus on three targets: developing small and medium-sized enterprises (SMEs), growing retail businesses, and increasing non-interest income.

Non-interest income is income generated not from interest but from fees and settlements. We started businesses such as enterprise co-operation, assets custody and cash management, attempting to profit by collecting handling fees. We felt that capital restriction was becoming increasingly stringent, so we needed to choose a business that could reduce capital consumption. SMEs consume relatively less capital, and retail banking business minimum required capital is less than investment banking, according to the Basel Committee. The capital consumption weight is 50 % for retail business, while that for wholesale business is 100 %. No capital is needed to generate non-interest income. As a result, we did our first transformation, which took five years. I remember we were meeting in Nanchang. Nobody wanted to do it as it is easy to do wholesale business, while retail business requires a lot of work.

But by 2009, our retail business already accounted for 30 % of our total assets, and the SME business was close to 50 % of our wholesale business, while non-interest income exceeded 21 % of our revenue. We considered the first transformation a success.

The global financial crisis took hold in 2009, and we expected more stringent restrictions on capital. We reviewed our first transformation and felt that we had done a good job in the retail business, undertaking the groundwork for China's retail banking. Our non-interest income was also leading, but the SME business had room for improvement. The key issue was that some medium-sized enterprises had assets of 100 million RMB. That was when we initiated our second transformation, targeting capital conservation. The first action was to reduce capital consumption and improve our pricing power. The second step was to reduce costs, control risks, and increase return on capital. This was the second transformation, with the main purpose being saving capital and improving pricing power. To achieve our goal, we needed to break SMEs into two further kinds of small enterprises: small and micro. We set up a small enterprise credit centre in Suzhou because, as we dealt with small and micro businesses, we could improve our pricing power, but our risk level also increased. If we wanted to have a clear analysis of each and every risk, our costs would also rise. So we had to find a way to control both risks and costs. To find that balance, we needed an examination and approval approach similar to that of mass production. We explored a new method that we tried out for five years in Suzhou, and then rolled it out to the entire bank.

As a result, small and micro enterprises are now under mass examination and approval with some preset indicators. The second transformation is still ongoing. We have encountered many difficulties, but we must keep moving on.

CMB's Core Values: Changing with Your Need, Changing with the Situation

Interviewer Chen: Excellent! Now let us talk about your sense of crisis, your philosophy of 'thriving in calamity and perishing in soft living', and your emphasis on acting before the change occurs. What do you think is the most severe challenge the banking industry is facing today? An how are you tackling it?

Ma: First and foremost, banking is a service industry, so understanding changes in customers' needs is critical. All these years our philosophy has been 'changing with your need', which means we should change our products and services according to customers' needs. This requires us to be sensitive to changes in customer situations and always stay ahead of the curve. As I said before, we strive to be a little earlier, a little quicker, and a little better in everything we do, so we should detect changing needs earlier than others can. Since customers' changing needs are closely related to the changing times, the other core value we have is 'changing with the situation.'

For example, while a bank is a micro enterprise, it is related to the macro economy, to history and to society. I always say that 'One who lacks insight into the future cannot judge the present; one who lacks understanding about the world cannot understand China; and one who lacks understanding of the macro cannot handle the micro.' As a bank president you must study economic, social, scientific and technological development trends; you must consider the micro enterprise in the macro context, against the backdrop of the world and the future. Only then can you study the macro, study the world, study the regular pattern, and study changing needs. For example, when we started the credit card business, nobody in China was offering them, and a large consulting firm wrote articles opposing the launch of RMB credit cards. Why? They believed that an overdraft is the basic profit model of the credit card. On the other hand, the Chinese like to save money and deposit it in the bank; the Eastern culture simply does not condone borrowing or overdrawing. Therefore, how would we make money?

So we hesitated: should we do it? First, we reasoned that China's economy would keep moving, and people would change their consumption values. Quite often China will take the path that developed countries in the West have already taken. Second, Taiwan, Hong Kong, Macau and Singapore, with similar Eastern cultures to China, already had very sophisticated credit card businesses. And third, changes in China would occur rapidly in the internet era. Based on these factors, we decided to start our credit card business.

Interviewer Chen: Does your credit card business make money?

Ma: It did not at the beginning, but we started to make money from the fourth year onwards. When we started the business, Sandy Weill, then president of Citibank, approached me to work co-operatively. Despite him being my idol, I rejected his offer. Why? Because I thought that if we worked with him and the credit card business became a success, people would say that this was because of Citibank. Moreover, the back office is critical for the credit card business. Working with Citibank meant that the back office would be in Singapore, under their control. Third, he knew that we were influential in China's debit card business. So we declined the collaboration proposal. Instead, we decided to work with Taiwan's China Trust Commercial Bank, not as a shareholder but as a consultant. We made an eight-year plan to reach a profit, but this was achieved in the fourth year. Later we found that 40 % of the profit was interest income. This finding surprised us: the Chinese also overdrew.

Interviewer Chen: Who are these people?

Ma: Some are rich folks, some are young people, similar to that in the West. Later I read *The World is Flat*, by Thomas L. Friedman, which says that ten bulldozers have levelled the earth, meaning that Western consumption values have influenced China. That is probably why we found ourselves in profit earlier than we had expected. And we have been making money ever since. The story of the credit card business reflects one of our beliefs in doing business. That means looking at a bank in the macro context and against the perspective of the future while making decision in the present. It also means we must act earlier, quicker, and be better in everything we do and at every stage of development.

Ma: With respect to 'thriving in calamity and perishing in soft living', everybody perceives the entire banking industry as a monopoly. Yet inside the industry, competition is cut-throat. Before China joined the World

Trade Organization (WTO), we were afraid that foreign banks would be likely to enter China; and that fear spurred us to action. In fact, since I joined CMB, we have always tried to instil a sense of crisis among our employees.

We have a concept called 'one three five': 'one' refers to one guiding principle; that is, the balanced growth of profit, quality and revenues all being equally important. 'Two' means the relationship between management and growth must be handled well without neglecting either. And 'three' means three rationalities: treating the market rationally, treating peer banks rationally, and treating ourselves rationally. Treating the market rationally means that you must stay composed in a heated market; you cannot just follow others blindly but must remain sensible. For example, in 2009, everyone was working on the government platform, but we loaned very little because we thought it was too risky. As a result, our loans were low in that year and saw a negative growth. During the road show I undertook in the United States, I explained why we had negative growth and why we loaned very little. Ultimately, our stock increased by 30 %. Nevertheless, when others were not lending during the period of control over the real estate market, we saw an opportunity and increased our loans at that time.

The second part is treating peer banks rationally. We should learn from banks that do a good job, regardless of their size. But if banks violate regulations or take risks that are too high, we should not follow their actions even if they perform better than we do. This is treating peer banks with reason. The third part is treating ourselves rationally. What does that mean? All these years we have stayed ahead of others, so it is easy to become complacent and be blindly optimistic. That is when we need a sense of urgency to help us stay alert. On our tenth anniversary we did not review our achievements; instead, we summarised eight major crises and twenty issues. Every year on the company's anniversary we spend a lot time talking about crises, which we think is an important thing to do. We all feel that CMB is endangered if we do not keep reinventing ourselves.

Interviewer Chen: You have very good lesson here: Prepare for danger in times of peace, and never become complacent because of past achievements.

Ma: Yes, CMB has always led the pack, but if we relax, others will catch up. That's why we treat ourselves rationally. We have a website for employees to post their concerns or opinions about anyone, including me, at any time, in any place, anonymously or otherwise. We all read these. When we went public, an employee in Chongqing wrote an article entitled 'Words of Warning at a Glorious Era—Where is CMB going?' using his real name, and asked many questions. I asked the management team to read and think about his article. We also rewarded this employee.

'Five' refers to five relationships. The first is the relationship between management and growth. Management capability determines how well we can grow. Second is the relationship between quality and profit. All profits must be subject to quality management. We call it risk pricing; that is, we profit by addressing risks. The third is the relationship between short-term and long-term interest. If banks fail to pay attention to long-term interest, they will not have long-term growth. For example, if you start a credit card business expecting to profit in the eighth year, but you leave the business in three years, you definitely will not do well. The fourth relationship is between shareholders, customers and employees. We belong to an association that stresses the social responsibilities of banks. We think that the shareholders' interests are our starting point; no one would buy our stocks without this. Where do shareholders' interests come from? From the market and customers, so we must also take good care of both of these. Who develops the market and customers? Employees do. Therefore, while the shareholders' interests are our ultimate concern, we must start with the employees' interests. We must care about how they feel and their interests. To us, people focus concentrates on customers and employees. These two and social responsibilities are our main concern.

We are keen to protect our employees' interests. Sometimes we are even in conflict with shareholders to protect the interests of employees. For example, we must first establish a salary system that motivates employees and guarantees their continuing performance. They will be well rewarded as long as they work hard. They are also entitled to pensions, social insurance and medical insurance. In addition, we must take care of their career paths. Our employees on average are less than 30 years old, so we must consider their future development. We offer many technical and managerial positions. Meanwhile, we create a pleasant company culture. In the past, we had only 'a gas station' but no 'coffee shop' (i.e. a basic, no-frills setting). Now we have both, and the coffee shop is the gas station, creating a better working environment. That is the fourth relationship.

The fifth is the relationship between rules and culture. Banking is a high-risk industry, and rules are extremely important. In fact, many rules and systems are established after paying a high price. So a bank must have stringent rules/systems and implement them firmly. On the other hand, we should also realise that it is people who devise rules, so they will definitely lag behind constantly evolving practices. And even laws often lag behind.

Interviewer Chen: Yes, the rules must keep pace with the times.

Ma: Rules are often rigid, passive and compulsory; normally they would not motivate people, only restrict their behaviours. For this reason, it is not enough to have rules alone; a viable company culture must be created. Culture consists of values and norms that guide our behaviours; when culture takes root, rules are implemented automatically. Therefore we must influence our employees continually with CMB's corporate culture.

CMB's Culture: Innovation, Service, People Focus and Risk Control

Interviewer Chen: What are CMB's core cultural values?

Ma: Our most distinguished core value is innovation. Why do we need an innovative culture? A company's culture is related to its genetic origins. CMB's origin were different from those of other banks. It was the first corporate legal entity among China's banks, an emerging economic entity. At that time people did not know about us or take us seriously, so we had to innovate for growth. If our services and products had not been better than those of others, we could not have stood out to attract customers and therefore would not have survived, let alone thrived. That genetic origin has determined CMB's innovation culture, which has been reinforced and consolidated through various crises.

Interviewer Chen: Do you take a top-down or bottom-up approach to innovation?

Ma: It can be both. In the past, employees tended to deem innovation to be the responsibility of management. Later, we emphasised that innovation came from the frontline because innovation is adapting to changing customer needs. We are in a service industry; so satisfying those constantly changing needs is the source of innovation.

The internet generated a need for online banking, and the availability of online payments has triggered a need for mobile payment e-banking. You must innovate if you want to capture and satisfy needs. And frontline employees are considered to be in a position to be first to detect such evolving needs. But at the same time they must be supported from the top with an incentive mechanism, a system and a culture that encourages innovation. We consider innovation to be an antidote, to keep from 'thriving in calamity and perishing in soft living.' Without innovation, CMB would remain stagnant and would be overtaken.

Our second value is service. As I said earlier, banking is a service industry. You must have better service than others to win customers. CMB aims to provide a dedicated service to our clients, covering even such aspects as attire and language. We constantly review variances in service and listen to customers' comments without letting up on our efforts. I personally handle customer complaints to enable the service culture to be deeply rooted among employees.

Our third cultural value is people focus. Young employees are CMB's most valuable resources, and they must be passionate about what CMB is striving to achieve. The last is the culture of risk management. We are not a state-owned bank; if we perform badly, the state will not offset our bad debts, and we shall harm both employees' and shareholders' interests. That's why we must nurture a culture that emphasises risk control.

However, excessive risk control could also have a negative effect, as everyone then becomes very cautious. The problem with our second transformation was that we were being extremely cautious; our non-performing asset ratio kept dropping to under 1 %, but at the same time our pricing power was also decreasing. We were being very risk-averse, ending up with high capital consumption and low pricing power. The most damaging effect was that employees lost both their risk-pricing capability and courage. Under these circumstances, we decided to carry out the second transformation and risk pricing. My management philosophy emphasises risk management on the one hand and bank management on the other, seeking to obtain the best balance between risk and profit. You cannot be too aggressive or too conservative. You must strike a balance.

Interviewer Chen: But sometimes it is very difficult to judge where is the optimal balance.

Ma: Yes, it is difficult to find the best balance between risk and profit. You must find it based on the information you have. Here is where the 'One Three Five' rule discussed previously can play a key role. For example, a focus shift from book profit to economic profit shows that you consider long-term interest. Book profit is what you make at the time, but if it comes from wholesale business or from consuming capital, it is less desirable. We should pursue economic profit, ideally from non-interest income, without consuming capital. Another example is that, in the past, we focused on big businesses; now we focus on small ones. We once practised extensive marketing; now we have adopted refined and precise marketing. The changes occurred during the transformation, and we have turned them into CMB's culture, well-known and practised by our employees. So I think that among all China's banks, CMB has a unique corporate culture. And that's why CMB can pursue group interests and maintain a stable performance. CMB is a sustainable company. It has a stable management team, consistent corporate strategies and a calm demeanour. CMB's steady growth provides investors with long-term investment value.

Interviewer Chen: Now that you have stepped down from the CEO position, are you concerned about CMB's future development?

Ma: No, not really. The new CEO, Mr. Tian, has been with CMB for a long time and is immersed in the CMB culture. He used to be a branch head, so he has an in-depth understanding of changes and can make timely responses. Moreover, though I had made constant changes down the years, I also had limitations. For example, I could not bring myself to dismiss underperforming associates who had worked for me for many years. Mr. Tian can be more detached from such baggage. In addition, I am already over 60 years old, while our employees' average age is about

30. Though I am a progressive learner, I and my employees belong to two generations, after all. I especially emphasise that not everything I did in the past was correct; I would be happy to see bold breakthroughs because that is the only way CMB can continue to grow. I firmly support changes.

Interviewer Chen: When you were the CEO of CMB, you must have encountered conflicts between personal relationships and business rationality. Could you share one or two typical incidents that gave you headaches? In looking back, how do you think you could have handled such conflicts differently?

Ma: I have many examples. For example, you deeply trust a branch head, but he stops performing after a few years. How do you handle it? You think he is not performing, but he thinks he is doing fine. You must make the necessary adjustment. He might resent the decision and take his case to the Board. But it is unnecessary to argue with him. You support your decision with facts so that everybody understands.

Another example occurred between me and the Board. Not long after I joined CMB, the Board passed a resolution to spin off CMB's online banking business and make an IPO for it. You know, the internet was burning money at that time. I had concerns about the decision. Online banking was an integral part of our business; how would we handle a separate listing? I told the Board that it was beyond my imagination.

However, the Board had made its decision. So I went to the United States and investigated three banks. First Security Bank, a purely online bank, was unable to continue at that time. Bank One once had an internal online bank but had already sold it. Wells Fargo had a 'clicks and mortar' model, a physical bank and an online bank that complemented each other very well. I decided that we should use that as our model. I told the Board that the purely online bank would not work if it went public separately. Using reason and facts, I convinced them to withdraw the resolution. Looking back now, if the online bank had gone public at that time, CMB would probably have failed to make it to the main board.

Interviewer Chen: Could you summarise your personal management philosophy, perspective, style and experience?

Ma: From a philosophical standpoint, four things are important for a service enterprise. First, change with the situation: formulate strategies according to situational developments. An enterprise should put itself in a macro context against the backdrop of the international environment and technological changes, constantly adjusting its position and strategy based on macro trends, and changing with the situation. Second, change with customers' needs, at two levels. One, customers are the anchor of the bank; you will not survive without them; you exist to serve them. If they do not exist, you will also cease to exist. Two, you cannot stop studying, because customers' needs change with the times. You must build this concept into the company culture, and do not make changes just for the sake of it.

Third, you should focus on people. For a bank, the most important productive forces are human resources. Fourth, you should achieve a balanced growth. A bank must deal with various contradictions, and a bank president must master the skills of co-ordination and balancing. Profit quality and revenues are a contradiction, as are risk and profit. The key is to strike a balance. Short-term and long-term is another contradiction; you cannot ignore either, so it is all about rationally allocating capital. These are my management philosophies. A bank president must constantly balance between the macro and the micro, the present and the future, the risk and the profit.

Commentary

Being the first Chinese private bank, the development and achievement of China Merchants Bank is significant in the economic reform process of Chinese private business, especially in the banking industry where private participation was very restricted and is still very limited today. The critical events that Weihua Ma illustrated during the first year of his management of the bank show how difficult it is for a privately owned bank to survive in a turbulent business environment, both in terms of governmental policy and customers' trust. Through capability enhancement, China Merchants Bank was able to expand strategically into different businesses, learning from existing models and innovating on their own and through alliances.

Similar to the insurance industry, China's banking industry is homogeneous in many ways. To stay competitive, CMB has been innovative and led the changes in the banking industry since the mid-1990s, which resulted in the remarkable transformation of the company. To Mr. Ma, staying innovative is to be 'a bit earlier, a bit faster, and a bit better in everything you do than your peers,' and is to make changes in synchrony with the customers' needs that are changing with the situation. Mr. Ma's sharp grasp of the driving forces of change and a deep understanding of the nature of banking make him a leader with vision and a manager with remarkable executive skills to implement that vision.

Besides vision and determination, it is also evident from his remarks in the interview that, for Mr. Ma, duality thinking is in his bones (Smith and Lewis 2011; Li 2012). He talks about balance in every aspect of running a bank: management versus growth, quality versus profit, short-term versus long-term interest, customers versus shareholders versus employees, rules versus culture, innovation versus risk control, macro versus micro, international versus domestic, Western versus Eastern, traditional banking versus e-banking and so on. The success story of CMB indicates that Mr. Ma is the person who can strike a balance in all these seemingly contradictory relationships.

References

China Entrepreneur Club (2013). Ma Weihua: The most innovative banker in China, 15 July. Retrieved March 26, 2015, from http://www.daonong.com/English/VIEWS/20130815/41323.html

CMB (2015a). China Merchants Bank. Retrieved March 26, 2015, from http://english.cmbchina.com/CmbInfo/

CMB (2015b). 2014 Annual Report, China Merchants Bank. Retrieved March 26, 2015, from http://file.cmbchina.com/cmbir/de9049e7-f1ce-4975-9b09-bc533a6a5173.pdf

FTSE (2014). About the FTSE China index series, FTSE document, December. Retrieved December 24, 2015, from http://www.ftse.com/products/downloads/About_FTSE_China_Indices.pdf

Li, P. P. (2012). Toward an integrative framework of indigenous research: The geocentric implications of Yin—Yang Balance. *Asia Pacific Journal of Management, 29*(4), 849–872.

Smith, W. K., & Lewis, M. W. (2011). Toward a theory of paradox: A dynamic equilibrium model of organizing. *Academy of Management Review, 36*(2), 381–403.

Part III

Leaders in Information Technology and E-Commerce Industry

6

If You Do Business for Money Alone, You Might Not Be Able to Make Money

Interview with Neusoft Corporation Founder and Chairman Jiren Liu

The interview was conducted by: Jianjun Zhang, Peking University, and Anne S. Tsui, Arizona State University.

Neusoft Corporation[1]

Established at Northeastern University, Shenyang, China in 1991, the history of Neusoft can be traced back to 1988, when Dr. Jiren Liu from Northeastern University worked with two other colleagues to set up a computer software and network engineering research lab with 30,000 RMB and three computers.

In 1991, a company was formed with the name Neu-Alpine Software Research Institute, as a joint venture with Japan's Alpine. After a merger with another university company, OPENSOFT System, the first National Engineering Research Centre for computer software was created in China in 1993; and the first university software park, Neusoft Park, was launched in 1995. To implement its own brand integration

---

[1] This section is based on information and news from the company website (Neusoft 2015a), 2014 Annual Report (Neusoft 2015b) and IACMR's *Chinese Management Insights*' publication on Neusoft in December 2011. According to the founder, Jiren Liu, 'Neu' in 'Neusoft' stands for Northeastern University.

© The Author(s) 2017   **145**
A.S. Tsui et al., *Leadership of Chinese Private Enterprises*, Palgrave Studies in Chinese Management, DOI 10.1057/978-1-137-40235-6_6

strategy, in 2001 Neu-Alpine was renamed 'Neusoft Co. Ltd.' The company developed further and created more joint ventures and strategic alliances with Toshiba, the Shanghai Baosteel Group, Philips, SAP, Intel, Harman, NEC, A&T, Huawei and Alibaba.

In 1996, Neusoft became the first listed software company in China (A share); and by 2004, it had become the largest offshore software outsourcing service provider in China. As the largest IT solution and service provider in China, Neusoft provides industry and product engineering solutions, related software products and platforms, and services through the seamless integration of software and services, software and manufacturing, and technology and industrial management capacity. By 2007, the company had already been listed for the fourth time in the 'Global Services 100' annual study of companies, ranked among the 'Top 10 to Watch in Emerging Asian Markets' companies, and named in the top 25 in the list 'Global Outsourcing 100' issued by the International Association of Outsourcing Professionals (IAOP). By 2014, Neusoft has been listed in 'Global Outsourcing 100' eight times by IAOP, and listed in 'Global 100 Software Leaders' three times by PwC.

In 2014, Neusoft had a revenue of 7.8 billon RMB, with net profits of 1.06 billon RMB. The accumulated financial reserve from undistributed profits had reached 2.88 billon RMB. By 2015, Neusoft had set up 10 software research and development (R&D) bases, 16 software development and technical support centres, eight regional headquarters and a comprehensive marketing and service network in more than 60 cities across China, with over 20,000 employees in total. In addition, Neusoft has set up three information institutes and a biomedical and information engineering school in China, in Dalian, Nanhai, Chengdu and Shenyang, respectively. Globally, Neusoft has subsidiaries across North America, South America, Asia (Japan), Europe and the Middle East, with products installed in 60 countries/regions around the world, including the USA, Italy, Russia, Brazil, Pakistan, and other countries in Eastern Europe, the Middle East and Africa.

As a software technology company, Neusoft has 'Beyond Technology' as its corporate philosophy and brand commitment. Engaged in building its core competence to create value for customers and society, Neusoft's strategies include open innovation, excellent operations and human resource (HR) development, determination to becoming a company well recognised and respected by employees, shareholders, customers and society alike. As a globally leading IT solutions and services provider, Neusoft also strives continuously to optimise its organisation and processes, develop leadership and employee competence, and commit to alliances and open innovation, to sustain its competitive advantages. Its particular competitive advantages are in telecoms, energy, finance, social security, health care, manufacturing, transportation and education.

Founder and Chairman Jiren Liu[2]

Born in 1955 in Dandong, Liaoning province, Dr. Jiren Liu is the founder, Chairman and CEO of Neusoft Corporation; he is also Vice President and a Professor at Northeastern University (NEU).

Jiren Liu earned his bachelor's degree in computer software from Northeastern China Institute of Technology in 1980 followed by his master's degree in computer application from the same institute. In 1986 he went abroad to study at the National Bureau of Standards (NBS) (later named The National Institute of Standards and Technology (NIST)) in the USA. In 1987, he returned to China and defended his doctoral dissertation at the Northeastern China Institute of Technology, which made him the first Chinese person to receive a doctoral degree in computer applications.

Dr. Liu founded Neusoft on the campus of Northeastern University in 1991 with the initial intention of attracting funding for research. Today, under the leadership of Dr. Liu, Neusoft has become the largest IT solutions and services provider in China. He also holds the position of vice chairman at the China Software Industry Association (CSIA), and is a standing member of the Chinese Association of Automation (CAA).

Because of his outstanding achievements, Dr. Liu has been awarded numerous honours, including the National Award for Excellence in

---

[2] This section is based on IACMR's *Chinese Management Insights'* publication on Neusoft in December 2011 with permission, complemented by public information from Bloomberg.com (Bloomberg 2015).

Science and Technology, China's Best Business Leader, Asian Innovator of the Year at the 6th CNBC Asia Business Leaders Awards, and Country Winner of Ernst & Young's Entrepreneur of the Year 2010 China. He was also named as CCTV's Top Ten 'China 2009 Economic Person of the Year,' and inducted into the Outsourcing Hall of Fame by the International Association of Outsourcing Professionals (IAOP). In addition, he is a member of the Chinese People's Political Consultative Conference (CPPCC). He has been given a variety of awards, such as National May Day Labour Medal, National Labour Model, Chinese Doctor with Outstanding Contribution, and National Top Ten Scientists and Technicians.

Trust Is Important, but Must Be Conditioned by the Institutional Foundation

Interviewers Zhang and Tsui: Please describe your management philosophy, perspective and style.

Jiren Liu (hereafter referred to as Liu): For a company like ours, the most important things are trust, delegation, transparency, communication and frankness. These are the most important aspects of our company value system. In the IT and service sector, the capability of the company comes from the capability of every individual. If you do not respect the employee, you are actually restraining his work enthusiasm and creativity, and your disrespect of him will result in his disloyalty. Our corporate culture and value system is something like that of universities: that is, to motivate everybody with passion and to realise the potential of each. Of course, if you only have trust and delegation without effective governance and transparency, it is easy to lose control. Therefore, we are always working to construct a strong system and process in order to avoid risk. We have invested a great deal in building a management platform such as an accounting system, human resource system, etc. Our company has an auditing and monitoring department, whose function is to monitor the behaviour of our managers. So, on the one hand we have trust, and on the other hand we have a relatively high level of institutional building.

Meanwhile, we emphasise optimising all aspects of our process managements. This process management started from our application of International Organization for Standardization (ISO) and Capability Maturity Model (CMM) standards to ensure reliable project delivery, and we try continuously to improve in all aspects of our management system. As the basis of trust, we have developed a methodology with continuous improvement such that we can structure employee behaviour within a basic framework while at the same time not restricting creativity and imagination. The benefit is that everybody has a sense of being an entrepreneur, and each person has his/her pride. Or we can say that everybody has a feeling that Neusoft has become the way it is today is because of each employee's efforts. This is the happiest thing for me. For example, Wang, the general manager of our Beijing branch, would think that 'It is because of me, Wang, that the Beijing branch has grown from being a few people to such a big branch in which most people own apartments and cars.' They see such achievement as a result of their own contribution, and see themselves as the masters of Neusoft. To put it another way, when everybody wants to achieve great success, I can focus more on institution building. This is the characteristic of management in Neusoft. As for humility, delegation represents one kind of humility from my point of view. But institutions have their authority, which cannot be compromised. In brief, we emphasise trust on the one hand, and system building on the other.

Interviewers Zhang and Tsui: Is there any tension between flexibility to adapt to China's environment, formality of process and the rigidity of institutions?

Liu: Sometimes there are conflicts and tensions, but in the process of developing a company, you must have trade-offs if you want the company to be long lasting. For example, efficiency might suffer when rules are too strict. But institutions/rules can avoid the risk of organisational death caused by too much flexibility. So, when the company is very small, flexibility is more important. But there is a bottom line that cannot be breached, which can cause organisational death. Birth and death are vital today now the company is so big, and flexibility today is more related to method innovation within the framework of rules. Our situation is that we cannot touch state laws and the bottom line (in terms of ethics values) of our company, which are unbreakable rules for all our employees. Of course, if we find that there are some ways of doing business that are better than existing procedures, we change our rules.

Interviewers Zhang and Tsui: What do you do if an employee makes mistakes?

Liu: I often say that we are not afraid of making mistakes, but there are two preconditions: one is that you cannot make vital mistakes, because with a vital mistake, you will not have the opportunity to make other mistakes. This is not allowed. Second, you cannot make the same mistake twice. Our key value of trust in Neusoft, however, means that making mistakes is acceptable. A young company cannot grow if you do not allow people to make mistakes, just as a child cannot learn how to walk without falling over. If you remove all those who make mistakes, nobody will take risks. So you have to allow people to make mistakes. In general, our tolerance of people making mistakes is relatively high. As long as the person does not have a personal motive for making mistakes and as long as the mistakes do not cause much harm, we tolerate them. If there is no tolerance for mistakes as a result of risk taking, the company will lose vitality, and employees will become bored.

If one breaches the bottom line, then we have to rely on the rule of law. But if somebody makes mistakes at work but does not bring serious harm to the company, we will tolerate them. As I said, it is impossible for any person never to make mistakes.

Interviewers Zhang and Tsui: When you originally introduced the rules on accounting and other formal procedures, you aimed at getting people to work under certain constraints. Did the people who used to be flexible feel uncomfortable about this?

Liu: There were a lot of complaints. Many people felt uncomfortable. Under the budget system, everything needs a budget, items listed in the budget must be actioned, and expenses that exceed the budget must be reported. This way of doing things is very different from the past. After their introduction, people were frustrated by the budget reforms. It took us almost one and a half years to implement the new system. Gradually, people in the functional departments improved their skills in calculation, almost matching those of the accounting staff. That is, during the process of introducing the rules, employees went from not knowing how to calculate costs to being able to manage themselves. People then have a common language of communication using the same rules.

When they complained, I did not try to persuade them, but strongly supported the executors of the new rules. This was not a subject for discussion. Rules are things that must be implemented. As a manager, you need to listen to various opinions, but you also have to have your own judgement. If you do not listen, you are not humble, but you cannot listen to others all the time. It is important to insist on principles. Principles and rules cannot be discussed.

Experience Is Fortune, and Every Experience Has an Impact on Me

Interviewers Zhang and Tsui: What experiences in your life had a profound influence on your business and management style?

Liu: It was during the Cultural Revolution, a time in which I experienced many things. Whether from the perspective of an individual or a family, I experienced what young people now can only get a sense of from movies. Those experiences helped me to be tolerant of many things as well as how to bear hardship. For example, in the early stage of our business, we often went to Beijing, sitting on the floor of a train and living in a basement. Sometimes we lived in an apartment with many people crowded in one room when we went to Beijing for an exhibition, for example.

I was also very fortunate to meet Professor Huatian Li—my mentor at the university. As one of his students, I benefited greatly from knowing him in terms of how to be a good person even more than how to be a good academic. He had graduated from Harvard University in the 1940s. He was familiar with Qian Xuesen and Qian Weichang (prominent scientists in China). They came back to China almost at the same time as he did. He developed the first computer in China. The reason I came back from the US after I had been a visiting scholar for several years was also because of his influence. He told me: 'It was before the founding of the new China when I came back. I actually did not live a good life after I came back. But I don't regret it because every country needs its people to contribute when the country is poor. Who will contribute if you do not? We cannot wait for others to contribute. So I encourage you to come back.' I was very moved. He was highly respected academically, but his living conditions were very bad. When Neusoft went public, we let our professor to have some shares. When we distributed apartments, we let him choose first. I was grateful to my professor.

One occasion that greatly impressed me was in 1981 when we went to a store. That store had expensive Philips electric razors. Professor Li asked the saleswoman to hand the razor to him to examine. The saleswoman looked at him and said: 'Mister, the price of this razor is more than 200 yuan. It is not 20 yuan', meaning 'Can you afford it?' The saleswoman further said that the product instructions were written in English. My professor insisted on having a look. The saleswoman was very surprised because the razor was very expensive, and few people ever bought one. My professor finally did not buy one. After we walked away, he said to me regretfully: 'Young Liu, it is very sad that our society judges people by their appearance.' I understood then why my professor did not respond to the saleswoman with 'How do you know I don't have enough money to buy it?' He was so calm, which greatly impressed me. I learned from him that a person could be humble when he was in fact most confident. Also, sometimes we did experiments in the laboratory until late and the cafeteria was closed. He would invite me to go back home with him, and cook soup for me. His honesty and integrity influenced me dramatically when I later founded my company.

I also have four years of precious experience as a worker in a steel factory. After I graduated from high school, I was assigned to work in the Benxi Steel Company. My job was gas maintenance. At the beginning, I thought it was a good job, something similar to being a nurse or a doctor. After I started work, I realised that it was actually a very dangerous job. My duties were to maintain the gas equipment. Gas is very poisonous and easily explodes. Some of my colleagues who had worked there for several years had had their faces burnt. But the good side of the job was that I had a lot of free time so I could do a number of other things, such as painting, playing basketball, taking care of the classroom for the factory instructors, etc. So I was very happy. Shortly after this, I was allocated to work in the labour union, where I developed my ability to interact with people. It was no surprise when I was recommended to go to university later on, since I got to know many people by helping them. I benefited greatly from those four years as a factory worker. I worked with the working class, facing various kinds of pressures and doing various kinds of tasks, which improved enormously my adaptability and ability to interact with different kinds of people. This experience shaped me to be more optimistic and more tolerant of difficulties and changes.

Interviewers Zhang and Tsui: How did your experience as a professor affect you as a business leader?

Liu: From my point of view, there are at least three benefits for a professor to move into business. First, a professor is romantic. He can feel a sense of achievement whether he succeeds or not. If he does succeed, it means that he has made a correct choice; and if he fails, that means the choice was wrong, which is also meaningful. Such an attitude leads to risk taking. The attitude of being playful with ideas might lead to value creation; however, if making money outweighs everything else, I might do things differently. Second, a professor doing business can have a long-term horizon. Academics tend to think of things from the perspective of social development and long-term trends, which equips them to be forward-looking. We linked with many industries in the very early stages, ahead of others by five or six years. For example, we entered the social security sector in 1995 when there was no social security system in China; we entered the telecommunications industry in 1991 when mobile phones had not yet become popular; and we entered utilities sector when there was only one power company in the country. Third, professors emphasise the development of human resources. The main purpose of education is human development. So we always focus on human beings and company culture, and an academic atmosphere is a guide for our company. Respecting employees and employee training are two of the key features of our company. Every year, we invite world-famous consulting companies to give us advice. We have also founded a leadership development centre. Leadership training ranges from collective training to one-to-one guidance.

Others see me as a modest person, but I am unwavering after I have made a decision. Examples of this abound: developing software parks, our stock market launch, our entering into the health care sector, our integration of brands, our joint venture with Alpine, the change of company name to Neusoft—all these things were met with resistance. But I am aware that I have to be persistent when I make these decisions. Professors are persistent when they insist on their theories, regardless of whether others accept them; once they think they are right, they will persist. Of course, you have to listen to the opinions of others. It is dangerous if you do not listen to others. I feel that the democratic part of a professor lies in listening to opinions from various people, then making a decision based on careful calculation and analysis. However, once it is time to make decisions and execute, steadfastness is a must.

Interviewers Zhang and Tsui: But how about being tough on people, not only on the problem?

Liu: I think that toughness does not have to be reflected explicitly but can be conveyed with a gentle attitude. When I insist on something, I would say 'This has been decided. Thank you for doing it.' Maybe my attitude is very modest, but that is tough enough, since there is no room for discussion.

From Doing Everything by Myself to Relying on the Team

Interviewers Zhang and Tsui: How do you position yourself in the company?

Liu: The most important thing I have to do is to decide on the strategic direction of the company. The second most important thing is to choose the right leaders. After I have decided on strategies, framework, principles, and found the right people, the next thing is to support the management team to execute the tasks. I seldom take charge of operations directly. Our team does an excellent job.

Interviewers Zhang and Tsui: Did you bring any particular management practices to your company?

Liu: At the early stage, when there was no MBA education in our country, and no professional courses on how to sell, I introduced a marketing strategy and the construction of a sales network. I invited a Japanese expert to address us. Then when we started to provide a service to our customers, I introduced ISO 9000 to improve the standard of our software and service. In 1996, when the company went public, we invited consulting companies to introduce professional management. We invited Hewitt to help us improve our wages system, and Interbrand to help us improve our brand strategy. We hired other companies to help us develop leadership, including one-to-one training. We also introduced the balanced scoreboard, 360-degree feedback and other management practices. Recently we have been improving our internal control system, introducing and optimising our institutional building to check risks. We are happy to see some results. When the Shanghai Stock Exchange, on its 20th anniversary, selected the ten best boards in China, Neusoft was included in the list.

After we have decided on our strategies, each department makes plans for implementation, and each has targets to meet. For example, the personnel of the HR department came to talk to me yesterday: 'I am so excited that we will receive an award for best employers this year on the 20th anniversary of our company. It is accredited by an international institution.' The accounting department has its own plans and initiatives. We also have a department of process improvement with its own agenda. So the final implementation and improvement come from each department. I only set the goals, and each department takes care of the methods and instruments that are going to be used to meet them. We have now created an environment in which, once I announce the goals and give them space to work, the employees do the rest.

Interviewers Zhang and Tsui: How did you come to recognise the importance of developing a marketing strategy and building a sales network in the early stages of the business?

Liu: It was because our abilities were not good at that time. A company has to do these things to survive. In addition, when the company was small, I had to do everything on my own. Let me give you an example of the kinds of initiatives we have had to take to expand our talent pool for the company. We invested in IT at three universities in order to develop talents. At the beginning of our collaboration with these universities, I discussed the design of the course in detail with the university team, the methodology and philosophy of teaching, and so on. After almost a year, the university team delivered a range of feasible solutions. They did such an excellent job in designing the curriculum that Neusoft received several awards, including an award from the Ministry of Education. I often talk to our management team about using the best tools and the best methodology to improve our management. When an organisation reaches a scale like ours, there will be problems if every functional department has to wait for orders from above and cannot develop its own solutions.

A Combination of Long-Term and Short-Term Focus, and of Software and Hardware Development

Interviewers Zhang and Tsui: To what extent does the uniqueness of Neusoft's development strategy and business model reflect the characteristics of the Chinese market environment? And to what extent is it the result of your strategic choice?

Liu: In terms of our business model, we attempted to find a way to keep our company growing continuously, and to increase our ability to avoid risks. And this model should allow us to avoid the danger of company death when we take risks. This is our principle: to identify our business model from the outset. When we decide on our strategy, the priority is to maintain a balance between risk taking and development. In the Chinese market, we first balance the international and domestic markets; and then balance the different market demands of various sectors at differing stages, which allows us to do both long-term and short-term business. Today we further balance international resources with domestic ones, and potentially might combine both software and hardware. As a result, it is difficult to find any company that is similar to us. Because we need our own characteristics and model to survive, we then have our own uniqueness. It will be problematic if we are similar to other companies. Our company is neither a Microsoft, nor an Infosys, therefore I always say that we are not following anybody else's way; we are going our own way.

To compete better among companies, we need to think and find a way in any environment. I like risk taking, but I will never take risks that will cause a disaster for our company. So from this angle, the choice of Neusoft is not a result that reflects the characteristics of China. Instead, it indicates more of our principles as a company attempting to survive. In the Chinese market, it is a basic principle to maintain a financial balance between long-term and short-term business. In the second year after we founded our business, I wrote an article entitled 'There will be no reality without a dream,' and said that a company will not thrive if it does not have a vision. But at the end of the article, I emphasised that it is impossible to realise your dream if you cannot take care of the reality of management in the present (short-term survival). If the multinational corporations (MNCs) had viewed China's market as the market in which they had to have an entrepreneurial spirit from the very beginning, smaller Chinese companies would not have had any opportunities. It was because MNCs did not have an entrepreneurial spirit as they had in their own early stages that gave us space to grow.

In brief, if we summarise the features of Neusoft using the metaphor of the art of war, I would say that the uniqueness of Neusoft does not come from country characteristics. We find our uniqueness only in the battlefield. Somebody said that Neusoft grew so fast because it fitted China's environment. The simple fact is that we did not know anything when we entered new sectorial markets. China's market was open back then, and any foreign company could have come in to exploit the opportunities. Somebody might have seen these opportunities but lacked resources; or somebody might not have entered because of the uncertainty of success in the future. MNCs failed because they did not have an optimistic view of China's future or they were very suspicious.

Interviewers Zhang and Tsui: You made and sold products in the early stages of the company. But later you found it was not good for business to do this, so you moved over to providing services. Did such a transition reflect more on the influence from the environment?

Liu: The US was the world leader in terms of software products. My experience in the States influenced me to become a product company, since there were so many excellent product companies in the States. But after I came back to China, I found that creating software did not work in China, since pirating was widespread, and intellectual property rights (IPR) protection in China was poor. So we made a business transition. That transition was important seen from today's perspective.

Interviewers Zhang and Tsui: Neusoft aims at 'letting everyone live in passion every day.' To what extent has it achieved this?

Liu: I think that we should make unlimited efforts to strive for this. Currently, I cannot confidently say that every employee lives in passion every day, but at least Neusoft is a company that emphasises sharing. As the founder of the company, I allowed employees to have shares from the beginning. Each department can then benefit from the company's growth, and everybody can improve their personal capabilities through the progress of the company. So, if you trust your employees, you will give them challenging tasks. As a matter of fact, there is no political struggle at Neusoft. Employees compete by showing their personal values and achievements. Everybody wants to behave better than others, and everybody wants to do more. This has become a feature of our company. So we do not control competition; there will be no growth without competition.

Interviewers Zhang and Tsui: In terms of competitive advantage, what is the strongest capability of Neusoft? How did Neusoft build up such a capability?

Liu: First, our business model makes our business very stable. Second, we can quickly deliver our solutions/services as a result of our efficiency in technology and HR management. We can anticipate demand for a product and quickly deliver our version of it, which keeps our business growing continuously. Third, as a technological firm, we have deep understanding of the industries to which we offer services. We not only own the technology, but we also gain knowledge continuously in the field. For example, our understanding of the social security and health care systems is the best in China, better than the MNCs'. Of course, this comes from our accumulation of knowledge over past years. In a word, our competitive advantage comes from our combination of business and technology. We now have an advantage in terms of brand and business scale over other domestic firms. Compared with MNCs, we have an advantage over them in flexibility, speed and cost. In addition, Neusoft wins not only through competition, but more through co-operation. Our company is quite open, and we cooperate with a large number of MNCs. We draw on many external resources to improve our competitive capability in an open environment.

You Will Be Humbled When Co-operating with Masters and That's How You Learn and Grow

Interviewers Zhang and Tsui: How did you choose your business partners?

Liu: We should look for the best business partners with whom to co-operate. Excellent business partners can bring you several benefits. First, their requirements and standards are high, which creates pressure for you to learn and improve. Second, you will become more open. Third, excellent business partners can bring you more resources, including marketing, branding and sales. If you co-operate with excellent companies, you will feel humility, but that can help you to make progress. Our co-operation with excellent companies comes from our conscious efforts. We push ourselves to co-operate actively with them. When you have several excellent business partners, there will be more people and companies that want to co-operate with you; then you will enter a virtuous cycle. We can say confidently that among our counterparts in China, we have the ability to find the best business partners in the world. Alpine is one of the best in the field of auto electric systems in Japan. In the past, some Japanese companies did not trust Chinese companies, but our successful co-operation with Alpine changed this view, which made our name known to the Japanese. The CEO of Alpine promoted us in Japan, saying it has a good partner in China. He wrote a book later which was read by a lot of Japanese. Because of our successful co-operation with Alpine, we also co-operated with Toshiba later on. Now we have many good business partners in Japan.

Interviewers Zhang and Tsui: How would you evaluate Neusoft for its competitive advantage and management quality? Why?

Liu: Compared to our dream when we first founded the company, I could not have imagined what we have achieved today. We can get a high rating now. But compared to my dream for the future, what we have achieved is just like the achievement of one's childhood. We were naïve and ignorant during the past 20 years. But we have been learning continuously. We are active. Therefore, what we have achieved is far beyond what we expected at the beginning. But if we look forward, we are just at the primary stage in this industry. When a country becomes increasingly wealthy, a greater demand for information and software will take shape; that is, from a basic demand to increased efficiency. I once raised a point in an international forum on innovation. The argument went like this: when you can make a lot of money without innovation, why would you innovate? If foreigners understand this, they will no longer make comments that there is not sufficient innovation in China. Because whatever you did brought you a fortune in the past 20 years—running a restaurant, buying land, buying stocks, etc. In contrast, making money by innovation was the slowest method as well as the most risky. However, in the future the situation will be changing. It is no longer easy to make money, so we have to innovate to do so.

If You Do Business for Money Alone, You Might Not be Able to Make Money

Interviewers Zhang and Tsui: What would you like to share with others in terms of your experience in founding and leading a company?

Liu: I feel that we should be more idealistic, more relaxed and not too serious when doing business. If one strictly follows what others have said and follows some doctrines, it is difficult to succeed. I think that management is more like an art than a science. If you treat it as a scientific doctrine, you will not have much space to expand. On the other hand, if you treat it as an art or a realisation of potential, and treat exploitation and creation as an exploration, you will gain more. Then you will not feel disappointed when you do not do well, and you will not be too proud when you do well, because the exploration of art is limitless. You will explore continuously, during which more interest and passion will be generated. So, I think that making a profit is a 'must' to do business; but if you do business only for money, you might not be able to make any money. It is necessary to combine the strategic objective of business with the interests of society. When you have the attitude of contributing to society, you might be able to get more. Therefore, the value of a company is not measured by how much it gains via various means in the market, but what it can contribute. If you consider serving customers and society as the contribution of your company, you will succeed.

Interviewers Zhang and Tsui: Could you have said this 20 years ago?

Liu: I was actually more relaxed 20 years ago, since I was a professor then. The original purpose of my doing business was to make some money to subsidise research. In comparison, I am under more pressure now, since I have 20,000 employees. We are more sensitive to money today. A basic question I have come to recognise over the past 20 years is this: what is the primary source of making money? This is not an abstract theory but a basic idea. When you contribute to others, you will find that others are more eager to give you money.

Interviewers Zhang and Tsui: What is the most important question that management scholars should pay attention to?

Liu: Our company has a slogan: 'Beyond Technology.' So I would propose something like 'go beyond management;' i.e. it might be better to approach management beyond management theory. Management concerns human behaviour and thought. It is not homogeneous, but affected closely by society and time. To study why some companies succeed is largely beyond the scope of current management theory. For example, management cannot tell you how to seize opportunities, which is critical for business success. The capability of seizing opportunities might come from one's entrepreneurial risk taking. Therefore, I think that, just like 'teaching a man how to fish is better than giving him a fish,' management study should focus on the methodology of methods, i.e. some kind of philosophy that can generate methods, instead of focusing on the methods themselves. I think management today should encourage more of an entrepreneurial spirit. The secret is not about the methods themselves, but about improving one's capability to use and improve these methods, create new methods or combine different methods. One final word, the most important thing is to help one to realise and improve one's abilities.

Commentary

Neusoft is a successful example of a Chinese university—industry innovation model, which was founded in the university and maintains industry leadership. Though Neusoft focuses on business solutions adapting to market needs, Jiren Liu emphasises academic values and influence from masters or leaders of the industry. Neusoft also manages the dual demands of long term versus short term, the combination between software and hardware, the integrative system between technology and humans, and the balance between corporate development and customer needs. Liu emphasises that a company succeeds only when it aims to contribute to the society.

Organisational literature often refers to CEO duality as meaning that the CEO serves as both board chairperson and chief executive officer (e.g. Baliga et al. 1996; Finkelstein and D'aveni 1994; Rechner and Dalton 1991). The organisational literature has another treatment of duality, which is a reconciliation of apparently incompatible and mutually exclusive imperatives and mechanisms (Farjoun 2010). Examples include organisational innovation duality at the firm level (e.g. Mastenbroek 1996) or paradoxical leader behaviours at the individual level (e.g. Zhang et al. 2015). Research in the Chinese context has highlighted the balanced view from the yin—yang perspective towards an integrative framework of contextual and indigenous research (Li 2012). The Chinese 'Middle Way' offers further explanation of the duality management system from a cultural point of view (Chen 2002; Fang 2011). Neusoft is one of China's indigenous technological firms whose management philosophy and approach illustrates the reconciliation of different elements. By tolerating small mistakes, it provides a trial-and-error learning process, as suggested in the literature, enabling innovation (e.g. Sosna et al. 2010).

References

Baliga, B. R., Moyer, R. C., & Rao, R. S. (1996). CEO duality and firm performance: What's the fuss? *Strategic Management Journal, 17*(1), 41–53.

Bloomberg (2015). Jiren Liu, Retrieved March7, 2015, from http://www.bloomberg.com/research/stocks/people/person.asp?personId=49857335&ticker=60 0718:CH

Chen, M.-J. (2002). Transcending paradox: The Chinese 'Middle Way' perspective. *Asia Pacific Journal of Management, 19*, 179–199.

Fang, T. (2011). Yin Yang: A new perspective on culture. *Management and Organization Review, 8*(1), 25–50.

Farjoun, M. (2010). Beyond dualism: Stability and change as a duality. *Academy of Management Review, 35*(2), 202–225.

Finkelstein, S., & D'aveni, R. A. (1994). CEO duality as a double-edged sword: How boards of directors balance entrenchment avoidance and unity of command. *Academy of Management Journal, 37*(5), 1079–1108.

Li, P. P. (2012). Toward an integrative framework of indigenous research: The geocentric implications of Yin-Yang Balance. *Asia Pacific Journal of Management, 29*(4), 849–872.

Mastenbroek, W. F. G. (1996). Organizational innovation in historical perspective: Change as duality management. *Business Horizons, 39*(4), 5–14.

Neusoft (2015a). Neusoft company. Retrieved March 6, and December 18, 2015 from http://www.neusoft.com/

Neusoft (2015b). 2014 Annual Report Summary. Retrieved December 18, 2015 from http://data.eastmoney.com/notice/20150327/2Wvl2W4puAIDAi.html

Rechner, P. L., & Dalton, D. R. (1991). CEO duality and organizational performance: A longitudinal analysis. *Strategic Management Journal, 12*(2), 155–160.

Sosna, M., Trevinyo-Rodriguez, R. N., & Velamuri, S. R. (2010). Business model innovation through trial–error learning: The Naturhouse case. *Long Range Planning, 43*(2–3), 383–407.

Zhang, Y., Waldman, D. A., Han, Y.-L., & Li, X.-B. (2015). Paradoxical leader behaviors in people management: Antecedents and consequences. *Academy of Management Journal, 58*(2), 538–566.

7

Building Lenovo into a Family Business Without Kinship

Interview with Lenovo Group Founder and Chairman Chuanzhi Liu

The interview was conducted by: Xiao-Ping Chen, University of Washington, and Weiying Zhang, Peking University.

Lenovo Group[1]

Lenovo was founded in Beijing in 1984 as Legend, and incorporated in Hong Kong in 1988. It acquired IBM's personal computer business in 2005 and agreed to acquire its Intel-based server business in 2014. As a Chinese multinational computer technology company with headquarters in Beijing, China, and Morrisville, North Carolina, USA, Lenovo designs, develops, manufactures and sells personal computers, tablet computers, smartphones, workstations, servers, electronic storage devices, IT management software and smart televisions. In 2014, Lenovo was the world's largest personal computer vendor by unit sales. Lenovo started its smartphone business from scratch in 2012 and had reached fourth place in the world by 2014.

We acknowledge Zhang Chen, a graduate student at Tsinghua University, for her transcription and initial English translation of the interview.

[1] This section is based on information and news from the company website (Lenovo 2015), Wikipedia (2015), and IACMR's *Chinese Management Insights'* publication on Lenovo in January 2013.

A.S. Tsui et al., *Leadership of Chinese Private Enterprises*, Palgrave Studies in Chinese Management, DOI 10.1057/978-1-137-40235-6_7

Lenovo has operations in more than 60 countries and sells its products in around 160 countries. In 2015, Lenovo revealed a new logo at Lenovo Tech World in Beijing, with the slogan 'Innovation Never Stands Still.' Its manufacturing bases range from Greensboro, North Carolina, USA and Monterrey, Mexico to India, China and Brazil. Lenovo's major research centers are in Yokohama, Japan; Beijing, Shanghai, Wuhan and Shenzhen, China; and Morrisville, North Carolina, USA.

Founder and Chairman Chuanzhi Liu[2]

Born in 1944 at Zhenjiang city of Jiangsu province in China, Chuanzhi Liu graduated from the Xi'an Military Communications Engineering Institution in 1966. Liu is chairman of Legend Holdings Ltd., Legend Capital, Hony Capital and Raycom Real Estate, and founder and honorary chairman of Lenovo. Under his leadership, Legend Holdings has become a conglomerate covering both investment and industrial businesses, and has developed a number of leading companies such as Lenovo, Digital China, Hony Capital and Raycom Real Estate. At the same time, he has nurtured a group of younger-generation leaders. With high aspirations, he continually initiates new business areas for the Legend conglomerate, taking it to new heights.

Chuanzhi Liu has contributed significantly to the Legend conglomerate in share structure reform, strategy development, business expansion, management methodology and culture, and talent nurturing. Under his leadership, Legend has accomplished numerous achievements that paved the way for its future.

Chuanzhi Liu is also a deputy to the 16th and 17th National Congress of the Chinese Communist Party (CCP), and a delegate to the 9th, 10th and 11th National People's Congress (NPC) of China. His other civil roles include vice president of the 9th and 10th All-China Federation of Industry and Commerce (ACFIC), a member of the Advisory Board of the School of Economics and Management of Tsinghua University,

---

[2] This section is based on IACMR's *Chinese Management Insights'* publication on Lenovo in January 2013 with permission, complemented by public information from Legend Holdings (2015).

guest professor of CEIBS (China Europe International Business School), Peking University, and Renmin University (China).

He has received numerous awards and recognition in China and globally, including: National Model Worker of China (1995), Asian Businessman of the Year (*Fortune* 2000), Businessman of the Year in China (*CCTV* 2000), Asian Star (*Business Week*, 2000), Top 25 Most Influential Leaders in Business (*Time* 2001), Outstanding Individual in Promoting China—U.S. Relations (National Committee on U.S.—China Relations: NCUSCR 2005), Fifty Faces that Shaped a Decade (*Financial Times* 2009), Business Leader in a Decade of Economic Development in China (*CCTV* 2009), Pacemaker—Most Influential Model Worker Since the Founding of New China (All-China Federation of Trade Unions 2009), Entrepreneur for the World Award (World Entrepreneur Forum 2010), and 10 Most Powerful Businesspeople in China (*Fortune/CNN* 2012).

Breaking the Conventional Wisdom

Interviewers Chen and Zhang: Mr Liu, over the past 30 years of founding and leading Lenovo, what accomplishments have given you the greatest pride?

Chuanzhi Liu (hereafter referred to as Liu): Since I started my business, I have overcome challenges that both the business world and academia view as being very difficult. Two accomplishments seem especially worthy of sharing.

The first accomplishment was Lenovo's acquisition of IBM PC—IBM's personal computer division. When we began the acquisition process, the business world thought we were like a snake trying to swallow an elephant. I recall clearly that we announced the acquisition on 9 December 2004. At the end of that month, I gave a lecture to an MBA class of about 90 students at the Guanghua School of Management, Peking University, Beijing. I asked the students to raise their hands if they thought our acquisition would succeed. Only three raised their hands, and two of them were Lenovo employees. It was obvious that almost everyone was pessimistic about our prospects. Today, the financial numbers alone demonstrate that the acquisition has been successful. Before Lenovo acquired IBM PC, the company had an annual sales revenue of about US$2.9 billion. In 2011, Lenovo had an annual sales revenue of US$29 billion, a tenfold increase in six years. Also, Lenovo's global market share rose from 2.7 % prior to acquisition to about 13 % in 2012, ranking second in the world.[3] However, financial numbers should not be the sole indicator of the success or failure of the acquisition. What is more important is that Lenovo now has a very good top management team, with both Eastern and Western executives on the team, and with Mr Yuanqing Yang as its head. At the same time, Lenovo has established a great corporate culture, and the employees—no matter whether they are from China or from Western countries—have all come to love Lenovo and view it as 'their' organisation. The company has good strategies and methods for formulating strategies, which delights me very much. Last year I retired as chairman of the board. I had retired once before, but then returned to the position when serious problems threatened Lenovo after the acquisition.

The second accomplishment is our diversification. At the end of 2000, when I led Lenovo's PC team to achieve the largest market share in China, I put some younger executives in charge. I worked with them to explore new areas—first venture capital, then private equity, and then real estate. At that time, I was lecturing in business schools. One MBA student, who was in the real estate business, warned me to avoid too much diversification, saying 'Mr Liu, we all recognise your achievements in the PC business. However, I think you should give up on going into other sectors. Otherwise, your lifetime reputation may be destroyed.' More than 10 years have passed, and the two fund management firms run by Lenovo Holdings are both top-ranking players in the industry in both capital size and financial returns. One is Hony Capital, a private equity firm that manages about 45 billion RMB. The other is Legend Capital, a venture capital firm managing about 13 billion RMB. The companies they invest in have developed substantially and have increased in value; so Lenovo Holdings is providing good returns. What's more, our real estate company is among the leading companies in China's real estate industry,

---

[3] Lenovo's global market share reached 19 % at the end of 2014, becoming the leader in the world, followed by HP and Dell, with 17 % each (Statista 2015).

though not yet in the top tier. It enjoys steady revenue and profit development, and I believe it will continue to grow in China's current drastically changing real estate industry. Therefore, I think we have done a great job in diversification.

Having True Owners Is Essential to Building a Long-Lasting Company

Interviewers Chen and Zhang: Those accomplishments have indeed impressed many in the Chinese business world. What factors contributed to your success in the two challenging endeavours?

Liu: I believe that if a company wants to sustain long-lasting success, having true owners is essential. Let me give an example. After Lenovo acquired the IBM PC division, we hired an international professional manager as Lenovo's CEO. However, this professional manager tended to focus more on current profits and stock prices, perhaps because these would have a direct impact on his career, prestige and income. Therefore he found it difficult to pay adequate attention to necessary long-term investments. Despite the board setting some general long-term investment requirements, he did not follow through with them. Specifically, before the acquisition, IBM's major product had been ThinkPad notebooks, which focused mainly on business customers and seldom reached general consumers. However, in recent years, the consumer market has been growing more rapidly than the business market worldwide, including in China. Therefore, IBM needed to take strategic action to address the trend. Emerging world markets, particularly in the BRIC (Brazil, Russia, India and China) countries, were witnessing rapid growth in numbers of PC users, but the IBM PC business had invested insufficiently in those areas before, so we had to compensate for the previous disadvantages. We needed new investments. For example, it would take three years and about US$750 million to invest in the IT systems necessary to manage supply chains alone, not including the investments necessary for other needs such as R&D and channel building. We would have had to deduct those investments from the current period profits and that would certainly have had a negative effect on stock prices. If the professional manager had a five-year term in office, his performance record might suffer in those five years because of the large investments. That's why he avoided making those important strategic investments. As a result, in 2009, during the global financial crisis, Lenovo's profitability dropped sharply, to a quarterly loss of more than US$200 million. Such a situation was almost inevitable because the financial crisis caused business enterprises to cut their costs, and IT expenditures were often the first to be reduced. When businesses stopped updating their computers, we had too few consumers in our customer base, so our business declined seriously. At first sight, the financial crisis appears to have caused the decline, but sound analysis shows that the problem was in fact related to strategy: the top executives were unwilling to invest for the company's mid-to-long-term interests.

True owners, on the other hand, will adopt long-term perspectives for the business rather than focusing on short-term profits. True owners will make necessary bold changes at key moments. I, for example, acted as director on behalf of the majority of shareholders. I was already about 65 years old then, but I still returned to the company and resumed the position as chairman of the board. Mr Yuanqing Yang then switched from being chairman to CEO. We collaborated and together we reversed Lenovo's downward spiral. Now, as we look back, we see that if Lenovo had not had true owners, such as I was, working on behalf of the majority of the shareholders, the company would have fallen totally off the cliff.

There have been several reasons for Lenovo's success. First, based on our many years of experience observing people during business interactions, we can recognise clearly those who will do well in certain industries and those who will not. When we recognise individuals as ideal leaders in a certain industry, we allow them to take charge as a true owner of that subsidiary company. Such true ownership mainly means ownership of wealth and property—we want them to be true owners in terms of property rights. Second, we establish a good culture so that leaders will feel that they, together with their employees, have true owner identity. Lenovo's long-time management philosophy and branding has also been a strong foundation for building such true ownership. These aspects enable our leaders to succeed in their respective industries. For example, when we first entered the real estate industry, we needed about 2 billion RMB as starting capital. However, we only registered 0.2 billion RMB as this capital, and obtained the rest through loans from the majority shareholders. What benefits did this approach bring to the leader of the real estate company? When the real estate company performs well enough to go for a stock market launch, the question will be how much the leader and his team should pay to buy their shares. If 2 billion RMB is counted as the total value of the enterprise, they will not be able to afford to buy them, but if we count 0.2 billion RMB as the total value, they will be able to purchase about 10 % to 15 % of the total shares. We considered that issue when we first started the business, so the leader and the top management team would understand that they are indeed the true owners of the company. I, as leader of the parent company Lenovo Holdings, played only the role of investment management, without getting involved in the business operations. Of course, we also have a set of measures for the parent company to use to monitor the management team after they formulate their strategies. Our successful experience with diversification illustrates the importance of having true owners for business enterprises.

In a survey of business enterprises, we found that the long-lasting companies are mainly family businesses. Family businesses are special because the leaders often view their companies as an integral part of their life, and their business as their lifelong career, to be passed to future generations. However, family businesses often hire and appoint people based on family relations rather than on talent and competence. A talk given by the Lee Kum Kee Company gave me some useful ideas for addressing this problem. At Lenovo, we have devised a set of methods we call 'building a family business without kinship.' By 'family business', we mean that our leaders should view Lenovo as their family business, as their lifetime career, and as an integral part of their life. 'Without kinship' means that we do not actually have family relations or blood ties here in Lenovo. Instead, we rely on shareholding mechanisms and organisational culture to form family-like relationships and emotional bonds. Achieving this goal of building a family business without kinship will require the effort of many generations. We have prepared well for my successors, but we must continue to work so that future generations of management teams can also inherit and pass on such a tradition.

The Biggest Challenge for Lenovo's Internationalisation Is Cultural Integration

Interviewers Chen and Zhang: You mentioned that people were pessimistic about Lenovo's internationalisation, but it turned out to be successful. In retrospect, what major challenges did Lenovo face in acquiring IBM's PC division and becoming an international company? How did you deal with those challenges?

Liu: We anticipated three major challenges before the acquisition. First, we considered that IBM had built the ThinkPad notebook into a well-known brand by spending many years and billions of dollars on it. Would consumers around the globe still value the ThinkPad brand once it had been acquired by a Chinese company? The second challenge was whether former IBM employees would stay with the new company. And the third challenge was whether individuals, from top management to frontline employees, could be integrated culturally. Would people from China and those from Western countries be able to work together smoothly and co-operatively? Would people from large enterprises and those from small ones work well together?

The first two challenges turned out to be relatively easy to deal with. We made adequate advance plans to assure that clients and vendors would recognise Lenovo as a truly international company. First, we established two headquarters, one in the USA and the other in Beijing. Second, employees who had been in charge of external contacts all remained in their positions, with no personnel replacements. Also, IBM sent out about 2000 sales people to help us talk to all the major clients. Because of these efforts, we lost almost no client contracts in the first year after acquisition, apart from some orders from the US military. This outcome showed that our clients accepted us as being sincere and legitimate. If we did not prove to be successful later, we could blame only our own inadequate performance. Without elaborating any further, I will just summarise that turnover was not a difficult problem.

The biggest challenge has been cultural integration. At the beginning of the 1990s, China's computer market opened up. Lenovo was an extremely small company struggling for survival when giant companies such as IBM and Compaq entered the Chinese market. Lenovo's technology, funding and management lagged so far behind those big MNEs, it was like a small sailing boat trying to compete with giant military vessels. The largest Chinese computer company at that time was 'Great Wall' (*Changcheng* 长城) and it was state-invested. Within just one year, 1993, the international brands entirely overwhelmed 'Great Wall.' Lenovo worked hard to compete with those international giants. We worked out a set of competitive business approaches, and they continue even today. In 2000, we gained a 27 % market share in China, far outpacing second-, third- and fourth-place international giants. Because of the time limit, I will not elaborate on the business approaches, but they enabled us to acquire the IBM PC division. However, at the time it was unclear whether the approaches would also work in the international market. If we simply continued using the approaches without fully understanding the international market, we might lose everything. A potentially serious consequence would be that Mr Yuanqing Yang, the CEO of Lenovo, might be dismissed because the company had failed to adapt to the international market. That would be a very big loss for Lenovo. So we took some protective measures in advance. We put Mr Yang in the position of chairman and hired a foreign professional manager as CEO. In that way we could learn about the international market by having a foreign leader run the business. And at the same time, we could test whether our previous approaches would continue to work. During this process, we found that our perspectives diverged greatly from those of the foreign leader. Mr Yuanqing Yang is very talented and knows the computer business very well, but at that time he was inexperienced in working with foreign executives. He confronted the foreign leader directly, which caused some tension. At that time, two US private equity (PE) firms that also took part in the acquisition and were shareholders who were also represented on the board and had their own directors, in addition to my position representing the majority shareholder. I realised that if the whole thing turned out to be all Chinese managers versus all US managers, the entire company would falter. Therefore, my primary job was to integrate the two sides and make them cohesive. We don't have the time to elaborate on this today, but I managed to do so. Ultimately, Mr Yuanqing Yang built a good top management team, and the board supported it.

That is the challenge of cultural integration we encountered. Different companies have different cultures, and Eastern and Western cultures are also different. I think Eastern and Western cultures are actually somewhat similar in their understanding of what constitutes good business behaviours, such as integrity and the fair treatment of employees. Individual companies can vary greatly in values and business philosophy, however, even if they are from the same Chinese or US culture. In Lenovo's case, I dealt with the culture issue rather indirectly and tactfully.

Interviewers Chen and Zhang: We are interested in the specific ways in which you achieved the cultural integration of the top management team. Lenovo's top management team has four Chinese executives and four US executives who work together quite well, but in the past the team encountered significant conflicts. What did you do to reverse the situation?

Liu: When we appointed Mr Yuanqing Yang as CEO, the board was concerned that when the original CEO left the company, the other key executives would also leave. My first step was to try to keep those key people in the company. Only after that would I be able to try to retain them in the long run. My first step for keeping them was quite simple. Because of the financial crisis, other jobs were difficult to find, so the external environment was working in our favour for a time. Another reason was that they would lose significant income if they resigned immediately. If they had a five-year term with only one year left, they would probably wait for a year before quitting. I think money is still persuasive in such situations. I worked with Mr Yuanqing Yang to devise a set of four-year incentive plans. During those four years, incentive pay for the executives was linked directly to the company's profits and was also at above-industry levels. Initially, those executives were somewhat suspicious. But after Mr Yang assumed leadership and adopted our business approaches, they proved to work, thus convincing the executives.

Another important difficulty was that the US executives did not want to work with the management team. Generally speaking, professional managers from Western countries tend to make decisions on their own. For example, when our previous foreign CEO wanted to acquire a Brazilian company, he asked the strategy officer to list the benefits of the acquisition and talked to the finance office about whether we had enough money to acquire the company. When the two officers agreed that the proposal would work, the CEO then held a short meeting with about 40 high-level managers and asked them to discuss and vote on the acquisition proposal. They could not know enough about the situation in such a short time, so many just acquiesced. Then the CEO brought the proposal to the board and said that management had already agreed. The board also did not know enough about the situation, so they also agreed. I had a lot of experience in running a business myself, so I asked how the proposal was actually passed, and then I knew that the managers had not discussed and considered it adequately.

So how does Mr Yuanqing Yang perform as CEO? He uses Lenovo's long-term approaches, called 'building up the team' (*Jian Ban Zi* 建班子). Among the eight top executives, some work in China, some in the eastern USA, some in Hong Kong, and some in Europe. They spend time together each month; for example, in Russia, India or China. They start by discussing more general and strategic issues (*Wu Xu* 务虚). That is, they discuss problems in Lenovo, future actions, and so on. This enhances their emotional exchange and mutual understanding. After they understand the more general and abstract issues thoroughly, they go on to formulate specific strategies. When formulating strategies, everyone must think carefully about what their responsibilities and roles will be in those strategies before they agree. Everyone must honour their words and really take on the new responsibilities. The top executives have come to realise that their words actually count, unlike the situation previously, when their opinions did not really matter. Because they can have a real impact and are truly recognised, and the CEO communicates with them continuously, the executives are now willing to speak sincerely rather than just to say pretty words. All these advances have allowed the business to perform better, and in turn the executives earn large bonuses. After four years, the company's performance far exceeded its initial goals, and the executives were earning more than before. They could also see the company's future promise; therefore they were more than happy to stay. At this time, none of these executives has left the company.

When I left the position of chairman, I reminded executives that their salaries should not be raised before raising frontline employees' pay. I suggested this because my calculations showed that the executives would enjoy high incomes once they reached the incentive plan target. If their incomes increased to high levels but employees' incomes remained the same, morale would suffer. Our employees in Europe and in the United States were very happy with the increased salaries. In particular, employees in Europe recognised that while almost all other companies were downsizing, only this Chinese company was raising salaries. I could not guarantee that this would make the European employees love the company, but they were able to recognise that Lenovo is truly an international company that sincerely cares about its employees. In this way, the organisation has become more cohesive and effective.

Developing Future Leaders Is Important to Maintain a Company's Vitality

Interviewers Chen and Zhang: In the 1980s, there were many companies even better-known than Lenovo, but today many are forgotten. Why do you think many of those then-famous companies failed to survive, whereas Lenovo is thriving? We know that some well-known companies, including family businesses, collapsed when serious leadership-transfer problems occurred. History abounds with examples of nations collapsing because of problematic leadership transfer. How have you dealt successfully with this problem?

Liu: Your first question is about why Lenovo continued to grow and develop, better than the other companies established at that time. There are several important reasons. Whenever state policies are changing, Lenovo thinks about its future steps in advance. For example, the Chinese government used to discourage importing computers from foreign countries to protect the domestic computer industry, and in particular to protect 'Great Wall,' by imposing high taxes and limiting import approvals. Therefore, at that time, many companies made money by taking advantage of the 'grey market' of foreign exchange and import approvals. We were not exempt from this strange phenomenon. But at the same time, we were actively learning about the management and development of foreign companies—their patterns, rules and experiences. For example, I learned a lot when I was a distributor for Hewlett Packard (HP). I studied its culture, marketing, channel management and so on. I also learned from Intel's and Microsoft's strategies. Therefore, when China applied to join the World Trade Organization (WTO) and the country's original domestic policies were about to disappear, fierce competition began; however, we were well prepared. Later, we further studied the industry's important patterns and discovered problems that foreign companies had ignored. For example, we found out that inventory turnover was in fact a big part of our costs. When we developed a sound understanding of those industry patterns, we beat the competition. The issue is essentially strategy formulation and execution, as well as fully using employee talent, so we have developed a theory of three elements of management, including building up management teams, formulating strategies, and strengthening teams (*Jian Ban Zi* 建班子, *Ding Zhan Lve* 定战略, *Dai Dui Wu* 带队伍). We have used this theory in managing our company, and I think it is still important to our survival.

As for the succession issue, the willingness to transfer leadership is related to what one values and pursues personally. When Lenovo became a big and successful company, I did not want to seize a large proportion of the fruits for myself. For example, if I have only 2 % or 3 % of the company's shares but every year I earn dozens of millions of RMB from that, it will be more than enough. In contrast, if I have a large proportion of shares but the company is small, what good is that to me? Therefore, I think it is important to motivate a wider range of people. When Lenovo was transforming its stock system, I made it possible for more people to have their own shares and to feel ownership.

My first aim is to run Lenovo's business well so that we can contribute more in taxes and contribute to China's economic development. When we have done that well enough, we can do other things to benefit Chinese society. Because of these personal values and guidelines, I am very happy to see that increasing numbers of young people are emerging into leadership positions. But, of course, when I select my successors, I am very careful to see that they are truly competent, and that their core values are consistent with mine. When I feel I have selected the right people and have offered them good opportunities, I will be very happy. And they will also respect me and appreciate my decisions.

The Principle for the Business—Government Relationship: Abiding by the Law but Allowing the Company to Survive

Interviewer Zhang: In China, the government is involved in a wide variety of areas, and many companies have failed to relate well to the government connection. Under your leadership, Lenovo has dealt successfully with the government. What is your experience of developing the company's core competences in an environment with high government intervention?

Liu: One painful experience in Lenovo's development was when the old planned economy had rules and policies that conflicted with the demands of the new market economy. Young people today might not understand what it was like. I will give you an example. In the early days of Lenovo, we developed a product called the Lenovo Chinese Character Card (*Lian Xiang Han Ka* 联想汉卡), a Chinese character system with one hardware card and software that would allow computers to display Chinese characters. In 1987, the government penalised us heavily because the government stipulated that the maximum selling price allowed was the total cost of the product's elements plus a 20 % markup. The government failed to recognise the added value contributed by R&D. Therefore, the government concluded that we set the price too high, and they were going to fine us 1 million RMB. Our total annual profit was less than 1 million RMB at that time. I, together with my employees, tried to find some relevant government authorities to solve the problem, but government officials would not agree to meet us because Lenovo was so small. We were in a really tough and embarrassing situation. The problem was still unresolved at the beginning of 1988, when we were recruiting some young college graduates, including Yuanqing Yang. Before they came on board, Lenovo's employees were generally conservative senior people who were more likely to obey rules and follow policies. These young newcomers suggested, however, that if the government was going to fine us, we could hold a press conference to make it known to the public. I thought about their proposal for two hours, and then responded 'Lenovo still wants to live, and we still want to do our business well. Our primary responsibility is to make the company successful rather than to fight unfairness.' This idea later became one of our important guiding principles. This world has much unfairness, so who should confront that? In addition to government leaders, scholars should work to confront it. Scholars should speak up to promote justice for the Chinese people and for all mankind. I am only serving Lenovo's employees. Therefore, I insist that the company should not become mired in unnecessary direct confrontations with the governments.

Another principle I insist on is that Lenovo should not seek unusual or illegal relationships with government officials to gain short-term benefits. That would also be very risky for our company. We have a special unit—our public relations (PR) department—to study and execute issues regarding what we should and should not do. We contemplate every problem and every action, rather than deal with our government relationships casually and randomly.

Lenovo's Core Culture: Do What You Say, With Your Heart and Soul

Interviewer Chen: What major challenges for culture building has Lenovo encountered when pursuing internationalisation? In Chinese companies, employees usually call upper-level people by their titles. I heard a story that when Mr Yuanqing Yang was trying to promote a team culture, he stood at the company entrance with a big board that read 'Call Me Yuanqing.' However, even his secretary did not dare to call him by that name. That was some time ago. I have heard that people now embrace team culture very well in Lenovo. How did this change happen?

Liu: This story describes something that is only superficial. What is really critical is that, after I became the chairman, I put my main effort into building a consistent culture and core values throughout Lenovo, for both Chinese and foreign employees. I cared little about other aspects, because the management team was already good at strategic issues. I embedded two slogans that serve as the core elements of our culture and can serve as the core for other cultural contexts in the future.

The first is: 'Do what you say.' Employees in our company did not always honour their words. For example, before I returned to Lenovo to become the chairman, we could seldom meet the budgets reported from below, for an amusing reason. I went to Europe to talk to a German manager, and asked, 'Why did you make a promise of success to the CEO even though you clearly knew that you could not meet the budget target?' He answered, 'That was because of my respect for the CEO.' Then I asked, 'Why didn't the CEO punish you after you failed to meet the budget?' He said, 'That is because of his generosity to subordinates.' It may seem good to have respect and generosity, but a company should never allow such dishonest practices. In the two years I was in office, Lenovo adopted the principle of 'do what you say', because it's utterly important to respect facts, tell the truth, and have sincerity and integrity. So we have set down the principle that you must think carefully before making promises, and you should keep your word and do what you say once you have made a promise. We have many rules for carrying out this principle and promoting the culture of 'do what you say.' For example, late arrival is not allowed at meetings; if you are late you will have to stand throughout the meeting. That may not work in the United States because people might view it as violating human rights. But in China, we take such policies and rules very seriously once they have been made and specified.

The second is: 'Do it with your heart and soul.' We can add to our cultural values in the future with values such as innovation. Once we set a core value, we take every single phrase very seriously. When the core values become more consistent and unified throughout the company, the employees will become an especially cohesive force.

Interviewer Chen: In terms of corporate culture building, do you think Lenovo still has challenges? Or do you think Lenovo has already done it perfectly?

Liu: Certainly, there are still big challenges. It will take a very long time for the company's culture to become deeply rooted. For example, Lenovo requires sincerity and integrity, and we ask employees to express their convictions sincerely to supervisors personally, rather than to merely speak some pleasant, meaningless words or do everything the supervisor says. However, this is challenging in China because of the Chinese culture and Chinese people's tendencies to hide their true thoughts. Therefore, Lenovo's leaders must model their actions consistently to gradually foster this culture of sincerity and respect for facts over the long-term. It takes a very long time for the corporate culture of an international company to permeate people's behaviours.

The Future Lenovo Should Be a Company with True Owners and a Well-Recognised Brand

Interviewers Chen and Zhang: Lenovo's acquisition of IBM PC division has been quite successful, and now more and more people are using ThinkPads. During security checks at airports, we have observed that ThinkPads are very popular. When I ask foreigners who are using them about the brands of their laptops, they often say 'IBM.' What do you think of this problem of brand recognition?

Liu: This shows the power of a brand. IBM spent so much time and money building the brand, and in the past Lenovo rarely did any brand marketing overseas. Is ThinkPad well-known today? Not so much yet, because it has been targeted primarily at business clients, and we still need to invest in marketing to make the brand familiar to consumers. Brand recognition means more in the consumer market and is not so important for business clients. Therefore, even in some countries where Lenovo has large sales revenues, the brand itself may not be that well recognised. This tells us that we still have much work to do.

Interviewer Chen: Please summarise in a few sentences your experience of building a successful and sustainable company.

Liu: The first important point for building a long-lasting company is to let it have true owners, which I discussed earlier. In the 1980s, Japanese companies developed better than did US companies.

The culture of Japanese companies was to make all the employees company owners. By the 1990s, US companies had outpaced Japanese ones, and Japanese companies could not even downsize when they were not performing well. Therefore, some think that using professional managers is better than following the Japanese system. But in Lenovo, we think both approaches have their problems. We think it would be better to designate the top management as owners, and for them to perform as owners. On the other hand, in terms of managerial discretion, material incentives and so on, lower-level employees may not necessarily be required to be owners—they may become owners if they want to, but problems arise if they are *required* to be owners. It's not the same for a company to have true owners and to make all employees into owners.

Commentary

Lenovo is one the most successful Chinese companies that has charted the road of internationalisation, and it is now a well-known brand outside China. The process of transforming a Chinese local company, Legend, into a global company, Lenovo, is still ongoing, but has passed some remarkable milestones. In 2014, Lenovo becomes the largest PC maker in the world. In 2015, the top management team had 15 members from diverse cultural backgrounds (Qiao and Conyers 2015). Mr Liu is without doubt the leader who brought the company to this stage. He had vision and determination, and he is always observing, learning, integrating, and then practising, what is most fundamental to a firm's long-term success.

In retrospect, the two most remarkable things Mr Liu did to ensure a smooth transition from Legend to Lenovo were (1) at the beginning of the acquisition of IBM PC, he let Mr Yuanqing Yang step aside, and hired foreigners to form the top management team. He did this to protect Yang from failure, and to provide him with a time window to observe, learn and prepare himself; and (2) he promoted a corporate culture emphasising 'Do what you say with your heart and soul,' which does not have any cultural flavour, but speaks to everyone's value system, and is essential to a firm's bottom line. The wisdom shining through these practices reflects Mr Liu's duality thinking.

References

Lenovo. (2015). Lenovo: Our company. Retrieved March 25, 2015, from http://www.lenovo.com/lenovo/us/en/our-company.shtml

Legend Holdings. (2015). Liu Chanzhi. Retrieved March 25, 2015, from http://www.legendholdings.com.cn/en/Leadership/FullBioLCZ.aspx

Qiao, J., & Conyers, Y. (2015). *The Lenovo way: Managing a diverse global company for optimal performance*. Beijing, China: China Machine Press.

Statista. (2015). Market share of PC vendors of PC shipments worldwide from 2011 to 2014, by quarter. Retrieved December 19, 2015, from http://www.statista.com/statistics/269703/global-market-share-held-by-pc-vendors-since-the-1st-quarter-2009/

Wikipedia. (2015). Lenovo. Retrieved December 16, 2015, from https://en.wikipedia.org/wiki/Lenovo

8

Let Employees Work for Themselves
Interview with HC360.com Founder and Chairman Fansheng Guo

The interview was conducted by: Jiwen Lynda Song, Renmin University of China, and Anne S. Tsui, Arizona State University.

HC360.com[1]

Founded in 1992, HC360.com (HC Group for the company and its subsidiaries) is a leading business-to-business (B2B) e-commerce service provider in China (People's Republic of China—PRC). Its core internet product is Mai-Mai-Tong, a strong online marketing platform, with professional services, and cutting-edge internet technologies that have made HC Group a reliable trading platform with full e-commerce services focusing on small and medium-sized enterprises (SMEs).

By providing professional information services and advanced internet technologies, in addition to tailor-made solutions on its Mai-Mai-Tong online platform, HC Group also leverages its strong traditional sales channels—*Business Information Catalogue, Yellow Pages in Chinese Industry, Industrial Research Report*—and various exhibitions to provide inclusive

---

[1] This section is based on information and news from the company website (HC360 2015a), 2014 Annual Report (HC360 2015b), and IACMR's *Chinese Management Insights'* publication on HC360 in April 2012.

© The Author(s) 2017   **185**
A.S. Tsui et al., *Leadership of Chinese Private Enterprises*, Palgrave Studies in Chinese Management, DOI 10.1057/978-1-137-40235-6_8

services and complete business solutions. Its online and offline services complement one another in a framework that has set a new standard for China's B2B business and has revolutionised the growth of China's e-commerce industry. Through more than 20 years of expansion, HC Group has established branches in 13 cities with a service team of about 2883 individuals to cover business in more than 100 cities in the PRC.

In December 2003, HC was listed successfully on the Growth Enterprises Market (GEM) of the Stock Exchange of Hong Kong, and became the first listed mainland Chinese company in information services and B2B e-commerce service industries. With more than 8.4 million registered users and as many as 8 million buyers in more than 70 industries, HC is China's most influential e-commerce service provider, offering customers multi-channel, all-dimensional online and offline supplementary services. HC Group has successfully hosted Top 10 Enterprises Awards for around 50 industry sectors, taking advantage of the Group's strong media resources and customer base, to help SMEs to build up brands and improve transactions.

HC Group is committed to providing professional and innovative services and products to meet both market and users' needs. Along with direct sales, agency sales and telemarketing, the group offers differentiated services and products to different types of clients with varied business solutions. In early 2009, the Group was granted ISO 9001 Quality and Management examination and its certifications.

In 2014, HC Group's revenue reached 966.6 million RMB, an annual increase of 15.39 %; with an EBITDA—earnings before interest, taxes, depreciation and amortization—of 277.6 million RMB, an annual increase of 28.27 %. The net assets of the group in 2014 was 936.3 million RMB, an increase of 59.92 % in comparison with 2013.

Founder and Chairman Fansheng Guo[2]

Born in 1955 in Beijing, Fansheng Guo is currently an executive director and the chairman of the board of HC. He founded the HC Group in October 1992, and is responsible for its overall strategic development and policy.

---

[2] This section is based on IACMR's *Chinese Management Insights'* publication on HC360 in April 2012 with permission, complemented by public information from Baidu (2015).

Soon after his birth, his family moved to the Inner Mongolia Autonomous Region as part of the movement called 'supporting the border areas.' In 1978, the second year of the restoration of the national college entrance exam, Guo was admitted to the Department of Industrial Economy, Renmin University, from where he obtained a bachelor's degree in industrial economics in 1982. Guo is regarded one of the 'elite generation in China', or those who had passed three demanding tests: the political movement that called for going to the countryside or mountain areas and working to re-educate city youth, joining the army, and passing the tough university national entrance exam.

After graduation, Guo served as a senior researcher for the Research Center under the Communist Party Committee of the Inner Mongolia Autonomous Region from 1982 to 1987. From 1987 to 1990, he served as a director of the Liaison Office and General Office of the Economic System Reform Institute under the State Commission for Economic Restructuring, and as the deputy director of the Western China Development Research Centre. During this period, he studied intensively issues concerning Western China's development and modern corporate systems. From 1990 to 1992, he worked as a manager in a state-owned business information company in Beijing before founding the HC Group. Starting with a few dozen employees and 74,000 RMB in 1992, HC Group is now a leading Chinese B2B company with more than 3000 employees and total assets of 3.25 billion RMB. Under Guo's leadership, the HC Group has created one landmark after another: in 2003, for example, when HC was listed on the Hong Kong Stock Exchange, 126 of the company's employees became millionaires overnight. Guo encourages his employees to expand into new markets and personally helped redbaby.com, zhongsou.com, and four other dot-coms under the HC Group umbrella to attract more than US$100 million of venture capital funds. Guo and the HC Group have also guided and assisted a dozen companies in their attempts to launch themselves on to the stock market.

Guo's interests are related mainly to family firms in China. He has participated directly in establishing stock options and profit-sharing schemes for several hundred domestic companies. He has also had great achievements in research on the economic development discrepancies between West and China, as well as on the Chinese economics and reform theory in the 1980s. For his achievements, he was recognised as a leading advocate and pioneer in China's knowledge economy arena. His research on economic systems and policy have laid down an important foundation for his business model and the management system of the HC Group.

Let Employees Work for Themselves

Interviewers Song and Tsui: Please describe briefly your management philosophy, perspective and style.

Fangsheng Guo (hereafter referred to as Guo): My management approach has developed gradually over time. Cloning others' managerial practices or copying extensively from outsiders is not my management style.

China's economic miracle of reform and opening since the 1980s has owed much to the vigorous growth of family firms that have boosted China's productivity greatly. During this historic time, Western management philosophies and modern enterprises could not guide Chinese entrepreneurs adequately. Rather, China's family firms had to explore and create their own management models. I have observed that the typical family firm exhibits a management model that generally begins with the first generation of family-firm leaders creating a variety of management models in accordance with their personalities or personal beliefs. As varied as these models were, they had one thing in common—high efficiency. Similar to European and Japanese management models, the Chinese models are deeply rooted in China's cultural and ethical characteristics, which are vastly different from those of Europe, Japan or the USA. Obviously, a unique Chinese management model must underlie China's economic boom.

The art of management is composed of adopting managerial thought processes and practising managerial skills. I believe management is nothing but the result of the absorption and re-creation of previous and existing managerial ideas by entrepreneurs. There will be no management at all without the presence of entrepreneurs. But, because China's political and cultural environment is so different from that of the West, Chinese entrepreneurs who are learners and thinkers will have management philosophies that will differ from those of their Western counterparts.

Interviewers Song and Tsui: What life experiences have deeply affected your business philosophy and managerial style?

Guo: Three aspects of my life have been most influential. First, my parents' instruction and my childhood environment taught me to respect knowledge and culture. I grew up in the Inner Mongolia Medical College (IMMC), which was, and still is, a gathering place for senior intellectuals. At that time, many professors who had taught or worked at universities were exiled to this college because they were considered to be counter-revolutionary, right-wing undesirables. Some lived in the same building as my family, and they taught me a great deal.

Second, as a soldier in the army I learned how to make the transition from being a civilian to being a solider. I learned to obey orders. Soon after enlistment I was promoted to lead a squad of more than 10 soldiers, all fellow intellectuals. Eight months later, I was promoted to team leader of another freshman squad.

From my life as a soldier I moved to life as a student at Renmin University, Beijing, where I gained valuable training in analysis, reasoning, statistics, economics and English. I count my excellent and outstanding classmates at Renmin as my most important accumulated wealth. From there, I learned how to make the transition from college to the workplace.

Third, after graduating from Renmin University, I went to work for the Chinese Communist Party Committee of the Inner Mongolia Autonomous Region (CIMAR) and later the Commission for Economic Restructuring (CER). CER helped me to develop my management philosophy. At that time, the CER gathered many young and bright elites. I had contact with Inner Mongolia's top decision-makers, many young and talented people who taught me a great deal. I learned how to leverage my theories, understanding and methods to affect these elite thinkers, which showed me the usefulness of ideology and theories. Between 1982 and 1987, my work at the CER helped me to gain a thorough understanding of how China's government works, and how to deal with Chinese officials. Now I am comfortable when dealing with government officials. I know how to quickly gain their friendship and trust.

At the CER, I studied enterprise reform and Western China's development. At that time, three other institutes existed: the Commission for Economic Development, the Commission for International Studies, and the Beijing Association for Young Economists. The four organisations grouped together were called TCOA (three commissions and one association). Even now, many still agree that TCOA gathered together many Chinese elites. Today, many TCOA members are exerting a decisive influence on China's politics and its economic development. Many have built life-long, deeply loyal friendships. They engage in top-class communications; and only top-class communications give birth to top-class Chinese firms. In my opinion, whether a firm is outstanding is not determined simply by its profit or scale, but rather by its exuberant vitality and its potential to lead the future development of other firms in our nation.

Leaders Are Born; Only Leadership Skills Can Be Learned

Interviewers Song and Tsui: How did you find, cultivate and develop your leadership capability?

Guo: I think leadership is inborn, not learned. Only leadership skills can be learned. I was the 'kid king' in my neighbourhood, and later the monitor for my squad in the army. I have a born leadership capability that propels me to lead, which in turn compels me to make constant progress. I am very comfortable leading a modern enterprise. I attribute my leadership capability to my parents, senior figures in the Chinese Communist Party. My mother was secretary general of the biggest hospital attached to the IMMC, and was a strong leader in maintaining harmonious interpersonal relationships. As a president of the IMMC, my father was a leader of many well-known professors and thousands of college students. His leadership came mainly from his moral and personal principles. For example, while the college allocated him a car, he never allowed me to use it. Following his tradition, I have never asked my company to buy me a car. Refusing to take advantage of public goods, and self-discipline are our family traditions, and I inherited a personality and a leadership style from my father.

No Management or Little Management Is the Best Management

Interviewers Song and Tsui: How are you positioned in HC's management?

Guo: When HC was first established, I had to be the entrepreneur, the manager and the leader at the same time, and to stay ahead of everyone else. As the backbone, I had to show full confidence in everything I did.

The second stage was when I turned 50, which was also the three-year anniversary of HC's listing on the Hong Kong Stock Exchange. I decided to hand over HC's internet business to someone more suitable, and chose to remain only as the navigator or spiritual leader. My most important job is to intervene in HC's business as little as possible——the less I manage it, the better. For example, I require my CEO to approve all expenditures, including mine. If such expenditures should not have been approved, I will reproach the CEO. If I forbid breaking established company rules and regulations even for myself, no one else will try to break the rules for themselves. Years of system development and culture cultivation in HC have taught me a basic truth: once a corporate culture is established successfully, it continues even without the founder's presence. As for my new role as a spiritual leader, I strive to encourage my employees to respect me and take pride in the assurance that I am a righteous man. Now I concentrate mainly on HC's public image and future development. This is how I define my position as CEO and as chairman.

I might have a third role in HC's future. When I retire completely from all managerial positions, I will then become a father figure to my employees. They might call me 'Old Uncle' or 'Father,' and their children might call me 'Grandpa.' I really look forward to taking such a role, reflecting the real joys of family life. Only after I have fulfilled this third transition will I consider myself to be truly successful, because my company will perform even better without my presence, but the ideology and mechanisms I designed and established will continue to guide them.

Interviewers Song and Tsui: Where do you get your confidence about your company's success, even with little or no management by you?

Guo: First, HC has a well-designed, fixed and unchangeable company system. Such a system allows us to turn even 'bad' employees into exemplary workers, let alone what we can do for 'good' ones. The system is founded on the employees' trust in our profit-sharing scheme, which can be described simply as a mechanism of 'working for yourself,' and family-type management. I am referring to the profit-sharing scheme, which means that employees share in the company's profits, depending on their peer-evaluated contributions to HC. End-of-the-year bonuses are allocated according to employees' actual contributions, not according to the proportion of shares employees hold (by the way, most employees do not hold company stock shares). Profits paid to shareholders are limited to 30 % of total annual profits; 70 % goes to the employees who hold no shares in the company.

Second, I try to observe from the sidelines. I keep quiet even when I see mistakes happening, as long as they are small and affordable. I intervene only when we cannot afford to let a mistake slide. That is one single basic principle I hold.

Third, after more than ten years of setting up and running a company, I think it is time to return to academic research. I am now studying the incentive effects of profit-sharing schemes on corporate governance. Any useful discoveries I make will contribute more to China's economy than to HC. That is one reason why I have decided to withdraw gradually, but not completely, from HC. If I let go of HC completely and it fails, my theory and research will be nothing but empty talk. Now I can teach profit-sharing because HC is a really excellent company, important to my life and my research. Establishing and then leaving HC is one of my most important life choices.

Interviewers Song and Tsui: You always say 'create wealth with knowledge, and change life with learning.' To what knowledge are you referring? How did you motivate workers to engage actively in learning? And how did you transform individual knowledge into organisational knowledge?

Guo: In my opinion, there are four types of knowledge. First, I regard knowledge as something that brings wealth and productivity. Second, I regard employees who fulfil their job requirements well as possessing knowledge, even if they have had only a primary education. Third, I believe that if superiors agree that an employee contributes well, that employee has knowledge. Fourth, people who work hard have knowledge, because they know their basic duties. So you see, we HC people have a rather pragmatic view of knowledge.

In HC, senior professional titles are not earned through examinations. HC has high school graduates, or even people of a lower educational level, as vice presidents. HC has created a good system that has made millionaires out of 126 of our employees. When their success stories spread, others follow suit and work harder. If you go to our data processing centre on any Friday night, you will find more than 100 of our people still working overtime, voluntarily. This is a vivid example of organisational learning. Simply requiring everyone in your company to continue to study will not succeed for long. Many people say outstanding performance does not necessarily make for excellent leadership. But I say if you cannot do your job well, how can you lead well? So I insist that leaders must be promoted from among excellent workers within the company.

Interviewers Song and Tsui: How do you select your managers?

Guo: Let employees try first. Without giving them a chance, how can you even know whether they are capable? Will a leadership aptitude test help you to identify potential leaders? Not at all. Everything in business management must be tried and tested before we adopt it. Such testing is the necessary cost of business management. When I have several thousand employees and only 20-plus department manager positions, I choose my candidates based not only on their previous job performance, but also on the following aspects.

First, are they willing to work overtime? HC employees are not allowed to leave work if their superior is still working. That may sound inhumane and ridiculous, but superiors are responsible for making subordinates feel that such a practice is reasonable and natural. So, if a superior does not want to work overtime, he or she cannot expect the employees to do so. Such thinking is possible under the right corporate culture. A corporate culture consists of a unique set of value-appraisal standards and codes of conduct. Under those standards and codes, employees will regard certain behaviours as natural and rational, though outsiders might see them as unreasonable. One Saturday I visited a company and saw that many employees were still working. I asked some why they were still working overtime on a Saturday. They said, 'We are not working overtime, we are working normal hours.' Do you think it is reasonable to work on Saturdays? Why do employees at that enterprise think it is natural to work at weekends?

Second, I appraise a potential candidate's job performance. Employees who fail to perform are not candidates for leadership.

Third, I place major value on their personal morality, which is a crucial index reflecting how they will lead and influence their followers in the long run. For example, if potential candidates ask subordinates to buy their meals or to falsify expenses, I shall never promote them. I value the virtues of humility and honesty the most. Leadership capabilities cannot be detected by mere testing or interviews.

Pool the 'Small Selfishnesses' of Each Employee and Create a 'Big Unselfish Enterprise' for Everyone

Interviewers Song and Tsui: In your opinion, how is the family firm system unique? What is the key to successful family firm management?

Guo: We must first define the family firm, which is an enterprise controlled and managed by one or several blood-related families. The uniqueness of family firms lies in its combination of property rights with management rights. Economists assume that human beings are naturally selfish. The more selfish we are, the harder we work for ourselves. Because I believe in the selfishness of human nature, I pool the 'small selfishnesses' of each employee and create a 'big unselfish enterprise' for everyone.

The Biggest Problem of Family Firms Is the Weak Character of the Family Head

The advantages of family firms are obvious. Briefly, first, they have lower management costs. Second, affection among members in a family firm is a natural managerial lubricant, and family wealth accumulation is one of the incentives used in their management. Better management of a family firm means creating more family-like affection among all employees within the boundaries of established rules and regulations. In my opinion, expanding the scope of family members is one of the most fundamental duties of managers in family firms. For example, managers can invent and modify a performance-based shareholding system to turn non-family employees into family employees, or into employees who are even more closely-related than family. After a comparison of all existing management modes, we can safely say that the family-firm business model is the most advanced and efficient management model for small and medium-sized enterprises. However, when SMEs grow bigger, can the bonds of affection inherent in family firms continue to function? In my opinion, the key to successful management of family firms lies in its patriarch. It is highly important that leaders in family firms regard themselves as the patriarchs of a big clan, and that they perform their patriarchal duties well. They must be fair, self-disciplined, industrious and thrifty in running their firms, and must practice what they preach. Only when they have morality and leadership capability, with well-designed regulations and mechanisms, can they manage rapidly growing enterprises successfully.

The Most Successful Management Is to Create Family-like Bonds Among All the Members in an Enterprise

Interviewers Song and Tsui: Do you see much conflict between *renqing* (personal favour and reciprocity) among family members and business ethics in family firms? How may a family firm deal with employee relationships among 'affection, reason and rules or regulations?' What is the relationship between law and *renqing* in managing an enterprise?

Guo: Modern management theories show a huge bias when they assume that family firms are full of conflicts between *renqing* and business ethics, accusing family firms of having overcomplicated interpersonal relationships and practising nepotism. While I agree that bias exists, and that we cannot achieve sustainable development in these firms until we can address these inherent problems, I see no point in eliminating affection and friendship in family firms. As I see it, the most successful management is not to eliminate affection and friendship, but rather to create a family-like bond among all the members in an enterprise. In the sense that blood relationships are inherent in family firms, I believe family firms are superior to non-family firms. Therefore, studying this special type of enterprise will surely bring fruitful results in both economics and management theory.

The law refers to tangible management that can be embodied by power and rights; *renqing* is intangible management. As intangible management is more effective than tangible management, *renqing* must be a more effective management means than the law. I think patriarchs of successful family firms must understand that the key to their success lies in *renqing*. A great family-firm leader needs to build up a modern corporate system and achieve business success simultaneously on the grounds of *renqing*.

Interviewers Song and Tsui: Behind each successful enterprise is a unique strategy or management style. What factors do you think influence HC's success?

Guo: Since both strategies and management can be imitated, they are not core competencies. Entrepreneurs are the scarcest resources of any enterprise, and they are also the most invaluable assets of HC. Some say that the most important determinant of business success is neither capital nor technology, but talent. But many enterprises have failed in spite of having those factors: they died suddenly, at their peak. These cases prove at least one basic truth: something is more important than funds, technology and talent. That 'something' is the core competency in an enterprise.

HC's unique management style and strategies stem from our *performance-based profit-sharing system*. How could HC excel even without top-down managerial interventions? The answer is that we rely on *renqing*, corporate culture, business ethics, autonomy and the voluntariness of our employees. Truly great management transcends tangible management to become intangible management. Only an enterprise that can complete such a transformation has a chance of becoming a world-class enterprise.

Enterprises that can continually turn numbers of talented employees into insiders are bound to succeed. Such a transition tests an entrepreneur's leadership capabilities. In a successful family firm, family-like affection is the inner core of its corporate culture, and culture is the scale of this affection. To cultivate family-like bonds among all enterprise members is the basic duty of entrepreneurs, and to regulate and standardise affection is a test of entrepreneurial leadership capability. Entrepreneurs are like parents to their enterprises, responsible for nurturing and raising the company. However, specific managerial approaches cannot purposefully create both culture and affection in a family firm. Rather, that must evolve during the course of independent and unique enterprise development. Actually, management itself is embodied by corporate culture, and corporate culture generally contains a certain degree of affection and *renqing*.

The Strongest Capability in HC Is the Motto 'Working for Yourself'

HC's strongest capability is our motto, 'Working for yourself', which stems from the performance-based profit-sharing system I mentioned above. You are actually working for yourself in HC, so why shouldn't you work hard? As an old Chinese saying goes, 'Those who win the heart of the people win the whole empire.' How to win the hearts of your employees? Give them higher salaries and bonuses!

Another determinant of HC's success is focus. Over these years working in e-commerce, I am now an expert in the B2B business. We have also successfully forged a top brand and turned loss into profit. Ever since its establishment, HC has concentrated on B2B business. From traditional B2B in newspapers and magazines to online B2B, our main business has not shifted. Now we are even more focused. We recently discarded trading in consumption goods to focus better on the core business of production information. Something of their own, a unique capability or know-how, is also needed for success. Our companies do not have patent technology as a barrier to newcomers. Thus we have adopted a management system to retain people by using profit sharing. Through sharing and giving to employees, we expect long-lasting success.

Interviewers Song and Tsui: Would you summarise the entrepreneurship and management experiences that you most want to share with others?

Guo: I would like to make three summary points about China's family firms: a good management system is the key to business success; sharing is beneficial to enterprise growth; and innovation brings greatness.

I observe that the greatest challenge is that most are not sufficiently down-to-earth. Some family-firm entrepreneurs spend more time playing golf than managing their enterprises. They spend very little time designing, establishing and maintaining good management systems, so their failure is almost inevitable. If managers in family firms continued to work as hard as they did when they first established their enterprises, if they were still the first to get to work and the last to go home, and if they took care of enterprise affairs personally, success would be certain.

Another issue is diversification. Some firms have very profitable main businesses, but when they diversify, profitability declines inexorably. Therefore bosses of SMEs must think twice before diversifying. They should remember that unifying their employees is always the top priority.

Finally, I advise bosses of SMEs and family firms to avoid worrying. As long as you work as hard as you did when you first started your business, you will survive.

Commentary

Though HC360.com is a publicly listed technology company, the corporate value that its founder, Fansheng Guo, has been instilling is the family culture and management style. Converting himself into a spiritual leader for the company, Guo empowers managers and employees at different levels to work for themselves, and to treat the company as if it is their own. The success of HC360.com consists of a dual system: a humanist management of the employees, and at the same time providing them with superior pay and opportunities to realise their dreams.

Along with its family culture and *renqing*, what distinguishes HC360 from other companies is its profit-sharing system. Research has largely established the role of profit-sharing for firm performance (Becker and Gerhart 1996; Kruse 1992; Yan 2008) and employee commitment (Florkowski 1992; Coyle-Shapiro et al. 2002). Allocating 70 % of profits to non-share-holding employees is unknown in any industry.

This is a distinctive feature that can be imitated easily (Barney 1991) but few companies, if any, would want to imitate it because of the unusual level of profits given to employees in contrast to that received by shareholders or retained by the owner. Through a significant level of profit sharing, and trusting employees to make independent decisions, Guo has succeeded in creating family-like bonds among all employees. Employees truly are 'working for themselves.' Combining a modern management system with a family culture within a technology sector is the unique dual leadership and organisational capability of the HC Group.

References

Baidu. (2015). Guo Fangsheng. Retrieved March 25, 2015, from http://baike. baidu.com/link?url=xBbYjrUlchM3tT7TidModOb__rWCA63uykVZ6Kts yKwqgYGDsWSxL_6EbNNjWudiDy5ioFP8kAmWZxxHxnvdj_

Barney, J. (1991). Firm resources and sustained competitive advantage. *Journal of Management, 17*(1), 99–120.

Becker, B., & Gerhart, B. (1996). The impact of human resource management on organizational performance: Progress and prospects. *Academy of Management Journal, 39*(4), 779–801.

Coyle-Shapiro, J. A.-M., Marrow, P. C., Richardson, R., & Dunn, S. R. (2002). Using profit sharing to enhance employee attitudes: A longitudinal examination of the effects on trust and commitment. *Human Resource Management, 41*(4), 423–439.

Florkowski, G. W. (1992). Support for profit sharing and organizational commitment: A path analysis. *Human Relations, 45*(5), 507–523.

HC360.com (2015a). Company website. Retrieved March 25, 2015, from http://hcgroup.hc360.com/English/index.html

HC360.com (2015b). 2014 Annual report. Retrieved May 20, 2015, from http://hcgroup.hc360.com/pdf/EW02280_report_150411.pdf

Kruse, D. L. (1992). Profit sharing and productivity: Microeconomic evidence from the United States. *The Economic Journal, 102*(410), 24–36.

Yan, R. (2008). Profit sharing and firm performance in the manufacturer-retailer dual-channel supply chain. *Electronic Commerce Research, 8*(3), 155–172.

9

Its Corporate Cultural Value System Is the Lifeline of Alibaba
Interview with Alibaba Group Founder and Executive Chairman Jack Ma

The interview was conducted by: Xiao-Ping Chen, University of Washington.

Alibaba Group[1]

The Alibaba Group was founded in 1999 by 18 people led by Jack Ma (Ma Yun), a former English teacher from Hangzhou, China, who aspired to help make the internet accessible, trustworthy and beneficial for everyone. Since its inception, it has developed leading businesses in consumer e-commerce, online payments, business-to-business (B2B) marketplaces and cloud computing, reaching internet users in more than 240 countries and regions.

When it launched its bid for inclusion on the New York Stock Exchange in September 2014, Alibaba Group raised USD 25 billion, the largest initial public offering (IPO) ever, surpassing a previous global record set by the Agricultural Bank of China Ltd. in 2010 with an IPO valuation of USD 22.1 billion, and beating e-commerce rivals such as Amazon and eBay.

---

[1] This section is based on information and news from the company website (Alibaba Group 2015), Steimle (2015), and IACMR's *Chinese Management Insights'* publication on Alibaba in August 2013.

© The Author(s) 2017   **201**
A.S. Tsui et al., *Leadership of Chinese Private Enterprises*, Palgrave Studies in Chinese Management, DOI 10.1057/978-1-137-40235-6_9

With its mission to make it easy to do business anywhere, the Alibaba Group operates leading online and mobile marketplaces in retail and wholesale trades, as well as cloud computing and other services, and provides technology and services to enable consumers, merchants and other participants to conduct commerce in the ecosystem. The Alibaba Group is a giant consisting of 25 business units, and is focused on fostering the development of an open, collaborative and prosperous e-commerce ecosystem. The now publicly listed Alibaba Group, including its affiliated entities, has some 35,000 full-time employees around the world (principally based in China) as of March 2015, up from 22,000 the previous year, and more than 70 offices in Greater China, India, the UK and the USA.

Some of the Alibaba Group's major businesses include Alibaba. com, Taobao marketplace, Tmall.com, Juhuasuan.com, Alipay, Alibaba Cloud Computing (AliCloud/Aliyun.com), Alimama.com, AliExpress, Ant Financial and CaiNiao. Alibaba.com, for example, is an e-commerce platform for small businesses, linking millions of buyers and suppliers around the globe. It offers more than 40 categories of goods, including apparel, electronics, health and beauty, agriculture and food, and industrial parts and tools. AliExpress is a leading global e-marketplace made up of small business sellers offering a wide variety of consumer products showing good value for money. It is dedicated to bringing unique products in more than 20 major product categories to its millions of registered buyers in more than 220 countries and regions. Each business in the Alibaba Group has gained a large market share around the globe, leveraging the economic power of China. The Alibaba Group, Taobao, Tmall.com and Juhuasuan have between them 231 million active buyers and 8 million sellers, and transact 11.3 billion orders per year. The huge market base makes Alibaba the largest online and mobile commerce company in the world by 2013 gross merchandise volume (GMV), according to the global marketing intelligence firm, IDC.

Founder and Executive Chairman Jack Ma[2]

Born in Hangzhou, Zhejiang province in 1964, Jack Ma (Ma Yun) is the lead founder of The Alibaba Group. After the company's debut in 1999, he served as Group chairman and CEO for more than a decade, with responsibility for overall strategy and focus. On 10 May 2013, he stepped down as CEO but remains as executive chairman and continues to shape the Group's business strategy and management development. With the launch of the Alibaba Group on the New York Stock Exchange in September 2014, Jack Ma became the richest man in China, according to *Forbes* 2014.

Jack Ma received his bachelor's degree in English from Hangzhou Teacher's Institute in 1988, and became a lecturer in English and International Trade at the Hangzhou Dianzi University. He was introduced to the internet during a trip to the USA in 1995. He founded the first internet company in China the same year, with family and friends, dedicated to website creation for enterprises. In three years, the company earned 5 million RMB. Because of this success, he was recruited to head an information technology (IT) company established by a department of China's Ministry of Foreign Trade and Economic Co-operation in 1998/9. But he soon returned to Hangzhou with his team to found Alibaba in 1999, starting with a focus on the B2B marketplace.

Besides his businesses in the Alibaba Group, Jack Ma also has more than a dozen other investments, from a soccer team to a film production studio. Currently serving on the board of SoftBank Corp., a leading digital information company that is publicly traded on the Tokyo Stock Exchange, he is also a director of Huayi Brothers Media Corporation, a company listed on the Shenzhen Stock Exchange.

Not only a business magnate, but also an active philanthropist, Jack Ma sits on the board of the Breakthrough Prize in Life Sciences with Mark Zuckerberg and Yuri Milner. During the devastating 2015 earthquake in Nepal, Jack Ma's Alibaba Foundation agreed to fund 1000 homes and send a team of 10 executives to Nepal. In 2009, Ma became a trustee of The Nature Conservancy's China programme and joined the global board

---

[2] This section is based on IACMR's *Chinese Management Insights'* publication on Alibaba in August 2013 with permission, complemented by public information from Wikipedia (2015).

of directors of the organisation in 2010; and since 11 May 2013 he has served as chair of The Nature Conservancy's China board of directors. He is the first Chinese citizen to serve on The Nature Conservancy's board.

Jack Ma has received wide recognition for his entrepreneurial and other achievements. He is the first mainland Chinese entrepreneur to appear on the cover of *Forbes* magazine, among other honours ranging from 'Top 10 Business Leaders of the Year' from China CCTV 2004, 'Young Global Leader' by the World Economic Forum in 2005, 'Asia's Heroes of Philanthropy' by *Forbes Asia* in 2010, and the 30th most powerful person in the world by *Forbes* 2014.

Jack Ma received further management education at Cheung Kong Graduate School of Business (CKGSB) and graduated in 2006. He also received an honorary doctoral degree from the Hong Kong University of Science and Technology in 2013.

Cultural Value: The Lifeline of a Company's Subsistence

Interviewer Chen: Mr Ma, thank you for agreeing to the interview. To start, would you please describe your management style, philosophy and perspective? And what experience in your life profoundly influenced your leadership style and philosophy?

Jack Ma (hereafter called Ma): In the past 30 years, management perspectives in China have undergone development, but no fundamental changes. I reached that conclusion by observing people, including myself. Countries and companies develop quite similarly. For example, both the US political system and its management system are based on similar Christian beliefs. Similarly, Japan's micro-management shows the same evidence. However, in China, because of the rapid economic growth in the past 30 years, and the lack of religious belief in the country, our management follows a less structured pattern. We must take parts from here and there, and nothing is our own. If Alibaba desires sustainable development, we must have a management system. But if we don't have a powerful and perpetual culture as the root, we cannot create the system. You learn from America; you learn from Japan. But you learn only their operations, not their Dao. So what is an enterprise's Dao? You may find me a little eccentric talking about Daoism, Buddhism, and sometimes Confucianism, and mixing them. Indeed, I have observed them all and then harvested meaning from China's ancient culture, from Tai Chi philosophy.

Interviewer Chen: Would you expand a little more about the particular Tai Chi doctrines you feel are meaningful?

Ma: Actually, Tai Chi's view on accommodation and transformation, yin and yang, ebb and flow, all thread through our company's management philosophy. A dialectic view on accommodation and transformation includes closely related concepts. The same goes for education and cultivation. Education is the school's responsibility, and cultivation is the family's job. We call it transformation by cultivation. I have thought about it for the past four years, and gradually formed my own perspectives on Alibaba's values and value system, and these are the concepts of belief and reverence. Belief means to be grateful for today and yesterday. Reverence means awe regarding tomorrow and the unknown. Weaving belief and reverence into our culture would form the core value for the basic design of all management systems.

That People Surpass Me Is My Greatest Wish

Ma: My thoughts about management have something to do with my teaching experiences. I was not the best, but certainly a good teacher, but I knew I couldn't be the best in China, so I decided to step into the business world. However, I applied the same rules I followed as a teacher to running a business. That is, teachers always hope their students will surpass them. That is the fundamental difference between me and other entrepreneurs and managers, who actually fear anyone overtaking them. But I'm the opposite. When I find talented workers, I want to train them to replace me as soon as possible. That's the characteristic of a teacher. Teachers always want the best for their students. If the student becomes a professor, or a mayor, or a big boss, teachers are as proud as if the achievement was their own. No teachers want their students to fail. So I never steal the spotlight from newly hired young people. If someone warns me about an employee who is trying to overtake me, I reply that I'm a teacher and that's the way it should be.

Another special experience is how I studied English. I began studying English when I was very young, not just the language but also the culture. I started chatting with foreigners around the West Lake when I was 13, taking them sightseeing while practising my oral English.

I hung around outside the Shangri-La Hotel for nine years, getting up at 5 am daily and walking to Shangri-La for a chat with people. I never skipped a single day! In talking with foreigners, I realised that the language was quite different from what I had learned in school and from my parents. The experience helped me to become more open-minded and more understanding about Western concepts. In addition, my experience in education keeps me interested in hiring, training, educating and inspiring talents. I worked as a class adviser previously, which meant recruiting good students. If they were not good enough, you had to 'fix' them. If things got too bad, you had to let them go. But my English learning experience helped me to understand the Western way, the Western mentality and systematic organisation. I think people in the West are quite good at methodology, and I embrace their managerial theories and principles. But it's hard for us to adopt their ways because our cultural foundations are quite different. So I must use Chinese culture as a base, while adopting Western principles and encouraging employees, young people, and ground-level managers to create their own ways, rather than allowing me, Ma Yun, to manipulate them. A boss should create reason and principle; a boss should look for the root and the spring of the corporate culture. I cannot build our corporate culture out of nothing.

As a teacher, I know how to use available resources. When I stroll in the rich Chinese cultural heritage, I feel the power of Confucianism, Buddhism and Daoism. In Daoism, the best leadership is not leading at all. What is leadership anyway? I think it requires sacrificing today for the future; the person who can sacrifice today to win tomorrow is a real leader. A good leader must be equipped with the excellent attributes of a professional manager. At the same time, the leader must be reliable and able to bear responsibilities not only for today but for tomorrow and the future. We habitually think about how to solve yesterday's problems, but it is more important to deal with what we must do today to solve tomorrow's problems. The Daoist perspective calls for walking your path naturally by following your understanding of the future rather than focusing only on past and present problems.

Grateful and Sharing Culture: Live Seriously and Work Merrily

Interviewer Chen: What exactly is the 'Dao' you see clearly?

Ma: The Alibaba Group is not supposed to be successful because we lack the necessary elements for success. We had no social resources, no 'sugar daddy' or rich uncle. I used to tell my colleagues that we picked up a gold brick from the street only by chance. We had two choices, to look for another brick or to hide it. The first choice is foolish; it is like a hunter standing by a tree waiting for a rabbit to crash into the trunk and kill itself. The second choice is insecure; someone might steal the gold. Instead, it's better to share it with others, show your gratitude, and everyone will be happy. The core of Daoism is letting things take their own course; the core of Buddhism is emptiness, the same inheritance as Daoism. What does it mean to let things take their own course? It means to stride ahead even though you know the result, for the process is what we really appreciate. If you can see that as your destination through life, you will not fuss over trivialities. Confucianism is the Chinese way of management: emperor and minister, father and son, ranking in layers, while Western Christianity has developed a more open system. We adopted what they have in common: gratefulness, sharing and openness.

I gave a talk at Harvard in 2002. After my talk, a CEO from a foreign company said that I was a mad man. He said he had been in China for many years, and didn't believe that my way of managing would work. I invited him to visit my company. After a three-day stay, he said 'Now I understand. Here you have 100 mad men just like you.' I agreed. People in a madhouse never admit they are crazy. People here are unified. Alibaba's culture was developed not through my own efforts, but through collective striving. Our culture is the result of cherishing the same ideals, following the same path, and pooling the same people. If you want to copy us, you have to copy our culture, conform to its theoretical foundation, and hire people who share your ideas. Many companies want to compete with Alibaba, and I'm like, hey, brother, you don't know what you're talking about. I have been waiting for 10 years. This whole e-commerce business is only one of my expressions, and no way could you compete.

Interviewer Chen: I went to your company for a meeting two years ago and saw that many meeting rooms are named after Jin Yong's martial arts novel.[3]

Ma: Jin Yong's martial arts novel is the most down-to-earth way of explaining Confucianism, Buddhism and Daoism. It cherishes brotherhood, loyalty, courage, emotion and conscience—what I have advocated in the company for years. Alibaba will eventually become the best money-making company, but I worry about losing our human sense. I want my company to be like a person, with feelings, consciousness, and a code of conduct. Alibaba is a service company, not a high-tech one. The higher the technology, the further a company may go from consumers. I cherish loyalty and friendship. One principle I advocate in the company is to live seriously and work merrily.

Interviewer Chen: People often say work seriously and live merrily. Why did you reverse it?

Ma: Because if you don't live seriously, life won't be serious with you. If you are unhappy at work, if you are working seriously, you cannot be innovative. Must you finish your work and then go off to be happy? Work seriously and live happily? That's foolishness! Some talk about balancing work and life. That's impossible! About four years ago, a person suggested that I give a lecture to teach our workers how to separate life from work. I talked for about 30 minutes, and suddenly I realised that I was talking nonsense, meaningless words, for I never separate my life from my work!

Interviewer Chen: It's uncommon in the business world for a 48-year-old CEO to retire. Your comments and action are quite daring.

Ma: Yes, I speak boldly, and that's my personality. If one day I begin to talk plainly and calmly, then something must be wrong with me. I say what I think, and I do what I say. If one day I do something different

---

[3] Jin Yong is one of the finest novelists of martial arts, with high influence in Chinese-speaking areas and communities.

from yesterday, then I admit that I was wrong but at the time I thought it was right. My actions match my thoughts; I never speak one way and think another. If I did, that would cause my employees and the whole of society to distrust me.

When you realise you have made a mistake, there are two possibilities: one is to hit the wall and keep hitting; the other is to turn back. So I have decided to give younger people a chance. However, their values must match with our long-term core ideas. I will pass the torch to the one who holds our values closely and is superior to us.

The Successor Must Come from Inside the Company

Interviewer Chen: Do you mean that the CEO who replaces you must be trained and cultivated by your company?

Ma: Of course. I already stated it in the corporate constitution: never allow outsiders to become CEO. Even if Alibaba is on the edge of bankruptcy, rescue troops from outside are forbidden. The new leader must have worked in the company for at least five years before the corporate constitution allows him to be a leader. You can come to work with us at the age of 30 and after five years you may be promoted to a higher level. The president of a country must be born there or have lived here for many years. If you don't love the country, you can only be a problem solver. I need a leader for this company! Chinese traditional medicine makes sense in this way: cure a person, not a disease. If the disease is cured but the person dies, what is gained? You may cure one disease, but how about others? I want the person to be cured, and I want to have someone who really loves the company, understands it, and is willing to bear the responsibilities. If this person can't be found, that's only because you didn't prioritise this requirement enough. If we hadn't written it into our corporate constitution, the board might say: hey, this person is not good enough, let's try another. The investors can never love the company more than you do. They talk like backseat drivers and could damage the whole ecosystem of the company. The worst scenario is that you could invite a wolf in who might think it is right to eat all the sheep. That's the only way he can prove himself; and that's partly why nine out of 10 mergers and acquisitions fail. We are solving the problem from the system level.

Succession—Fix the Roof on a Sunny Day

Interviewer Chen: Right from the beginning and up to the present, you have taken different roles in Alibaba. At different times, how have you positioned yourself in the company's management? What circumstances would make you come forward or step aside?

Ma: If the company is in danger, I will always throw myself in and try my best to help. That is my responsibility. When the company is succeeding it's time for me to leave. Furthermore, when the company is at its best time, it is time to start reforming because you must fix the roof on a sunny day. If you wait for a rainy day, you might slip and die. Fix the roof on a sunny day; stay at home and relax on a rainy day: that's a corporate responsibility. Let others set off celebratory fireworks.

Interviewer Chen: And now you have decided to retire. Does that mean you have been successful in finding your successor?

Ma: I have groomed several successors. I'm now persuading them to see the challenge as picking up a gold brick on the street just as I did earlier. I spent 10 years, especially the first few years, trying to give back to society gratefully. The new CEO should also be grateful and willing to share by returning wealth to society. A CEO must sacrifice for others and do a better job than others.

Long ago I drove out those I felt would not be good partners. I'm not going to cause trouble for the man I pick. I will fix the trouble myself. In the past three years, while I was training future leaders, I found their weaknesses and let them work hard to overcome them.

CEOs Must Have Vision, Tolerance and Strength

Ma: And that's the course the CEO must take. If you were a general fighting on the frontier, and one day I called you to withdraw from the burning battlefield to work in the backroom for three years, it would be like putting you into cold storage at your peak. And then when you are at your lowest point, I suddenly inform you that you now can go somewhere to work. This way, I trained the most sturdy and durable men. If two people are both powerful and vigorous, I can assign them to different jobs. The emperor who killed his brother to secure his position was stupid. That's not the Daoist way and it is definitely not Buddhist either. If I can't get this right, that's my problem, not theirs. What happens if the two confront each other before I figure a way out? I have three prerequisites for a CEO: vision, tolerance and strength. Compared with others, you need further sight and a bigger heart to endure wrongful treatment. The heart gets bigger by experiencing injustice, and man gets tougher only by suffering unjust treatment. Strength is endurance. If a guy returns smiling after rounds of being beaten up, then he is the one I want to be my successor.

Interviewer Chen: How many men in your company have you 'beaten up' like this?

Ma: Oh, a lot. As a teacher, how can you not criticise people, not discipline them, and not encourage them? When I criticise someone, he will feel pain and anguish, will curse me, will think it's impossible to work for me, and will feel terribly mistreated. But this training system is cultural, and it has actually fostered today's system of competition. No other internet company in China has a system like this.

If something is wrong, and I tell the person so, I then watch his attitude. If he admits his mistake, there is no problem. I worry most when he doesn't admit it, because he will make the same mistake tomorrow. I will never use a general who always wins. I choose one who has failed often but sometimes succeeded, because his failures would make him more careful. A man who has never failed will fall hard when he does so, and then you will be dead. If he is not open, and he is easily discouraged and easily loses control, you should ignore him after punishing him. After three months, if he still can't dig himself out, you call him in and have a talk.

If he comes on his own initiative, you can tell after half an hour whether he has really changed or is just trying to please you. Talk with him, let him open up, breathe out all toxins. Some people have broad minds; they treat this procedure as using their face to mop the floor, or to actually gain dignity. I criticise someone in every meeting, but they are OK, no matter the criticism. I keep criticising until they can't take it anymore, not only the CEOs but every manager. I have now structured the company into 25 business units, with 25 young business leaders, each with three to five assistants. I have spent a lot of time building up this graduate class, so-called *Feng Qing Yang* (wind blow gently). Several times a year I teach them about the values of our corporate culture.

But it's not feasible to teach everyone in just one way. Everyone has a different personality. I hope my company can be like a zoo of different animals with different characteristics. If everyone is the same, then the company becomes a farm, raising a bunch of pigs or chickens. With different animals, a company can have a good ecosystem. You must know how to deal with different people. Otherwise, you can't deal with society, and you can't get along with your clients. A leader must suffer, endure and have vision to stand out compared with his employees. I died thousands of times, and have no fear of another death. Young people can easily catch up with your skills, but courage is what makes a leader.

The Corporate Mission Has to Keep Up with Social Development

Interviewer Chen: As the founder of an enterprise, you really emphasised the building of a corporate culture. What is the ideal culture for Alibaba? How did it form and get sustained? Please give some detailed examples.

Ma: In the twenty-first century you must understand your mission and your reason for existing. In past centuries, companies could prosper simply by having good luck. Today, big companies must solve social problems if they are to solve their own company's problems. Only then can the company last for ever. Alibaba has tried to solve social problems such as unemployment, and to answer needs for innovation. It is not simply a company, but an ecological system. The difference between poor scholars and me is that they use their knowledge to change the world, but I use my actions to change everything, from the bottom up. I've nurtured people who were born in the 1980s and learned about the internet when they were little.

To me, the company mission comes before a value system; with mission and value created, then vision is demanded. Afterwards, strategy is laid out before the organisational structure is created, followed by the determination of talents and culture. All these constitute a whole system. I did not understand that in the past, but I have gained more understanding over time and have created something systematic of my own. Today's Alibaba is not built by stitching pieces, but by mission value management. Then action is confirmed, and staff learns how to proceed step-by-step. Our corporate culture can be summarised by four simple words: open, transparent, sharing and responsible. These words correspond with my understanding of the internet.

The internet has developed so rapidly because it is open, transparent, responsible and sharing. A company's corporate culture must be merged with the internet culture and with society's future, or it will be over. In my view, the internet is our future. Whether we are willing or not, society will become more open, transparent, responsible and sharing. If your company has such a culture, it will naturally get stronger. I personally believe that our company is the most open in China, at least in its strategy. I can always share my strategy with others.

Even our intranet has been open to the public for two years. We are reconstructing it. When it's done, anyone can find out who is doing which project. You can watch, but you can't comment on our webpage. You can comment somewhere else, but if everyone gives an opinion about our business, that would ruin everything. So you see, I didn't emphasise democracy, but I'm democratising internally. Of all I did in 2012, I am most proud of the democratic reform.

Morality Is the Core Value of Our Culture

Ma: I believe we have inherited much of value from our ancestors. Of course, that doesn't mean we refute Western ways. They are more advanced than we are, so their knowledge is part of the world management doctrine. I just offer food for thought. After my retirement, I hope to make some valuable contributions to companies like ours. Let me tell you a few stories. Sometimes we invite people, for example, to come to teach marketing. But if they teach us how to sell combs to monks, I won't ask them back because they are teaching us to be liars: monks don't need combs. We are talking about how to create customer value, and you are teaching us how to sell combs to monks and calling that a typical case? That's nonsense.

Here is another story. Once I decided not to hire a person who was very good at communication, logic and management at the job interview. We were ready to hire him, but he concluded the interview by saying that he would bring a lot of customers when he came here to work. Then I changed my mind. I said, 'Thank you, but let's find another opportunity to work together.' I could see that when he left our company, he would take away some of our customers as well. That's the moral problem. I don't encourage employees to open their own businesses. Joining Alibaba is to help others open businesses. We have 7 million sellers in our platform. Join us if you want to help them, but if you want your own business, then you'd better stay away. If you want to be one of those 7 million people, I will certainly support you. So, when I talk about the open, transparent, sharing and responsible culture, it's also about acting and convincing others.

Interviewer Chen: I heard that your core value system is the 'Six Meridian Swords': putting the customer first; embracing changes; solidarity and co-operation; integrity; passion; and dedication. How was that system established? What role has it played in Alibaba's development? How has it influenced employees?

Ma: Well, I didn't devise this system on my own. The first year, the founders discussed it several times behind closed doors. We started from the 1995 Chinese Yellow Pages, and went through pain and struggle, but never gave up. We discussed what unified us. We didn't do well in business, but we stuck together. Why?

We discussed and wrote down the reasons and then combined them into nine items defining our reasons for persistence. From then on, every newcomer had to follow the nine items, which became the basis for employee performance appraisals. Rather than measuring sales performance, we assessed values and were determined to pass them down. After some time, we refined the nine items into six, the so-called 'Six Meridian Swords', which make up 50 % of employee performance evaluations. If you don't stick with our core values, you must leave. Regarding performance, I have discovered that small companies tend to prefer people with good performance but bad values.

It's true they make more money, but the money is from dishonest dealings, and may cause the company to remain dishonest for ever. When employees of that generation become company leaders, the company will be weak because they have got used to taking dishonest advantage. That's why the biggest hurdle for small companies is the 'wild dog.' On the other hand, the hurdle for big companies is the 'little white rabbit': people who perform badly but get along with others well.

I 'killed' two 'wild dogs' in 2002 when I proposed 'one yuan profit.' The company had serious losses, and at the beginning of the year we had a meeting, and asked what Alibaba could do to survive in the internet business, where everyone was giving kickbacks, a violation of our basic principles. The meeting began at 8 am and lasted until 4.30 pm. All complained that we couldn't live like that any more. At 4.30 pm, I concluded the meeting and said, 'Remember this, as the founder, I would rather close the company than give kickbacks, because that's the behaviour we hate so much. We want to make money, but if we rely on kickbacks to make money, then we will fall one day just like the others. I don't want to do that. For people who support giving kickbacks, you can choose to leave today. That's my principle.'

Six months passed. Our calculations showed that we had about 800,000 RMB revenue. Sales from two employees made up 50 % of our revenue; but both had given kickbacks.

So I fired them, firmly and decisively. And through that self-cleansing, from 2005/2006 onwards, the company began to form its own value system. And we sent a clear message: give kickbacks, kill; bring old customers to a new job, kill; start from little things and no fake books; visit only three customers, fire.

Interviewer Chen: What do you mean about visiting only three customers?

Ma: If I find out that a salesman planned to visit five customers daily but visited only three and still reported five, I'm going to fire him. If he cheats on those little things, how can I trust him again? If he is honest,

I will not fire him for visiting only three customers instead of five. But if he lies to me, how can I trust him any more? How can we work together? These systems and details are the first culture base built in Alibaba.

Make Integrity a Big Deal

Interviewer Chen: Your Company's Articles of Association clearly define integrity. The company reportedly has a special department to ensure integrity. And you also have a dedicated 'sensing officer' to detect whether anything is going wrong. Even so, something went wrong in 2011; that is, the B2B customer incident, and the shopkeeper incident at ju.taobao. com in 2012. Can you discuss these incidents?

Ma: Today I can proudly say that what I did regarding those incidents is incomparable in terms of integrity among companies of our size or smaller in China. I went to the Central Discipline Inspection Committee and initiated the exposure of both incidents, in 2011 and in 2012. We must understand what we should overplay and what we should downplay. We need to make a big deal about integrity but downplay business performance, because integrity is related closely to our cultural roots. This ecosystem, this platform we are building is for thousands of ordinary people to use, which is very similar to a government operation. The question is how to build it. It was in 2009, I was completely immersed in Taobao and Alipay, working on our future strategy, so I entrusted Alibaba to Wei Zhe's team. They were under tremendous pressure after taking it over, especially when Fujian, notorious for forgery, was rampant with gangs of swindlers. They came to Alibaba pretending to be suppliers to defraud money from foreigners. We reported them to the police, but nobody took any action.

The ultimate problem is that we don't have power. The Alibaba system has 350 million people and more than 34 million companies within it; I am operating in an ecosystem of over 600 million people. If 1 % are bad guys, I have 6 million scoundrels.

When we found that there was a little over 1 % in duplicitous business, I told Wei Zhe that if he had replaced the person in charge of that business four months before, he would have been considered as having taken action; but now, if I didn't fire him, Alibaba should fire me. So the whole team was dismissed. One may find it hard to imagine—pulling out the CEO and his entire team. I was determined to make a big deal out of it.

Many people still thought it was definitely a storm in a teacup. But this was a cancer and had to be rooted out; otherwise the cancer cells would spread quickly. It was not evil behaviour that we hated; rather, we hated indifference to evil behaviour.

Interviewer Chen: But why did Taobao have problems after that?

Ma: I did an even better job with the Taobao incident. I thoroughly analysed the whole situation and found that the real problem was with the senior management of the Taobao system. The internet was developing so fast that we neglected Alibaba's strict training system in our basic process of recruitment and training. At that time I felt it was really hard to run a small enterprise, so I offered free service. Actually I offered free service three times. The purpose of the first time was not to beat others; it was because we had no clue about the business model and did not know whether what we were offering was useful or not. Therefore the starting point was to explore and define a model.

Later I said we would have to charge for the service after five years, but then came the financial crisis. OK, let's keep it free, then. After free service for a time, the business amounted to 700 billion RMB in that year. In a 700 billion RMB free market, it is natural you have all kinds of people. We desperately needed people, so various job candidates were introduced by employees, or recruited as interns, and some even offered cash when seeking a job. Corruption was outrageous at that time.

Immunity Can Be Supported Only by Core Values

Ma: It was really scary. What should we do? I told my colleagues that this had to be handled seriously. However, nobody was free from contamination. It was really a social problem, not just for us. The most important thing was to cultivate our immunity, the core of which is our values, our systems and our interests. Under these circumstances we set up the integrity department with six employees. Probably no other company in China has an integrity department.

Our integrity department is very efficient. What we want is not a fire brigade but a fire prevention team to solve fundamentally both technical and system problems. It is not difficult to solve system problems. We adopt an 'interlink assurance' policy that binds supervisors and subordinates in the recruitment process, meaning that today I am your boss, so I am accountable for what you do, and I shall shoulder responsibility together with you if you do something wrong. I request my direct reports to tell me the truth. If they hide the truth from me, I will be blamed if anything goes wrong.

I also observe people when I talk to them. If I find that someone has something in his hands, something must be wrong. This is what a 'sensing officer' does. If someone does not look into my eyes, he is either not happy with me or hiding something from me. I will have a chat or a drink with him. If I cannot see the problem, then it is my problem, using the wrong people or neglecting my supervisory duty, and my boss has to bear the responsibility too. This is the first level of interlink assurance. Otherwise everybody can say they are not aware of the issue, and it will always be someone else's responsibility. I want to hold everybody accountable.

Second, I investigate each reported customer complaint. Competition for customers is cut-throat. If we all sell tea, and you take bribes from a seller, others will blow the whistle. I learned that from Lee Kuan Yew.[4] I deal with those who are involved in bribery if the investigation confirms the report. Once we confirm that a shop has practiced bribery, that shop is closed for ever and can never re-enter the Taobao and Alibaba system. Their reputation is ruined, which is a terrible thing for many people because they will never be able to do business again. The industrial and commercial authority inspections are not as frightening as doing business at Taobao nowadays. The closing of the business at Taobao is worse than going to jail.

Regarding whistleblowing, if one of your employees receives a report letter, the shop will be closed if the claims are found to be true. So the one doing the bribing is also afraid, as he knows that many people can blow the whistle on him. If your employee does it, other employees can report

---

[4] Lee Kuan Yew (1923–2015) was the first Prime Minister of Singapore, recognised as the nation's founding father.

it; if you give money, your employees would definitely know, and if they report it, your shop will be closed. That's why I deal with the source. Our interlink assurance system, our cultural system and our technical system all support our efforts. We have hidden lines encrypted in all our programs that keep track of every single footprint 'walking in the snow.' Once I sense you, I will definitely chase you no matter how far you run, and bring you back to jail. By this I am telling employees that even if you have taken the money, you will not dare to spend it as you will fear getting caught. This is how we operate—six people, reporting with real names, and immediately investigating reports. Reporting with real names is a commitment.

I feel that this system is working well. Of course, we are still improving it. Meanwhile, we have resumed recruitment and are accepting interns. To us, interns are a social responsibility, not cheap labour. Based on our capability, we can train 100 interns, who come to us to learn, not to work.

From the perspective of management, issues are inevitable as long as there are people and organisations. These issues are not necessarily bad problems; it largely depends on our corporate spirit. When the water is too clear, there will be no fish. We are in such a social environment, and I get to understand many things through my experience of handling those incidents. It all boils down to whether you are willing to challenge, whether you are willing to take responsibility, and whether you are willing to sacrifice yourself for the future. I have never felt ashamed of myself; I show my wounds to people, not to you but to my employees, and hope they will remember what I have done in the history of Alibaba. Perhaps my employees will ask the CEO in future years years: 'Ma Yun did this, so why can't you?'

As chairman of Alibaba, I have three missions. The first regards Alibaba's current influence. Today, Alibaba has influenced consumption styles, production and manufacturing styles, and lifestyles, and its impact will keep on increasing. If I were just a CEO, I would operate the company following corporate logic. But as the chairman I must look at the company from the perspective of a prime minister, as I must ensure that the company keeps abreast with the progress of society.

Some people say Ma Yun has no responsibilities. The truth is, I have many responsibilities on my shoulders, but I must keep quiet. My religion teaches me to map out my strategies from a national and global standpoint.

My second mission is to build a talent training base, and to build our culture; and the third is public welfare. What's public welfare to Alibaba? It's waking up the kindness. If you have kindness, your products will be good, and your kindness will affect others. Alibaba does public welfare; our existence contributes to the employment of 10 million Chinese people and the survival of over 1000 small enterprises. How we do things will affect what numerous households purchase; therefore, products and services must come from kindness. I told my colleagues to do the right thing and not to make me come back to correct their faults!

Interviewer Chen: In all these years of running the business, have you ever encountered conflicts between interpersonal relationships and business rationality? Looking back, how do you think conflicts between relationships, loyalty and business rationality should be handled?

Ma: This is a rather complicated question. Without feelings we are just machines. It is natural that people will get close to one another eventually. But if we focus too much on human relationships, we cannot form an organisation or a company on a scale that could impact society; instead, we can just affect ourselves. In general we are doing fine in this respect, including the departure of some founding partners, including my wife. She was the no. 2 employee of Alibaba. But we had no choice.

But leaving does not necessarily mean the relationship is ruined. My wife can be mad at me, but I am not angry with her, as I know that she does not work for me today. As a CEO, I try to stick to the commitment. I told everyone that they can hate me, but that will not make me give up my commitment.

Interviewer Chen: Lastly, would you like to share your best experiences in starting and managing a business?

Ma: My experience in starting a business is to start with things that make you happy, and to start with the easiest rather than the most difficult things. My management philosophy is 'use people with doubt and use those whom you doubt.' From a management perspective, I believe in letting people use their own judgement instead of telling them what to do. Starting up a business is to entrust people who excel; to use people with doubt focus more on a person's capability than his/her integrity. In Chinese, the word trust consists of two parts—trust and entrust. I've always believed that we should use people with doubt and use those you doubt. To give different types of people a try. It turns out many talents are discovered by those of whom I had doubts.

Management is a long-term process, entrusting people who excel and entrusting people with the power to make decisions are two different levels. We have people who are in their seventies but still like to use their judgment and make decisions by themselves. It makes them feel accomplished, but at the same time, they have deprived others of something they want to do. You have the power; do others have to kill you to get the chance to make decisions? You can have your own life only if you entrust people with the right to make decisions. Life is important, and so is happiness. I think as Chinese enterprises improve, more people will focus on charity work.

I absolutely agree that today's business leaders should assume social responsibility, and many of them have done that. Meanwhile it is really important for us to think about this issue. We have not developed a clear understanding about what money is and how to manage donations. Bill Gates (founder of Microsoft) has his foundation to manage donations; but which foundation can we donate to in China?

I believe what we really need is to build up a charity system. The amounts donated won't matter as long as we have a sound charity mechanism. I don't think merely donating can solve all the problems, though, and currently the most urgent problem is to awaken people's social consciousness. China's prosperity could not have been be achieved without the hard work of countless entrepreneurs, and that's our biggest contribution to Chinese society.

Commentary

In the internet service industry, it is no exaggeration to say that integrity is the most important quality a company must have, as it is the foundation on which to build consumers' trust and confidence. In China's social environment, where cheating has been prevalent, integrity becomes even more important for a company that wants to last for at least 102 years.

That is why Jack Ma emphasises integrity, and has decided to take extreme measures to ensure that it becomes the 'DNA' of Alibaba. He 'kills' the 'wild dogs', fires those who are dishonest, has formed an integrity committee within the company, appoints those with 'long noses' as sensing officers, established the 'interlink assurance' system, and built a footprint tracking device on the internet to make sure that no one can get away with cheating. Ma exemplifies the ethical leadership that has emerged in the literature (Resick et al. 2006). It is also evident that he has a strong focus on people and people development, and it is through rigorous HR activities such as recruiting, training, socialising, performance evaluation and incentive mechanisms, that Alibaba has been able to build a corporate culture that is open, transparent, sharing and responsible. Ma's leadership, values and personality have strongly imprinted the culture of Alibaba (Schein 2010). It is also remarkable that he is able to integrate Daoism, Confucianism and Western management thoughts as well as develop his own philosophy of management and practices in grooming his successors, dealing with crises, and leading Alibaba to become one of the most important players in the Chinese economy and beyond (Ma and Tsui 2015).

References

Alibaba Group. (2015). Alibaba Group. Retrieved March 28, 2015, from http://www.alibabagroup.com/en/global/home

Ma, L., & Tsui, A. S. (2015). Traditional Chinese philosophies and contemporary leadership. *The Leadership Quarterly, 26*(1), 13–24.

Resick, C. J., Hanges, P. J., Dickson, M. W., & Mitchelson, J. K. (2006). A cross-cultural examination of the endorsement of ethical leadership. *Journal of Business Ethics, 63*, 345–359.

Schein, E. H. (2010). *Organizational culture and leadership*, Vol. 2. Hoboken: John Wiley and Sons.

Steimle, J. (2015). A beginner's guide to Alibaba Group. *Forbes.com*. Retrieved March 26, 2015, from http://www.forbes.com/sites/joshsteimle/2015/01/26/a-beginners-guide-to-alibaba-group/

Wikipedia. (2015). Jack Ma. Retrieved March 26, 2015, from http://en.wikipedia.org/wiki/Jack_Ma

Part IV

Leaders in Construction and Real Estate Industry

10

Successful Business through Moral Conduct and Integrity

Interview with Beijing Vantone Holdings Founder and Chairman Lun Feng

The interview was conducted by: Xiao-Ping Chen, University of Washington.

Vantone Holdings Co. Ltd.[1]

Established in Beijing in 1993, Vantone Holdings Co. Ltd. (hereafter Vantone) is one of China's largest and most innovative professional real estate investment companies. The company's business is concentrated in high-growth urban areas such as Beijing, Shanghai, Tianjin, Hangzhou and Chengdu. With its value-driven and innovation-oriented strategies, Vantone specialises in real estate investment with two major businesses: direct investment and fund investment. The company's business activities range across real estate development, commercial properties, fund management and asset management.

We thank Zhonghua Gao for her initial English translation of the interview.

[1] This section is based on information from the company website (Vantone 2015a), Annual Reports (Vantone 2015b), and IACMR's *Chinese Management Insights'* publication on Vantone in August 2012.

© The Author(s) 2017   **225**
A.S. Tsui et al., *Leadership of Chinese Private Enterprises*, Palgrave Studies in Chinese Management, DOI 10.1057/978-1-137-40235-6_10

Because of its active social promotion and innovative architectural design, Vantone is one of the best-known brands in China's real estate industry, with several real estate products established as a reference in their corresponding segment, such as 'Xinxin Homeland', 'International Series' and 'Huafu series', in the high-end city residential business. Vantone's real estate development includes concern about environmental issues. Being the first Chinese real estate company to make a commitment to reduce carbon emissions in the real estate industry, Vantone Real Estate was named the 'Most Valuable Real Estate Company' in the 2013 China Real Estate Ranking. In November 2015, the Vantone Centre in Hangzhou received the Gold Certificate of LEED (Leadership in Energy and Environmental Design) from the U.S. Green Building Council (USGBC), becoming the first of this type of commercial property project in China. By the end of 2014, Vantone Real Estate possessed total assets exceeding 14.2 billion RMB.

In recent years, Vantone Holdings has focused more on expanding its fund management business. In 2010, its successful establishment of commercial real estate funds led to private real estate investment trusts (REITs) fund innovation in China. The fund management business exceeded 20 billion RMB by 2013, among the highest in the real estate company fund rankings. In terms of asset management, Vantone Property won the 'Top 10 Service Quality of China Property Service Enterprises' award in 2013. Vantone Holdings and Vantone Real Estate have been recognised among the Top 10 of Wealth Creation Capacity, Top 10 Most Outstanding Contributors of Chinese Settlements in Ten Years, among other awards.

Vantone was also the first mainland property developer to expand into Taiwan. The high-end resort condominium project 'Vantone l Taipei 2011' laid a solid foundation for the company's overseas business development. In 2009, Vantone participated in the reconstruction of the World Trade Center in New York, and invested in the 'China Center New York.' The project began in 2015 and provides a high-end platform for both commerce and culture communication between China and the USA.

Vantone also actively promotes and participates in social activities to contribute to a better society. In 2008, the Vantone Foundation was established, committed mainly to building eco-friendly communities, and to researching and developing new technology. Vantone Holdings donates 1 % and Vantone Real Estate donates 0.5 % of their profits to the Vantone Foundation annually. Other societal projects include the Vantone Academy and the Vantone Museum, established in 2009. As a valuable real estate brand in China, it has been recognised in the Top 100 Enterprises in Economic Contribution, and as Outstanding Corporate Citizen in China, and Model Enterprise of Responsible Real Estate in China.

Founder and Chairman Lun Feng[2]

Born in Xi'an in 1959, Lun Feng founded Vantone in 1991 and has served as its president since then. He is a general partner at Vantone Investment Group. He has served as chairman of Beijing Vantone Real Estate Co. Ltd. since 1995 and its director since 2 June 2008; chairman at the China Center New York LLC, and chairman of the board of Vantone International Group's (VIG's) close affiliate, the Vantone Enterprise Group. He personally orchestrated the acquisition of Shanxi Securities and the Wuhan Investment Trust Company. He also serves as vice chairman of the Urban Housing Development Commission of the China Real Estate Association, and the rotating chairman of the Real Estate Chamber of All-China Federation of Industry and Commerce. He helped to establish and serves as venture director of China Minsheng Banking Corporation.

Known as the 'Property Thinker' in China, Lun Feng initiated the American real estate model that calls for turning powerful developers into professional real estate investment companies. He actively promoted the progress of the industry as an innovator and pioneer. He co-sponsored the establishment of the China Urban Realty Association (CURA) in 1999, and acted as its second rotating chairman. In 2001, he published a paper entitled 'Follow the Good Example of Vanke', which strongly advocated that enterprises should be socially responsible. These efforts continued with Lun

---

[2] This section is based on IACMR's *Chinese Management Insights'* publication on Vantone in August 2012 with permission, complemented by public information from worldsofceos.com (Worldofceos 2015).

Feng's planning and promotion of a large-scale TV documentary 'Housing Remodel China' in 2003, which actively promoted the development and moral enhancement of China's real estate industry; and with continuously promoting the industry's integrity, self-discipline and rights protections when he served as the rotating chairman of the Real Estate Chamber of the All-China Federation of Industry and Commerce (ACFIC) in 2005.

He established the Society of Entrepreneurs & Ecology (SEE) in June 2004, with almost 100 renowned Chinese entrepreneurs, and served as executive director and president of the board. Committed to desertification control and environmental protection, SEE has emerged as one of the most well-known non-governmental environmental protection agencies, and one of the largest non-governmental organisation (NGO) incubators in China. In April 2008, Lun Feng initiated the Vantone Foundation.

Lun Feng has a bachelor's degree in economics from Northwest University of China, a master of law degree from the Party School of the Central Committee of the Communist Party of China (CPC), a master's degree in public policy (MPP) from the Lee Kuan Yew School of Public Policy at the National University of Singapore, and a juris doctorate from the graduate school of the Chinese Academy of Social Sciences. He has also held posts in the Party School of the Central Committee of the CPC, the Publicity Department of the Central Committee of the CPC, the National Reform Commission, and the China Institute for Reform and Development from 1984 to 1991 before founding Vantone. His writings include the best-selling books, *Savage Growth* and *Voluptuous Aspirations*, reflecting 'the spiritual history' of Chinese private enterprises.

Successful Business Through Moral Conduct and Integrity

Interviewer Chen: Please describe briefly your management philosophy.

Lun Feng (hereafter referred to as Feng): My management philosophy is very simple: 'Be moral and be creative.' It is extremely important to stick to moral values and follow laws, regulations and national policies.

At Vantone, we follow established rules for handling at least 70 % of the issues we encounter. We try to solve ambiguous grey-area problems creatively, but always adhere to the moral bottom line. For example, as a real estate development company, one of our main businesses is to secure land from the government. In China, one might use various approaches to obtain land, but our basic principle is 'never bribe.' Where money is really needed, we spend it openly, for example, by sponsoring a beach volleyball match. If we encounter personnel problems, our basic principle is to make these affairs public, so that we can deal with them following consistent principles. With this approach, our company has built a good reputation, long-term credibility, and an ethical and transparent culture, which has allowed us to avoid legal troubles for almost 20 years.

Certainly, we have paid a good deal for following these values; for example, we were not able to obtain the land we were seeking, so in the short term, moral principles can be costly. However, in the long run, benefits accrue. First, our well-deserved good reputation has helped us win the approval of projects, especially when good reputation was the contractors' key requirement for maintaining trust. Thus our good name made us their best choice to partner with.

Interviewer Chen: What life experiences influenced your management philosophy?

Feng: My management philosophy has the influence of both external and internal factors as well as accidental triggers. From the day it was founded in 1991, the general public has paid a great deal of attention to our company. With external forces watching us so closely, we became more self-aware and self-disciplined.

The six co-founders of Vantone are men with lofty ideals: Wang Gongquan, Pan Shiyi, Wang Qifu, Yi Xiaodi, Liu Jun and me. Starting our business in Hainan, we encountered many challenges. We spent two days reflecting on our vision and goals. After these two days of heated discussion and debate, we reached a consensus on our mission: to create an enterprise that could help to save the world, create wealth, and perfect the self. At the time, the *China Youth Daily* reported this mission. Since then, we have been clear about our basic principle of doing business; that is, we do not just do it to make money. More important, we want to benefit society by following the 'benefit self and benefit others' principle.

The accidental trigger happened after 1993, when our company was transformed into enterprise groups. We invited Mr Wang Luguang, who grew up in a military family and attached special importance to rules and laws, to serve as a long-term company monitor. I reported all company activities to him almost weekly for more than 10 years until he passed away in 2005. Mr Wang held us to high standards. Another meaning of 'be moral and be creative' is to correct errors and apologise for mistakes. Over the years, we have gradually become habituated to being monitored and to correcting any errors that surface.

That is why our company has never encountered legal troubles, which has enabled us to focus entirely on analysing the market, optimising our business operations, and building effective teams. I will say that Vantone is pure, and we are happy to show it.

Morality and integrity are also reflected in our self-conscious and self-disciplined company governance and financial management. Our company sponsors an Annual Introspection Day and has set up self-monitoring systems, including an internal control system. These practices have allowed us to establish a value system that is something of a religion guiding our behaviour unconsciously. I am confident that these safeguards will keep us out of trouble, even when I'm gone. As it is, I spend about 180 days a year on the road.

Interviewer Chen: What roles do you play in your company?

Feng: I see myself in three roles. First, I founded Vantone, so I have legitimate source for my authority, which lends some mystique in the view of the younger generation. Second, I am the strategic leader of our company, and I focus on the company's development, transformation and governance. Fortunately, the past has shown every Vantone transformation to be on the right track. When we choose a strategy, we rely on the general manager's competence for implementation. Fortunately, Vantone has a very competent top management team. My third role is being a mentor. I love to read and think, and have read many books and articles, especially those dealing with the real estate industry. I know the industry's history and its most important people, so I have the background information to help others solve problems. I also prefer to influence others through communication rather than through my status. I respect people and treat others equally.

The Stranger Principle and Continuous Innovation

Interviewer Chen: What management practices have you introduced to Vantone? Why did you introduce these practices?

Feng: Vantone's management practices have three distinct characteristics: transparency, adherence to the 'stranger principle', and continuous innovation.

Transparency may require being transparent to investors, but it also requires that the actions of internal management are also transparent. When we first established our business, we six co-founders established the transparency principle: All employees know the salaries of everyone else, and no one may have a second income. Employee identities are clear to all. If an employee obtains a passport or emigrates to a foreign country, everyone should know. We have continued this principle since our foundation.

We also advocate the important stranger principle, because an acquaintance culture weakens the implementation of a fair system. Generally speaking, when companies deal with strangers, they exclude potential problems caused by personal relations and reciprocal gestures, such as *renqing* (human obligation) and *mianzi* (face). Independent investors and independent board members are like that. However, when doing business with acquaintances, it is much harder to stick to rules completely. For example, when an acquaintance asks for the reimbursement of certain expenses, a company might relax their rules by 40 % to 50 %, a problem related to the acquaintance culture. Vantone encourages the treatment of all clients as important strangers and sticking to the rules.

On the other hand, the stranger principle doesn't mean that our employees cannot introduce competent friends as potential employees. On the contrary, we encourage our employees to recommend their friends, but we require them also to take responsibility. An employee will be rewarded for introducing a friend who performs well and makes valuable contributions to the company. In contrast, the employee will have a damaged performance appraisal if the friend performs poorly or causes company losses. In this way, employees are particularly cautious about recommending friends, and objective rules and systems remain fair and unbiased.

In addition, Vantone greatly values learning, training and development as the premise for career progress. All our employees receive wide-ranging cultural values and basic skills training at our company school, Longshan School. We also send senior managers to pursue advanced MBA and EMBA courses. For example, I attended chief executive officer (CEO) training at Cheung Kong Graduate School of Business and the China European International Business School, and will apply for a master's degree at the Lee Kuan Yew School of Public Policy at the National University of Singapore to learn more about Singapore's political system and operations. Our company invests approximately 3 % of revenue in research and development (R&D) to encourage innovation. We often say that Vantone has no one to depend on, so we must rely on ourselves. Vantone's share price has been increasing continuously. One reason may be the significant interest in our new concept, the three-dimensional city. Another reason may be Vantone's solid financial performance indicating a worthwhile investment.

Interviewer Chen: I'm interested in the three-dimensional city concept. Can you talk about the progress of this project?

Feng: The three-dimensional city can be seen as the subversion of the traditional city model, as well as the transformation of a psychological pattern. We have made good progress towards acquiring the land, location and funding, and we are ready to break ground. Meanwhile, we have circulated on the internet our novel describing a love story in a three-dimensional city. A paper edition of the novel was published in March 2011, and it has become very popular and prompted people to imagine life positively in a three-dimensional city.

I personally feel that there are many advantages associated with innovation, including a strong co-operative culture. We work with others to create something new. They may be bosses from private companies, managers from state-owned companies or foreign companies, or people from different projects, companies and investment institutions. We have two kinds of potential partners: people with high ability, and people with good ethics. People with high ability can make a lot of money, and people with good ethics are willing to give money to others.

Interviewer Chen: You have said 'Vantone is a typical private company that has made many mistakes, as other private companies have.' Can you describe in a few sentences the mistakes private companies often make? What do these mistakes mean to the growth of private companies in China?

Feng: Private enterprises often make different mistakes depending on their development stages. In the early stages, a company grows fast because it makes money easily. However, the ability to make money is totally different from the ability to run a company, and a new company's managers often do not know how to operate a company. Like teenagers in adolescence: their bodies grow quickly but their minds develop slowly. This period represents a socialisation process through which children become adults. Similarly, if a company in this period cannot learn to grow up, it will stay small and won't last long.

Diversification is the second common mistake private companies often make. After the initial success, CEOs often feel overconfident and tend to view their accidental success as being their destiny. They start to take their companies into multiple business fields to achieve lateral development, and eventually fail because they lack the necessary skills to meet challenges from such blind diversification.

The third mistake private companies make is that they rely on political connections for success. Some are even obsessed with power and politics. In Wu Bi's recent book, *Revolution and Business*, the author describes four major institutional changes since the early twentieth century in China. With every institutional change, private enterprises were forced to choose a side, and if they chose the wrong side, they would lose their entire business. In contrast, the stable social institutions in British society, for example, mean that a company needs to concentrate only on markets and products. In China, the relationship with the government must be considered alongside other factors. Therefore, companies have four choices: (1) actively participating in institutional change; (2) cooperating completely with the current institution; (3) gradually fitting into the system; and (4) going abroad to compete in the global market with a stable institution. My sense is that companies that depend on political connections for success in China often fail in a pure market environment.

Another type of mistake is relying too much on the capital market. These companies attempt to gain capital through the launching of their companies on the stock market, and then spend too much time on capital manipulation instead of focusing on the internal management, operation of the company, or on product/service innovation to meet customers' needs.

The Most Cost Effective Organisations Have Good Values

Interviewer Chen: You often mention the importance of 'time and persistence.' Without values that go beyond individual interests, people cannot unite to fight to succeed. These values can help organisations overcome their greatest fears and achieve goals at the lowest cost. What experiences have brought you such an inspiration?

Feng: This inspiration came from my observations and thinking about religious organisations. I like traveling and have been to many Asian, European and Middle Eastern countries, where I witnessed the powers of various religions. First, religious organisations are civilisation's oldest organisations; second, their members receive no salaries but instead contribute money to the organisation; some even sacrifice their lives for its benefit. Third, many religious organisations have their own brands. Compared with Coca Cola's US$4 million annual expenditure on maintaining its brand, isn't it true that religious organisations maintain their brand at the lowest cost?

But how do you explain this? I have a simple answer. Religious organisations rely on values rather than mechanical systems or restrictions in guiding members' behaviours. Management costs decrease dramatically when organisational values have been fully internalised. Vantone's emphasis on integrity and self-discipline are the steps we have taken in this direction.

Interviewer Chen: Can you describe occasions when you encountered situations that presented conflict between personal relationships and business rationality? In retrospect, would you have handled such conflicts differently?

Feng: The real estate industry faces countless ethical challenges, especially in dealing with people who are interested in investing in real estate or land. For example, a private company's CEO, a friend of our senior manager, sent his department manager to negotiate with us about one project. This manager offered a profitable price but asked for a 'kick back.' We were faced with several ethical decisions: first, should we report this unethical request to the CEO? Second, would it be worthwhile to give the 'kick back'? If we gave the kick back, would we benefit? Obviously, giving the kick back went against our ethical code. On the other hand, if we refused, we might offend both the CEO and the manager. After some debate, we decided to sacrifice potential profits, risk offending our friends, and terminate our co-operation.

Another problem we encounter in the real estate industry is that many acquaintances ask for discounts when they purchase properties. Sometimes they control the land, and if you refuse to give them a discount they will deny your land application. Whether to hold to your principles or to compromise to get land is a dilemma we often face. Our choice is to stick to long-term principles by giving up short-term interest. We would rather suffer a loss of profit by sticking to our moral code.

Interviewer Chen: Finally, what are the most important points you would like to convey?

Feng: First, and most important, is the 'be moral and be creative' principle. The second is the 'learn to step back and not fight for your personal interest' principle. Often in the business environment, people like to win, and they will negotiate for many hours just to gain a few dollars. To me, it is not worth the time and energy to win just a few dollars at the expense of a harmonious relationship with a business partner. In contrast, I prefer to compromise financial interest to save time and relationships, because harmonious relationships established in negotiation will benefit our future co-operation. In addition, since I make concessions, I can encourage others to do the same, and that will make doing business easy and enjoyable. We had such experiences when we were raising funds for our three-dimensional city project. It was difficult because investors were experienced negotiators, and they were so good at calculating everything. Many problems occurring during our negotiations really annoyed me. I decided to let others get whatever they asked for, and we reached satisfactory agreements that allowed us to achieve our goal of breaking ground for the project, which is the result I really wanted.

In summary, it is most important to do the right/moral thing, and to learn to step back. Once you follow these guidelines, you can conquer the world.

Commentary

'Being moral and creative' is the first principle that Lun Feng credits for the success and sustainability of Vantone in the real-estate industry in China. While being moral and ethical prevents Vantone from being involved in corruption scandals, this simple commitment also provides the foundation for long-term sustainability. However, sticking with this principle often has negative effects in the short term. In this sense, being creative offers Vantone the possibility of adapting continuously to or creating market demand, which in turn integrates moral leadership to differentiate the company from its competitors.

Innovation has long been argued to be the key to firms' gaining and sustaining competitive advantages (e.g. Lengnick-Hall 1992; Ireland and Webb 2007). Creativity as the foundation allowing innovation to occur in an organisation has also attracted the attention of both scholars and practitioners in recent decades (e.g. Amabile 1998; Grant 2013). Particularly in the Chinese context, creativity and innovation are popular in terms of business models and strategy renewal (Zhang and Zhou 2015), which are considered to be important ways for Chinese indigenous private firms to gain a significant part of the market share, against their opponents, state-owned enterprises (SOEs) and foreign multinationals. Van Kleef and Romme (2007) argue for capability development to foster a company's competence to innovate in more sustainable ways, since business has shifted its focus from competitiveness to sustainability. The ecological and innovative design of Vantone in its real estate business is one example connecting innovation with sustainable management. On the other hand, a phenomenon in China's real estate and related industries is the high degree of corruption. Being moral and ethical has been particularly important for the sustainability of the firm's management and survival in the long run. A new paradigm of humanistic management emphasizing ethical treatment of all the stakeholders of a firm away from the economic model is another shift in the management field (Melé 2009; Tsui & Jia, 2013).

References

Amabile, T. M. (1998). How to kill creativity. *Harvard Business Review*, (September), 77–87.

Grant, R. M. (2013). Nonaka's 'dynamic theory of knowledge creation' (1994): Reflections and an exploration of the 'ontological dimension.' In G. Von Krogh, H. Takeuchi, K. Kase, & C. G. Canton (Eds.), *Towards organization knowledge: The pioneering work of Ikujiro Nonaka*. London: Palgrave Macmillan.

Ireland, R. D., & Webb, J. W. (2007). Strategic entrepreneurship: Creating competitive advantage through streams of innovation. *Business Horizons, 50*(1), 49–59.

Lengnick-Hall, C. A. (1992). Innovation and competitive advantage: What we know and what we need to learn. *Journal of Management, 18*(2), 399–429.

Melé, D. (2009). Editorial introduction: Towards a more humanistic management. *Journal of Business Ethics, 88*, 413–416.

Tsui, A. S., & Jia, L. D. (2013). Calling for humanistic scholarship in China. *Management and Organization Review , 9*(1): 1–15.

Van Kleef, J. A. G., & Roome, N. J. (2007). Developing capabilities and competence for sustainable business management as innovation: A research agenda. *Journal of Cleaner Production, 15*(1), 38–51.

Vantone (2015a). Vantone Holding. Retrieved December 11, 2015, from http://www.vantone.net/

Vantone (2015b). Annual reports of Vantone Real Estate. Retrieved December 11, 2015, from http://www.vantone.com/investor/index

Worldofceos (2015). Lun Feng. Retrieved March 20, 2015, from http://www.worldofceos.com/article_out.php?AID=601628&page_from=dossiers/lun-feng

Zhang, Y., & Zhou, Y. (2015). *The source of innovation in China: Highly innovative systems*. London: Palgrave Macmillan.

11

Managing with Simplicity, Transparency, System and Responsibility

Interview with Vanke Group Founder and Chairman Shi Wang, and CEO Liang Yu

The interview was conducted by: Xiao-Ping Chen, University of Washington.

Vanke Group[1]

Established in 1984, China Vanke Co. Ltd., is the largest residential property developer in the People's Republic of China (PRC). Vanke annually provides homes for more than 400,000 households, and had a total sales revenue worth 140 billion RMB by the end of 2012. Vanke has focused on major regions such as the Pearl River Delta, Yangtze River Delta and Bohai-Rim region, and now has a business presence in more than 60 cities across China. Since its stock market launch in 1991, the company's revenue and net profit have grown at compound annual rates of 30.2 % and 34.3 %. Forbes identified Vanke as one of the most admired Chinese companies, and as the best Asian company. Internationally renowned media such as *Investor Relations* (now *IR*), *The Asset* and *Asiamoney* (now *GlobalCapital Asia*) have presented the company with awards for 'Best Corporate Governance' and 'Best Investor Relations.'

---

[1] This section is based on information and news from the company website (Vanke 2015), and IACMR's *Chinese Management Insights'* publication on Vanke in April 2013.

© The Author(s) 2017   **239**
A.S. Tsui et al., *Leadership of Chinese Private Enterprises*, Palgrave Studies in Chinese Management, DOI 10.1057/978-1-137-40235-6_11

Vanke, committed to leading China's green movement in the real estate sector, responded actively to China's environmental challenges by minimising its environmental impact on construction and home use. The company developed the National Construction Research Centre in 1999 to research prefabricated (prefab) home building and eco-building technologies. In 2007, it was the first Chinese company to introduce prefab construction (PC), building 50,000 square meters of prefab homes. That number increased twelvefold in 2008 and doubled again in 2010. In 2012, Vanke built 2.7 million sq m of residential homes (20 % of the total) in this industrialised way, in the process saving 360 hectares of forest. Currently, Vanke has built one in every two Green Three-Star homes in China (the highest eco-building standard certificated by the Chinese government). It is committed to building all properties in the industrialized way and in compliance with national green standards implemented since 2015. As a result of its excellent performance in corporate governance and ethics, Vanke has been honoured as one of 'China's Most Respected Companies' eight consecutive times.

Vanke has made diligent efforts during its development to fulfil its social responsibility in the society. In 2008, Vanke donated 124 million RMB to construct public buildings in the areas heavily affected by the Wenchuan earthquake, with 17 technical measures in place to improve the structural safety of the buildings and ensure the highest level of earthquake resistance. In the same year, the Vanke Foundation was established with the approval of the Ministry of Civil Affairs and the State Council. Since then, donations for charity projects have exceeded 59 million RMB, including, in 2011, 17.95 million RMB being provided to finance projects related to the treatment of serious illness among impoverished children, and environmental protection.

Founder and Chairman Shi Wang[2]

Born in 1951, Shi Wang is the founder and chairman of the Vanke Group. Since founding Vanke in 1984, his leadership has shaped its corporate vision, ethics and management strategies. Before beginning his

---

[2] This section is based on IACMR's *Chinese Management Insights'* publication on Vanke in April 2013 with permission, complemented by public information from China.org.cn (2014) and WWF (2015).

entrepreneurial adventure with Vanke in 1984 at the age of 33, Shi Wang completed five years of military duty, was employed as a furnace worker, studied at Lanzhou Jiaotong University, and worked for the Guangzhou Overseas Trade and Economy Commission. He is one of a massive group of officials who became businessmen during the early stages of China's economic reform. Shi Wang made his first profits in the animal fodder business, providing him with a million RMB for further business development. In 1984, he founded the Shenzhen Exhibition Center of Modern Scientific and Education Equipment, the predecessor to China Vanke Co. Ltd.

Mr. Wang was the executive director of the One Foundation and the Shenzhen Mangrove Wetlands Conservation Foundation, China's first public foundation. In 2004, he co-founded the Society of Entrepreneurs & Ecology (SEE), China's largest environmental network of private sector business leaders. In 2010, Wang was named as one of the 25 most influential business leaders in China by the Chinese edition of *Fortune* magazine. He was elected chairman of the China Entrepreneurs Forum in July 2011.

A passionate mountaineer, Wang reached the peak of Mount Everest from the north side in 2003 and the south side in 2010. He is the eleventh person to accomplish '7 + 2'—reaching the Seven Summits in 2004, and the North and South Poles in 2005. His mountaineering experiences inspired his global vision of environmental sustainability. He was invited to join the US Board of the World Wide Fund for Nature (WWF), and the World Economic Forum Global Agenda Council on Governance for Sustainability, focusing on forest conservation, biodiversity and climate change. Shi Wang was a visiting fellow at Harvard University in the USA, and Cambridge University in the UK, specialising in business values and ethics. He also teaches at numerous universities, including Peking University, Columbia University, MIT, HKUST, and the National University of Singapore.

The interview with Mr Shi Wang was joined by Mr Liang Yu, the CEO of Vanke. Born in 1965, Liang Yu joined Vanke in 1990, was appointed general manager in 2001, and is now president and chief operating officer. He also served as vice president of the China Real Estate Association in 2006, and has been chairman of the Vanke Foundation since 2008. China Central Television designated him the 2012 Economic Champion. Mr Yu received a bachelor degree in international economics from Peking University in 1988, and was appointed as a research fellow of the Counselors' Office of the State Council in 2012. In his leisure time he enjoys long-distance running, mountaineering and cycling.

Managing with Simplicity, Transparency, System and Responsibility

Interviewer Chen: Thank you for accepting our invitation to be interviewed, Mr Wang. Could you describe your management philosophy, management style and management concept, and then talk about the experiences in your life that have influenced your philosophy, style and management concept?

Shi Wang (hereafter referred to as Wang): The modern enterprise system is a product of Western culture, religion and civilisation. In running a modern enterprise, my approach is simple—copy and learn. While I have been quite 'local' for most of my life—I did not study abroad, and I was one of the worker/peasant/soldier students—I am very receptive to Western ideas. Besides, I experienced the Cultural Revolution, so Chinese traditional culture has a very limited influence on me, or I can say no influence at all. When I was young I read many masterpieces of Western literature: works of French writers such as Balzac, Hugo and Stendhal; the English writer Dickens; and some Russian writers such as Tolstoy and Dostoyevsky. My initial education about the West was from these literary masterpieces.

Respect Others: Create a Platform for Young People to Shine

Interviewer Chen: Among these books, which were your favourites or impressed you the most?

Wang: From the perspective of personal struggle, it was Stendhal's *The Red and the Black*—Julien's struggling, social climbing, doing everything to get what he wants—impressed me tremendously. From the standpoint of humanist thought, Dickens's *David Copperfield* influenced me the most. My knowledge of capitalism and of the French Revolution came from this book. In terms of personal life experience, I was a soldier, worker, worker/peasant/soldier student, office worker and teacher before I went to Shenzhen. Looking back now, one thing about that experience saddens me: every time I wanted to express myself, I was repressed. As a result, I became a good boy and always tried to behave myself.

When I was an office worker in Guangdong, I was never a minute early to work or a minute late leaving work. This way people could say nothing about me, and I did not stand out in any way. Basically I only needed to spend 10 % of my energy on my work. Ironically, the leader appreciated it this way—he liked me for not being ambitious or individualistic, and not showing off. It was really scary. I thought if I continued in this way, I could already see my whole life clearly: the highest position I could get would be an assistant bureau-level official, and anything above that would not be determined by my effort or ability. What's the point of life then? At the time, studying abroad began to be popular, and I really wanted to go. It so happened that the Special Economic Zone (SEZ) was being established, and I was already married and had a child, so I decided to stay in China and make some money before going abroad. I had a clear idea that if I managed a company and if I was capable, young people working for me would not have to experience what I had as a young man, always being resigned to whatever came my way and compromising. If I managed a company, I would do it according to the humanist concepts and ways of the West. This idea has been very clear in my entire business career, and it still is. I wanted my dream to come true; I was a strong individualist; I was eager to show my capabilities and prove what I could do. One year after I went to Shenzhen, I made some money, and then started my own business, which continues today.

My Ideal Reform Is the Liberation of Humanity

Interviewer Chen: Does that apply to the way you treat your employees and managers?

Wang: I want people to respect me, and I want to use my talents. Similarly, we need to create an environment for young people where they are respected and can use their capabilities. They should not have to repeat what I went through.

This is something Western. The Western model has a very simple logic. The first assumption is that people are evil and need systematic restrictions. For the Oriental modern enterprise, we assume people are good and have no need for restricting systems. If you suspect someone, you don't hire that person, and you work with good people only. In the West, they believe that good people can sometimes be wicked. I often reflect about myself: am I good? Of course I am good. Do I have a wicked side? Unfortunately, I do. Therefore, since I have a wicked side myself, how can I require other people to be 100 % good? This logic is very clear when I run my business.

You asked about my management philosophy. It is quite simple: learning everything from scratch. I have certainly made many mistakes in the process, and quite often I am too idealistic. But my basic principle is respecting people. First, assume that people are ugly and need system restrictions; second, practice transparent management; and third, adhere to norms of ethics. If I take bribes, how can I possibly maintain my dignity? Obviously making money should not be the only purpose. I think the biggest problem we have in China today is that making money has become the one and only purpose, to such an extent that any mean tricks can be employed. Idealism is completely out of the window. Surprisingly, I have found that others find these principles unacceptable. They say, 'You don't give or take bribes? Not possible.' I don't give or take bribes, and I forbid the company to do so. This is our corporate culture. It cannot be that the boss does not give or take bribes but allows his people to do it. Believe it or not, that's what we do, and it is easy to prove. Vanke has a history dating back 30 years. Even one case of bribery in our history would ruin our credibility and reputation.

Simple Management, No Nepotism

Wang: I went to Shenzhen in 1983, accumulated some capital, and established Vanke in 1984. From 1983 to 1999, about 15 years, I basically did everything myself, big or small. But then I became very vigilant about an issue. You know, under the influence of Oriental culture, quite often leaders and family enterprises distrust other people and employ only those connected with them by blood, geography, history as classmates, and so on. I have no relatives or friends working in Vanke. I have eight siblings, but they do not work for Vanke. No employees are linked to me, directly or indirectly, not even my university fellow students or army comrades.

Interviewer Chen: Have they ever approached you?

Wang: Yes. But I have also been firm about another principle. Before I started the business, goods such as flared trousers, video recorders and sunglasses were easy to get in the South of China as it is close to Hong Kong and Macau. But I refused to buy anything for my relatives, not because I did not want to spend the money but because I have eight siblings; if I bought things for one, I would offend all the others; and if I wanted to buy for all of them, I could not get the same price or model and it would be seen as unfair. Even if they gave me money and asked me to buy for them, I would not do it. If I did not buy for anyone, I could not offend anyone. I have held that principle in managing a company. I refuse requests from everyone, and gradually they get used to it and don't ask again, including university classmates. Of course, they are angry, but that is just temporary. In China, we have an unwritten rule: that is, 'criminal law does not apply to senior officials,' meaning systems and rules apply only to people under you, not those above you. I want to behave in the opposite way—harsh to the top and lenient to the subordinates. If all bosses could be like this, that principle would naturally become systematic. And it is similar to the principle of no bribery. When an official knows that you don't use bribes, he won't ask again. An interesting incident occurred when I was in Shenzhen. I heard that a deputy mayor in charge of real estate was being prosecuted. I could not believe it because to me he seemed quite honest and helped me to get things done as soon as I asked him, without asking for a bribe. So I thought he was upright. Actually he did take bribes, but not from me, and I became an umbrella for him. Everybody knows Wang Shi does not bribe. If the deputy mayor did business with me, he thought that would prove that he was clean.

The same occurred with the mayor of Shenzhen two or three years ago. He also took bribes and I did not believe it either. When I called, he helped me. I did not even have to buy him dinner. But he did take bribes from other people.

Transparent Management: Only One Accounting Book

Interviewer Chen: It is easy for you as you have the Vanke brand. But at the beginning, you were on the same footing as everybody else; how did you survive then without bribing?

Wang: When I started the business, the planned economy still dominated the country. Only Shenzhen had implemented a market economy. Anyone who went there would find that only trading or importing/exporting businesses were profitable. I chose to sell corn. I was quite puzzled about how to transport corn to Shenzhen and then to the feed plants. The answer was in a railway carriage, but we didn't have any carriages. Someone suggested I should use a red envelope of bribe money to get the carriage, but instead, I brought two cartons of cigarettes as a gift.

Whether a gift is a bribe or not depends on the amount of money and the purpose of the gift. If your purpose is to obtain extra commercial interests, it is bribery. Obviously, I was giving cigarettes to get two railway carriages, so it was technically bribery. But ironically, my gift was rejected. The guy just smiled at me, declined the cigarettes, and offered me the two carriages. I was confused: you don't accept the cigarettes but you agree to give me the carriages? He explained that he had noticed that I was carrying corn with a group of labourers. One sack of corn was 150 kg, so he thought I was hardworking and tough. I was dressed like someone from the city, handsome, but willing to carry heavy sacks, so he wanted to help me. Before I left, he asked whether I knew the market rate of bribery. I answered no. He told me a red envelope of 400 RMB was necessary for two planned carriages. I was too far from the market rate with my gift of 20 RMB.

We can use Maslow's hierarchy of needs theory to explain this case simply; he needed nothing material from me. He was touched by my behaviour and wanted to help without asking for anything in return. But what he did also did not affect his other money-power trade, that is, 2000 RMB for 10 carriages. The key is the behaviour you demonstrate to them. If people see that you are honest, they will treat you honestly. Actually, I made mistakes throughout those years, but most people appreciated how we gradually shaped the Vanke style, formed our own competitiveness, and made management simple. If you give or take bribes, you must think about how to cook the books, how to maintain two sets of accounting records, and it becomes very complicated. Vanke has only one set of accounting books. Besides, we never evade taxes. Paying tax just means that I make a little less money, but why should I live in fear trying to hide things? If I were dishonest, I could be ruined if any accounting people decided to inform against me.

Quite simply, our accounting does not accommodate bribery. If you try to disguise payments, you must find excuses for expenditures, such as through entertainment, but Vanke's financial system forbids this. Besides, if anything happens in the market, I will bear the brunt. In the real estate industry, bribes in tens of millions of dollars are common. My first-line managers do not bribe because they cannot balance the books, unlike some companies that can disguise payments. Vanke is present in 50 cities where, occasionally, mayors get caught in bribery. We have normally been among the top two companies operating locally for more than a decade, so we automatically become suspects. How can Vanke be clean? But investigations always show that we are innocent.

Take up Mountain Climbing; Run Vanke by Corporate Culture and Teamwork

Interviewer Chen: You said that from 1983 to 1999 you were very hands-on and on top of everything. What happened after that? How did your role change?

Wang: First, I noticed that many CEOs tended to have problems when they approached retirement, so I decided to leave Vanke when I became fifty-something. But I did not say I was retiring. I was actually 46, and it was in 1997. I wanted to send two messages to the employees: Vanke could do well without me, and I could leave Vanke for a bigger platform to better use my talents.

I hoped the team system and the corporate culture, rather than a certain individual, would run Vanke. I believed that Vanke could sustain itself by relying on the system, so I thought of leaving the CEO position. But I did not do it until 1999, at which time I stepped aside completely.

Interviewer Chen: Do you still feel connected? I remember when Bill Gates quit: Steve Ballmer was CEO, but Gates just could not be hands-off, so he still attended and spoke up at every meeting, and the two had fights. Did you have that kind of struggle?

Wang: I went through a painful time, but I overcame it within a month. Remember, I stepped aside voluntarily. But the day after I made the announcement, I felt ... Well, I slept well in the evening, but the next day when I went to work, nobody was in the office. I was told that they were having the General Meeting. I asked why I was not informed. Then I realised that I was no longer CEO. I had the urge to go to the meeting, but I suppressed it, fidgeting all the while.

The first month is critical. You either pass or you fail. But what should I do next? I knew it would be hard to stay in the company. So I decided to go and climb mountains.

Interviewer Chen: From what I know, you were probably the first or among the first Chinese enterprise founders to introduce a professional management system, especially among real estate companies. You have a unique way, and you insist on *not* being the majority owner of Vanke. Why?

Wang: System and teamwork are the fundamentals of Western management. We Chinese like to adopt the best parts of Western ideas while still basing our operations on Chinese theories, critically absorbing the good part. To me it is simple, I just copy and use.

Interviewer Chen: In addition to the professional manager system, have you introduced other unique management practices?

Wang: The team is responsible for specific management practices. I will let Liang Yu answer this question.

Yu: We have introduced many management practices, such as performance appraisal, the balanced scorecard, which at first was very helpful but after a while we saw problems. For example, the process is too tedious, and puts too much stress on KPIs (key performance indicators). Management thought is too 'ceremonial.' When we act, we consider four aspects—elements of the balanced scorecard. But after a time, it seems we are only accountable for the process, or for a certain indicator. For example, one indicator of information submission is the quantity of information submitted by subsidiaries. But this is an inaccurate indicator, as they may skip critical information that should be reported. So later I simplified the process with constant modification and improvement.

Managing with Simplicity and Transparency

Interviewer Chen: Well said. Wang Shi, you once said, 'Simple rather than complicated, transparent rather than opaque, rules/norms rather than tricks, responsible rather than indulgent.' How does Vanke's management team implement these philosophies?

Yu: The most important is 'simple rather than complicated,' meaning simple personal relationships. My boss has no classmates or close friends working in Vanke. Neither do I. This way we have simple personal relationships. If two employees get married to each other, one must leave. It may not be fair or reasonable to our friends or relatives, but it is fair to our employees. For example, I bought an apartment for my parents within our apartment complex. Nobody ever came to visit them during the Chinese New Year because they know that I forbid that.

Another important guideline is a simple way of working. For example, an employee has no need to second-guess what the manager wants. The only important thing is to do the job well.

Interviewer Chen: But aren't personal relationships and family the most distinct characteristics of Chinese culture?

Wang: In this respect, Vanke is more stringent than many multinational enterprises. In Vanke's early days, people often knocked at my door, either to seek help or to build a relationship. I knew what they wanted, so I did not open the door. I said 'You did not let me know beforehand, so I will not let you in. If I went to visit you without telling you first, would you agree even if it seemed it was just a social visit? So I think I am being fair.' After trying twice, he would not come again.

Interviewer Chen: So that is 'simple rather than complicated.' What about 'transparent rather than opaque'?

Yu: Nothing is better than transparency for solving problems, as a system cannot be exhaustive. How can we best make judgements? Open discussion is perhaps the best way. Transparency requires norms. With transparency you cannot hide anything. Therefore, sometimes you can just make a simple judgement; that is, are you doing something that could be openly discussed. For example, you would not tell people that you take gifts home, so do not do it.

Interviewer Chen: Wonderful. What about 'norms rather than tricks'? That seems hard to implement in private companies in China.

Yu: We are very Westernised in that respect. One thing is very clear; Vanke definitely would not ask employees to sacrifice their self-interest for the interests of the company. We make it very clear that if you spend 100,000 RMB to save the company taxes of 10 million RMB, and the 100,000 RMB ruins your future, the company will not protect you even if it has gained 10 million RMB, as you have harmed both the company and yourself.

Customers Are Partners; Employees Are Assets

Interviewer Chen: I would like to ask about your company's core values. I heard that you have printed the four core values on the back of every employee's card: 'Customers are always our partners; employees are the assets of Vanke; a sunlit system; sustainable growth.' It can be said that these values are deeply rooted among the employees. How were these values formed? What role have these values played in Vanke's growth? What specific effects do these values have on employees?

Yu: We can grow only by satisfying the needs of customers. Among all of Vanke's appraisal indicators, only one is linked to all employees: customer satisfaction. As early as the year 2000, we engaged Gallup to conduct a customer satisfaction survey. You may sell housing this year and make money, but if you fail to provide good service, you hurt your future customers. In the process, we have come to understand more about our customers. In the beginning, good products were enough; now there must be good service and good neighbours. We have a good neighbour measure in the satisfaction survey. We can check how many other homeowners a homeowner knows, how many friends they have among the other homeowners. Caring neighbours are the key to harmonious communities. We need not only acquaintances but also friends. Our data show that every homeowner has 12 friends on average, someone close enough you can ask to look out for you when nobody is at home.

If homeowners have fewer than 12 friends in a certain apartment complex, we ask the property manager to organise events to connect and facilitate communication among these homeowners. The results of the survey are linked to bonuses; both the four best companies and the bottom four must file reports with me regarding specific growth and rectification goals, and implementation actions.

Interviewer Chen: That is to say, the most important appraisal indicator is to cultivate good neighbours in the housing estates.

Yu: Eventually it will be reflected in customer satisfaction and loyalty, and customer loyalty will affect people in choosing whether to buy our houses or recommend our houses to others. We identify different needs of homeowners based on phases: those who have just bought the apartment; those who have just moved in; and those who have lived there for more than three years. One of Vanke's management approaches is to identify weaknesses. We can do that through surveys and rectification. This is built into the work plan throughout the group and is linked to employees' bonuses.

The 'Sunlit System'

Interviewer Chen: How about the 'sunlit system'?

Yu: The 'sunlit system' is actually a norm that guides our direction. Our Sunshine Declaration must be signed. We tell people about the website, how to file complaints, a hotline for tip-offs, to contact personnel, etc. We have this arrangement so that every agreement must be signed, making it convenient for everybody. All new employees, as well as suppliers and co-operation partners need to sign the Sunshine Declaration, because in that way, we can pass our cultural values on to them. We also hold a supplier conference to talk about this. Our first agenda item in the conference is not to introduce senior management, but rather to tell them where the fire escape is. Safety first. Then we start the normal agenda and definitely talk about our expectations concerning the honest operation that contributes to our win—win situation.

Interviewer Chen: Wonderful. The last one is 'sustainable growth.'

Yu: Sustainable growth is our goal. Quite often people want to overtake us. We are fine with that. It is really difficult to stay in the No.1 position for a long time. It is tough, and is not important. I say we are not No. 1 in every field, but we do want it to be an industry leader.

Balance Business Rational and Interpersonal Relationships

Interviewer Chen: One more question for Wang Shi. In all these years you must have encountered conflicts between interpersonal relationships and business. You mentioned that you made it clear that none of your friends or relatives can work in Vanke.

Wang: I'll give you an example. I left Vanke (I won't elaborate on the reason) for one year and came back, only to find that my cousin was working there. She had graduated from Jilin University, majoring in international finance. While I was away my mother had managed to get her a job at Vanke. After I returned, I let her go, but leveraged my social connections to get her another job. That was at the beginning of the 1990s, and it was easy at that time to find a job with a degree in international finance from Jilin University.

Interviewer Chen: So your mother was not that upset?

Wang: Of course, she was very angry. She said, 'Don't you need talent? Hasn't your cousin got talent? Jilin University is a great school, and the major in international finance is good too. She worked in the personnel department, and people have made good comments about her.' I said, 'Yes, right, but I have two assumptions: she has talent, or she does not have talent, as I cannot say all the graduates of Jilin University are talented. Of course, let us assume she is talented, then it would be easy for her to find a job. Why must she work in her cousin's company? If she has to do that, that means she is not talented, and she will discredit me.' My mother was not happy for a while, and then we moved on. No big deal.

Interviewer Chen: So basically, to you, business supersedes everything else.

Wang: Of course, that is my principle. The logic is clear: she is the cousin of the chairman and the founder, how would people be able to work with her? It would definitely be inconvenient.

Actually sometimes it is quite painful handling internal issues, which is one of the greatest challenges in running an enterprise. We've got talented people from everywhere. They all think they are the best and cannot work with each other. For example, we recruited two people: one was appointed as the executive vice general manager, and the other as the sales manager. Vanke was a trading company then, and those were very important positions. But the veteran employees did not like this arrangement. They asked a vice general manager to talk to me about their objections. So I talked to the two new appointees, but they said 'Since you hired us, you cannot listen to the older employees any more. Like it or not, they will have to accept it.' I was stuck in the middle.

I mediated between the two sides. The two newcomers made it very clear that either they or the veteran employees had to leave. The veterans said that although they did not like the new arrangement, they would accept it if I insisted. After a lot of thinking, I made the painful choice. The veteran employees were willing to compromise, but the newcomers were intransigent, so I chose to let the two of them go.

This case taught me that I could not recruit new people from outside. 'Airborne troops' would not work. Talent must be trained internally. For example, people such as Liang Yu have been working in Vanke since they graduated from university. Quite often I also wanted to bring in some new employees, such as from multinational companies, but it did not work out. When internal people feel they have no hope of climbing higher, it is difficult to maintain the impetus for trying. China has few successful stories about using 'airborne troops.' Vanke has experienced a long development process and has its own reserve of talent for both business and management.

A Talent Reserve Is the Cornerstone for Vanke's Sustainable Growth

Interviewer Chen: Regarding the nurturing of talent, does Vanke have a solid talent reserve now?

Wang: We are doing a terrific job in this respect. Vanke has some turnover, you know, including senior managers.

Yu: The main reason for our turnover is that people want to start up their own businesses. Nowadays the environment is ideal for new start-ups. By leaving Vanke they can realise financial freedom that they could not get if they stayed with the company. So they give it a go. Another reason is room for growth. Vanke is a mature company. We have many vice presidents and only one president. On the other hand, just before being listed, some small companies try to hire our people as presidents after consultants suggest that they hire people from professional companies to improve their stock price.

Many people are concerned about our turnover, but our performance remains good, and we can fill vacancies in one day. We have many capable people waiting to be promoted, and we can also continue to train our own talent.

Interviewer Chen: Time is running out… Finally, regarding starting and managing a business, can you summarise what you think are the most important aspects to share with others?

Wang: With respect to starting a business—first, the most important thing is to hold on to your integrity bottom line. Of course, I did not expect that this bottom line would eventually become advantageous. Second, in running a business, you should follow the fundamentals of Western management theories; that is, practise the basic ideas that business schools are teaching, such as sustainable development, ethics and transparency, and yes, social responsibility. In short: simplicity, no tricks, following rules, and assuming responsibility. Just these four points. Managing Chinese enterprises is very tough. You can reap rewards as long as you follow the rules, but you must be very patient and clear-minded. Many people ask me what methods Vanke adopted for success. I reply that rather than following methods, we are just idealistic. Vanke provides young people with a platform for realising their talents. This is actually Vanke's idealistic pursuit.

Commentary

In China's real estate industry, where bribery was perceived as the 'norm', Vanke has insisted on integrity in operating its business and has won its position in the market through its professionalism and Westernised management systems. It is evident that Mr Wang and Mr Yu are both strong believers and practitioners of Western management philosophy, which emphasises simplicity and transparency. They are determined to stick to the fundamental values of business practices that are contradictory to the basic cultural values of Chinese society, such as *renqing*, *mianzi* and *guanxi* (Chen et al. 2013). It is quite interesting that, unlike other business leaders interviewed for this book, Mr Wang and Mr Yu do not hold dualistic views about the Western and Chinese management philosophies, nor do they try to integrate them or embrace each depending on the situations that arise. They simply believe that Western professionalism is what can make a company sustainable; and the success of Vanke seems to support their belief.

For Mr Wang, the principle of business foundation is the liberation of humanity as the initial motive for his entrepreneurial actions. Since creativity is the foundation for organisational innovation (Amabile 1998), releasing humanity may provide the base to allow creativity and innovation to occur in organisations and business. Thus, potentially a human-based management such as humanist management rather than an 'economic-man' model could be the basis for long-term sustainability management (Melé 2009).

References

Amabile, T. M. (1998). How to kill creativity. *Harvard Business Review*, (September), 77–87.

Chen, C. C., Chen, X.-P., & Huang, S. (2013). Chinese *Guanxi*: An integrative review and new directions for future research. *Management and Organization Review, 9*(1), 167–207.

China.org.cn (2014). Wang Shi. Retrieved March 20, 2015, from http://wiki.china.org.cn/wiki/index.php/Wang_Shi

Melé, D. (2009). Editorial introduction: Towards a more humanistic management. *Journal of Business Ethics, 88*, 413–416.

Vanke. (2015). China Vanke Co. Ltd. Retrieved March 22, 2015, from http://www.vanke.com/en/

WWF (World Wildlife Fund). (2015). Wang Shi. Retrieved March 22, 2015, from https://www.worldwildlife.org/leaders/wang-shi#close

12

Providing the Best Products, Treating Employees Well, and Working for the Public Good

Interview with Tecsun Homes Founder and Director Shengzhe Nie

The interview was conducted by: Qing Qu, Tsinghua University, and Pingping Fu, The Chinese University of Hong Kong.

Tecsun Homes Co. Ltd.[1]

Tecsun was established in 1992, and registered as a wholly-owned subsidiary of Federal Tecsun, Inc. of the United States in 1997 in the Suzhou Industrial Park (SIP). The company specialises in research, development, design and manufacture of American-style modern wood and steel homes. Tecsun (Suzhou) Homes Co. Ltd. is one of the most talked-about enterprises in China for its value-based management and sustainable human resources (HR) management. The Tecsun Employee Code of Conduct (the 'Code'), spelling out the company's rules and regulations, has been hailed as the 'Management Bible for Chinese enterprises.' Before its third edition was published in 2013, a half-million copies had been sold and it had undergone 28 printings.

---

[1] This section is based on information and news from the company website (Tecsun 2015), and IACMR's *Chinese Management Insights'* publication on Tecsun in June 2014.

© The Author(s) 2017   **257**
A.S. Tsui et al., *Leadership of Chinese Private Enterprises*, Palgrave Studies in Chinese Management, DOI 10.1057/978-1-137-40235-6_12

In 1998, Tecsun joined the National Association of Home Builders of America, and it became the first Chinese builder to named member. In 2003, the Chinese local government's Jiangsu Science and Technology Office labelled Tecsun as a 'Jiangsu New and High Technology Enterprise', and it received certifications of quality control (ISO 9001: 2000) and environmental management (ISO 14001: 1996). In the following years, Tecsun continued with research and development (R&D) and achieved further quality certifications. Its villa construction projects won several national and provincial awards for their ecology and quality.

Tecsun holds 70 % of the market share and has annual sales of about 400–500 million RMB (about US$25,000,000–US$31,000,000). By 2014, Tecsun had fixed assets of 200 million RMB, manufacturing and operations facilities in Suzhou, and a new manufacturing and R&D base, 'Tecsun Kunshan Park', was under construction.

In 2005, the Tecsun Value Manual 'Tecsun Staff Regulations' (the 'Code' book) was published and launched on the Chinese national market. It conveys Tecsun's management experiences and practices. The company states its core values as 'honesty, diligence, care, no shortcuts.' These core values have inspired the company's many unique rules, as expressed in the 'Code' book. The Appendix lists the ten cardinal rules in the 'Code' book, which contains rules for different aspects of the employment relationship with the company. Tecsun puts an emphasis on training, especially with technical professionals, considering it as one of the critical success factors in the company's strategy. Every year the company sponsors training trips for the management team and key technicians to the USA, Canada and Finland, with the purpose of learning about high quality service and products.

Tecsun also contributes widely to society. In 2003, the company donated funds to the Tecsun–Luban (Xiuning) Technical School of Carpentry. In 2004, Tongji University's Tecsun Institute of Housing Technology was founded. In 2005, Tecsun (Xiuning) Primary School was founded, to serve students from poor families, with a donation from Tecsun, which provides the pupils with free clothing, meals, living quarters, transportation and tuition. By the end of 2014, Tecsun had donated more than 60 million RMB to different charity foundations, for the poor, for schools and for cultural projects, to aid the development of China's Western region.

Founder and Director Shengzhe Nie[2]

Shengzhe Nie is the founder of Tecsun. Born in 1965 in Xiuning, Anhui province, he received his bachelor's degree in Chemistry from Sichuan University in 1985, and later studied in the USA. In addition to being the chief executive officer (CEO) of Tecsun, Nie also participates actively in education as an adjunct professor and executive director of research for several higher educational institutions. He is a deputy executive member of the Committee of Wood Framed Buildings at The Architectural Society of China, editor of the magazine *The Chinese Art*, and associate editor of *Cross Media Studies*. Nie's publications include plays, poems, critiques, books, short novels and hundreds of research papers. He has also participated in making movies, TV series and dramas.

Nie's management philosophy can best be summarised in the following bons mots:

- Without pride, one cannot perform well; without glory, one cannot be self-confident; without self-dignity, one cannot be responsible!
- Tecsun will always be a just, noble and conscientious company. Rather than give in to evil to survive, Tecsun would close down!
- Chinese traditional culture has always revered the educated and disdained the uneducated. I hope we can abolish that perception and learn to respect labour.
- People who fail to follow rules are unreliable! Nations that fail to follow rules are unreliable!
- Swiss watches have lifelong warranties because they never break down. The world needs many enterprises like Swiss watchmakers, with products that may be small but are of supreme quality, for the market's long-term peace and stability.

---

[2] This section is based on IACMR's *Chinese Management Insights'* publication on Tecsun in June 2014 with permission, complemented by public information from Baidu (2015).

Tecsun's Responsibility: Providing the Best Products, Treating Employees Well, and Working for the Public Good

Interviewers Qu and Fu: We would like to know about your management philosophy, your management style, and the perspective you adopt when thinking about management issues.

Shengzhe Nie (hereafter Nie): It is both simple and complex to accomplish things within the Han culture in China. We talk daily about enterprises and entrepreneurs, but entrepreneurs and businessmen are distinctly different. Arthur Schopenhauer (1788–1860, German philosopher) said that business is the lubricant of human civilisation, built on high-quality commodities. Many so-called entrepreneurs in China, particularly real estate developers, are totally unable to play such a role in an industrial civilisation. They do not contribute to civilisation because they do not produce the high-quality products that civilisation needs. Does China have entrepreneurs who produce high-quality commodities? Yes, Lu Guanqiu[3] is one. He started early in 1969 making agricultural machinery parts, later becoming a key supplier for Mercedes Benz and BMW, and today manufactures hybrid vehicles. Kazuo Inamori (Japanese entrepreneur, known as the 'business saint' in Japan) is a relatively conservative and traditional entrepreneur. His most famous quote is that profits without sweat cannot count as profits. Although this statement reflects a misunderstanding of finance, his point is thought-provoking. Without the experience of setting up and managing Kyocera, he could not have successfully rescued Japan Airlines. He knows how to do everything well with high standards.

Interviewer Qu: To which standards are you referring?

Nie: It is actually very simple. All buildings should have no water, rain or wind leakage as basic construction requirements. If China's

---

[3] Lu Guanqiu (1948–), founder and chairman of the board of directors of the Wanxiang Group, is one of the most well-known entrepreneurs in China. He is praised as 'the evergreen tree of the Business World.'

manufacturing industry lacks a good foundation, other industries will fail. I feel that our nation should follow a development path in which 'Made in China' becomes 'Meticulously Made in China' and finally 'Created in China.' 'Meticulously Made in China' is an indispensable step. A company in Japan has only around 40 employees but has an output worth more than US$2 billion by producing all the dust bearings in the world. Similarly, in the motor-car and high-speed-rail industries, once the manufacturer puts on a screw cap, say, it should not come off without the use of a special device to remove it. This is what I mean by 'meticulous' making.

If China's construction industry fails to create and adhere to basic standards, our houses will not last long, and eventually we shall have to demolish them and dispose of them as trash. So you ask, what are the responsibilities of entrepreneurs? The first is to give the best products to customers. Customers choose you and your products because they trust you. Therefore, the first and most important responsibility is to give them the best products. Without that, other responsibilities are basically empty talk.

The second responsibility is to treat employees well. Employees have chosen to work for a company in the hope that they can be happy and grow there.

So I believe that entrepreneurs have these three social responsibilities. After fulfilling the first two responsibilities, if entrepreneurs still have financial resources left, they can invest in public undertakings. However, if companies fail to do the first two well, they will only hurt society more by investing in those public undertakings.

China has generated the second-largest gross domestic product (GDP) in the world because the country has 1.3 billion people. As the economy has grown, people have become carried away and have neglected to take the indispensable steps needed to develop from *Made in China* to *Meticulously Made in China* to *Created in China*. China's overall business environment has problems, including in the enterprise environment and supply chain. Our standards are that we must strive first of all to provide high-quality products at reasonable prices.

The World Needs Many Enterprises like Swiss Watchmakers

Interviewer Qu: Did your previous experiences and exposures contribute to the development of your management thoughts?

Nie: I think so. For example, I compared my (Chinese) Zhongshan watch that cost 38 RMB to Shanghai's Baoshihua watch and to a Swiss watch. When you see that the Swiss watch offers a lifelong warranty, you realise that it is because Swiss watches do not require repairs. Then you further realise that Swiss watchmakers work for small companies that have changed little for 100 years. That observation made me aware that the world needs level-headed people.

We lack the craftsman's mind and spirit. The more some real estate companies grow, the more harm they will do. While they provide temporary housing, they leave construction waste in their wake. In 1994, some at the Frankfurt World Construction Conference expressed concern about how the future will handle China's construction wastes, knowing that China's buildings will be future trash. Of course, some companies are attempting to learn how to recycle and dispose of such rubbish. Do some entrepreneurs behave responsibly? Yes. Lu Guanqiu is one. He avoids the media and stays out of sight. Some Chinese enterprises conscientiously make outstanding products. More than 10 years ago, I said that the internet was important because it has been built on the foundation of a well-developed manufacturing industry. The parasitic service industry is totally meaningless without the manufacturing industry.

Our Chinese culture grants social status to people who give orders but do no physical work, believing that 'those who work with their brains rule and those who work with their hands are ruled.' If we fail to change that mindset, then China's manufacturing industry has no future, let alone a future for meticulous manufacturing. People should be equal despite their positions, jobs or professions.

Articles of Association: The Basis of a Company

Interviewer Qu: Can you share the source of the thoughts and specific rules in the Code? Did you borrow from your own experiences at home or abroad?

Nie: Tecsun is a management experimental field for transforming Chinese culture. I wrote every word of the Tecsun Employee Code of Conduct. I did not borrow specific clauses from other companies such as GE (General Electric) or Boeing, but I did some cultural benchmarking. For example, places such as Hong Kong influenced me in terms of behavioural norms and people's restriction of their own rights. I also included many of my own reflections. For example, when you have rights, you must first consider what you cannot do rather than what you can do. These are Western legal concepts. I gather observations that align with human civilisation and summarise them as provisions in the Articles of Association, which are the basis of our company. For example, we stipulate there that the board of directors should not modify the rules on power restriction. If the board proclaims 'quality is not negotiable,' they are indicating that the company would be dissolved if we failed to achieve quality. This differs from our penalty provisions, which are specific rules based on the company's foundation; that is, the Articles of Association.

People need knowledge, experience and common sense. If you lack knowledge, you must have experience; if you lack both knowledge and experience, you need common sense. It would be detrimental if Tecsun regarded power as being paramount.

Profit Exceeding 25 % Is Exorbitant and Represents Disrespect for Consumers

Interviewer Fu: How has Tecsun built its competitive advantages? Have you changed your positioning as the company has progressed through the developmental phases?

Nie: This is similar to your first question about entrepreneurial responsibilities. How do we deliver the best products to our customers? Technical and service guarantees are most critical. Technical guarantee means that we continually conduct research and development (R&D). Over the past 15 years, we have raised our average price only once, by about 14 %. At the same time, the price of the principal material of electric wire, copper, has risen several dozen times. We have kept our prices low because our R&D efforts absorbed much of the cost. Furthermore, we persist in delivering the best quality housing. Our housing construction cost is about 80 % of the renovation cost of a locally built house under the same standards. Our price includes a large refrigerator, washer, dryer, white furniture, air-conditioning, lights and sanitary appliances, all ready to move into apart from a bed and bedding. You can imagine how competitive we are! Our quality is twice as good and our price is about 30 % cheaper, so nobody has the guts to say they can compete with us.

Interviewer Qu: Some 20 % or 15 % lower would be good enough. Why do you go as low as 30 %?

Nie: Because our profits are already 15 %–20 %. We believe that once profit exceeds 25 %, it is exorbitant and indicates disrespect for consumers. If our profits drop below 15 %, we shall increase prices because, with profits that low, any managerial negligence could cause loss. We think the best profit range is our current 15 %–20 % level.

Help Employees Complete with Dignity Their Last Task in Life: Death

Interviewer Fu: Tecsun is stable in the wooden villa market, and you are also involved in education and trading in construction materials. Do you have plans for future growth? Do you have an idea of Tecsun's future in 20 years or even 50 years time? Or is Tecsun just an experiment in which nature will take its course?

Nie: I have a realistic, basic requirement: Tecsun will not close down for at least 10 years after I die. Why 10 years? I want people who have gone through thick and thin with me to live well. We have a reserved pension fund, and I plan to increase it to 1–2 billion RMB during my lifetime. I cannot let my company grow too big. I must limit the number of people for whom I assume responsibility. If I had 4000 to 10,000 employees, I could not afford to be responsible for them all. The world has many poor people, but I will first help those I know. My employees are close to me, so I will provide for their old age. I am the boss of Tecsun, and I must solve Tecsun's issues. I have created a two-committee system; both committees are on the same level. The pension committee can invest only 50 % of the pension fund; and the management committee ensures that the other 50 % remains in the account.

We have another rule regarding headcount increases after my death. Tecsun can hire one employee only to replace another. Otherwise, people would rush to join Tecsun to enjoy our benefits. The total number of our employees cannot be changed; otherwise people will bring their townsmen to join the company after I die, and they will quickly bleed the company dry. I know human nature well.

I just care about my employees. They are my fellow workers, and I must help them to complete with dignity their last task in life, the task of dying. How we can leave this world happily, without regret.

Interviewer Fu: The last time an employee was sick, you vowed to save him even if you had to auction off the company.

Nie: For many years, the Chinese have treated the less privileged with indifference, which is the result of influence from the dross culture. This is terrible. I told our employees that if they suffer from kidney failure, I can donate one kidney. Of course I cannot donate two kidneys, as I cannot die to save them, but I have no use for one kidney anyway; it will rot after I die. We must say what we really think, so people will feel we are trustworthy and equal. For this employee you mentioned, we spent over 6 million RMB to treat him, because 95 % of his body was burned.

As a matter of principle, though the employees are not owners, I care about their existence; we have the same rights to life and survival. It is difficult to convince my family that it is right to pass a huge fortune to my employees rather than to my children. I asked them if they knew anything about the descendants of Zhu Yuanzhang.[4] No matter how great and powerful an individual may be, their descendants become prodigal after three or four generations and have little relationship to you anyway. My family supports me 100 %. In fact, if people around you are happy, they will return their happiness to you.

Interviewer Fu: Apparently Western culture strongly influences Tecsun's management style. Tecsun has Thanksgiving, Christmas holidays and appeals hearings, which are very Western style, but then they are distinctly Chinese in character. The West has no equivalent to your Tecsun employee code of conduct.

---

[4]Zhu Yuanzhang was the first emperor of the Ming Dynasty (1328–1398). Though born into a poor family, he remained in power for 30 years.

Nie: No, there is none. This year is the 40th anniversary of the establishment of diplomatic relations between China and Malaysia. The Tecsun Employee Code of Conduct is being translated into Malaysian. A Malaysian professor who understands the Chinese language proposed that when Malaysia's Prime Minister Najib visits China, Premier Li Keqiang will give him the Malaysian version of the Code. I don't think that US enterprises need this kind of Code of Conduct because Americans have already learned such behavioural norms from their families and through their education, from primary school to university. US employees are grateful when I present Christmas bonus cheques of $200 or $500 at our headquarters, but seem to doubt whether they deserve the money. But in China, people take it for granted, which reflects the cultural difference. I cannot turn China into the United States. I just want a guideline on how to build a good company. I never expected that the Code would be so popular and sell so well. We already have an English version, and now we will even have a Malaysian version.

The Tecsun Employee Code of Conduct Originates from the In-depth Analysis of Human Nature

Nie: Actually the Code is an outcome of in-depth analysis of both human nature and Chinese culture, which is based on my understanding of the Western civilisation, which includes the rule of law through Christianity and Catholicism, but not the religion itself. God is watching us, so we cannot lie or be envious. Why does the Bible advise so strongly against jealousy and lying? It is because they are two biggest scourges to human beings. You can see that jealousy poisons human civilisation and is terrible with or without power. After I analysed those observations, including their effects on bureaucracy, I wrote the Employee Code of Conduct according to Chinese characteristics.

Interviewer Qu: Have any Western principles guided the Code?

Nie: Scholars once proposed 'universal values', but the Code presents behavioural norms. Applying universal values to develop behavioural norms makes them universally acceptable. I think honesty, diligence, care and no shortcuts are the most important values.

Interviewer Qu: Do you think China's traditional cultural teachings from the Four Books and the Five Classics have value in modern business and social management?

Nie: No, not much. The wheat and chaff are all mixed in Chinese traditional culture. It is very hard to separate the two. Too much rhetoric and literal beauty can be harmful. For example, I write a love poem that may be beautiful as a poem, but as a guiding principle for romance, it fails. For example, 'Facing the sea with spring flowers blossoming, and from tomorrow on I will write to my lover.' Although that creates an artistic conception, it is impossible as romantic advice. Chinese traditional culture includes much impracticality. If two out of ten rules and regulations are unattainable, the remaining eight mean nothing.

So how can we use Chinese traditional culture? We must clarify paradoxical elements that appear right but are in fact wrong. For example, we find contrasting idioms in Chinese traditional culture such as 'One may be poor but never cease to be ambitious' and 'Poverty stifles ambition.' How should you decide when and how to use them? You must clarify that 'One may be poor but never cease to be ambitious' is used for motivating people. However, imagine that you, Professor Qu, feed me every day of my life, but I am too poor to ever buy you anything, not even dumplings. Then poverty stifles my ambition. Chinese culture has many such examples. The most outstanding characteristic of Chinese traditional culture is the lack of standards.

Interviewer Fu: Can you share some real examples and tell us how you dealt with challenges and difficulties in your growth process?

Nie: Actually we have not encountered any difficulties, except perhaps we have too many orders to handle. When you become No. 1, your only challenge is how to push your limits.

Some have tried to undermine our credibility. But we make products for a niche market of consumers with strong character and who are good analytical thinkers. Consumers in the niche market do their research and know the market well. Furthermore, we have good word-of-mouth references. If people start bad rumours about us, they are only advertising our name and incurring disdain for themselves. For example, we have a simple way of dealing with commercial bribery. When some companies approached us for kick-backs, we simply tell them no kick-backs or we drop the deal. When the customers understand our procedures, they stop attempting bribery. Information about our projects is publicly available. If we sign a contract with an agent (a third-party arrangement), others will investigate and find out why the signatory of the contract is not the proprietor, and the deal will be revealed. Therefore, companies must be clean. They should not only avoid enabling any corruption, but also fight it resolutely and wisely. All these years, we have had no lawsuits or legal disputes.

Interviewer Fu: Some provisions in the Code seem extreme; for example, the fact that company policy strictly forbids playing cards even if it doesn't involve money.

Nie: Gambling is forbidden. In card playing, money may not be lost but precious time is, because card playing can be endless and people cannot always control their desires and play long into the night. You might not have a good rest; you might have a fight; you might have a car accident the next day because you were tired, and then one thing leads to another. This can be an endless waste of time. Generally speaking, we let it go if there is no complaint, but in essence it is illegal according to our Code.

Even with all those rules, Tecsun cannot guarantee 100 % that employees will not play cards. From time to time, some will play cards until 3 am. Once they experience that high from playing cards, they will keep playing until they are exhausted. Then, of course, they will need rest but instead some might have to drive 500 miles to provide post-sales service the next day. If we cannot eliminate such damaging behaviour, the company will suffer. We cannot allow that to happen. I made the policy based on my full understanding of human nature.

Keep at Arm's Length with Government Officials

Interviewer Qu: Tecsun has had numerous visitors throughout the years. What advice and recommendations do you give to these visitors who come to learn from Tecsun? Do you know of any success stories coming from these visits?

Nie: We Chinese often fail to understand that Rome was not built in one day. Everybody is eager to succeed, but it takes five to 15 years to progress from establishing values to becoming like Tecsun. Most want to learn how Tecsun uses the least amount of resources to manage the most people and make the most money. That is impossible.

On the other hand, the world gives entrepreneurs a lot of leeway, but many ruin themselves. You will definitely be ruined if you make fake and inferior products. If you collude with government officials, you will also be ruined when they lose power. Let me give you an example. Some people read the first four books of the *Biography of Hu Xueyan*,[5] written by Gao Yang, and thought they understood Hu. But they failed to read the last two volumes: *Vanish* and *Tragic End*, which are the most important. Hu thrived financially because of his relationship with General Tso,[6] but collapsed after Tso passed away. His story shows that business—government collusion, while it can be beneficial for a short time—is dangerous, shameful and bound to come to a miserable end.

If our company is to be healthy, we must rely on products, costs and services. Keep a short-term, arm's length relationship with government officials. I am a good friend of many officials, but we will never have any business relationship. For example, I avoid doing business in the city where a friend serves as a government official. Our perpetual principle is: Stay away from dangerous collusion with officials and speculators, always provide good products and you will be invincible.

Therefore, if you have a humble heart and try to do the right things, you can be like Tecsun. That is really not difficult in China. Most Chinese lack conscientiousness but are eager to succeed, so you can easily stand out and become No. 1 if you put your heart into it.

Interviewer Qu: Would it be more difficult for the Tecsun model to succeed in a more competitive industry other than real estate?

---

[5] Hu Xueyan (1823–1885), a Chinese business celebrity in the nineteenth century, was the richest businessman in the late Qing dynasty, but his life ended miserably after he failed in the silk market.

[6] Zuo Zongtang (1812–1885), generally referred to as 'General Tso' in the West, was a Chinese statesman and military leader in the late Qing dynasty.

Nie: It would be more difficult but still possible. For example, software companies such as Kingdee and Yongyou Software face cut-throat competition, but they are excelling in their chosen area. For example, Kingdee is very good in industrial accounting, while Yongyou Software UFIDA is fantastic for commercial accounting. It all boils down to treating your consumers well. If an entrepreneur wishes to sell shepherd's pie wontons, he begins by using fresh meat and the best vegetables. Customers soon recognise the quality and come back for more. It is the same with everything else. It is also important to have people of good quality, particularly bosses. You must foster cultural justice, and establish a complete and complementary set of management/supervisory systems to function as effectively as an immune system. In China, supervision is most important. In fact, people worldwide can be problematic if they are unsupervised. Supervisors must first control, and reward later. Be kind to people and allow them legitimate compensation so that they can have easy, peaceful and good lives. If bosses are duplicitous, workers will distrust and disrespect them.

Interviewer Qu: In addition to humility and proper behaviour, what else can Tecsun teach about management systems?

Nie: All regulations and rules should be humanist and accepted by employees. Anything related to people, as are regulations and rules, should have the common principle of being acceptable. All employees must agree that your directives are right; and they must follow the directions even though that might be difficult at first. There is also a difference in expression between English and Chinese characters. Using Chinese characters, a statement may read something like this: 'Pay attention!' But English would put the speaker in a lower position by saying 'May I have your attention, please?' The difference in that expression demonstrates that English is less bureaucratic than Chinese. However, since employees would not understand if I wrote in English, the Code book is in Chinese. However, I added comments and explanations after stipulations so that employees could understand the reasons for the rules. For example, after I stipulated that employees must chew gum, I explained that the rule was to prevent bad breath from disturbing colleagues. Another rule says: 'When you see that a colleague is sick, you must stop whatever you are doing and take him/her to the hospital, or make sure he/she receives timely care.' Following this rule I added: 'Because when you are sick you will also need such help.'

The Soul of Management Lies in Education

Interviewer Qu: You are engaged in many businesses now, and you also have many hobbies. Do these hobbies add value to your management of Tecsun? Or can we say that the company is not a major part of your life now?

Nie: The *21st Century Business Review* published an interview with me entitled 'The Soul of Management is Education.' In China, most universities are acting like enterprises; they are selling diplomas as products. Enterprises must then become universities and re-educate university graduates. So in China it is most important for business managers to educate employees to be worthy of their salaries. Most are singleton children, and their parents have taught them that as long as they have good grades, they will succeed. They are spoiled. That's why I want to enhance the area of education, and I use culture to educate.

If any student in your Executive MBA (EMBA) class wants to know about Nie Shengzhe, tell him to go to see *The Bygones of Huizhou*, showing at the National Grand Theater in Beijing. This play demonstrates my management philosophy well. While it is a traditional opera, it adopts the Hollywood narration style and is so exciting that you won't even want to take a break in the middle. It advocates justice, integrity and the nobility of love. The investment in the play is 3 million RMB, and the box office take is already over 20 million RMB. It will eventually exceed 100 million RMB. This is unprecedented in the history of Chinese traditional opera. How is this possible? This is consistent with my management philosophy: caring about the existence of others, the existence of the actors and audience. Guiding audiences and educating employees are the same—the soul of management lies in education! I explore human nature in this play through the theme that officials should be modest and that ordinary people should be tolerant of officials for positive social interactions.

Interviewers Qu and Fu: Can you share recommendations for others in the business community?

Nie: First, truth has only one standard. Similarly, all entrepreneurs should follow one standard: to perform their responsibilities well. Second, entrepreneurs must respect anyone and anything related to the enterprise. For example, to relate well with their customers, they must make good products. To relate well with their employees, they must take good care of their workers. They must tell the truth to anyone interested in the company. I would like to add that I dislike the popular term *implementation capacity*. I see it as a false and empty concept that evokes selfish thoughts of 'me': 'Do you implement my orders?' Because of its high-powered distance culture, the Chinese people consider implementation capacity from the perspective of 'How do I implement your orders?' Instead, the term *implementation capacity* should indicate how we create a working atmosphere so that colleagues will collaborate to solve problems at a lower cost but with a higher quality.

However, once you use the term *implementation capacity*, it becomes a complicated question of whether people below you implement your decisions. Some people might say 'What right do you have to give me orders?' For example, if I order you to make me a cup of tea, you might spit into it and I would not know. Yes, my order has been implemented, but badly. Implementation makes sense only when everybody truly feels happy.

That's why the term *implementation capacity* evokes thoughts regarding implementation of orders rather than questions about how well the orders will be implemented, or who will be responsible. Terms such as *implementation capacity* or *the science of success* are nonsense.

Commentary

Though it may sound inhuman from the view of Western standards, when playing cards is forbidden in workers' spare time, the Tecsun Code for Employees reflects the reality of a humanist approach to managing employees in the Chinese construction industry. Shengzhe Nie's explicit instructions regarding the conduct of employees shows his care for his employees, the existence of others, the quality work of Tecsun, and the final products and services provided to customers. The moral leadership (Gini 1997a, b; Sergiovanni 1992) extends beyond the obligations and benefits listed in the Code of Conduct, also to cost—price consciousness for customers and ethical interactions with suppliers. The correctness of the way of being is a foundation for business sustainability (Olson et al. 2003) and success of Tecsun, which at the end of the day is a family business with Mr Nie as the main shareholder.

On the one hand, the particularity of its business model and its position in a niche construction market with high quality and relatively low price has ensured the success of Tecsun from the outset; while on the other hand, Mr Nie's management philosophy seems to be the source of the business model. The unusual management of the employees includes treating them well (Pfeffer and Veiga 1999), to guarantee their life success up until their deaths, and extend their responsibility to a broader society if there are more resources available. Mr Nie's philosophy is based on self-reflection over a long period, based on reading, the experience of both Western and Chinese culture, and observing human nature in depth.

Appendix

Ten 'cardinal rules' of the Tecsun 'Employee Code'

1. Employees must never gossip with colleagues or anyone else about other colleagues or about the company. Blaming or ridiculing colleagues irritates them, damages the company image, and brings no benefit to the perpetrator.
2. The company will never adopt time clocks. Employees are expected conscientiously to avoid arriving late or leaving early. Employees can take time off as needed, but must be 100 % dedicated to work during working hours.
3. Employees must be hygienic. They must take regular showers, preferably each day, brush teeth at least once daily, and have a haircut at least monthly.

4. Employees who do not complain about disappointing treatment or rejection and who work for the company's best interests will be given 200 RMB for each incident.

5. Sick employees are not allowed to work. Violators will be fined 50 RMB to 100 RMB each time they do. Minor ailments such as colds, but not influenza, are not included in this rule. The company values employees' lives as its most precious fortune. Thus workers must not risk their lives for the collective or national sake of the company.

6. Employees who make unintentional mistakes at work and report their mistakes to their supervisors will pay a symbolic fine of 1 RMB; employees who try to conceal mistakes will be punished heavily.

7. Employees must not play mahjong, card games or electronic games with colleagues or other people at any time (except for the three days before and immediately following the Spring Festival), whether for gambling or entertainment purposes, because people addicted to gambling will waste much time. Violators will be asked to resign.

8. Employees can entertain up to ten family members once a year at the company's expense; not to exceed 60 RMB per person. Family members include spouses, children, parents of the wife and husband, and other immediate family. Employees who submit fake invoices will be deemed fraudulent.

9. At the company's expense, employees will purchase supplies annually for each child enrolled in school, from primary school to graduation from university. The purchase may include such items as stationery, shoes or clothes. The cost should not exceed 200 RMB each time.

10. Tecsun employees do not need managerial approval for claiming expenses. Anyone can submit expense invoices to the finance department, but all employees should carefully heed the instructions provided by the financial staff, 'Serious Reminders—Statement before Reimbursement': Vouchers for reimbursement must be true and compliant with the *Financial Reimbursement Rules*. Otherwise they are fraudulent, against the rules, and perhaps are even illegal, and will be severely punished, causing lifelong consequences. If you are unsure about the authenticity of the reimbursement vouchers, please carefully confirm that vouchers are correct before beginning the reimbursement process. Please note that we consider this issue to be extremely serious.

Numerous readers have shared their thoughts about the Code book on the internet. One reader said: 'The first time I browsed these rules I felt fortunate that I was not a Tecsun employee because the rules and regulations appeared very stringent, harsh and impersonal. However, the more I read, the more I felt the pride that Tecsun employees must feel. In the end, I was deeply impressed by the seemingly simple words and plain writing style. Tecsun teaches its employees not only how to do a job; but more important, it teaches them how to be upright people. Tecsun's values of "honesty, diligence, care and no shortcuts" seem simple at first glance, but they caused me to think... Why should we be like these people? We should because this is the only way to have a meaningful life and for our company to become stronger and more sustainable. Most important, such behaviour will earn respect.'

References

Baidu. (2015). Shengzhe Nie. Retrieved March 23, 2015, from http://baike. baidu.com/link?url=hBU9dr9mkCjU8Eii_fFzodWM29ZS-XbKd5m2tqUpjS8J-3rxsmUoPNFJfPNyIljDmPIEDmE9qushH1arcOF8J_
Gini, A. (1997a). Moral leadership and business ethics. *Journal of Leadership & Organizational Studies, 4*(4), 64–81.
Gini, A. (1997b). Moral leadership: An overview. *Journal of Business Ethics., 16*(3), 323–330.
Olson, P., Zuiker, V. S., Danes, S. M., Stafford, K., Heck, R. K. Z., & Duncan, K. A. (2003). The impact of the family and the business on family business sustainability. *Journal of Business Venturing, 18*(5), 639–666.
Pfeffer, J., & Veiga, J. F. (1999). Putting people first for organizational success. *Academy of Management Perspectives, 13*(2), 37–48.
Sergiovanni, T. (1992). *Moral leadership.* San Francisco: Jossey-Bass.
Tecsun. (2015). Tecsun website. Retrieved March 23, 2015 and January 17, 2016, from http://www.tecsunhomes.com/homepage.asp

Part V
Leaders in Consumer Goods and Retail Industry

13

My Dream Relies on the Team to Realise

Interview with Li-Ning Company Founder and Chairman Ning Li

The interview was conducted by: Jianjun Zhang, Peking University, and Anne S. Tsui, Arizona State University.

Li-Ning Company[1]

Established in Guangdong (China) and with the 'LI-NING' trademark registered in 1989, the company was founded by Ning Li, a well-known Chinese gymnast, after he retired from competing. Li-Ning Company Ltd. was the first leading sports brand enterprise in China. More than twenty years later, it has become a leading Chinese sports brand in the People's Republic of China (PRC) and is exploring international markets.

Headquartered now in Beijing, the company provides mainly sports goods, including footwear, apparel, equipment and accessories for both professional and leisure purposes, primarily under the Li-Ning brand

---

[1] This section is based on information and news from the company website (Li-Ning 2015a), annual reports (Li-Ning, 2011, 2014, 2015b, c), and IACMR's *Chinese Management Insights'* publication on Li-Ning in September 2011.

© The Author(s) 2017
A.S. Tsui et al., *Leadership of Chinese Private Enterprises*, Palgrave Studies in Chinese Management, DOI 10.1057/978-1-137-40235-6_13

name, leveraging the high reputation of the founder in the sports area. By brand marketing, research and development (R&D), design, manufacture, distribution and retail capabilities, it has established itself well in the Chinese market with various international collaborations. In addition to its core Li-Ning brand, the Group also manufactures, develops, markets, distributes and/or sells sports products under several other brand names, including Double Happiness (table tennis), AIGLE (outdoor sports), Lotto (sports fashion) and Kason (badminton equipment), which are either self-owned or licensed to/operated through joint ventures.

In terms of distribution, it has had a nationwide retail network in the PRC since 1997. Its extensive supply chain management system, distribution and retail network is primarily through the outsourcing of manufacturing operations and distribution via franchised agents, though the company also directly manages retail stores for the Li-Ning brand. By the end of 2010, when its highest revenue (9.455 billion RMB) was achieved, the company was operating 7915 Li-Ning brand retail stores (7333 franchised and 582 operated directly) in 1800 Chinese cities, as well as setting up sales points in Southeast Asia, Central Asia and Europe. Its international markets have always been only a small part of its core business.

At the beginning of the company's creation, it sponsored the Chinese national team in the Asian Games in 1990. Then in 1992, again the Chinese national team taking part in the Barcelona Olympic Games was sponsored. Sports sponsorship, strategic alliances and agreements with international partners were common practices of the Li-Ning Company as it grew. To name just a few: its strategic alliance with the National Basketball Association (NBA) since 2005 resulting in a range of agreements with NBA players such as Damon Jones, Shaquille O'Neal, Chuck Hayes and Baron Davis; a strategic partnership with Swarovski AG since 2005; the official partners providing sportswear for the Swedish Olympic Delegation and Spanish Olympic Delegation in 2007; and other types of agreements, as, for example, with the Sudan National Team, an Ethiopian marathon athlete, the Argentine Basketball League, and the United States National Table Tennis Team.

The group has a strong focus on R&D. It set up its first design and R&D centre in Foshan, Guangdong, in March 1998, and now there are centres in mainland China, Hong Kong and Portland, Oregon, in the USA. Several of its designs based on its own R&Ds have been recognised by the German 'iF Design Awards'; and China's 'China Innovative Design Red Star Award' and 'The Most Creative Organization' in consecutive years. Being recognised as 'My Favourite China Brand', the Li-Ning Company also has been honoured as 'The Best CCTV Employer' and 'The Best Company to Work For' awarded by different national and international institutions.

Since the Li-Ning Company was listed on the Hong Kong Stock Exchange in June 2004, its sales have increased steadily, reaching 9.478 billion RMB of revenue in 2010 at the peak of its sales, with an EBITDA (earnings before interest, taxes, depreciation and amortization) of 1.759 billion RMB. As a result of market saturation, the company has been facing huge challenges, with a reduced turnover and for the first time had an operating loss in 2012 which continued in 2013 and 2014. To address competitive constrains, the Li-Ning Company transformed its board of management and approved its new business strategy named the 'Channel Revival Plan' to renew downstream channels. This resulted in a reduction of numbers of retail stores to 5915 in 2013 (4989 franchised and 926 operated directly) and further to 5626 in 2014 (4424 franchised and 1202 operated directly). Li-Ning returned to be the Interim Chief Executive Officer (CEO). In addition to tighter control over the wholesale processes of products, it has also connected products R&D and retail capability with the business environment driven by the internet with digitalised sports business. As a result, the group reached a positive EBITDA and operating cash flow in 2015, according to Interim Results.

Founder and Chairman Ning Li[2]

Ning Li, born in 1963 in the south of China, and founder of the Li-Ning brand, is the Group's Chairman and Executive Director. His primary responsibility is to formulate the Group's overall corporate strategies and planning. The name of the company was created from his own name as an outstanding athlete in the twentieth century.

Before his entrepreneurial activities began, Ning Li was a gymnast with a worldwide reputation. He first came to fame in the 6th World Cup Gymnastics Competition in 1982, when he won six gold medals in the men's artistic gymnastics events, an unprecedented achievement. After this, he was known as the 'Prince of Gymnastics' in the PRC. Two years later, in 1984, Ning Li again demonstrated his extraordinary capability in the 23rd Olympic Games held in Los Angeles. He won six medals: three gold, two silver and one bronze, making him the athlete who won the most medals of that Olympic Games. Since then he has been considered as a hero sportsman in the PRC, admired by most Chinese people. In the 17 years of his gymnastic career, Ning Li won a total of 14 world champion titles and 106 gold medals in different national and international gymnastics competitions. For his extraordinary achievement, he became the only Asian member of the Athletes' Commission of the International Olympic Committee (IOC) in 1987.

On retiring in 1989 from his athletic career, Ning Li first joined the Guangdong Jianlibao Beverage Group, and soon initiated the idea of the Li-Ning brand with the aim of creating the first national sports goods brand, as another way to contribute to the development of the sports goods industry and its community. This reflects on his ongoing spirit of 'originating from sports, and dedicated to sports.' For his entrepreneurial achievements, he was honoured as the '2008 CCTV Businessman of the Year.'

Even after his retirement from his athletic career in 1989, he continued to contribute to the sports community from different angles. From 1993 to 2000, he served as a member of the Men's Artistic Gymnastics

[2] This section is based on IACMR's *Chinese Management Insights'* publication on Ning Li in September 2011 with permission, complemented by public information from China.org.cn (2009) and Wikipedia (2015).

Technical Committee of the International Federation of Gymnastics, of which he is now an honorary member. In 1999, he was voted one of the 'World's Most Excellent Athletes in the 20th Century' by the World Sports Correspondent Association, and in 2000, he was listed in the International Gymnastics Hall of Fame, becoming the first Chinese person to achieve this recognition. In 2008, in his capacity as the representative of leading Chinese athletes, Ning Li lit the cauldron at the start of the Beijing Olympics.

In addition to his athletic achievements and entrepreneurial activities, Ning Li is also a hard worker with a continuous desire to learn. He obtained his bachelor degree in law from Peking University, Beijing, in 2002, followed by an Executive MBA (EMBA) from the same university. He also received an honorary technical doctorate from Loughborough University in the UK in 2001, and a degree of Doctor of Humanities honoris causa of The Hong Kong Polytechnic University in 2008.

As well as pursuing his own learning and putting what he has learned into practice, Ning Li is also concerned with the educational and developmental opportunities of others. He is actively involved in charities via the 'Li-Ning Fund Association' and generously supports active and retired Chinese athletes and coaches with 'The Chinese Athletes Educational Foundation.' These funds aim to provide subsidies for further education and training for athletes, and to support educational development in impoverished and remote areas in China. For his socially responsible activities, in October 2009 Ning Li was appointed by The United Nations World Food Programme (WFP) as China's first 'WFP Goodwill Ambassador against Hunger.'

My Dream Relies on the Team to Realise

Interviewers Zhang and Tsui: Please describe your philosophy, perspective and style of management.

Ning Li (hereafter referred to as Li): As far as I am concerned, the most important thing is to find a successful way to do business, including what kind of business you are doing, how to do it, the necessary knowledge and skills, the choices of managers and employees, the transformation of the business, etc. How to organise various kinds of resources effectively based on business need is the unchanging key in management. Since the 1990s, the markets and products relating to our business have changed many times. Consequently, our company has undergone corresponding transformation and change. With the accumulation of experience, technologies and capabilities, we have experienced a gradual shift in decision-making from 'one-man, top-down' to a comprehensive, organisation-wide approach. Such decisions are executed through the integration of human resource (HR) management. However, any change and adjustment within the organisation is goal-oriented, based on the needs of the business.

As I was once an athlete, sports are my personal pursuit and interest, which originally motivated me to move into business. Undoubtedly, my own dream and passion have always been there, influencing the whole process of founding and running the company. Such a dream and passion are reflected in the direction of any transformation, the identity of the company, the corporate culture and the value system. However, in the process of market competition, it calls for a strong, organic system of organisation with skills in administration, finance and human resource management to keep the company competitive and vigorous. I hope that Li-Ning can become a professional company, providing specialised/approved products for the market, which cannot be achieved by the efforts of a single individual. To reach this target, we need a strong professional team.

In brief, my passion and dreams were the original drivers in founding the company, while the building of the professional team and organisation capacity is a continuing task to sustain success. I have been moving professional management forward continuously, which might be a unique character of Li-Ning, compared with other domestic companies.

Interviewers Zhang and Tsui: What experiences in your life significantly influenced your business and management style?

Li: The most important thing is being an athlete. It makes me passionate in pursuing a dream. Initially, I benefited from years of hard training, which helped me to realise the importance of having clear goals while continuously pursuing a dream. Such passion and perseverance has led me to be persistent as well as to be confident in overcoming difficulties.

In managing my company, the key revolves around transforming the dream of one man into the goals of an organisation, transforming a single person's knowledge and capability into the capacity of a professional concern, and finally winning the business.

Interviewers Zhang and Tsui: What experience inspired you in this?

Li: I traced it to my experience of studying at Peking University, when this idea became clear in my mind. In my classes, I studied many business cases and could see the difference compared to Chinese firms, where one person usually makes all the decisions. In Western companies, a team of professional managers make the decisions. Moving from management by one person to that by a team matches my perspective well.

When I was an athlete, to produce an Olympic champion was the dream of all Chinese people, because that could prove our ability and raise our national pride. I, myself, was able to win a gold medal to realise the dream of the Chinese people. But to create a first-class sports brand needs support from many areas, such as technology, finance, sales and management, etc. Though it is my own dream, it relies on many other people to realise it.

Interviewers Zhang and Tsui: To realise that the success of a company depends on teamwork involves a major change in mindset. How did you effect this transformation?

Li: The sports experience gave me the opportunity to come into contact with some international brands relatively early, such as Coca-Cola, McDonald's and Adidas. The success of these major companies inspired me. Meanwhile, I learned a lot from my coach and teammates. I am very grateful to them. Even today, I still admire my coach and consider him to be my father, and I still treat my teammates like my brothers. When I was in the national team, even when I was the youngest, I was appointed to be the captain. This might indicate my talent and my unique understanding of the sport. Such a mentality might also be related to my personal values. There is a technique in acrobatic gymnastics, that involves four gymnasts forming a human tower. Audiences always focus on the top person, but actually, without the support of the other three team members, this arrangement could not be achieved. I use this example to show that personal success relies on team support, which is also extremely important when doing business.

Professionalisation: A Difficult But Necessary Road

Interviewers Zhang and Tsui: How do you position yourself in the company?

Li: First, I consider my dream and passion as the spiritual pillars of the company. Second, it is my responsibility to make strategic choices concerning the company's direction and development. The two CEOs after me respected and valued my opinions, but I also encourage them to make decisions independently. If I am too powerful, they will become too weak to make independent decisions. Very often, having an overpowering leader may result in employees being too careful around him or her, and deprived of the opportunity to develop organisational capacity. This should be constructed through market competition; only through market competition can an organisation make constant progress and remain vigorous. Of course, I must participate in decisions concerning the life of the company, the shareholders, or basic values, but for detailed decisions, I step back.

This kind of style is also related to my experience as an athlete. In my training, my coach always gave me a lot of space. When making plans, from the volume of training and the understanding of actions to technical choices, my coach always gave me great discretion to decide, experience and transcend. This is very important. Coaches who emphasise too many details would decrease athletes' independence. I have two main coaches, one in the national team and the other in the provincial team. Though they have different styles, both of them have given me room and influenced me significantly.

Interviewers Zhang and Tsui: Did you bring any particular management practice into your company? Why did you do so?

Li: In 1996, I introduced professional management to the company and removed nepotism. I let my relatives and other top managers who were my teammates leave the company. Many people think that I must have suffered a lot of pressure; actually I didn't. In fact, from the beginning, I did not think that I should have to take on the burden of taking care of my relatives and be forced to run the company like a family business. The tradition of family and regional culture affects company values and the way in which the company is managed. Because of my fame, many people, such as my teammates or fellow villagers, came to join the company. This gradually developed into a kind of family culture. So, in 1996, I made a firm decision and asked my relatives to leave the company, with the purpose of providing promise and hope for the rest of the employees: they would not have to worry about their origins, they should just focus on what they would be doing and whether they could make a contribution. At that time, the scale of the company was small, and some of the top managers complained that professionalisation was too early and would hurt efficiency. But this action (i.e. adopting professionalisation) in fact established a very good culture and atmosphere in the company. People come to Li-Ning to pursue their dreams, and they don't need to worry about their relationship with anybody. Everyone has a fair chance to succeed.

Meanwhile, I also realised that professionalisation is very difficult in China. When the whole society has not developed a good understanding of professionalism, and where many people are faced with temptations, it is extremely difficult for professionalism to show the 'noble spirit,' i.e. the spirit of sacrifice. Many private firms in fact have the mentality permeating certain kinds of state-owned enterprises, such as irresponsibility, inefficiency and lack of vitality. These were not what we wanted, and we introduced professionalism to improve management.

Interviewers Zhang and Tsui: Have you experienced conflict between personal emotions and business rationality? How do you think they should be dealt with?

Li: No, I have not. In fact, when I asked my teammates and relatives to leave, none of them complained. But the general manager did not understand me. He thought that my solution was too simple. He also thought that transparency and professionalisation would affect efficiency in a negative way. In my view, while short-term efficiency might be affected, professionalisation would ensure long-term efficiency. Of course, we made a generous arrangement for those people who left, which not only reflected our personal courtesy, but also showed our conformity to the social norm. We must maintain mutual respect and friendship.

Interviewers Zhang and Tsui: At the beginning of your business career, when you made the first batch of sports shoes, you failed because of their inferior quality even though your team worked hard. You decided to destroy the shoes. Did you hesitate at all in this action?

Li: No, I did that with no hesitation. After throwing out the inferior products that couldn't be sold, the only thing we could do was to look continuously for what could be sold. This is the basic requirement for a product. As a new team, making mistakes is to be expected. I was able to do a few things to encourage continuous improvement, however. First, I took responsibility and blamed no one else for the problem. Second, I gave the team space to pursue the right thing with their passion. After all, they all wanted to create an excellent brand. This kind of so-called lenience or tolerance is partly related to my experience as an athlete. As athletes, we suffer a lot of failures, even though people may only see or remember our successful and honourable moments. As the proverb says, failure is the mother of success.

Interviewers Zhang and Tsui: Is there anything that you cannot tolerate?

Li: Benefiting oneself at the expense of the company, such as taking kick-backs, are among the acts that cannot be tolerated. Such situations happen occasionally. This phenomenon has very complex social roots, because China's social environment is very complex, and the legal infrastructure is not sufficient or effective. Therefore, the key is to establish an effective mechanism to prevent and constrain such behaviour within the company. We try to maintain a balance between two difficulties. On the one hand, we should avoid such actions to protect the value of the company, but on the other, we should ensure cost-effectiveness. For example, a single item with fifty cents higher in cost often means a loss of profits in billions of dollars.

Interviewers Zhang and Tsui: You often mention that you are a passionate person. How can you transmit your passion to the company's employees and motivate them to work with passion towards a dream, instead of just being a 'salaryman'?

Li: I still think that professionalisation is very difficult in China. In China, self-sufficiency is a thousand-year-old tradition, and universal social welfare has not been established in the process of industrialisation.

As a result, it is not easy to shape employee attitudes during the process of professionalisation. Because of the inadequate social security, rapidly changing social environment and numerous opportunities, it is difficult for Chinese people to settle down in a job or a career; therefore, it is more difficult to enforce professionalism with basic values and ethics. With the exposure to various temptations such as free-riding, the value of professional managers is easily challenged.

In 2004, after our launch on the stock market, we adopted stock options and other measures to improve the income of our key employees. We also strengthened training on passion and dreams. But still some managerial actions brought harm to the company. I don't think this is an individual problem; it is a social one. Employees come from society, and they are inevitably influenced by certain popular yet harmful values in society. Of course, I also recognise that the cost of human resources will increase during the process of professionalisation. In the final analysis, the solution to this problem is dependent on the overall progress of Chinese society.

Interviewers Zhang and Tsui: This is really a dilemma for Chinese entrepreneurs. Entrepreneurs in the West operate in a mature society, where professional ethics have been well developed. This task of professionalisation is on the shoulders of entrepreneurs in China.

Li: In Western society, people who do not conform to professional ethics will be expelled from the market, and it will be difficult for them to find another similar job in the industry. In China, the cost of job mobility is very low. You don't even need a certificate or documents. The role of reputation has not been established in Chinese society; therefore, reputational loss does not exert effective constraints on people. Without such a professional reputation mechanism, it is difficult to have external constraints on professional managers. The primary responsibility of the business is to grow, to be responsible to shareholders, and to be responsible to our employees. Companies have social responsibilities, but we cannot take all the responsibility for society. But improving organisational capacity and professionalism is important to help the business succeed and survive.

Further, without passion, it is difficult for our company to make progress. The company's daily work is trivial with little value, such as sewing and making a garment. If employees are not passionate and only care about wages, it would be difficult for the company to be creative and competitive.

We only Deserve a Bronze Medal Now, But We Are Flexible for Change

Interviewers Zhang and Tsui: From the perspective of competitive advantage, what do you think is the strongest capability of the Li-Ning Company?

Li: Compared with our domestic competitors in the industry, the strength of our company is our capacity in managing a brand. However, there is still much more room for us to transform this capacity efficiently into company development and profit.

In addition, Li-Ning is developing a relatively strong organisational capacity. Since the 1990s, we have experienced various changes: from millions to billions in revenues, from single to multiple products, from single level to multilevel markets, the Li-Ning Company was always changing. Such experiences have given us strong organisational capacity in turbulent environments. For example, in the late 1990s, when we first introduced enterprise resource planning (ERP), which required new processes and new ways of doing things, many people felt it difficult to adapt and complained to me. But I firmly insisted on pushing this change forward, and finally we succeeded, with the organisation's capacity being promoted to a higher level.

Let me give another example. As the first publicly listed company in Hong Kong in this industry, we experienced tremendous challenges. We faced huge pressure to transform a traditional and indigenous enterprise into a modern company that conformed to Hong Kong's laws and regulations. All our managers and accounting staff underwent a painful process, like a process of transformation from being a caterpillar to a butterfly. Though everyone was very tired, and resistance was frequent, they all followed and grew, so that during the process we gained a better understanding and made progress. We can say that the strength of our organisational capacity is reflected very well in these two experiences—the introduction of ERP and the listing on the Hong Kong stock exchange. Of course, there is still room for us to improve our commercial organising capacity.

None of the changes was personal, but organisational and systematic. Change seems like a permanent task. The capacity for organisational change can help us to find the right direction, seek more resources and more space to develop, and eventually bring more benefits. This unceasing transformation will make our organisation more flexible. Therefore, I am determined to embrace change.

Interviewers Zhang and Tsui: What would you like to share with others in terms of your experience in founding and managing a company?

Li: We can see a condensed picture of Chinese economic development since the 1990s through the window of our company's growth and development journey. For now, it is probably too early to share my thoughts on management with others, because our ideas might be outdated, and our ways of doing things still need improvement. For example, professionalisation is a unique feature of our company, but it is still difficult to judge when we can confidently claim that professionalisation has been achieved. It took the Li-Ning Company three years to complete the current so-called professionalisation, but whether this is the true professionalisation we want is still unclear. Even though we have given up some family or regional culture, we still need to generate efficiency from the professionalisation. We still need to manage the balance between business efficiency and basic values.

Interviewers Zhang and Tsui: If you were asked to make an assessment of the Li-Ning Company in terms of gold, silver and bronze medals, what do you think you have achieved?

Li: At the current stage, I would say we have reached the bronze level. Of course, any evaluation depends on the criteria. I think that we still have too many things to improve. What we have achieved might be just like this: we succeeded only because we were bold enough and started earlier than others. When the market was in its early stages, competition was not intense. As long as you are brave enough, you will succeed. However, our so-called success won't bear the scrutiny of detailed analysis from a business, management, skills or marketing point of view. So perhaps we still don't have anything to be proud of, and we don't have successful lessons to promote just now. The reason I would give Li-Ning a bronze medal instead of gold or silver is because we still have a lot of things to do, to create new needs, make more commercial gains, or influence consumers' behaviour in the society. To create new products and needs, we have to rely on organisational capacity rather than individual capacity.

Commentary

Called after the founder, Ning Li, a well-known Chinese sportsman (one even considered as a national hero when he won some of the first medals for China in the Olympic Games), the Li-Ning Company quickly became famous in the Chinese market. Through the rapid expansion of the retail business of sports products, the Li-Ning Company has a strong brand position in the market. Mr Li and his company faced the challenge of professionalising their team, upgrading the company's organisational capability, and adapting the business model through constant transformation, as required by the changing market and business environments.

From the interview, we sense an extraordinary humble man who leads by personal example, with passion, discipline, perseverance, moral character and self-reflection. Though humble, he is also a man with great inner strength and a high level of moral integrity. His behaviour and values fit the definition of 'moral leadership' (Gini 1997a,b; Sergiovanni 1992) and 'ethical leadership' (Brown and Treviño 2006; Brown et al. 2005). Sports goods and sportswear is an extremely competitive industry, demanding constant product innovation and transformation. The company has been facing tough and constant domestic and international challenges and a reduced market position. With determination and discipline, Mr Li is leading his company again in this redemption process, with market focus, product innovation, morality and ethics constantly transforming Li-Ning Company to adapt to the new business environment.

References

Brown, M. E., & Treviño, L. K. (2006). Ethical leadership: A review and future directions. *The Leadership Quarterly, 17*(6), 595–616.

Brown, M. E., Treviño, L. K., & Harrison, D. A. (2005). Ethical leadership: A social learning perspective for construct development and testing. *Organizational Behavior and Human Decision Processes, 97*(2), 117–134.

China.com.cn (2009). Li-Ning: Legend of Chinese brand. Retrieved December 26, 2015, from http://www.china.com.cn/economic/zhuanti/xzgjjlsn/2009-07/23/content_18190398.htm

Gini, A. (1997a). Moral leadership and business ethics. *Journal of Leadership & Organizational Studies, 4*(4), 64–81.

Gini, A. (1997b). Moral leadership: An overview. *Journal of Business Ethics, 16*(3), 323–330.

Li-Ning. (2011). Li-Ning 2010 annual report. Retrieved March 15, 2015, from http://www.irasia.com/listco/hk/lining/annual/ar71068-ew02331.pdf

Li-Ning. (2014). Li-Ning 2013 annual report. Retrieved March 15, 2015, from http://www.irasia.com/listco/hk/lining/annual/ar122630-e02331.pdf

Li-Ning. (2015a). Li-Ning website. Retrieved March 12 and December 26, 2015, from http://ir.lining.com/en/global/index.php

Li-Ning. (2015b). Li-Ning 2014 annual report. Retrieved December 26, 2015, from http://www.irasia.com/listco/hk/lining/annual/ar139406-e02331.pdf

Li-Ning. (2015c). Li-Ning 2015 interim results. Retrieved December 26, 2015, from http://ir.lining.com/en/ir/presentations/pre150813.pdf

Sergiovanni, T. (1992). *Moral leadership*. San Francisco: Jossey-Bass.

Wikipedia. (2015). Li-Ning. Retrieved March 12, 2015, from https://zh.wikipedia.org/wiki/%E6%9D%8E%E5%AE%8

14

Chinese Companies Need Strong and Open-minded Leaders

Interview with Wahaha Group Founder, Chairman and CEO, Qinghou Zong

The interview was conducted by: Anne S. Tsui, Arizona State University, and Katherine Xin, China Europe International Business School.

Wahaha Group[1]

In 1987, Qinghou Zong and two partners borrowed 140,000 RMB and started their entrepreneurial venture in Hangzhou: Wahaha. The first year was a hard period of exploration and learning, and Zong was selling ice cream, soft drinks and exercise books from a tricycle. It was not until the second year that Wahaha made remarkable profits, by producing nutritional drinks. Zong chose the name 'Wahaha' for his company; the literal translation is 'laughing child,' which means a happy child. Wahaha initially aimed to tap a niche in the market for a 'children's liquid nutrient. With Chinese single-child families, and the parents' full concern for

---

[1] This section is based on information and news from the company website (Wahaha 2015), Sull and Wang (2005), other public information (Sugawara 2014), and IACMR's *Chinese Management Insights'* publication on Wahaha in June 2012.

A.S. Tsui et al., *Leadership of Chinese Private Enterprises*, Palgrave Studies in Chinese Management, DOI 10.1057/978-1-137-40235-6_14

their single child, Wahaha was a resounding success from the beginning. Nowadays its product covers eight categories and has more than 150 products, including dairy drinks, bottled water, carbonated soft drinks, fruit juice, tea drinks, health foods and canned foods.

Wahaha is the largest and most profitable beverage company in China, with more than 150 branches and 60 manufacturing bases in 29 provinces nationwide, total assets of 30 billion RMB, and 30,000 employees. Since 1997, Wahaha has been ranked number one in the Chinese beverage industry in terms of all business performance indicators. Despite the present harsh and complex global economic development, Wahaha continues to excel. In 2010, Wahaha ranked eighth in revenue and first in profits among China's top 500 privately-owned enterprises. In 2014, the company reached 72 billion RMB of revenue and gross profit before tax of 12.9 billion RMB. Not listed on any stock exchange and with accumulated financial liquidity, Wahaha exercises conservative financial management with no outstanding loans.

Wahaha is a typical example of an ordinary Chinese company without a significant political or other outstanding background (e.g. Li-Ning). It achieved success by taking advantage of opportunities offered by the market economy when China opened up. Its success in leveraging marketing capability could also be reflected in the company's entry into China's cola market in 1998, challenging Coca-Cola and Pepsi-Cola (Pepsi) by introducing China's own version of cola: Future Cola (*feichang kele* 非常可乐). Since then, the market share of Future Cola has maintained third position in the Chinese soft drinks industry.

In 2004, Wahaha established a formal business strategy to promote innovation in all lines of business, including products, equipment and management. Learning, leveraging and innovating has been an essential motto for Wahaha employees. With a 10 billion RMB investment, Wahaha imported 400 world-class automated production lines from developed countries such as the USA, France, Germany, Japan and Italy. This upgraded Wahaha's National Technology Centre and realised fully automatic production processes from bottle-making, batching, filling and packaging. Recognising its outstanding performance, Wahaha has been the recipient of multiple awards such as 'National Advanced Enterprise of Quality Management,' a 'Chinese Enterprise Management

Special Contribution Award' and 'China's Most Respected Company;' as well as being recognised by the State Council of China as one of the top, most competitive, private Chinese enterprises.

Dominating the Chinese domestic beverage market, Wahaha has also diversified not only in terms of products and vertical integration, but also with regard to geography. After two decades of strenuous efforts exploring international markets, nine major categories of Wahaha's products have been sold to more than 30 countries and regions in the world, with annual sales close to 20 million USD by 2014. The principal exporting countries include the USA, Canada, Russia, Japan, Korea, Singapore, Italy, the UK, United Arab Emirates (UAE), South Africa, and many more. The chief products exported include instant foods such as bottled tea beverages, bottled water, milk drinks, mixed congee and wet noodles.

Founder and Chairman Qinghou Zong[2]

Born in 1945 in Jiangsu province, Qinghou Zong is the founder, chairman and CEO of Hangzhou Wahaha Group Co. Ltd. He created the principal brand: Wahaha (Laughing child), and has led the company to continuous growth and success. He and his family ranked first on Hurun's 2012 China Rich List and remained at number three in the Hurun Rich List in 2015 (Hurun 2012, 2015).

Zong had an ordinary life before the start of China's market economy, similar to many others of his generation. After high school, he worked as a manual labourer on a farm before becoming a salesman, and later moved to Hangzhou to become a sales manager and a project contractor. His entrepreneurial success came when his Wahaha Nutritious Food Factory achieved high performance nationwide in China. He has served as chairman of the board of directors and CEO of the Wahaha Group since 1991.

Before his entrepreneurial success with Wahaha, Zong prepared himself first by studying enterprise management at the Hangzhou Workers

---

[2] This section is based on IACMR's *Chinese Management Insights'* publication on Wahaha in June 2012 with permission, complemented by public information from Hurun Institute (2012, 2015) and Wikipedia (2015a).

Amateur University between 1981 and 1983, then leadership and enterprise management at Zhejiang Television University and Zhejiang Municipal Party School in 1987 and 1988. Today, he is not only an active participant in social political activities (i.e. Representative of the 10th and 11th National People's Congress, vice president of Zhejiang Chamber of Commerce and the Zhejiang Federation of Industry and Commerce, and vice chairman of the China Beverage Industry Association), but he is also accredited MBA Instructor at Zhejiang University.

In addition to being the recipient of several awards in recognition of his achievements (e.g. National Excellent Entrepreneur, and The First Chinese Entrepreneurs Entrepreneurship Prize), Zong is also a civic-minded business leader who shoulders his share of social responsibility. As principal owner (estimated 80 % of the total shares), Wahaha has made donations to areas such as education, social welfare and humanitarian efforts for the Wenchuan earthquake, responded to the call to invest in disadvantaged areas across China to help in job creation, and was honored as the National Advanced Unit for supporting the migration work of the Three Gorges Project, Poverty-Alleviation Project, China Charity Prize, and so on.

Leading with Authority and Benevolence

Interviewers Tsui and Xin: Thank you for giving us your valuable time. Please describe your management philosophy.

Qinghou Zong (hereafter referred to as Zong): Many Chinese enterprises borrow management practices from foreign companies, but these practices do not always work in China because the country has different conditions, a unique culture, and is at a distinctive stage of development that differs from much of the world. Chinese managers should explore management methods that fit China's unique conditions, culture and development. Chinese companies need strong, open-minded leaders who put people first and are kind and tolerant towards their employees, and leaders who lack authority will find it difficult to manage Chinese companies. When employees make mistakes, leaders must point them out explicitly while giving the employee involved a second chance to put things right. Open-minded leaders should also practice what they preach and treat others as they would like to be treated. *People-foremost* means that the leader always considers employee interests and assumes responsibility for increasing employees' incomes and standards of living. I require employees to be disciplined and to obey orders. On the other hand, I am always nice to them. As a result, very few would say anything unfavourable about me. I listen to many points of view before I make major decisions, learning from Mao Zedong's idea of democratic centralism.[3]

Interviewers Tsui and Xin: You mentioned that a leader should consider employee interests. How did Wahaha put that idea into practice?

Zong: In 1999, we established an employee stock ownership plan giving company stock to employees who have worked with Wahaha for more than a year. As stockholders, employees should work much more proactively. In addition to basic salaries and bonuses, they also enjoy annual profit-sharing. Several years ago, Wahaha bought some affordable houses in Hangzhou for more than 3000 RMB per square metre. We then sold the houses to employees for 1200 RMB less per square metre per person. If a couple worked for Wahaha, they would pay 2400 RMB less per square metre. In recent years, we also built some low-rent houses for married employees in Hangzhou, Xiaoshan, Fuling and Chengdu. And we pay tuition fees from kindergarten to junior high school for the children of all employees.

Interviewers Tsui and Xin: What gave you the idea of considering employee interests?

Zong: I grew up in a poor family. I started working for a living after I graduated from junior high school. I was only 16 years old. I worked part-time here and there and then went to work in the countryside, as most young people did at the time. I stayed on the farm for 15 years before returning to Hangzhou. Life there was very tough and it taught me about the hardships under-privileged people faced. Also, I know very well that it is impossible for anyone to build and develop a company alone. You must motivate employees to work with you.

---

[3] Democratic centralism is a Leninist term, with 'democratic' referring to the freedom of members of the political party to discuss and debate matters of policy and direction; and 'centralism' referring to all members being expected to uphold the decision once it has been taken by majority vote. In China, Democratic centralism is stated in Article 3 of the Constitution (Wikipedia 2015b).

Developing a Family Culture: From Employee (Small Family) to Company (Big Family) to Country (National Family)

Interviewers Tsui and Xin: Can you describe any unique management practices at Wahaha?

Zong: We call our corporate culture *family culture*. We use the motto 'Love your small family, develop our big family, and serve the country.' Employees have their own small families. Wahaha is our big family. Employees regard their work as a lifelong career, and so they increase their capabilities continuously in developing the big family. On the other hand, Wahaha must consider employee interests by sharing growth results and continuously improving their standard of living. After we have achieved a strong big family, we should then also serve our country and assume our social responsibilities. However, good wages and benefits may breed laziness. Therefore, we use a competitive promotion system to encourage motivation to work hard.

Interviewers Tsui and Xin: Wahaha is a big family, and you are a paternalistic leader. We understand that you have no vice general manager positions, no small top management team. You make all the decisions. Does this create too much dependence on you?

Zong: We do not have vice general manager positions, to avoid conflict between employees. Some state-owned firms have a factory manager and a party secretary, each with their own teams of managers. Conflict occurs between these different coalitions. Our department heads are equivalent to vice general managers. They are responsible for their work areas. I can discuss with them on an equal basis, but they cannot challenge my authority.

When the company was small, I had to be concerned with everything. As we grew larger, we added hierarchical delegation. Reporting to me are 18 functional heads for the entire company; they are the general managers of the 150 divisions (subsidiary companies), the sales managers in the provinces, and the head of our R&D function. I divided production into eight regions, with a management centre in each region. These eight management centre heads also report to me directly. We have regular monthly meetings with the sales heads, production heads, and even the heads of major suppliers. These monthly meetings are to plan and negotiate sales, production and delivery.

The 18 functional departments are responsible for the operation of the whole company. Our divisions act as production workshops, with quality control departments, facilities departments, financial departments and administrative offices. The sales company is in charge of marketing and sales. It has sales branches in each province, under the charge of provincial managers. Each province is divided into multiple districts with district managers in charge. Sales companies meet monthly with those branches and deliver products to them to co-ordinate production and arrange delivery plans.

I have always regarded my employees as my children. Some new employees prefer to call me Manager Zong, but many long-time senior employees call me Big Brother, which makes me feel warm. Employees obey and greatly respect me. They rely on me a lot, which could be a problem. So I have empowered them by giving them chances to make decisions. Then I give them feedback to help them correct their mistakes. In other words, I allow them to make some mistakes. When the company was small, it could not afford mistakes. But now that it is bigger, we can afford some trial-and-error if the mistakes are not too serious.

Interviewers Tsui and Xin: Have you ever experienced conflicts between personal emotions and business rationality?

Zong: We had that kind of conflict in 1991 when we tried to merge with the Hangzhou Canned Food Factory. At the time, we had more than 100 employees and tens of millions of cash in the bank. Hangzhou Canned Food Factory had more than 2000 employees and more than 60,000 square metres of production area, but the company was insolvent and failed to pay its workers. In the beginning, many of our employees did not understand why we wanted to acquire such a factory. I told them that the merger would enlarge our scale, enabling us to grow faster, as well as to have higher incomes and better welfare.

The feedback from Hangzhou Canned Food Factory was also negative. Their employees called the merger 'a smaller fish trying to swallow a larger one.' Their mid-level managers were extremely resentful, fearing they would lose their jobs after the merger. Hangzhou government representatives talked with them for three days, but failed to persuade them to accept the merger. Then I had a meeting with them. I suggested that they look at the merger from another point of view that would revise their perception of which company was the smaller fish and which was the larger one. Was the bigger fish the company that had poor products, a small market share and couldn't pay its workers? In contrast, demand for Wahaha's products was so strong that it exceeded our ability to meet it. We had sufficient cash and our employees enjoyed high salaries. Despite having fewer employees, we were not necessarily a small company. I assured them that they would enjoy much better income levels. I also promised, to ease the mid-level managers' concerns, that we would not lay off workers after the merger. But I also told them about our performance evaluation system. Those who failed the evaluations would be fired, no matter who they were.

After the merger, the Hangzhou government sent in an integration team. The government was concerned about any instability arising from the merger and planned first to engage in ideological and political work. But I believed the priority should be to restore production, since the only way to eliminate instability was to give workers jobs and then pay them. I convinced the integration team to focus on production first. It took only one month to restore production.

Interviewers Tsui and Xin: What factors have led to Wahaha's success?

Zong: To be successful, a company needs comprehensive competences such as production, technology, R&D and marketing management. Apart from these factors, I see three other reasons that have led to our success.

First, we focused on our core business, to become the largest and most-profitable beverage company in China and among the leading companies in the world. We have invested heavily in buying world-class equipment and technology to ensure that our products are of top quality. We have expanded our production scale to ensure low costs. Unlike some beverage companies that outsource their production, we do it ourselves to lower costs and improve efficiency. For some time, real estate development profits were so high that many manufacturing companies joined in. But not us. Why? Because our core business kept us fully occupied. How would we have the time and energy to manage another, totally unrelated business? In the beverage industry, there are many competitors who will quickly copy any new product you introduce and cause prices to drop rapidly. Therefore, we have to grow very fast to keep up the economies of scale. When you are big enough, competitors cannot compete on price. We did not launch on the stock markets either. We have cash, and stock market membership has its disadvantages. Quite often shareholders do not think in the same way as the company, which might affect company decision-making.

The second reason is continuous innovation. Competition is fierce in our industry. With homogeneous products and price wars, companies lack pricing power, which yields razor-thin profits. We must be innovative and introduce new products constantly to gain pricing power. We have an R&D Academy specialising in innovation, and we are willing to invest however much is necessary. Our R&D investment-to-sales-revenue ratio is about 3 %, mainly because we have very high sales revenue.

Our innovation can be divided into three stages. The early stage was innovation in formulation. When smoothies were hot in the market, all the companies in the industry produced and sold versions of them. The standard packaging was six bottles of smoothies of the same flavour. We introduced a small innovation by packaging six bottles of different flavours together. As a result, our products outsold all our competitors. When all the companies were selling calcium milk, our innovation was adding vitamins A and D, which help the human body to absorb calcium. The second stage was imported innovation. Our growth has given us the financial resources to buy advanced international technologies and facilities. For example, we bought technologies from the USA for producing purified water with lower costs and with a better flavour than competitors had produced. The third stage was self-dependent innovation. Take our Nutrition Express as an example. We added 15 nutrients to milk. Many competitors copied this product later, but ours has the best flavour.

The third reason is our marketing network—our corporate sales network—which consists of two subnetworks. One is our own network—our nationwide sales branches. The other is the distribution system. Our account managers work with our first-level agents by helping them with sales as well as supervising them. The key is to ensure that the agents produce profits. The process is as follows: at the beginning of every month, the first-level agents deposit into our account money that we use to deduct their payables. At the end of each month, we pay the agents 1 %

interest of the deposit if they sell out of all the products. Thus we ensure the collection of receivables. Agents also find it favourable, as the 1 % monthly interest rate is higher than bank loan rates. Many of our agents were very small companies at first. They have grown with us to become large, highly loyal, and guided by the faith that we will honour their credibility. Now we have more than 6000 first-level agents.

If You Want to Make Money, You Must Ensure that Others Also Make Money

Interviewers Tsui and Xin: How did you devise such a good idea as to pay 1 % interest of the deposit as a reward?

Zong: We didn't have such a method at first. Although our products sold well, we could not collect all the receivables. Our Nourishing Oral Liquid sold so well that demand often exceeded supply. But we still had bad debts until we instituted this method. Our agents accepted it willingly because our products sell well. After all, the 12 % annual interest rate is higher than the profit margin of many industries. Anyway, if you want to make money, you must ensure that others also make money. Only then will they co-operate with you.

Interviewers Tsui and Xin: How did you establish your distribution channel?

Zong: Our distribution channel has changed with the development of the market environment. Before China established its market economy, we used the country's planned sales networks as our distribution channel. But with China's reforms, these networks suffered, because wholesale markets emerged. So we turned to the wholesale markets, especially in rural areas. Then competition among wholesale markets became so fierce that everyone had to play the price card. We began to build our own distribution network. First we had one agency in a single district. Later we had one in every county. Now every agency covers 200,000 to 300,000 people.

Interviewers Tsui and Xin: What is Wahaha's goal?

Zong: To be one of the 500 strongest companies worldwide. Most top-500 companies in China are actually tops in terms of scale, not strength. We want to have real top strength.

Interviewers Tsui and Xin: How do you define *strength*?

Zong: Profitability. Many manufacturing companies have profit margins that are too low to resist the temptation of real estate development, which enjoys excessive profits. We had profit margins of about 30 % in previous years. With rising costs in recent years, the margins have decreased to around 15 %–18 %. I attribute our profitability mainly to our efforts to ensure product quality and lower costs through investing in advanced technologies and facilities.

Interviewers Tsui and Xin: Wahaha broke with Danone in 2009 after 13 years. What lessons from this can you share with other business leaders?

Zong: In 1995, Danone wanted us to consider a co-operative venture. At that time, they had just entered the Chinese market. They had a poorly performing factory in Guangzhou. We were willing to establish a joint venture (JV) with them, for two reasons. Danone ranked sixth in the world's food industry, and we hoped to learn from their management expertise and advanced technologies. Also, we were responding to the local government's call to attract foreign investment. But after setting up the JV, we found that Danone contributed little beyond an initial investment of 300 million RMB. We operated and managed the JV. The products used our brand. Their directors were located as far away as Hong Kong. In spite of these problems, we performed well. We provided them with a return of 40 %–50 % annually. In 1996, the year our JV was established, sales revenue was RMB 900 million RMB. In 2006, sales revenue reached more than 14 billion RMB and profits were more than 1 billion RMB. In 2007, they wanted to buy our non-JV branches at net asset value. We disagreed. They attacked us through the media and brought it to the attention of the Hangzhou government, Chinese government, and even President Sarkozy of France. They sued us worldwide, in France, Italy, the USA, Hong Kong and China. We won all the cases. Our co operation with Danone was an early one in China, and we were too inexperienced. If we can draw a lesson from this, we learned that you must see clearly whether the potential partner is really sincere about co-operating with you. If they just want to invest some money and then effortlessly reap the benefits, you should avoid the deal.

Interviewers Tsui and Xin: Will you consider co-operating with other companies in the future?

Zong: We will if the potential partner has good products or advanced technologies. But the co-operation must be on an equal footing and for mutual benefit. We will consider no co-operation that involves only financial investment.

Interviewers Tsui and Xin: Wahaha has been focused on its core business. Have you considered diversifying?

Zong: Chinese companies have had two different views regarding diversification. In the early years, the popular view was that you should not put all your eggs in one basket. At that time, many companies were quite diversified. They all collapsed eventually, which led to the view that diversification was too risky.

We would consider three points. First, whether we needed to diversify, and actually we need to do so at present. We have a lot of cash. The beverage industry is over-competitive. It will be hard for us to develop further if we have only one core business. Second, we would ask whether the industry we want to adopt offers growth potential. Monopoly industries are poor alternatives. Third, we would consider whether we had the capability to diversify.

We will first consider diversifying up- and downstream, then into high technologies. We are careful. Last year, we set up a biological engineering institute to develop health foods. In 2002, we started producing children's clothes, which fits the Wahaha brand well. Now sales revenue for this business is more than 100 million RMB, with profits of more than 20 million RMB.

Interviewers Tsui and Xin: What management expertise would you like to share with young business leaders?

Zong: First, you must have dreams. You won't act if you have no dreams. Then you must be a down-to-earth doer. Third, you can't keep all the profits: you must ensure that all stakeholders benefit, and you must avoid being tempted by excessive profits. Last but not least, to be successful, you must work with your employees.

Commentary

Characterised by a paternalistic leadership (Farh and Cheng 2000; Pellegrini and Scandura 2008) style, Qinghou Zong has devoted his life to building the Wahaha empire, after having a harsh early life experiences, like many of his generation in China. The economic opening and growth of the consumer market brought an external environmental opportunity for Wahaha. However, it is the constantly enhanced organisational capability, especially in terms of innovation capability, that has paved the road to the success for Wahaha. Today, with strong branding in the beverage industry in China, Wahaha enjoys an unbeatable leading position by continuously adapting to the changing business environment.

Based on a culture of family (small, big and national), Mr Zong has modernised the company's management practices, combining Chinese cultural traditions with Western systems such as stock options to share ownership with employees. With high morality and integrity, the leadership style is strongly rooted in the Chinese cultural context along with authoritarianism and benevolence (Farh and Cheng 2000). By constantly transforming itself and developing new products to adapt to the demand of the market, Wahaha faces challenges of future diversification, especially into technological sectors, and succession issues.

References

Farh, J.-L., & Cheng, B.-S. (2000). A cultural analysis of paternalistic leadership in Chinese Organizations. In J. T. Li, A. S. Tsui, & E. Weldon (Eds.), *Management and organizations in the Chinese context*. Basingstoke: Palgrave Macmillan.

Hurun Institute. (2012). Hurun Rich list 2012. *Hurun Report*, 24 September. Retrieved December 28, 2015, from http://www.hurun.net/EN/ArticleShow. aspx?nid=Hurun Institute

Hurun Rich List. (2015). *Hurun Report*, 15 October. Retrieved December 28, 2015, from http://www.hurun.net/en/ArticleShow.aspx?nid=14678

Pellegrini, E., & Scandura, T. A. (2008). Paternalistic leadership: A review and agenda for future research. *Journal of Management, 34*(3), 566–593.

Sugawara, T. (2014). Wahaha is a drinks giant in China, but CEO Zong thirsts for more. *Nikkei Asian Review*, 28 March 2014. Retrieved March 26, 2015, from http://asia.nikkei.com/Business/Companies/Wahaha-is-a-drinks-giant-in-China-but-CEO-Zong-thirsts-for-more

Sull, D. N., & Wang, Y. (2005). *Made in China: What Western managers can learn from trailblazing Chinese entrepreneurs*. Boston, MA: Harvard Business School Press.

Wikipedia. (2015a). Zong Qinghou. Retrieved March 20, 2015, from https://en.wikipedia.org/wiki/Zong_Qinghou

Wikipedia. (2015b). Democratic centralism. Retrieved December 28, 2015, from https://en.wikipedia.org/wiki/Democratic_centralism

Wahaha. (2015). Wahaha website. Retrieved March 20 and December 28, 2015, from http://www.wahaha.com.cn/

15

Building Strong Relationships with Customers

Interview with Five-Star/Kidswant Founder and Chairman Jianguo Wang

The interview was conducted by: Xiao-Ping Chen, University of Washington, and Bin Gu, Arizona State University.

Five-Star/Kidswant[1]

Five-Star Holdings Ltd., founded on 18 December 1998 with 236 million RMB registered capital and headquartered in Nanjing, is a diversified investment enterprise engaged in modern service industrial chain and supply chain management, real estate, finance and investment, and specialised operations. Five-Star Holdings established the famous and successful Five-Star Electric Appliances chain, which achieved the top three position in the industry in only six years. In 2006, they formed a joint venture with Best Buy, the world's largest home appliances enterprise. In early 2009, Five-Star Holdings was officially spun off from Best Buy.

Today, Five-Star Holdings uses its advantages in brand, funding, management and human resources (HR) to help start-up businesses implement

---

[1] This section is based on information and news from the company website (Five-Star 2015), ifeng. com (2015), and IACMR's *Chinese Management Insights*' publication on Five-Star/Kidswant in September 2014.

© The Author(s) 2017   309
A.S. Tsui et al., *Leadership of Chinese Private Enterprises*, Palgrave Studies in Chinese Management, DOI 10.1057/978-1-137-40235-6_15

strategic transformation, create new businesses, and train talent. Five-Star chain brands include Huitongda, Kidswant and Hos Joy, all of which have been praised for their new business models. Five-Star now has more than 10 subsidiaries in different industries, with more than 3000 employees.

The subsidiary Kidswant is an emerging maternity—infant—child speciality retailer, providing integrative products and services in the field of children's growth and development. The business model of Kidswant is innovative and pioneering: it provides a one-stop solution for customers. Targeting medium- to high-income households with infants and children up to 14 years old, Kidswant is expanding its store network all over China. By July 2015, Kidswant had opened 80 stores in more than 20 cities in China, with an average space of 5000 square meters per store.

Founder and Chairman, Jianguo Wang[2]

Born in 1960 in Suzhou, Jiangsu province, Jianguo Wang obtained a bachelor's degree in economics in Jiangsu Communist Party School in 1992, and then a master's degree in administrative management in Nanjing University in 2000. In 2003 he received his MBA from the Australian National University and graduated from the Chinese Enterprise CEO Class of Cheung Kong Graduate School of Business, China.

He achieved early career success as section head of the Price Division of the Jiangsu Provincial Department of Commerce. Later he became the general manager of Jiangsu Provincial Corporation of Hardware, Electric Appliances and Chemicals, which was converted into Jiangsu Five-Star Electric Appliances Co. Ltd. Mr Wang led this transformation and became the president of Five-Star Electric Appliances. Through the joint venture formed with Best Buy, Mr Wang became the senior vice president of Best Buy Asia Pacific. After selling all his stocks of Five-Star Appliances to Best Buy, Mr. Wang founded and became the current chairman of Five-Star Holdings Group Co. Ltd., where he founded, invested in and led different businesses, including Kidswant.

---

[2] This section is based on IACMR's *Chinese Management Insights'* publication on Five-Star/Kidswant in September 2014 with permission, complemented by public information from Maigoo.com (2015) and ifeng.com (2013).

Jianguo Wang is vice director of China Household Electrical Appliances Association, vice president of Jiangsu Youth Chamber of Commerce, executive vice president of the Jiangsu Federation of Commerce, guest professor at Nanjing University of Science and Technology, guest professor of Southeast University, Nanjing, and special guest lecturer on the MBA programme of Nanjing University.

In 2008, the Ministry of Commerce and the Ministry of Personnel awarded Jianguo Wang the honorary title of 'Model Worker of the Country's Commerce System.' In 2009, he was named as one of '60 Jiangsu entrepreneurs affecting China's economy in the 60 years after New China was founded.' In 2010, Jianguo Wang, Jack Ma, Yuzhu Shi, Feng Yu and Guojun Shen established Yunfeng Capital,[3] dedicated to investing in areas such as the internet, consumer products, and new energy.

Incubating the Internet Business Model: From Managing Commodities to Managing Customers, From Meeting Demands to Creating Demands

Interviewer Chen: Please tell us how you founded Five-Star Appliances, sold it to Best Buy, and then started a new business to become chairman of Five-Star Holdings?

Jianguo Wang (hereafter referred to as Wang): After graduating from university, I worked for 10 years in a government agency, and for another 10 years in a state-owned enterprise. My most important discovery was that I liked business activities. I thought commerce in China was extremely underdeveloped, mainly because Chinese people had always valued industry and agriculture but despised commerce. Consequently, the government undervalued commerce. Government officials were happy to inspect industrial parks and farms but felt 'degraded' if they had to inspect shopping malls. Besides, you rarely saw a party secretary or

---

[3] Yunfeng Capital was established in January 2010, named after Ma Yun of Alibaba and Yu Feng of Target Media. It is a private equity firm in China set up by successful entrepreneurs, pioneers and industry leaders. More information can be found on http://www.yfc.cn/en/

a mayor with a commercial background; most government officials came from industrial or agricultural sectors. Once I tried to arrange a meeting with the mayor in charge of logistics in Yancheng city, Jiangsu province, but he said he had no time for me because, as he said, he had to receive an 'important customer.' Later I learned that the important customer was one of my suppliers who ran a small factory. At that time I was running a 10 billion RMB shopping mall, while his factory yielded just tens of millions. But he was more important because he owned a factory. Why does a factory seem more important when my shopping mall pays more taxes? China's attitude towards commerce was really backward, though commerce guided its production.

That is why I stayed in the commercial world after selling Five-Star Appliances to Best Buy. I continued to believe that commerce represents a huge opportunity. Consumption, investment and export are the three drivers of China's future development. I believe that internal demand is the most important driving force of the economy. That realisation led me back to the business world.

Interviewer Chen:What was your goal in returning to business? You had already accumulated capital from Five-Star Appliances, so making money was no longer the driver. Also, how did you choose what business to focus on?

Wang: My research revealed that the internet was having a tremendous impact on business operations. I decided to give it a go, but did not think that I should start from scratch, so I positioned myself as an investor. I would recruit investors, but I would dedicate myself to a new business model to help ambitious young people create successful businesses. My vision was to help aspirational people to build their dreams. I told my shareholders that even peasants sow seeds after harvesting. I persuaded them to invest some of the several hundred million US dollars we had received from selling Five-Star Appliances to Best Buy. They were very supportive. Previously I had started from the bottom with one enterprise. Now I would start from the top and take a holistic view of the information society to get a more complete picture of future business development.

We decided to define our direction using a scientific approach. We hired a consulting firm to investigate the market and formulate a strategy. A few months later, they recommended four targeted groups our business should focus on: children, the ageing population, the wealthy, and women. I could not cover all four, and chose to target the kids' market. My team and I went to the United States, the United Kingdom and South Korea to study businesses related to children. Then we went to Taiwan and Hong Kong to observe all businesses related to children in China. I watched, thought, and discussed my ideas with my team members regarding specific methods to approach the huge market relating to products for children in China, where 24 million babies are born every year. At that time, we defined our target segment as children from minus one (prenatal) to 14 years old, split into four to five age groups, a population of around 360 million. We observed that China had no brands dedicated to such a huge market. We could not think of any store a consumer might visit to buy for children. We knew that was not the case in foreign countries. The United States has several brands, such as Babies 'R' Us and Toys 'R' Us. So does the United Kingdom, but not China. That was the opportunity.

To acquire an international perspective for approaching the business seriously, we studied the US, UK and Japanese models thoroughly. Then we hired Americans to design our logo and Taiwanese to design our business model. One of my ideas was to change from managing commodities to managing customers. In the past, all retail stores managed and sold commodities, but no one cared about customers. My experience at Best Buy showed me that I should focus on customers. I started to think about how to categorise and interact with customers, and how to ascertain customer value.

The second idea was to change from meeting demands to creating/guiding demands. Meeting demands is fundamental; creating demands and then meeting them hits a higher level. Young parents lack experience in raising babies. Consequently, they are open to recommendations.

Once we clarified those two concepts, we worked to make them operational. My team converted concepts to strategies, strategies to actions, and actions into something operational and measurable.

The First Step to Managing Customers: Listen to Them

Interviewer Chen:You did not use consulting firms this time?

Wang: No, we figured it out for ourselves. We opened our first Kidswant store using the shopping mall model rather than the department store or supermarket model. Department stores target individuals; supermarkets target housewives; shopping malls target families. Thus we wanted our first store to be in a mall. Jianlin Wang, the founder and CEO of the Wanda Group, was ready to open his first shopping mall, Wanda Plaza, in Nanjing. We offered to rent a space of between 5000 and 6000 square meters. At first he was surprised that we would need such a big space for a kids' store. I explained that we would do more than selling commodities; we would add a playground, a photo studio, a hair salon, and swimming facilities. He eventually agreed. Of course, he suffered no risk. All our rental contracts were fixed for more than 10 years.

Now the store revenues have grown from 30 million RMB to nearly 200 million RMB. I have continued to explore new ideas while running this business. Before, all I did was conclude transactions, make money, and pay back the loan as soon as possible. Now my mindset has changed. I keep studying business patterns and ways to differentiate our company from others and stay ahead. For example, initially we followed the 'purchase store' model—a premium look with spacious aisles, bright lighting, and image displays for all brands. I expected it to be a hit, but few customers showed up. We started to get nervous. What should we do? The only way was to talk to customers, listen to their complaints, and gather their feedback. I even had dinner with some customers. I concluded that Chinese wives and mothers were all very price sensitive and liked bargains, whether they were rich or poor.

They said that the store was so brightly lit and the aisles were so spacious they assumed the prices must be high. Some remarked that the shelves were closed so they could not touch or experience the commodities. We immediately remodelled and re-designed everything, blocking up where necessary and opening shelves so customers could touch and experience the products. This is what understanding and listening to customers mean. Customers started to come, and then we focused on the optimisation of commodities and services. We introduced photo services and then experiential activities such as drawing, calligraphy, a sand-play box, and painting competitions. Later we incorporated cultural elements such as singing, dancing, tourism and social activities. Gradually we developed the Kidswant business model.

The Second Step for Managing Customers: Provide Free Commodities and Services, and Keep Customer Data

Interviewer Gu:So far, you have spoken about Kidswant's offline activities. When did you start your online activities?

Wang: We have never departed from internet thinking, which more or less came from Jack Ma of Alibaba. I have had significant exchanges with Jack Ma through my personal association with the Yunfeng Fund. He often asks me questions about commerce, because I am in the retail industry. When we opened the first Kidswant, I invited him to visit. He asked many questions, such as traffic volume and customer loyalty. I couldn't give him straight answers because I did not have them. But I quickly recognised the strengths in internet thinking, especially regarding customers and customer orientation. But how could we apply concepts such as free services and traffic flow to bricks-and-mortar stores? I define traffic flow as the number of customers visiting.

Then we started collecting customer data—the number of daily customers, the number of items average customers bought, and the amount of money they spent. I realised increasingly that I must learn from the internet and attract customers by offering free services. We started offering courses for expecting mothers, followed by courses for new mothers. Then we established the community mothers' programme. Our continually offered free programmes have had several effects. First, people are often surprised that a bricks-and-mortar store offers free services. Our employees feel that they are not really salespeople but are the caretakers of customers.

For example, they remember customers' age, personality, facial expression, and even ways of speaking. If you ask our employees what Kidswant does, they won't say that Kidswant sells maternal and child products. Instead, they say Kidswant manages customer relationships.

At first I feared that 'managing customer relationships' might sound a bit vulgar. I told the general manager that we should mention managing customer relationships only in private; that employees would find the goal awkward. He said, 'I understand what you say, Boss. But at the beginning this is the only way for our employees to understand what it means to manage customer relationships.' So we told employees that everything we do is to maintain good customer relationships, to speak kindly, and to compliment them. As a result, our employees seem to accept this approach and have learned to praise and compliment customers. They also distribute small gifts and business cards and record customer phone numbers—all for managing relationships. But in addition to managing relationships, we also sought improvements and upgrades. So later we proposed managing customer data, information and files.

Interviewer Gu: That is an internet concept.

Wang: It means quantifying customer relationships by calculating transaction amounts and individual customer contributions. If a customer spends 800 RMB in Kidswant a year, what is the purchase frequency and gross profit generated? If a customer spends only 15 RMB, that results in a low margin, low purchase amount, and high cost. How do we increase our assets? How do we increase the number of customers? How do we increase customers' consumption power? How do we convert a customer into a club member and increase the amount of each transaction? We appraise our performance using data instead of previous assessment methods. We no longer use daily sales as an indicator. First, we look at the number of members; that is, customers who buy at least twice a month. Second, we look at the conversion rate; that is, the ability to convert ordinary customers to members. Third, we consider the amount of each transaction; and fourth, the sales amount per customer. Those key performance indicators guide my management team. The more customers I have, the greater my customer assets. If one customer spends 1000 RMB a year, 10 customers will spend 10,000 RMB, and 100 customers will spend 100,000 RMB. That is how I measure customer assets.

The Third Step for Managing Customer Relationship: Build Strong Relationships

Wang: After managing customer assets successfully, we still thought we could do more. Brainstorming came up with the current drive to build strong customer relationships through an interpersonal bond with customers. We categorise generation 1 and generation 2 stores. The Nanjing store is now a generation 3.5 store, and we are developing generation 4 stores. Generation 4 stores must have door-to-door + service + culture + recreation + social + a place for mother members while their children are engaged in various activities.

Interviewer Gu:It is interesting that you classify your stores by generation, like Web 2.3, 3.0, and 4.0.

Wang: Yes, constant generation update is another internet characteristic; we incorporate advanced technologies whenever we can. All these years, while my team and I have pondered current issues, I have also been considering the future.

Powerful Back-End Management: From Functional Responsibility to Customer and Process Responsibility

Interviewer Chen: What measures do you think are especially effective in motivating employees to build customer relationships passionately and diligently?

Wang: First, it is difficult to 'transplant' internet genes into a traditional enterprise: genes are inherited. But I knew we could change the culture. Culture is an atmosphere established when every employee works and behaves consistently within it. I hoped to change the traditional commodity-oriented culture to a customer-oriented one: whatever the circumstances, we focus on customers. Second, regardless of an employee's function—HR, finance or purchasing—ultimately each employee is accountable for the customer results, not functional results alone. The transition was not as easy as it appeared. It was extremely difficult to change the culture. Employees tended to think that if they worked in the

HR department, they were responsible only for recruitment and training. If they worked in the finance department, their job was to control costs and manage budgets. They might say 'Customer happiness is not my concern. Frontline staff manage customer satisfaction.' Such traditional ideas are hard to change. We tell employees repeatedly that if we stick to past practices of working by function, we cannot survive. Losing customers means losing everything.

In addition to instilling these ideas, we broke down walls separating the different functions by weakening some functions and central positions and strengthening customer service functions. We consolidated the entire finance function and built a strong back-end and small front-end. Our 'golden triangle' concept means that two or three people serve one customer.

In another step, we combined the 'virtual' and the 'actual.' We consider the organisation to be an entity for studying and formulating policies, but in actual operations the virtual organisation takes the lead. For example, I am a virtual team leader; previously I was just a department head, but now even the general manager listens to me. This way more people take responsibility. Employees can now assume the functions performed by department heads and general managers in the past. As the many layers are removed, the organisation becomes flattened. Currently we have no layers for virtual functions; thus we have improved efficiency and added vitality by changing the organisational culture. We call this *employee-driven* change. Employee-driven rather than boss-driven, employees are automatically motivated.

Interviewer Chen: How long did it take for employees to completely accept the reform?

Wang: I set an example by practising what I advocated. If you do not take part but just order people to change, it won't work. I stepped aside and let the sales-team leaders speak. When Kidswant started, store managers expected me to discuss everything with them. I felt that they should not continue to rely so heavily on me, so I told them that I would be absent and that Mr Xu, the store manager, would be chairing all the meetings when I was not there. I also told them that this was Mr Xu's decision. People got nervous, as there were so many decisions to make.

But I was determined. One evening I told them that I would definitely *not* be available. They had to decide how to handle their problems and tell me about it the next day. I said 'I don't care how you decide, I just need results.' They kept calling and asking what to do. They said 'This is serious; you'd better come, Boss.' I replied that I had important things to attend to, and asked them to stop calling me. Actually I was right there; I was circling the building in my car five or six times. I knew there was a chance that they might make a major mistake that would have a big impact on me and on the company. But I restrained myself from going upstairs.

Mission of Middle Management: Supporting Frontline Employees

Interviewer Gu: The Kodak company presents a case study: one reason it failed was that middle management failed to execute top management's plans. Is your company in a similar situation?

Wang: Middle managers such as department head or HR director are very important, as are store managers. But my analysis showed that frontline employees were the most important, so I let them direct the frontline operations. Take advertising, for example. In the past, if the frontline wanted to organise an event, they had to send a request for approval to middle management and then to top management. The process mistakenly implied that the advertising was conducted for the management. So I decided to eliminate the approval system but keep the right of review. Is your advertisement effective? If not, you will be penalised. But you have the right to advertise. Another reason to delegate authority to the frontline is that, in the internet and information era, consumers dominate. The most important goal is to attract consumers. Frontline people, being at the front-end, understand consumers the best. Then what about middle management? They serve the frontline by providing support and resources.

Interviewer Chen: This thinking hugely challenges the traditional thinking of management.

Wang: Under our structure, middle management plays a less important role. Their main responsibility is to help the frontline and to solve in a timely way the problems employees encounter. If the managers can't solve the problem, I will replace them. Frontline employees are the most important. We evaluate and quantify their performance directly, such as the number of customers they manage. For example, a frontline employee receives 5 RMB for obtaining a member customer. If the customer makes another purchase, the employee gets another 5 RMB. If the customer becomes a regular purchaser, spending, say, 300 RMB a month, the employee gets another 3 RMB. Under this model, employees conclude transactions. Middle management does not conduct business; it provides a service.

Interviewer Chen:Do you link the income and bonuses of middle management to employees under their supervision?

Wang: Middle management appraisal is based on overall company performance. The appraisal mechanism has multidimensional indicators adjusted by weight as required. For example, if a middle manager has focused on training his team and new employees, that target will be weighted more highly. If I add new requirements this year for developing customers, I will increase the weight for that target. The system allows flexibility to allocate weighting based on targets.

Full Delegation Within the Core Cultural Value System

Interviewer Chen:Western management theories consider delegation to be a very important topic. Many talk about doing it, but they don't really 'walk the talk.' How did you turn the concept into practice?

Wang: The precondition for delegation is that you must have a solid system. Without data or information, you probably would not dare to delegate. I am not afraid to delegate because I am on top of everything. I know the gross margin, and I can make sure that no commodities or money will be lost. Our data monitoring and central control systems are both very strong. Moreover, my philosophy is that our job is not to catch employees who make mistakes but to set up a system that prevents them from making mistakes. From this perspective, cultural education and the establishment of values are extremely important.

Interviewer Chen:What are your company's core values?

Wang: Very simple. First are integrity and pragmatism. I define integrity basically as no lies—do not tell lies internally, and do not deceive people externally, as simple as that. Employees will be fired, without exception, if they cheat customers, make false statements, harm anyone inside or outside the company, or resort to any deceit. Pragmatism means no empty words or empty talk. Our meetings are straightforward. We skip niceties such as 'Dear guests' or 'Dear Professor.' We just say 'I have a few things to report today.' Excessive politeness is not allowed.

I am quite demanding. If you fail to meet the target, tell me why but don't give excuses such as weather conditions, holidays, or too few customers. If employees try to give excuses in meetings, they have to leave. You say this year we have a tough macroeconomic situation and there is market regulation, but our business is not big enough for the macro economy to impact it. Just do your business. These are our values.

Interviewer Chen:What other values do you have in addition to integrity and pragmatism?

Wang: Respect for individuals, meaning that we encourage everyone to make the best use of their strengths. Specifically, when we talk about others, we must talk first about their strengths before we discuss their weaknesses, because we think it is easier to exploit advantages than to overcome weaknesses.

We also value independent innovation and the pursuit of excellence. We consider any beneficial improvement to be innovation. I contribute 3 million RMB from my personal account to reward innovation, and I choose the winners. We have very positive results. We think wisdom comes from employees, not from top management. We have a company motto, 'The goal is carved on the rock, and the ways to reach the goal are written on the beach.' The goal is set in stone, but the paths can be rewritten and erased. Innovation creates new paths.

Interviewer Chen:How did you create your company culture?

Wang: To provide cultural guidelines, you tell employees what you value, what you advocate, and what you oppose. I emphasise honesty and credibility. If you are reliable, employees and partners are willing to work for you and with you. The entire company spends much time building our company culture. For example, we encourage competition between teams because moderate competition can drive individual progress. But you must guard against those who will slander, attack or step on others, because such behaviours will destroy team spirit. You cannot encourage victory built on harming others; instead, you must stop that behaviour. We must be very clear about our message when praising or criticising. You may praise lavishly those who succeed and help others to succeed. Guidance is critically important for judging leaders. If some get to the first place by harming others, we definitely cannot recognise them.

Interviewer Chen: So you don't just look at the results alone but also look at specific behaviours to achieve the results.

Wang: Yes. For performance appraisals, we advocate team success instead of individual heroism. But when I give praise, I always praise individuals. Let me use a metaphor here. If you are a coachman, do you whip the horse or the carriage? The horse will not feel the pain if I whip the carriage, just as the individual will not feel pride if I praise the team. I must direct praise to the deserving individuals.

Therefore appraisals are focused on individuals rather than units. For example, I only talk about how the general manager is performing, not how the store is doing. Why? Because the unit, as the carriage, is irrelevant; the store manager must take full responsibility. As a result, all my ranking lists and letters of recommendation are individually based.

'Exploit' the Role Model in Innovation

Interviewer Gu: Generally speaking, how do you make successful bottom-up innovations known to the company as a whole?

Wang: The purpose of innovation is not to solve individual problems but to provide demonstrations, examples or role models. If a store has a most effective practice, it becomes a role model that will be introduced to others. We copy best practices using the role model concept. For example, if an employee is skilled in explaining company culture, she will be selected to explain it to the entire group and to others on a speaking tour. If another employee has achieved an unusually high gross margin as a result of his skills in purchasing, he will be responsible for spreading his expertise.

Anyone can be a role model. One does not have to be a leader. The point is that you give them an opportunity to speak; their manager will also be praised; and it all becomes a driving force for the rapid adoption of innovation.

People Orientation, Continual Innovation Amid Changes

Interviewer Chen:Please summarise your management philosophy, style and concepts, especially for readers who want to start their own businesses.

Wang: Ultimately, it comes down to people. Regardless of the type of enterprise or the stage of enterprise development, employees and customers are the most important assets. Companies must choose the right people, use them the right way, and bring out their passion and enthusiasm. Furthermore, we must satisfy their need for learning and growth. Put simply, the first point is to stick to a human orientation.

The second point is to build a good corporate culture that can adapt to the internet and information era. Many companies say that culture is immutable. I disagree. Culture must adapt to the new environment through continuous innovation. Change itself is the only thing that remains unchanged. But the change is not blind; it is adaptation.

My personal experience provides a good illustration of subversive change from working in a government agency to a state-owned company, to a private company, to a joint venture, and finally to a private innovative business. Without change, I would still be working in a government agency somewhere. Over the past decades I have come to another important realisation: keep it simple. Simplify complexities to make it easy to accomplish more. Many companies fail not because they lack ideal conditions but because their organisation, relationships and processes are too complex. I promote simplicity: no meetings if a phone call will suffice; no sitting if standing can solve the problem; no meetings lasting more than an hour. I believe in timely communication and timely solutions.

Interviewer Chen:This also means high transparency and low information asymmetry?

Wang: Yes, my advice reflects our company fundamentals. A company is basically in trouble if it cannot make fast decisions or if people evade responsibilities. If a company is aware and agile, its employees can solve problems and take responsibility. If a salesperson is not afraid to say 'Leave this to me. I will come back to you with a solution after talking to my boss,' then that company is full of life. Our company is like that.

Commentary

The initiation and creation of Kidswant was through scientific management tools outsourced to a professional consultancy. This is in contrast to most other start-ups that practise 'learning by doing' (Christensen 1997; Cope and Watts 2000; Tsang 2002). Nonetheless, Kidswant still went through its own 'trial and error' process. Though experienced in retailing business for other industries and products (i.e. Five-Star Electric Appliances), Jianguo Wang had to interact intensively with potential customers to learn about this industry, and had to adjust the business model when the first store was not a success. Now holding a strong brand in its segment, Kidswant has renewed the whole management process to adapt to business needs, and apply internet logic to their business model even though most of the business is still offline. The simplistic and pragmatic approach of delegating power to the frontline employees enables bottom-up innovations and to successful management of customer relationships.

Different from his earlier entrepreneurial experience, Mr Wang was able to define an interesting market with great potential and carry out a field study of the business model in different advanced economies to build up a benchmarked model. Through accumulated entrepreneurial experience, observations and reflections, Mr Wang brings internet concepts creatively into the retailing business, incorporating free services, building a database and centralising the management control system, and a fair reward and compensation system. With his intelligent management of the process in spite of tension and disagreement (Zhou and George 2003), this eventually enables innovation and creativity to flow, and decisions to be taken by frontline employees (Cadwallader et al. 2010), which turned the business of Kidswant in the direction of success and prosperity.

References

Christensen, C. M. (1997). Making strategy: Learning by doing. *Harvard Business Review*, (November–December), 141–156.

Cadwallader, S., Jarvis, C. B., Bitner, M. J., & Ostrom, A. L. (2010). Frontline employee motivation to participate in service innovation implementation. *Journal of the Academy of Marketing Science, 38*(2), 219–239.

Cope, J., & Watts, G. (2000). Learning by doing—An exploration of experience, critical incidents and reflection in entrepreneurial learning. *International Journal of Entrepreneurial Behavior & Research, 6*(3), 104–124.

Five-Star (2015). Five-Star Holdings website. Retrieved March 23 and December 18, 2015, from http://www.fsh.cn/

ifeng.com (2013). Jianguo Wang. Retrieved December 18, 2015, from http://finance.ifeng.com/people/comchief/wangjianguo.shtml

ifeng.com. (2015). Five-Star Holdings surpassed 10 billion RMB in five years. Retrieved March 23, 2015, from http://js.ifeng.com/business/brand/detail_2015_03/01/3598543_0.shtml

Maigoo. (2015). Jianguo Wang. Retrieved December 18, 2015, from http://mingren.maigoo.com/683.html

Tsang, E. W. K. (2002). Acquiring knowledge by foreign partners from international joint ventures in a transition economy: Learning-by-doing and learning myopia. *Strategic Management Journal, 23*(9), 835–854.

Zhou, J., & George, J. M. (2003). Awakening employee creativity: The role of leader emotional intelligence. *The Leadership Quarterly, 14*(4–5), 545–568.

Part VI

Leadership Insights from the Founding Private Firm Entrepreneurs

16

A Concentric Model of Private Firm Leadership in China: Insights from Founding Entrepreneurs

As discussed in Chap. 2, there has been little empirical research focusing specifically on executive leadership in Chinese private enterprises. The existing literature is composed mainly of large-sample survey studies of executive leadership, with no distinction between firms with different ownerships. Given an extremely dynamic, complex and inhospitable environment, both institutional and social, we argue that the emergence and success of the vibrant private economy can be ascribed primarily to the exceptional leadership of the founders of private enterprises as well as the other leaders who have worked with them. To further develop this insight, we interviewed 13 carefully selected and extraordinarily successful Chinese leaders of private firms to gain an in-depth understanding of their unique backgrounds, management practices and thoughts on leadership. Chaps. 3 to 15 contain the interview transcripts. In this chapter, we present the results of the content analysis of these 13 interviews.

The entrepreneurial leaders interviewed come from four distinct industries, with three in the financial services (China Merchants Bank, Fosun, and Taikang Life Insurance), four in computers, information technology and e-commerce (Alibaba, HC360, Lenovo and Neusoft), three

© The Author(s) 2017   **329**
A.S. Tsui et al., *Leadership of Chinese Private Enterprises*, Palgrave Studies in Chinese Management, DOI 10.1057/978-1-137-40235-6_16

in construction and real estate (Tecsun Homes, Vanke and Vantone), and three in the consumer and retail industries (Kidswant, Li-Ning and Wahaha). We first analysed the background of these 13 founders/leaders. Following that, we performed an 'attribute content analysis' to detect the presence of the four traits (determination, discipline, duality focus and divinity belief) introduced in Chap. 2, while remaining open to the possibility of additional attributes based on the perspectives of these 13 leaders. Third, we followed an independent open coding procedure to identify patterns of management with a 'thematic content analysis.' A detailed description of the content analysis methods is provided in Appendix 16.1.

Below, we first present profiles of the 13 leaders, then discuss the results of the attribute content analysis (at the individual leader level), and the results of the thematic content analysis (at the organisational level). We perform a cross-industry comparison of the leaders' management principles (thoughts, beliefs and associated practices). Integrating the results of the attribute analysis and thematic analysis, we develop a concentric model of Chinese private firm leadership, and conclude with a discussion of the implications of this model for future research and practice.

Background and Current Profiles of the 13 Entrepreneurs/Leaders

Table 16.1 presents the profiles of the 13 leaders in the four different industries across three main categories: *previous experience* (Table 16.1a) before their entrepreneurship (educational background, previous work experience and institutional relationship); *current activities* (Table 16.1b) in addition to their primary entrepreneurial activity (in social contributions, business associations, university collaboration and political participation); and *personal achievement* (receiving entrepreneurial awards, other outstanding domestic and international recognition), summarised in Table 16.1c.

Table 16.1a Pre-entrepreneurial experiences of 13 private firm leaders

Type of experience	Financial industry	Technology industry	Real estate industry	Consumer industry	Total
University education	3/3 Dongsheng Chen and Weihua Ma: PhD in Economics; Xinjun Liang: BSc in Genetic Engineering	4/4 Chuanzhi Liu: BA in Radar; Jiren Liu: Dr. in Computer Science; Jack Ma: College Degree in English; Fansheng Guo: BSc in Economics	3/3 Lun Feng: Doctor of Jurisprudence; Shi Wang: BA in Drainage; Shengzhe Nie: BA in Chemistry	2/3 Qinghou Zong: Hangzhou Workers Amateur University; Jianguo Wang: Bachelor of Foreign Economics	12/13
Work experience	3/3 Dongsheng Chen: Associate Editor of the journal *Management World*; Weihua Ma: Governor of PBOC Hainan Branch and Chief of SAFE Hainan Branch; Xinjun Liang: Lecturer at Fundan University	4/4 Jack Ma: English Teacher at HangZhou Dian Zi University; Jiren Liu: Professor at Northeastern University; Chuanzhi Liu: Researcher and Administrator at Chinese Academy of Sciences; Fansheng Guo: Office Director of China Economic System Reform Institute	3/3 Lun Feng: China Institute of Reform and Development; Shi Wang: Guangzhou Overseas Trade and Economy Commission; Shengzhe Nie: Top manager at USA Federal Tecsun	3/3 Qinghou Zong: School-run Enterprise Sales Department Manager; Ning Li: Gymnastics Athlete; Jianguo Wang: General Manager of Jiangsu Provincial Corporation of Hardware, Electric Appliances and Chemicals	13/13

(continued)

Table 16.1a (continued)

Type of experience	Financial industry	Technology industry	Real estate industry	Consumer industry	Total
Government positions	2/3 Weihua Ma: Multiple government positions at regional and national level; Dongsheng Chen: Ministry of Foreign Trade and Economic Cooperation	1/4 Fansheng Guo: Multiple governmental positions at regional and national level	1/3 Lun Feng: Multiple governmental positions at regional and national level	1/3 Jianguo Wang: Several governmental positions at provincial level	5/13

Notes: 1. University education refers only to that undertaken before the entrepreneurial experience
2. Work experience refers to the job immediately before their first start-up business or private business experience (for non-business founders)
3. Information is taken from company websites or various public open sources on the internet such as Baidu.com, Worldofceos.com, mingren.maigoo.com, Google, Sohu, Wikipedia and Forbes. Please accept our apologies for any errors or omissions
4. The entries for previous experience are illustrative examples and may not be exhaustive
5. The number in each cell (e.g. 3/3 or 2/3) refers to the number of leaders with the referenced experience

Table 16.1b Current activities of 13 private firm leaders

Sub-elements	Financial industry	Technology industry	Real estate industry	Consumer industry	Total
Social contribution	3/3 Foundation, subsidies and donation (Taikang Life Insurance Co., Ltd./Dongsheng Chen; China Merchants Bank/ Weihua Ma; Fosun Group/Xinjun Liang)	4/4 Foundation, subsidies and donation (Neusoft/ Jiren Liu; Alibaba/Jack Ma; The Lenovo Group/ Chuanzhi Liu; HC360.com/ Fansheng Guo)	3/3 Foundation, subsidies and donation (Vantone/Lun Feng; Vanke Group/Shi Wang; Tesun/Shengzhe Nie)	3/3 Foundation, subsidies and donation (Wahaha Group/Qinghou Zong; Li-Ning Company/Ning Li; Kidswant/Jianguo Wang)	13/13
Business association	3/3 Weihua Ma: Vice president of China Enterprise Directors Association; Xinjun Liang: Vice president of China Youth Entrepreneur Association; Dongsheng Chen: Vice president of Insurance Association of China	2/4 Chuanzhi Liu: Vice chairman of the All-China Federation of Industry and Commerce in 2002; Jiren Liu: Vice president of China Internet Association	3/3 Lun Feng: Vice president of the Real Estate Association of China, Federation of Industry and Commerce; Shi Wang: Vice president of Shenzhen General Chamber of Commerce;Shengzhe Nie: Deputy executive member of the committee of Wood Framed Buildings of China Architecture Association	2/3 Qinghou Zong: Vice resident of the Chinese Health Food Association; Jianguo Wang: Executive Vice president of Jiangsu Federation of Commerce	10/13

(continued)

Table 16.1b (continued)

Sub-elements	Financial industry	Technology industry	Real estate industry	Consumer industry	Total
University collaboration	2/3 Weihua Ma: Vice chairman of the Board of Ji Lin University; Dongsheng Chen: Part-time Professor at Nan Kai University and Northwestern University (China)	2/4 Jiren Liu: Vice chancellor of Northeastern University; Jack Ma: Awarded an honorary doctoral degree by the Hong Kong University of Science and Technology	2/3 Shengzhe Nie: Professor and Doctoral Supervisor of SiChuan University; Lun Feng: Committee member of HuPan College;	3/3 Jianguo Wang: Guest lecturer at Nanjing University of Science and Technology; Qinghou Zong: MBA Tutor at ZheJiang University; Ning Li: Awarded honorary doctorate from different international universities	9/13
Political participation	2/3 Xinjun Liang: Municipal People's Congress Standing Committee; Weihua Ma: CPPCC Member	2/4 Jiren Liu: CPPCC Member; Chuanzhi Liu: Deputy of the National People's Congress	0/3	2/3 Qinghou Zong: Deputy of the National People's Congress; Ning Li: Deputy of the National People's Congress	6/13

Note: 1. Information obtained from company websites or various public open sources on the internet such as Baidu.com, Worldofceos.com, mingren.maigoo.com, Google, Sohu, Wikipedia and Forbes. Please accept our apologies for any errors or omissions

2. The entries for current activities are illustrative examples and may not be exhaustive

3. The number in each cell (e.g. 3/3 or 2/3) refers to the number of leaders with the referenced activities

Table 16.1c Personal achievements of 13 private firm leaders

Sub-elements	Financial industry	Technology industry	Real estate industry	Consumer industry	Total
Entrepreneurial recognition	3/3 Weihua Ma: China's Most Influential Leader Award; Dongsheng Chen: Chinese Economic Leadership Award; Xinjun Liang: The Management Innovation Award of China Young Entrepreneurs	4/4 Chuanzhi Liu: Asian Star; Jiren Liu: CCTV China Economic Figures of the Year; Jack Ma: CCTV China Economic Figures of the Year;Fansheng Guo: Management Guru of Family Business	2/3 Shi Wang: Chinese Real Estate Industry Leader; Lun Feng: The Most Popular Top Ten Entrepreneurs	2/3 Qinghou Zong: CCTV China Economic Figures of the Year; Ning Li: Distinguished CEO Award	11/13
General recognition	2/3 Xinjun Liang: Shanghai Ten Outstanding Young Persons; Weihua Ma: Outstanding Contributor to Civil Society in 2011	3/4 Jack Ma: Most Generous Philanthropists; Chuanzhi Liu: Model Worker; Jiren Liu: May I Labour Prize	1/3 Lun Feng: Special Contributor of the Year	1/3 Ning Li: 20th Anniversary Special Contribution Award of Project Hope	7/13
International reputation	3/3 Xinjun Liang: '2011 Chinese Business Leader of the Year' at the Horasis Global China Business Meeting in Valencia, Spain; Weihua Ma: 'Asia's Excellent CEO' by Institutional Investor in 2011; Dongsheng Chen: China's Most Influential 50 Business Leaders in 2012	3/4 Jack Ma: 'The world's greatest 50 leaders' by Fortune in 2014; Chuanzhi Liu: 'Global Top 50 Most Influential Thinkers' by Thinkers 50 in 2013; Jiren Liu: 'China's Most Influential 50 Business Leaders' in 2012	1/3 Shi Wang: One of 25 most influential business leaders in China, 2010; 'Fortune Forum' in Hong Kong, 2001	2/3 Qinghou Zong: 'The China Mainland's Richest Man' by Forbes in 2013;Ning Li: 'The 10 Most Respected Chinese Entrepreneurs' by Forbes in 2009	9/13

Note: 1. Information obtained from company websites or various public open sources on the internet such as Baidu.com, Worldofceos.com, mingren.maigoo.com, Google, Sohu, Wikipedia and Forbes. Please accept our apologies for any errors or omissions

2. The entries for current activities are illustrative examples and may not be exhaustive

3. The number in each cell (e.g. 3/3 or 2/3) refers to the number of leaders with the referenced achievements

Previous Experience

From Table 16.1a, we can see that almost all of the 13 successful private entrepreneurs had obtained a high level of education before embarking on their entrepreneurial activities. Many of them had also engaged in continuing education, earning higher educational degrees during their entrepreneurial activities. For example, Fosun's Xinjun Liang earned an EMBA degree (Executive Master in Business Administration) and was in the process of pursuing a doctorate in business administration (DBA) at the time of the interview. Vantone's Lun Feng earned a Master's degree in Public Policy from the National University of Singapore. Ning Li, who did not have a university degree before his entrepreneurial activity, completed a Master's degree in business administration and a law degree, both from Peking University, Beijing, after he founded Li-Ning Sports Co. The educational background of the leaders in the technology industry is particularly remarkable, because all of them worked as a researcher, scientist, lecturer or professor in a research unit or in higher education institutions prior to founding their firms. In sum, 12 of the 13 leaders earned a university degree with diverse specialisations (e.g. computing, chemistry, engineering and economics) before initiating entrepreneurship, and the majority of them engaged in continuing education afterwards.

Another common feature of the 13 leaders is that all of them have worked in different types of organisations (e.g. public institutions, state-owned enterprises—SOEs, privately owned enterprises—POEs and educational institutions) before starting their own business, or their first private business morphed from being a state firm (in the case of Weihua Ma). However, no consistent pattern could be detected between their work experience and the industry in which they chose to start a business, with the exception of Ning Li (who stayed in a sports-related field) and two entrepreneurs in IT-related industry (who were computer engineers by training). So what motivated them to start their own businesses? According to Jiren Liu of Neusoft, his initial purpose was to obtain research funding to further develop a software program. However, after he received orders from a Japanese company, ALPINE Electronics, Inc., he realised the significant business implications of his software. Shi Wang of Vanke was motivated to 'jump into the sea' of business because the civil service, in which he worked, discouraged performance.

Interestingly, in this sample of leaders, some leaders in all the industries, except those in the retailing/consumer industry, had previously worked as civil servants. We speculate that might be because, in the retailing industry, a government background could not offer any competitive advantage. On the other hand, in real estate, technology or the financial services industries, government connections from previous civil service experience may have been useful with the initial establishment of the business.

Table 16.1a shows that five leaders had held governmental positions previously. Dongsheng Chen of Taikang Life Insurance worked from 1983 to 1988 in the International Trade Research Centre of the Ministry of Foreign Trade and Economic Cooperation before working as Associate Editor for *Management World*, a journal of the China State Council's Development Research Centre. Weihua Ma of China Merchants Bank served in multiple government positions at both provincial and national levels, including as deputy director and deputy secretary general of the Economic Planning Committee of Liao Ning province, director of the Party Office on the CPC Liao Ning Committee and CPC An Hui Committee, deputy director of the General Office of the People's Bank of China (PBOC), deputy director of the Finance and Planning Office of PBOC, and governor of the Hainan branch of PBOC, and chief of the State Administration of Foreign Exchange (SAFE) Hainan branch. Clearly, there is an inclination for the entrepreneurs with economic expertise to start their businesses in a financial services industry, in which they can take advantage of their macroeconomic planning ability and their government connections.

Current Activities

As shown in Table 16.1b, in addition to their businesses' contributions to China's GDP and employment, these 13 leaders have made contributions to Chinese society through non-business activities such as making social contributions, including financial donations, establishing business associations, developing university collaborations, and engaging in political participation.

All 13 leaders and their corresponding firms have established explicit formal mechanisms to contribute to society, including foundations, subsidies/sponsorships or donations. Being socially responsible emerged as an explicit aspiration for most of these leaders even though we had not pre-specified this question in the interview protocol. Social responsibility is one of the seven management philosophies discovered in the Zhang et al. (2008) study. It seems that these leaders have ingrained social responsibility in the corporate culture to encourage compassion towards both internal (employees) and external (e.g. customers, suppliers, community) stakeholders. For example, Qinghou Zong of Wahaha refers to the 'family' at three levels: the small family of each employee; the big family of the company; and the further extended family of the nation/society. He states that 'after we achieve a strong big family, we should also serve our country and assume our social responsibilities.' Many of these leaders have established corporate foundations as part of their socially responsible actions, such as the Wahaha Foundation, the Alibaba Foundation and the SEE mentioned in Chap. 1.

As well as social contributions through donations and foundations, many of these leaders (10 out of 13) also actively participate and assume leadership roles in business associations of their profession or industry at regional or national levels. There is also a high level of collaboration with universities (nine out of 13), ranging from serving as the chairmen of the boards of universities to serving as guest lecturers or instructors. A number of entrepreneurs (six out of 13) also participate in political activities, such as serving as elected members of the People's Congress or the China People's Political Consultative Conference at national, provincial or township levels. This is consistent with the incidence of political engagements among the chairmen or CEOs of highly successful listed private firms (Li and Liang 2015). In sum, the high level of participation on all these extra-entrepreneurial activities reflects a high level of social consciousness among these successful private entrepreneurs.

Personal Achievements

From Table 16.1c we can see that the 13 leaders have certainly achieved great success and received recognition from many places. We categorise these recognitions into three types: (1) entrepreneurial recognition—awards related explicitly to their entrepreneurial success; (2) general recognition—awards not related to their business directly; and (3) international reputation—mentions or awards given by international entities. We observed that almost all of the leaders interviewed have received type 1 recognition for their business achievement or leadership achievement (11/13). Furthermore, more than half of them (seven of the 13) also received type 2 recognition for their philanthropy or their outstanding and exemplary leadership of the economically disadvantaged or for special groups such as the young or retired athletes. Nine of the 13 leaders have received type 3 recognition. For example, Jack Ma was recognised as one of the world's 50 greatest leaders; Chuanzhi Liu was recognised as one of the Global Top 50 Most Influential Thinkers; and Weihua Ma was named as 'Asia's Excellent CEO' in 2011.

The commonality shown in the profiles of the 13 leaders offers us some insights regarding those who lead successful private enterprises in China. It is evident that higher education and continuing education are essential; in addition, having the ideals and ambition to do good for society are strong motivating forces driving their success. In the next section, we report on the leadership traits and attributes beyond their demographic characteristics that might be responsible for the entrepreneurs' extraordinary achievements.

Results of the Attribute Content Analysis

The purpose of the attribute analysis is to offer a model of private-firm leadership attributes, building on the preliminary four Ds model we deduced from the survey studies in Chap. 2 and the discussions in Chap. 1 on the institutional contexts. Appendix 16.1 provides a description of the coding process. The initial coding was based on the four attributes (four Ds): Determination, Discipline, Duality focus and Divinity belief. A new attribute emerged from the coding of the first interview that we labelled as 'Reflective Thinking.' The definitions of these five attributes and associated keywords or key phrases can be found in columns one and two of Table 16.2, respectively. Using paragraphs as the units of analysis, we report the percentage of paragraphs containing ideas, words or phrases that are related to an attribute based on the responses of the leader to the questions of the interviewer. If an interview text has 50 paragraphs and 20 of them mention ideas or actions related to discipline, say, the result is 40 % (20/50). If 10 of them mention the ideas or perspectives related to divinity belief, this result is 20 % (10/50). The use of percentages adjusts for the length of the interview text and provides a sense of the relative dominance of the attributes for each leader. Given five attributes, each would have a 25 % chance of being mentioned. Hence we define a high level of the presence of an attribute if it is reflected in more than 30 % of the text (paragraphs), a medium level in 15 % to 30 %, and a low level in less than 15 % of the text. In Table 16.2, we report the percentages of the attributes for the leaders in each industry, giving an overall presence of the attribute in an industry while protecting the identity of individual leaders. The 'Total' column is the average level of presence across all 13 leaders. The last column is a comparison of the presence of the attributes across the four industries.

This table provides information on leader attributes both within and between industries. In addition to analysing the text in terms of the degree of presence of any of the five attributes, we also identify quotations that illustrate the attributes. Tables 16.3a, 16.3b, 16.3c and 16.3d. offer some illustrative quotations by leaders for each of the attributes in each of the four industries.

Determination—A Basic Requirement to Succeed

Determination refers to having a firmness of purpose, strong commitment, courage and perseverance. From Table 16.2, we can see that, among the five attributes, determination has the lowest presence based on the words

Table 16.2 Relative presence of attributes among 13 private firm leaders

Attributes and definitions	Keywords/phrases	Financial Services (3 leaders)	Technology and E-C (4 leaders)	Real Estate (3 leaders)	Consumer Retail (3 leaders)	Total (average of 13 leaders)	Comparison across industries
Determination: The quality of being determined; firmness of purpose	Commitment, courage, persistence, patience and perseverance	Low (5 %–10 %)	Low (5 %–10 %)	Low (0 %–5 %)	Low (5 %–10 %)	Low (5 %)	Low across all industries
Discipline: A form of self-control and control of others through establishing and consistently enforcing a set of rules or a structure	Structure, rules, principles, responsibility, control, teamwork and co-operation, pragmatism/realism, enforcement and consistency	Medium to high (20 %–40 %)	Medium to high (25 %–50 %)	High (35 %–50 %)	High (30 %–55 %)	High (38 %)	High across all industries
Duality focus: An ability to deal with two opposing forces or contradictory requirements simultaneously	People and task focused, short and long term, keep authority and give autonomy, self and others, divergent thinking, East and West, yin and yang	Low to medium (10 %–30 %)	Low to medium (10 %–20 %)	Low to medium (5 %–20 %)	Low to medium (10 %–25 %)	Medium (16 %)	Low to medium across industries

(continued)

Table 16.2 (continued)

Attributes and definitions	Keywords/phrases	Financial Services (3 leaders)	Technology and E-C (4 leaders)	Real Estate (3 leaders)	Consumer Retail (3 leaders)	Total (average of 13 leaders)	Comparison across industries
Divinity belief: An acceptance of the existence of a higher force that is looking after humanity, and one's duty to show gratitude for one's fortune	Gratitude, Golden Rule, humility, integrity/ morality, transparency/ openness, powerlessness, people development/ coaching, transcendence	Low to medium (10 %–25 %)	Low to medium (10 %–25 %)	Medium (20 %–25 %)	Low to medium (10 %–20 %)	Medium (18 %)	Low to medium across industries
Reflective thinking: Part of the critical thinking process referring specifically to the processes of analysing and making judgements about what has happened and has been learned	Inspiration and self-reflection, querying and curiosity, reflecting when practising, analogical analysis, metaphorical thinking, foresight, perspective	Medium to high (20 %–45 %)	Medium to high (15 %–35 %)	Low to medium (10 %–30 %	Low to medium (10 %–30 %)	Medium (24 %)	Low to high across all industries

High: above 30 %
Medium: 15 % to 30 %
Low: below 15 %

Table 16.3a Illustrative quotes on leadership attributes in the finance industry

Attributes	Finance industry sample quotes (3 leaders)
Determination The quality of being determined; firmness of purpose.	**Ma (CMB):** '... The process was a long story. From establishing the representative office at the beginning to making it a branch later, we dealt with Wall Street and the Federal Reserve for eight years. I wrote a book entitled *On Wall Street* to record the process.' **Liang (Fosun):** '... We take a lot of time to optimise our operations. There are innumerable examples. I can provide numerous details of current or past cases.'
Discipline A form of self-control and control of others through establishing and following a set of rules or order.	**Chen (Taikang):** 'I often tell my employees that we must consider framework and structure first. The greatness of your ambition determines how far you can go, and the size of your framework determines how large your market can be and how far your vision can go.' **Ma (CMB):** '... Banking is a high-risk industry, and rules are extremely important. Actually many rules and systems are established after paying a high price. So a bank must have stringent rules/systems and implement them firmly.'
Duality focus An ability to deal with two opposing forces or contradictory requirements simultaneously	**Liang (Fosun):** '... The most important thing in Tai Chi is tolerance of yin and yang. If you think yang is right, you must clearly know that yin causes yang. Never try to eliminate conflicts or rivals. You must discover the co-existence of their interests.' **Chen (Taikang):** '... China is a big country with huge regional, cultural and climatic differences, so we must allow a balance between consistency and flexibility. We need to pass on our core company cultural values, but to compete in the market, we must respect special features of different markets.'
Divinity belief An acceptance of the existence of a higher force that is looking after humanity and one's duty to show gratitude for one's fortune.	**Chen (Taikang):** '... My advantage is that I understand the decreed fate (*Zhitianming* 知天命) ... Unlike younger people, I know the history of the past century. My historic experiences coalesce to form an integral framework in my mind ... These experiences give me the foundation for making good judgements.' **Ma (CMB):** '... though I had made constant changes all these years, I also had limitations. ... While I am a progressive learner, I and my employees belong to two generations after all. I especially emphasise that not everything I did in the past was correct; I would be happy to see bold breakthroughs because that is the only way CMBC can continue to grow. I firmly support change.'

(continued)

Table 16.3a (continued)

Attributes	Finance industry sample quotes (3 leaders)
Reflective Thinking A part of the critical thinking process referring specifically to the process of analysing and making judgements about what has happened and has been learned.	**Liang (Fosun):** '... we became an asset management company. Why? Because our cash flow output conflicted with the size of our investment demand, and the conflict was quite striking. We had to choose: Should we increase the debt rate to make investments? Slow our investments? Or find another way out? We chose to find another way out: asset management.' **Chen (Taikang):** 'As a company with 15 years of rapid growth, we still lag behind leading firms in maturity and technical competence. But our overall framework has been well established; we are now strong enough to compete with big firms for talent, which is the most important prerequisite for building a great company.'

of the 13 leaders, while discipline has the highest—it is consistently high across all the leaders. The low frequency of the mention of determination is not surprising, for two reasons. First, these leaders have already reached a high level of success. Their determination was important in the early days when they were building their businesses. Furthermore, several leaders (e.g. Liu of Lenovo, Ma of CMB, Feng of Vantone, Guo of HC360) have already retired from the day-to-day management of the firm and are serving as chairmen of their boards, focusing on strategic issues of the firm. To them, determination is still necessary when introducing new processes or changes that might disturb the status quo. For example, Liu of Neusoft said (Table 16.3b), 'Developing software parts, our IPO, our entering the health care sector, our integration of brands, our joint venture with Alpine, the change of company name to Neusoft, and all these things met resistance. But I am aware that I have to be persistent when I make these decisions.' Liang of Fosun reflected on the long time it took to optimise operations. Li of the Li-Ning Company devoted much effort to 'continually seeking what can be sold' (Table 16.3d).

Most of the stories of determination are about struggles in the earlier years of their business venturing. For example, Jack Ma of Alibaba recalled the importance of perseverance in the early stages of the company when building a customer base (Table 16.3b): 'We started from the 1995 Chinese Yellow Pages and went through pain and struggles, but

Table 16.3b Illustrative quotes on leadership attributes in the technology and E-commerce industry

Attributes	Technology and E-commerce industry sample quotes (4 firms)
Determination The quality of being determined; firmness of purpose	**Liu (Neusoft):** '...Developing software parks, our IPO, our entering into the health care sector, our integration of brands, our joint venture with Alpine, the change of company name to Neusoft, all these things met with resistance. But I am aware that I have to be persistent when I make these decisions.' **Ma (Alibaba):** 'We started from the 1995 Chinese Yellow Pages, and went through pain and struggle, but never gave up.'
Discipline A form of self-control and control of others through establishing and following a set of rules or order	**Guo (HC360):** 'They must be fair, self-disciplined, industrious, and thrifty in running their firms, and must practise what they preach. Only when they have morality, leadership capability and well-designed regulations and mechanisms can they successfully manage rapidly growing enterprises successfully.' **Liu (Lenovo):** '...we have set the principle that you must think carefully before making promises, and you should keep your word and do what you say once you have made the promise. We have many rules for carrying out this principle and promoting the culture of 'do what you say.' For example, late arrival is not allowed for meetings; if you are late you will have to stand throughout the meeting.'
Duality focus An ability to deal with two opposing forces or contradictory requirements simultaneously	**Ma (Alibaba):** 'When I stroll in the rich Chinese cultural heritage, I feel the power of Confucianism, Buddhism and Daoism. In Daoism, the best leadership is not leading at all. What is leadership anyway? I think it requires sacrificing today for the future; the person who can sacrifice today to win tomorrow is a real leader.' **Liu (Neusoft):** 'Sometimes there are conflicts and tensions, but in the process of developing a company, you must have a trade-off if you want the company to be long-lived. For example, efficiency might suffer when rules are too strict. But institutions/rules can avoid the risk of organisational death caused by flexibility.'
Divinity belief An acceptance of the existence of a higher force that is looking after humanity and one's duty to show gratitude for one's fortune.	**Ma (Alibaba):** 'I gradually formed my own perspectives about our values and value system, the concept of belief and reverence. Belief means to be grateful for today and yesterday. Reverence means awe regarding tomorrow and the unknown. Weaving belief and reverence into our culture would form the core of value for the basic design of all management systems.' **Liu (Lenovo):** 'Lenovo requires sincerity and integrity, and we ask employees to sincerely express their convictions to supervisors personally, rather than just speak some pretty words or obey everything the supervisor says ... Lenovo's leaders must consistently model their actions to gradually foster this culture of sincerity and respect for facts over the long term.'

(continued)

Table 16.3b (continued)

Attributes	Technology and E-commerce industry sample quotes (4 firms)
Reflective thinking A part of the critical thinking process referring specifically to the process of analysing and making judgements about what has happened and has been learned	Liu (Neusoft): '…Compared to our dream when we first founded the company, I could not have imagined what we have achieved today. We can get a high rating now. But compared to my dreams for the future, what we have achieved is just like the achievement of one's childhood. We were naïve and ignorant 20 years ago. But we have been learning continuously. We are active. Therefore, what we have achieved is far beyond what we expected at the beginning. ' Guo (HC360): 'In my opinion, whether a firm is outstanding is not determined simply by its profit or scale, but rather by its exuberant vitality and its potential to lead the future development of other firms in our nation.' Ma (Alibaba): 'The Alibaba system has about 350 million people and more than 34 million companies living within it; I am operating an ecosystem of more than 600 million people. If 1 % are bad guys, I have 6 million scoundrels.'

never gave up.' Wang of Vanke recalled how he did everything in the first 15 years of his company. He said (Table 16.3c) 'I went to Shenzhen in 1983, accumulated some capital, and established Vanke in 1984. From 1983 to 1999, about 15 years, I did everything myself, big or small.' Zong of Wahaha described how he worked on a farm for 15 years before returning to his home city of Hangzhou to start his business. He said (Table 16.3d), 'life was very tough and it taught me about the hardship unprivileged people faced.'

As these quotations illustrate, it is hard to imagine how a business can succeed, or even survive, without determination, firmness of purpose, and a strong will in its leader. Such perseverance is especially important in the early stages of economic reform, given the difficult institutional environment in which these leaders had to operate and the obstacles they had to overcome without government support, relative to that of state-owned and foreign firms (see Chap. 1). Thus the leaders have internalised and subsumed the trait of determination as they have experienced increasing success; it is no longer a significant explicit part of the vocabulary for successful leaders. This explains the low frequency of its occurrence in the interview texts.

Table 16.3c Illustrative quotes on leadership attributes in the construction and real estate industry

Attributes	Real estate industry sample quotes (3 firms)
Determination The quality of being determined; firmness of purpose	**Wang (Vanke):** 'I went to Shenzhen in 1983, accumulated some capital, and established Vanke in 1984. From 1983 to 1999, about 15 years, I basically did everything myself, big or small.' **Nie (Tecsun):** 'We have kept our prices low because our R&D efforts absorbed much of the cost. Furthermore, we persistently deliver the best quality housing ... Our quality is twice as good and our price is about 30 % cheaper.'
Discipline A form of self-control and control of others through establishing and following a set of rules or order	**Feng (Vantone):** 'We also advocate the important stranger principle, because an acquaintance culture weakens the implementation of a fair system. Generally speaking, when companies deal with strangers, they exclude potential problems caused by personal relations and reciprocal gestures, such as *renqing* (human obligation) and *mianzi* (face).' **Nie (Tecsun):** 'The first and most important responsibility is to give the best products to your customers ... The second is to treat your employees well. After fulfilling the first two responsibilities, if entrepreneurs still have financial resources left, they can invest in public undertakings. However, if companies fail to do the first two well, they only hurt society more by investing in public undertakings.'
Duality focus An ability to deal with two opposing forces or contradictory requirements simultaneously	**Wang (Vanke):** 'System and teamwork are the fundamentals of Western management. We Chinese like to use the best part of Western ideas while still basing our operations on Chinese theories, critically absorbing the good part. To me it is simple, I just copy and use.' **Nie (Tecsun):** 'We believe that once profit exceeds 25 %, it is exorbitant and indicates a disrespect for consumers.'
Divinity belief An acceptance of the existence of a higher force that is looking after humanity and one's duty to show gratitude for one's fortune.	**Feng (Vantone):** 'Morality and integrity are also reflected in our self-conscious and self-disciplined company governance and financial management. Our company sponsors an Annual Introspecting Day, and has set up self-monitoring systems, including an internal control system. These practices have allowed us to establish a value system that is somewhat of a religion guiding our behaviour unconsciously.' **Nie (Tecsun):** 'We lack the craftsman mind and spirit. The more some real estate companies grow, the more harm they will do. Though they provide temporary housing, they leave construction waste.'

(continued)

Table 16.3c (continued)

Attributes	Real estate industry sample quotes (3 firms)
Reflective thinking A part of the critical thinking process referring specifically to the process of analysing and making judgements about what has happened and has been learned.	**Feng (Vantone):** '...Private enterprises often make different mistakes depending on their development stages. At the early stage, a company grows fast because it makes money easily. However, the ability to make money is totally different from the ability to run a company, and a new company's managers often do not know how to operate a company. Like teenagers in adolescence, their bodies grow quickly but their minds develop slowly ... Similarly, if a company in this period cannot learn to grow up, it will stay small and won't last long.' **Wang (Vanke):** 'I often reflect on myself: am I good? Of course I am good. Do I have a wicked side? Unfortunately, I do. Therefore, since I have a wicked side myself, how can I require other people to be 100 % good? This logic is very clear when I run my business.'

Discipline—To Ensure Consistency, Meritocracy and Professionalism

Discipline is a catch-all word to include having self-control, being principled, assuming responsibility, insisting on consistency and enforcement, and merit-based resource or reward allocation decision-making. Based on the frequency of being mentioned, it appears that control and monitoring of the operation, to ensure consistency or reliability of action, are most important in these leaders' minds. On average, about 38 % of the text (paragraphs) are related to the idea of a disciplined or principled way of organising and managing the firm. The words of Chen of Taikang Life Insurance capture this idea well (Table 16.3a), 'we must consider framework and structure first. The greatness of your ambition determines how far you can go, and the size of your framework determines how large your market can be and how far you vision can be.' Structure and systems are important to most firms, but particularly for financial institutions with a high degree of risk. Ma of CMB said (Table 16.3a), 'a bank must have stringent rules/systems and implement them firmly.' Guo of HC360 mentions (Table 16.3b), 'self-discipline, industrious, thrifty in running their firms,' and the need for 'well designed regulations and

Table 16.3d Illustrative quotes on leadership attributes in the consumer and retail industry

Attributes	Consumer retail industry sample quotes (3 firms)
Determination The quality of being determined; firmness of purpose.	**Li (Li-Ning):** 'After throwing away the inferior product that couldn't be sold, the only thing we could do was to continuously seek what can be sold. This is the basic requirement for a product.' **Zong (Wahaha):** 'I grew up in a poor family. I started working for a living after I graduated from junior high school. I was only 16 years old. I worked part-time here and there and then went to work in the countryside, as most young people did at the time. I stayed on the farm for 15 years before I came back to Hangzhou. Life there was very tough and it taught me about the hardships unprivileged people face. Also, I know very well that it is impossible for anyone to build and develop a company alone. You must motivate employees to work with you.'
Discipline A form of self-control and control of others through establishing and following a set of rules or order.	**Li (Li-Ning):** '…Only through market competition can an organisation make progress constantly and become vigorous. Of course, I must participate in decisions concerning the life of the company, and concerning the shareholders or basic values. But for detailed decisions, I step back.' **Zong (Wahaha):** '…We will (enter into joint venture) if the potential partner has good products or advanced technologies. But the co-operation must be on an equal footing and for mutual benefit. We will consider no co-operation that involves only financial investment.'
Duality focus An ability to deal with two opposing forces or contradictory requirements simultaneously	**Li (Li-Ning):** 'The two CEOs after me respected and valued my opinions, but I encouraged them to make decisions independently. If I am too powerful, they will become too weak to make independent decisions.' **Wang (Kidswant):** 'All these years, while my team and I pondered current real-world issues, I have considered the future.'

(continued)

Table 16.3d (continued)

Attributes	Consumer retail industry sample quotes (3 firms)
Divinity belief An acceptance of the existence of a higher force that is looking after humanity and one's duty to show gratitude for one's fortune.	**Zong (Wahaha):** '...Chinese companies need strong, open-minded leaders who put people first. Leaders who lack authority will find it difficult to manage Chinese companies; in other words, Chinese companies need strong and open-minded leaders who are kind and tolerant of their employees.' **Wang (Kidswant):** '...Very simple. First are integrity and pragmatism. I define integrity basically as no lies—do not tell lies internally, and do not deceive people externally, simple as that. Employees will be fired, without exception, if they cheat customers, make false statements, harm anyone inside or outside the company, or resort to any deceit.'
Reflective thinking Part of the critical thinking process referring specifically to the process of analysing and making judgements about what has happened and has been learned.	**Wang (Kidswant):** 'Why does a factory seem more important when my shopping mall pays more taxes? China's attitude towards commerce is really backward despite commerce guiding production ... I continue to believe that commerce represents a huge opportunity. Consumption, investment and exports are the three drivers of China's future development. I believe that internal demand is the most important driving force of the economy.' **Li (Li-Ning):** 'Compared with our domestic competitors in the industry, the strength of our company is our capacity to manage a brand. However, there is much room for us to transform this capacity efficiently into company development and profit.'

mechanisms.' Liu of Lenovo emphasises the culture of 'do what you say' (Table 16.3b), which consists of thinking carefully before making promises, and 'do what you say once you have made the promise.' Feng of Vantone advocates (Table 16.3c) the 'stranger principle' to ensure fairness because 'an acquaintance culture weakens the implementation of a fair system ... When companies deal with strangers, they exclude potential problems caused by personal relations and reciprocal gestures, such as *renqing* (human obligation) and *mianzi* (face).' Li of Li-Ning Company shares a similar philosophy. Within five years of founding the company, Li decided to introduce professionalisation and asked his relatives, fellow villagers and past sports teammates to leave the company. After he relinquished his CEO position, he made a genuine effort to step back from detailed decision-making and to focus only on strategic issues (Table 16.3d) 'concerning the life of the company, concerning the shareholders or basic values.'

The leader that best exemplifies a strong approach to discipline is Nie of Tecsun Homes. He developed a detailed Employee Code of Conduct with over 30 rules that apply to a variety of employee behaviours ranging from personal hygiene to punctuality, from a restriction on gambling to the reporting of expenses. Focusing on the company as a whole, he emphasised the discipline of providing the best products, treating employees well, and working for the public good, in that order. He said (Table 16.3c), '...if companies fail to do the first two well, they only hurt society more by investing in public undertakings.'

In summary, successful leaders emphasise discipline in their organisations by designing rules and defining standards to ensure consistency and reliability in both actions and decisions, by themselves and their employees. Discipline ensures transparency, meritocracy and professionalism, essential ingredients of an efficient and effective organisation. It is not surprising that these 13 successful leaders all demonstrate a high level of discipline, as expressed in their thoughts and words when describing their management philosophies and practices.

Duality Focus—Embracing Conflict, Balance and Opposites

A duality focus refers to the leader's orientation and capability of balancing two or more opposing forces or satisfying contradictory requirements, whether objective or perceived. Leaders with a duality focus pay attention to both people and task issues, both operational and strategic issues, both current and future challenges, both self and other interests, both internal and external contingencies and so on. They show an appreciation for both the East and the West, the new and the old, the present and the past, and see the need for both stability and change, consistency and flexibility, autonomy and control. They have a 'both/and' rather than an 'either/or' mentality, a core idea in both Confucianism and Daoism and captured by the term 'yin/yang' (Fang 2012; Jing and Van de Ven 2014; Ma and Tsui 2015). However, it is not simply a perspective or mentality; duality is reflected in the leaders' actions and decisions. This is an important distinction from the attribute of 'reflective thinking' that will be discussed below. Reflection and learning from past experiences may or may not reveal a duality focus.

Based on the analysis of the interview texts, words relating to duality focus are present in 5 % to 30 % of paragraphs, with an average of 16 % across all 13 leaders. As Liang of Fosun said (Table 16.3a), 'The most important thing (in Tai Chi) is tolerance of yin and yang. If you think yang is right, you must clearly know that yin causes yang. Never try to eliminate conflicts or rivals. You must discover the co-existence of their interests.' Chen of Taikang Insurance said (Table 16.3a), 'we must allow balance between consistency and flexibility. We need to pass on our core company culture values, but to compete in the market, we must respect special features in different markets.' Liu of Neusoft reflects on the need for duality in perspective with these words (Table 16.3b): 'Sometimes there are conflicts and tensions, but in the process of developing a company, you must have trade-offs if you want the company to be long lived. For example, efficiency might suffer when rules are too strict. But institutions/rules can avoid the risk of organisational death caused by flexibility.'

Keeping an eye on both the present and the future, Wang of Kidswant shared these words (Table 16.3d), 'All these years, while my team and I pondered current real-world issues, I have considered the future.' Wang of Vanke saw the merit of blending the East and the West. He said (Table 16.3c), 'We Chinese like to use part of Western ideas while still basing our operations on Chinese theories, critically absorbing the good part (of both the East and the West).'

We observe as much within-industry variation (e.g. 10 % to 30 % in the finance industry, 5 % to 20 % in real estate, and 10 % to 25 % in the consumer/retail industries) as there is between industries. No clear pattern of significant differences exists between industries. The leaders with an apparent higher level of duality focus have a wide range of education (from a bachelor's degree to a doctorate). It is not clear that the Chinese traditional philosophies of Confucianism or Daoism are the major sources of their duality thinking. Only two of the four leaders make reference to these sources. However, duality focus is present among all 13 leaders, with an average of 16 % of the interview texts relating to this attribute. While it is lower relative to the attribute of discipline (which has an average of 38 %, with a range from 20 % to 55 %), duality focus is clearly a defining characteristic of these successful leaders.

Divinity Belief—Uncompromised Integrity, Gratitude and Compassion

This is perhaps the broadest concept, relative to the other four. At the most fundamental level, it is a belief in the existence of a higher force that is looking after humanity and governing the universe. In other words, it is a belief that one's fortune or misfortune is not entirely within the control of a human person. Leaders with this belief have a sense of humility because the human person is small relative to the grand universe (Ou et al. 2014); they express gratitude for their blessings, and follow the Golden Rule (treat others as you would like to be treated by them). They tend to treat others with generosity, forgiveness and integrity. They are interested in developing followers and encouraging them to reach their highest potential. These leaders locate the source of this divinity belief in the intellectual and philosophical teachings of Confucianism, Daoism, Buddhism and Christianity. In fact, the Golden Rule is a core doctrine in most religions and philosophical teachings (Robinson 2016). Formal religious belief is not a necessary condition, however, for an individual to have a high level of morality and integrity, to express gratitude, and to be kind and compassionate. Leaders without a religious faith can also be high in self-transcendence and low in self-enhancement.

The results of the attribute content analysis suggest a moderate degree of variation in the presence of the divinity belief among the 13 leaders. There is also a similar degree of variance between leaders within the same industry. For example, in the technology and e-commerce industry, the presence of the divinity belief attribute is 10 % for one leader and 25 % for another. In the financial services industry, the range is between 10 % and 20 %. Across all 13 leaders and four industries, the presence of divinity belief ranges from low (10 %) to medium (25 %), with an average of 18 %. Again, similar to duality focus, we do not detect any systematic pattern between having a divinity belief and the leaders' background or the industry in which they operate. This individual difference attribute seems to be present in varying degrees among all successful Chinese business leaders, at least among the private-firm entrepreneurs.

The element of humility within divinity belief can be seen in the words of Ma of CMB (Table 16.3a), 'I also had limitations ... I especially emphasise that not everything I did in the past was correct.' Liu said (Table 16.3b), 'Lenovo requires sincerity and integrity, and we ask employees to sincerely express their convictions to supervisors personally, rather than just speak some pretty words ... Lenovo's leaders must consistently model their actions to gradually foster this culture of sincerity and respect.' To Feng of Vantone (Table 16.3c), 'Morality and integrity are also reflected in our self-conscious and self-disciplined company governance and financial management ... to establish a value system that is somewhat of a religion guiding our behaviour unconsciously.' Wang of Kidswant also emphasises integrity, defining it as 'no lies,' both internally and externally. He says firmly, (Table 16.3d), 'Employees will be fired, without exception, if they cheat customers, make false statements, harm anyone inside or outside the company, or resort to any deceit.' Honesty is a core principle underlying the employee code of conduct at Tecsun Homes. Employees are trusted to submit expenses claims without supervisory review, but if these are found to be false, they will face severe punishment causing 'lifelong consequences.' Nie is known to stand by his motto 'Tecsun will always be a just, noble and conscientious company. Rather than give in to evil to survive, Tecsun would rather close down!'

Zong of Wahaha exemplifies the spirit of both humility (open-mindedness) and compassion (kindness) through these words (Table 16.3d), 'Chinese companies need strong and open-minded leaders who are kind and tolerant of their employees.' His early experiences of hardship and poverty developed in him a high level of compassion for people without privileges. He purchased apartments at market value and sold them to his employees at greatly reduced prices. Nie of Tecsun Homes has developed a system with high integrity, responsibility and transparency that protects customers and employees first, and then contributes to society. He has found other real estate companies that grew at the expense of society to be irresponsible and disgusting. He said, 'the more some real estate companies grow, the more harm they will do. Although they provide temporary housing, they leave construction waste.' Nie takes pride in looking after the company's employees and has put aside a large pension fund to ensure they will live a decent life and die with dignity. He said, 'I want people who have gone through thick and thin with me to live well.'

Overall, the four D attributes account for about 76 % of the content in the 13 interviews. This is noteworthy because the interviews were designed and conducted independently of and before the development of the four attributes. These findings suggest the centrality of these attributes of the leaders, while leading and managing their entrepreneurial firms on the road to success and sustainability. These findings corroborate those of the the large-sample survey studies described in Chap. 2, in which the leaders were from firms with different ownership structures and across a wide variety of industries. Next, we turn to the new attribute that emerged from this set of interviews: that is, reflective thinking.

Reflective Thinking—Critical and Integrative Thinking, Learning, Sense Making and Meaning Making

This attribute refers to the critical and step-back thinking process that involves analysing, making sense about what has happened, and making meaning about the world based on experiences, observations and wide-ranging reading interests. Reflective leaders think about bigger and more long-term issues based on their critical analyses of the problems they or others have experienced. For example, they contemplate the role of business and its relationship to stakeholders beyond shareholders (including customers, employees, suppliers and so on) and on the role of the government relative to business for the progress and harmony of society. They engage in self-reflection and use analogies and metaphors in their language. They have a high level of curiosity about the world and take time to step back and look at the big picture or to think about the cosmos. Reflective thinkers are learners (Conklin 2012; Rodgers 2002), which is an important quality of strategic thinking that Mintzberg (1994) claims to be necessary for visionary leaders and managers. To be more specific, Mintzberg (1994: 108) states that strategy making is so complex a process that it 'involves the most sophisticated, subtle and, at times, subconscious elements of human thinking'; and strategic thinking is about *synthesis*, involving 'intuition and creativity.' While such learning may influence the CEOs' decision-making and actions, reflection usually does not necessarily have implications for action. We observed the largest variation in the presence of this attribute among the 13 leaders. The percentages range from low (10 %) to high (45 % or more) with variance both within and across the industries. In the finance industry, the attribute is reflected in 20 % to 45 % of the interview texts, while in the real estate and consumer/retail industry, it is from 10 % to 30 %. Among the 13 leaders, three show a relatively high level (35 % to 45 %) of reflective thinking, and three leaders have a low level (less than 15 %). There seems to be more reflective thinkers among leaders in the financial (average 33 %) and technology industries (average 24 %) than among the leaders in the real estate (19 %) or consumer/retail industries (20 %). The overall average level is 24 %, higher than for duality focus (16 %) and divinity belief (18 %) but lower than for discipline (38 %). This suggests that reflective thinking is also a defining attribute of these successful leaders.

This statement by Liu of Neusoft illustrates reflective thinking, 'Compared to our dreams when we first founded the company, I could not have imagined what we have achieved today ... We were naïve and ignorant 20 years ago. But we have been learning continuously ... what we have achieved is far beyond what we expected at the beginning.' Guo of HC360 reflected on the nature and purpose of the firm (Table 16.3b), 'whether a firm is outstanding is not determined simply by its profit or scale, but rather by its exuberant vitality and its potential to lead the future development of other firms in our nation.' Chen reviews the progress of Taikang Life Insurance with this statement (Table 16.3a), 'As a company with 15 years of rapid growth, we still lag behind leading firms in maturity and technical competence. But our overall framework has been well established; we are now strong enough to compete with big firms for talent, which is the most important prerequisite for building a great company.' Ma of Alibaba sees himself as operating an ecosystem rather than a company (Table 16.3b): 'If you look at Alibaba as an ecosystem, we have about 350 million people on the platforms and more than 34 million companies living within it. I am operating an ecosystem of more than 600 million people.' Wang of Kidswant ponders on the question of the role of business in society and government. He realised that the status of commercial activities lags behind that of manufacturing perceiving that Chinese society continues to value production more than commerce. So he asked (Table 16.3d) 'Why does a factory seem more important when my shopping mall pays more taxes? China's attitude towards commerce is really backward despite commerce guiding production.' Reflection is not only directed towards the external world but also internally, as Wang of Vanke indicates (Table 16.3c), 'I often reflect on myself: am I good? Of course I am good. Do I have a wicked side? Unfortunately, I do. Therefore, since I have a wicked side myself, how can I require other people to be 100 % good?' Through self-reflection, the leader becomes more detached from him/herself and gains a more balanced perspective on human needs, relationships, life, meaning, purpose, progress, society and the universe. Nie of Tecsun, in expressing admiration of the extremely fine craftsmanship of Swiss watchmakers, also provides an example of reflective thinking. He said that China needs more entrepreneurs such as Swiss watchmakers. This is not determination, not discipline, not duality focus, and not divinity belief. It is reflective thinking.

Summary

We obtained the confirmation of four attributes from the interviews of the 13 leaders and observed the emergence of a fifth attribute. The rate of 38 % for 'Discipline'—the highest frequency of mention by the 13 leaders—is worth further discussion and elaboration. We offer several explanations for the salience of discipline in these leaders' minds. The first is related to the business environment the leaders face. In China's transitioning economy, private businesses have to deal with governmental control over many aspects, whereas many governmental officials engage in 'rent seeking' behaviours. The recent anti-corruption movement initiated by President Xi represents an effort to restore public confidence in the government; however, the number of corrupt officials being imprisoned every week, and the amounts of money they have embezzled, are astonishing. To ensure that their business will survive and not be taken down along with the corrupt government officials, the leaders of private businesses need to have strong discipline in walking the thin line between bending the law and breaking it.

The second explanation for the significance of discipline in the thinking of these leaders is related to organisational management. Even today, the majority of private businesses in China are family owned, and typically they have relied on the traditional philosophy of 'person governs' rather than the modern management philosophy of 'system governs.' The 'person governs' principle provides the leader with a great deal of freedom and flexibility in all aspects of management, with the leader having few restrictions on his or her actions. These leaders have high agency, as suggested by Chen and Lee (2008) in their analysis of Chinese leadership. On the other hand, when adopting the principle of 'system governs,' the leaders need to be role models in complying with rules and regulations. In this sense, the 13 leaders we interviewed are proud of the professional managers who run their businesses, based on the principle of 'system governs.' The 'system governs' idea is also consistent with the teaching of Legalism introduced about 2,000 years ago, 250 years after the introduction of Confucianism and Daoism (Ma and Tsui 2015). It is an early Chinese form of bureaucracy, emphasising clear divisions of labour, detailed job descriptions, well-defined rewards and punishments, transparency, meritocracy and fair enforcement. The 'system governs' idea is also consistent with modern professional management.

Finally, we speculate that the salience of this attribute is highly related to the leaders' self-discipline in their professional and personal lives. It is not uncommon to hear that a successful entrepreneur has been sent to jail because of gambling excessively, seeking prostitutes, or having children out of wedlock. Many of the richest people on the Hurun list since 2006 have been imprisoned, and the media has also reported incidences of a 'second-wife village' in several cities in China. Living in a society with pervasive materialism and hedonism such as is developing in today's China, it requires extra effort and self-discipline not to let oneself follow the social norm of questionable behaviour.

The new distinguishing attribute that we found in this set of leaders but was not obvious in previous large-sample survey studies is reflective thinking. Interestingly, it was mentioned, though not featured in the interview study, by Zhang et al. (2008). We speculate that the emergence of this attribute is highly related to the educational backgrounds and life experiences of these leaders. As noted earlier, they had all achieved at least one university degree, with a few also earning a master's or doctoral degree; thinking and learning have been an integral part of their development. They are also highly rational and analyse issues from a detached perspective. These leaders put themselves in the big picture and view themselves objectively via a third-person perspective to reflect on their own strengths and weaknesses and to learn both from their own mistakes and from the lessons of others in contemporary and historical settings, local as well as global. We suspect that this unique attribute might be the one that sets these 13 leaders apart from the many private business leaders included in previous large-sample studies and, as a result, sets their firms apart from the millions of other private firms in China.

We should mention that the presence of this attribute could not be an artefact of the research method; that is, the interview questions forced the leaders to 'reflect' on their life and past experiences. If it is a method artefact, we should have more leaders scoring highly on this attribute than the 24 % we found based on the systematic coding.

Results of the Thematic Content Analysis

In this section we present the results of the thematic content analysis of the interview texts to identify management thoughts and leadership practices in the 13 companies. In other words, we wanted to determine both their ideas (thoughts) and their actions (practices). We first present the distinctive management thoughts and leadership practices within each of the four industries. Then we identify and discuss the commonalities across industries. Finally, we present the less common and industry- or company-specific management thoughts and leadership practices.

Leadership in the Financial Services Industry: Risk and Credibility Management, Differential Management and Innovation

The three private enterprises (and founders) in the financial, insurance and investment industry are the Fosun Group (Xinjun Liang), Taikang Life Insurance (Dongsheng Chen), and China Merchants Bank (Weihua Ma).

A predominant characteristic of management priority in the financial services industry is *risk management* and upholding the credibility or reputation of the company. When a financial institution loses its credibility, its business could be ruined, and it is most likely that the company would become bankrupt. Managing credibility and risk is a principal concern for the three leaders, as it could be a matter of life or death for their companies. For example, a situation occurred at China Merchants Bank's Shenyang branch in 1999. The origin of the crisis was only a rumour, but the situation could have adverse impact on the Bank had Mr Ma not managed the crisis appropriately. Of course, the support from the Central Bank of China and the local government (a result of Mr Ma's strong government relationships gained from his prior experience) also contributed to the successful resolution of the situation during this process.

Money or capital is the essential product of the financial industry, which flows to different destinations to create higher value, and which in turn pays back to the depositors or investors, accompanied by correspondent services. The *differential management* between earnings and the cost of capital is the principal business model for companies operating in this industry, and all three leaders acknowledged that. China Merchants Bank transformed its business model in 2004, which included increasing income from non-interest business (reaching over 21 % of revenue); serving micro and small enterprises; and increasing retail business that follows a similar rationale, though requiring a better balance between risk management and cost control. In addition to low capital costs and high earnings, structural cost is another key for financial performance. That is, high efficiency in business processing and in sales creates higher value added. China Merchants Bank improved internal management to achieve efficiency, using standardisation and integration to reduce costs and enhancing their high reputation with branding.

This differential management approach is also present in the Fosun Group, which underwent a transformation from industrial operations to investments, and then to asset management and insurance service. This value chain reduces capital costs and increases value-added in their products and services. Fosun looked for cheap resources (capital) and projects to invest in; in addition, the company replicated the business model and methods across these investments, which allowed for efficiency in terms of mass production and lower unit costs through economies of scale. Its premium pricing increases value-added with brands and sustainability of resources such as technology and capital. One of the techniques Fosun has used is buying when the invested project/enterprise is cheap and selling at its peak. Some European companies, declining in value, have recently been acquired on this principle, notably, with which it has formed a strategic partnership: French holiday resort chain Club Méditerranée SA and the British travel company Thomas Cook (Hu 2015).

Taikang Life Insurance Company bases its management practices on the philosophy of providing steady, professional, amiable, innovative and honest service. Most of these elements focus on building a reputation of quality services for clients, who provide low-cost capital for later investment. With the trust of their clients, the insurance and asset management business model could be sustained in the long run. Based on logic similar to Fuson's, Taikang Life Insurance commits itself to practices such as specialisation, standardisation, marketisation and internationalisation to achieve economies of scale that reduce structural costs and provide value-added activities.

In contrast to the risk-controlling nature and conservative image of the financial services industry, all three firms place a great emphasis on *innovation*, considering it to be a relevant element in their success. On the one hand, there is a certain degree of monopoly in the financial industry because its entry barriers are high, including requiring a large amount of capital, there are many strict regulations, and it is difficult to obtain an operating licence. So those who are able to enter this industry share numerous common features and offer similar core products. In such a context, the initial market was highly concentrated, with fierce competition based on the same business model and operating logic. To gain competitive advantages for long-term survival and development, the companies have to be innovative.

The forward-looking leaders in Fosun, Taikang and China Merchants Bank have relied on innovation to bring about critical transformations in their business models. The motto of Chen, at Taikang Life Insurance, is 'to innovate is to be the first to imitate' and 'to learn from the West.' Imitation worked for Taikang because the financial industry in China was still in its infancy at that time (early 1990s). Nonetheless, while imitation could be a helpful initial step, self-generated innovation is necessary for long-term sustainable development and superior performance (Peng et al. 2009; Zhang and Zhou 2015). For example, in spite of the comment of imitating the West and benchmarking insurance companies in mature markets, Taikang did not just 'copy and paste' an identical model. Indeed, the company analysed different models and selected the optimal option by blending them to form a unique Taikang approach.

A similar approach can be observed in the China Merchants Bank. Though their decision to launch a credit card business was based on the model in Western countries and in other Chinese contexts such as Hong Kong, Taiwan and Singapore, Weihua Ma rejected the idea of co-operation with CitiBank. His rationale was that he did not want China Merchants Bank's success to be attributed to the partnership with CitiBank. Fosun even created its own unique business model by focusing on China's growth in the consumption market through leveraging global resources such as products with European brands and origins. The entrepreneurial spirit of Liang in Fosun won him several innovation awards for entrepreneurs.

Leadership in the Information Technology and E-Commerce Industry: Humanistic Approach, Dual Systems and Tolerance of Mistakes

In this highly technology-related industry (IT solution providers, personal computers, e-commerce and related services), four enterprises and their leaders (Neusoft: Jiren Liu; Lenovo: Chuanzhi Liu; HC360.com: Fansheng Guo; and Alibaba: Jack Ma) offered their insights on how to do business successfully in China.

The leaders of the four technology firms pay a great deal of attention to a *human touch in managing* their enterprises. For Ma of Alibaba, ensuring that employees are happy at work is key to becoming innovative. He uses the motto 'live seriously, work happily.' Ma also emphasises morality and values in the culture of the company. Performance assessment at Alibaba does not focus on sales performance, but on a value assessment of employees. Similarly, he rejects recruiting managers who are excellent in sales but morally questionable. At Alibaba, leadership succession must come from within the company, because that is the only way the candidates will be socialised to the corporate culture and values. Similarly, both Liu of Lenovo and Guo of HC360 claim a family culture. For Liu, Lenovo is a family without kinship. In other words, he has set up a culture in which every employee and manager considers the company to be his or hers. HC360 is listed on the Hong Kong Stock Exchange, but it still possesses a family business culture. Guo plays the role of the 'spiritual' father of this 'family' business. He cultivates a family culture by giving 70 % of annual profits to employees through a profit-sharing scheme, thus aiming to encourage employees to feel that they are 'working for themselves.' Guo is serious about being a spiritual leader and navigator rather than intervening in the day-to-day management of the enterprise. He believes that 'no management is the best management,' reflecting a core Dao spirit of 'invisible leadership.'

While Liu does not claim Neusoft to be a family business, there is also a family culture and a human touch in his leadership style. He trusts his employees and empowers them to release their imagination and creativity fully. In this way, employees feel the growth of the company is being created with their participation, and they perceive themselves to be contributors to, and owners of, Neusoft. In Liu's view, a technology company needs to go 'beyond technology.' A humanist approach to management places emphasis on the people who create knowledge in this knowledge-intensive industry, where high employee turnover is common (Zhang and Xu 2014). Based on a strong corporate culture with a family value system and trust, the company gets a return on loyalty and passion in the workplace. Employees perform at a high level because the company is part of their family, and they are working for themselves and for the benefit of their own lives.

These technology firms do not only rely on soft systems such as corporate culture; they also develop hard systems, such as organisational structure, processes, and human resource management systems, to be consistent with the culture and ensure success. It is a *dual system*, like the two sides of a coin. For example, both Liu of Neusoft and Ma of Alibaba mentioned their audit departments specifically, which investigate any unethical or illegal behaviour. Liu of Neusoft emphasised that a company needs to implement a strong system and procedures to prevent any risks resulting from trust and empowerment. Accountability is built into the system, such that a superior is required to be responsible for the behaviour of his/her subordinates. Liu of Lenovo insists on 'do[ing] what you say' to ensure personal responsibility and accountability. Only a combination of reliable structure, system and procedure with a culture of 'do your best with heart and effort' can make the 'family business without kinship' function appropriately.

Since the technology industry requires intensive knowledge content and continuous innovation, constant learning in both the technology content and changing market conditions is necessary to sustain successful performance. *Tolerance of mistakes* is another feature in this industry, as reflected in the words and actions of these leaders. As long as the mistake is not fatal, Guo from HC360 will simply ignore it. Ma of Alibaba and Liu of Neusoft emphasise that the only rule is not to repeat the same mistake, as part of learning is avoid repeating mistakes. Moreover, tolerance of mistakes is part of the culture of taking a certain level of risk and venturing in business. In the opinion of Liu of Lenovo, Japanese companies faced a challenge in their second generation of professional managers, who became conservative and risk-averse. While the level of risk needs to be moderated and handled carefully in order to avoid any fatal hazards, risk-taking is part of the entrepreneurial adventure, as past experience never guarantees future success. Only through methodical learning, continuous innovation, the encouragement of certain risks and a tolerance of mistakes can a company keep pace with the fast-moving developments in this industry.

Leadership in the Construction and Real-Estate Industry: Ethicality, Simplicity, Market-Orientation and Business Sustainability

The three leaders in the real-estate and construction industry are Lun Feng (Vantone Holdings), Shi Wang (Vanke properties), and Shengzhe Nie (Tecsun Homes).

While successful companies have always emphasised a strong corporate culture, the three leaders in this industry emphasise in particular *moral and ethical principles*. The nature of the businesses in these three private enterprises differ in that they are positioned in different segments of the industrial value chain. Vantone's major business is real estate and industry development complemented with fund and asset management. Vanke specialises in residential property development, and Tecsun manufactures upmarket villa homes. However, all three leaders agreed that the company's and individuals' morality is essential and equally important for their success. Because of the strong ties with government (which is necessary to acquire the land for real-estate development and to obtain a construction licence, etc.) and the importance of other stakeholders in the sales chain for competitive pricing, the real-estate business is generally considered to present significant challenges to a company seeking to avoid the scandals of corrupt behaviours such as bribery. Nevertheless, these three extraordinarily successful private enterprises are not only exemplars for not engaging in illicit behaviours (at both individual and corporate levels), but also demonstrate strong ethical and moral role models for others to follow. All three companies have firmly stated their principle of transparency, reporting any bribery intent, or cutting the business deal, and are willing to sacrifice short-term benefits in order to stick with the legal bottom line and ethical principles. This discipline of unfailing adherence to ethical conduct has contributed to their long-term sustainability. Beyond the legal compliance and moral correctness, they also emphasise value creation for customers, the well-being of employees, and social contribution. While it may sound utopian and lofty, Vantone has long stated that its mission is 'to create an enterprise that could save the world, create wealth, and perfect the self.' Its basic principle in its business is not 'just do it to make money,' but 'do it to benefit society' by 'benefiting self and benefiting others.'

Wang of Vanke also began his entrepreneurial career with a similar idea (and has maintained this idea throughout his entire business career). In Vanke, young people are encouraged to develop their capability and apply their talents to benefit both the company and society. Tecsun's Employee Code of Conduct has sold more than half a million copies. It is hailed as the 'Management Bible for Chinese Enterprises.' This Code is a demonstration of founder/CEO Nie's concern for the quality of life of his employees. Nie created an employees' pension fund from his own income. Indeed, vowing even to auction off the company if necessary to save an employee's life, Tecsun once spent 6 million RMB to provide a cure for a sick employee. The value system of Tecsun to contribute to society and to create value for customers is also reflected in its pricing policy: it considers a profit margin of 15 %–20 % to be reasonable. If profits exceed 25 %, Nie considers it shows a disrespect for customers. Through this humble approach, the business model of Tecsun has been unbeatable by any other competitors in the market, making it unique and sustainable.

The three leaders further insisted on a *market focus and innovation for business sustainability*. They are cautious about relying on government relationships. Tecsun's Nie referred to the example of the once richest businessman in the Qing Dynasty, Xueyan Hu. Hu had a tragic end; his business empire collapsed when his good friend in the government, General Tso, passed away. Nie has therefore chosen to stay away from the government but instead has focused on a niche market segment in order to be the best. Tecsun's products are well positioned in the market and sustained by constant research and development (R&D). He has focused on both quality and cost, claiming that his houses offer twice the quality with a 30 % cheaper price. While the cost of raw materials has increased significantly in recent years, the price of Tecsun's homes has increased only once in 15 years—by 10 %. This low cost but high quality is sustained by R&D that absorbs the increased cost of raw materials.

Along the same lines, Wang from Vanke dedicates its real-estate business to residential development, in which it establishes sound branding, a good reputation and customer loyalty. Unlike its principal competitors who have expanded without much restriction, the focused strategy of Vanke allowed it to overcome the crisis when the government intervened and the market became strictly controlled. In a mature market, the only way to succeed is to introduce differentiation in the target segment. In this case, product quality is not enough. Vanke leads with innovation in the market, by providing post-sale service and the notion of 'good neighborhood.' To enhance customer satisfaction, the company engaged Gallup to conduct a survey of its customers. Employees' performance appraisal is related to the indicators in this customer satisfaction survey. For example, 'good neighborhood' is measured by how many other homeowners a homeowner knows, which symbolises a harmonious community. If the survey results show a low score on this item, the property manager is expected to organise social activities for the residential house owners, providing an opportunity for them to get to know each other and to build a better neighborhood and relationships. With the strong reputation of Vanke in the market, customers were willing to wait for their product launch to market in 2012 when the purchase was restricted.

Feng from Vantone considers diversification to be a common mistake that private enterprises make when they have their first success. Many private firms do not have the market capability to handle such diversification. Instead of relying on political connections or the capital market, Feng prefers to focus on product and service innovation to meet customers' demands. 'Being moral and creative' is the often emphasised principle that Feng promotes both within the company and in society. Vantone invests 3 % of its annual revenue in R&D. Vantone created a new concept of a three-dimensional city, a subversion of the traditional city model, transforming a psychological pattern.

With a market focus and a customer-oriented innovative business model, Vantone, Vanke and Tecsun stick with *humanist and simple management principles* to support their successful entrepreneurial paths. Known as the 'Property Thinker' in China, Feng from Vantone actively promotes ecological, humanist and technological moves in the real-estate industry. He emphasised several times in his interview that his management philosophy and principle is 'very simple: be moral and be creative.' This simplicity is reflected in the execution of the principle, 'not only keep it on paper—but do what you say.' Most of the company's other principles are extensions of this fundamental idea of simplicity. Being moral and maintaining value adherence, as in a religious organisation, is highly effective and with a low co-ordination cost. Being creative by introducing innovative products and services helps to differentiate the company in a highly competitive market. Sticking to these ideas and keeping it simple enhance efficiency in the implementation process. This is relevant because Chinese society and culture often emphasise complexity, including the usage of *guanxi* (interpersonal relations), *mianzi* (face) and *renqing* (human obligations). Despite the effectiveness of *guanxi* practices in certain business circumstances (Chen and Chen 2009; Chen et al. 2013; Chen et al. 2004; Zhang and Zhou 2015), *guanxi* also creates problems for management and business dealings, especially in the real-estate industry. For example, acquaintances may ask for discounts when purchasing properties. Therefore, Vantone applies 'the Stranger Principle' to maintain a fair system. According to this principle, employees are to treat all clients as important strangers, and to apply the rules universally and equitably with no favoritism.

Similarly, Wang from Vanke also appreciates the humanist concept and believes that the liberation of humanity is the ultimate goal of life. He advocates Western logical thinking and is very much against the Chinese traditional culture elements of *renqing* and *mianzi*. To simplify interpersonal relationships in the company, he firmly refuses to allow any of his related family members to work there, which he illustrated, during the interview, with an example of how he dismissed a cousin from the company. At the same time, he and his management team highly respect people and give them the chance to develop their potential; in addition, they promote tolerance as an important value. Even though many Chinese companies have expressed very good principles, claiming employees as their assets, in practice, they do not always adhere to these principles. In the case of Vantone and Vanke, however, it is the simplicity of their management philosophy and adherence to it that drive their continuous success and sustainable development.

'Do what you say' is also the way of Tecsun. The well-known Tecsun Code of Conduct has major effects on employees' behaviour by influencing their day-to-day work and life. It is practised effectively in the company, and people can see how it works, modelling respect and trust to oneself and others. Since all behavioural requirements are explicitly written and executed, it makes management, and life in general, simpler. The effectiveness of the rules also depends on whether the one who designs the code follows the same rules. In this case, Nie's act of spending a large amount of money to save the life of one of his employees provided a testimony that he really cares about his employees; he trusts and respects them.

Leadership in the Consumer Goods and Retail Industry: Branding with Innovation, Building Organisational Capability and Engaging in Constant Transformation

For the retail industry, we analysed the management thoughts and practices of three leaders: Ning Li (the Li-Ning Company), Qinghou Zong (the Wahaha Group), and Jianguo Wang (Kidswant). While the three companies are grouped under the umbrella of retail and consumption, the specific market in which each operates is very different: Li-Ning specialises in sports-related goods such as clothing and sporting equipment; Wahaha is involved principally in food and drink production and sales; and Kidswant offers integrated services and products for children from birth to 14 years and their families. Despite these differences, however, they share some similarities in their management philosophies and practices.

First, these three companies have a strong emphasis on *branding with innovation* as they operate in a highly cost-conscious market. The Li-Ning brand is well known in China, and is named after its founder Ning Li. His gymnastic accomplishments as an Olympic gold medallist earned him the admiration of the Chinese people. Currently, Li-Ning is a reputed sporting goods brand not only in China but also around the globe. The Li-Ning Company has a controlling interest in Double Happiness (China), a well-known brand of table-tennis-related sports products, and an alliance with the international company, Lotto (Italy), an established sports fashion brand.

Beyond branding, research and development (R&D) is also important for innovation in product development and quality improvement. Even though the company is positioned in a high-end segment of the industry, cost efficiency is critical, because to stay competitive needs a large volume of product sales. This large volume also means that a variation of several cents per unit may be related to a big difference in profit or loss. Further, the manufacturing base of the overall industry has been shifting gradually from the Four Asian Tigers to China, and now to Vietnam, as multinationals seek lower production costs.

The Wahaha Group has also been focusing on its economies of scale by growing market share and sales volume. The group has been spending 3 % of its revenue on R&D, a relatively high ratio for a company in the retail/consumer industry. It is engaging in three forms of innovation: (1) Improvement innovation, such as improving packaging to attract consumer purchases; (2) Imported innovation by purchasing advanced machinery from the West to reduce production costs and improve product quality (e.g. improving or creating new flavours); and (3) Independent innovation by developing new products that can increase pricing power in the market. With innovative ideas, high quality products and first-class marketing capabilities, Wahaha is now the strongest brand in the Chinese beverage industry, having earned a large market share, and it has begun to exploit this strong brand prestige by diversifying into the children's garments industry.

In the case of Kidswant, the parent company, Five Star Holdings, has extensive experience in building and managing brands in several industries. Kidswant CEO Wang identified a huge market, with 24 million babies born every year, and 360 million children aged from birth to 14 years old. Now that China allows urban couples who are single children themselves to have a second child, the population in this age group will become even larger. Wang observed that China had no brand dedicated to such a huge market. Today's Kidswant enjoys a strong reputation as a speciality kids' products and services chain store with an innovative business model. Innovation is encouraged strongly in all areas to improve efficiency and effectiveness. Employee rewards have been established for continuous innovation, with the ultimate objective of satisfying customers: innovations are focused on building a strong and close relationship with them. This requires not only creating customer needs but also listening to customer experiences. For example, the initial spacious and luxurious design of stores aimed at the high-end segment where Kidswant wanted to position the brand did not encourage customers to enter. After talking to customers, including having dinner with selected customers, Wang discovered that Chinese mothers are very price conscious regardless of whether they are rich or poor. A store with a spacious and luxurious design discouraged entry because customers presumed the products and services would be expensive. Responding to customer opinions, a modification in design successfully changed the flow of customers' visits. The offer of free services such as children's cultural events, experience-sharing sessions, expectant mother, new mother and grandparent clubs have also increased customer flow into the stores.

All three leaders claim that a company's success is not an individual effort, but a result of its overall *organisational capability* to create and serve customers' needs and, ultimately, to create and keep customers' loyalty to the company and the brand. Based on the efforts of all company employees through teamwork, high organisational capability was built up through the company's system in different areas, including a special emphasis on customer relationship management and sales network. Kidswant has an innovative business model that transforms their frontline store employees from salespersons to caretakers of customers. A strong customer relationship management culture has been instilled in the mindset of all employees in such a way that it forms an organisational capability oriented towards customer satisfaction. Customer satisfaction becomes the ultimate performance indicator for all levels of employees and managers, with specific measures in accordance with the company's current objectives and the job function of the employee. For example, the frontline employee's performance is assessed by the number of members in various clubs, the number of customers converted into club members, the amount of each transaction, and the sales amount per customer. Frontline employees are expected to provide a rapid response to resolve any customer issues, as they are in direct contact with customers. They can also make decisions on sales advertisements as they think appropriate without gaining approval from store managers. In this way, the services to customers are on time, flexible and effective. The function of managers is to serve the frontline employees and to enhance the employees' capability to satisfy customers' needs.

All three leaders talked of the importance of their reliance on their management teams and the strength of teamwork. They empower their management teams, give them autonomy, and help them with decision-making only when absolutely necessary. Zong from Wahaha admitted that his paternalistic management style could be a potential problem in the development of his subordinate managers, and has made an attempt to correct these mistakes. In this way, the company is not dependent on one single individual but on the overall organisational capability to improve managerial decision-making abilities.

Wahaha developed a creative method for collecting receivables which benefits both the company and the sales agents in the distribution network. At the beginning of every month, the first-level agents deposit money into an account that Wahaha uses to deduct the agents' payables. At the end of the month, Wahaha pays the agents 1 % interest on the deposit if they sell all the products. In this way, Wahaha ensures the collection of receivables, and agents earn interest on the deposit. This 12 % annual interest rate is higher than the profit margin of many industries. Wahaha demonstrates a high capacity to resolve the typical headache of collection in the retailing industry and distribution channels.

Li from the Li-Ning Company has also spoken on the necessity of team reliance for the success of an individual leader. While he personally participated in the first clothing design, the first factory construction, the first store's location selection and decoration, and the first advertisement's photography and design, he firmly believed that his dream of creating a first-class sports brand relies on a team of managers and employees to work together on that challenge. As with his success in the world of sport, he analogized leadership to the gymnastics technique of 'Four Arhat,' during which audiences may focus on the top person, but actually, without the support of the bottom three people, this position could never be achieved. To achieve the passion and mission of creating an international sports brand, Li is focusing on building a professional management team. With accumulated experience, technologies and capabilities, the Li-Ning Company has experienced a gradual shift from one-man decision-making and direct top-down process to a comprehensive and collective organisational decision-making process based on capability enhancement. Li has even said that a leader must not be too strong. If a leader is too powerful, his or her follower-managers will become too weak to make independent decisions. An overpowering leader may result in employees who are too careful and may deprive them of the opportunity to develop organisational capacity.

These three companies in the consumer goods industry, with retailing and distribution networks, engage in *constant transformations to adapt to the changing environment*, including their corporate culture. The Li-Ning Company undergoes constant transformation to keep pace with the market environment. Within five years of its founding, Li recognised the need to professionalise his company. He asked his family and teammates from his sports environment to leave the company. He saw this as a painful but necessary step to introduce professionalism and to give all employees the expectation of developing their careers in the company regardless of their origin or relationship with the founder. The determination to embrace changes has brought unceasing transformations to the organisation, making it more flexible and able to adapt to an increasingly demanding market.

Similarly, Wahaha has undergone a constantly changing process in its growth path. When it was still based in a small factory, Wahaha acquired another factory with 20 times more employees. The success of this acquisition and merger brought Wahaha a higher production capability, enabling it to satisfy the high demand from the market. Meanwhile, the company also transformed the culture of the acquired company, which was a state-owned enterprise (SOE). When Wahaha grew larger, hierarchical levels were added to the organisational structure to take on different responsibilities. Reporting directly to Zong were 18 functional heads of corporate services, 150 divisional general managers, the general sales managers in each province, and the head of R&D. He deliberately avoided having a position of vice general manager, to prevent conflict and competition between people. He learned this from noting the experiences of some SOEs that often have conflict between different coalitions. Another significant transformation in Wahaha is the adaptation of distribution channels and sales networks in order to keep up with environmental changes. At the beginning, nationally planned sales networks monopolised Chinese distribution channels, and these are the only possible channels for Wahaha. With China's reform and development of a market economy, wholesale markets emerged, and Wahaha turned to these, especially in rural areas. However, competition among wholesale markets was eventually so fierce that price became the most sensitive factor, allowing companies to enter and remain in the market. It was then that Wahaha decided to develop its own distribution network. The company grew from having one agency in a single district to one in every county, with each agency covering 200,000 to 300,000 of the population.

Constant transformation is also a characteristic of Kidswant. In this era, even a chain store cannot ignore the internet. By applying internet thinking to the retailing business, the business model of Kidswant became unique and innovative. The model was not imposed from the beginning, but instead has evolved and been updated constantly, to adapt to demands from the environment. This was done through reflection and interactions with stakeholders such as clients, employees, partners and even suppliers. The corporate culture was also changed in accordance with the transformation of the business model. The most influential change has been in the managers' attitudes, from functional power and activities to customer-oriented support activities, in which the frontline employees have become the real power executors to satisfy customers' needs and have been converted into virtual leaders for their specific events and activities.

Summary

We have identified the primary themes (i.e. management thought and associated leadership practices) for each industry, based on a thematic content analysis of the interview texts. In the first two steps of the thematic content analysis, our focus was on identifying the major themes among the firms within an industry. Three to four themes emerged for each industry, with a total of 14 themes across the four industries. Interestingly, all 14 themes seem to be relatively independent and capture unique management thoughts or leadership practices. In the third phase of analysis, we looked for potentially common themes across industries.

Comparison Across Industries

The major themes that emerge in an industry may or may not be unique to that industry. To identify potential commonalities and differences across industries, we applied these themes to the companies in the other three industries. Generally, there has been insufficient recognition of industry effects in organisational research, which could be a very important and influential contextual factor for these firms operating in different industries (Child 2015; Spender 1989).

Appendix 16.1 describes the procedure used in this cross-industry comparison. We organised the results of this comparative analysis into four groups, based on the extent of similarity among companies in the four industries on the 14 themes. The first group was 'General common themes across industries,' consisting of four themes that are strong in all four industries. The second group is 'Frequent common themes,' consisting of four themes that are absent from one or two companies across the four industries. The third group, 'Less frequent common themes,' consists of three themes that are absent from most of the companies across the four industries. The fourth group, 'Industry and company specific themes,' has three themes that are absent from more than four companies across industries while being strong in one industry. The results of this comparative analysis are presented in Table 16.4.

General common themes in management philosophy and leadership practices across industries

There are four common themes underlying successful entrepreneurship across the four industries: innovation, moral and ethical principles, market focus, and organisational capability. In Chap. 1, we described the difficult conditions for POEs, where entrepreneurs had to rely on their creativity to identify and cultivate sources of support. Given highly uncertain government policy and the hypercompetitive business environment, innovation is important for all businesses to enable them to stay alive, and to gain and sustain a competitive advantage. Innovation is necessary to create new products and approaches in each company's specific industry. Innovation is important for retaining talent (as emphasised by Chen of Taikang Life Insurance). Innovation can be carried out in different functions of the company and in different formats. For example, Taikang's nursing community for elderly people is an innovative market approach; Wahaha's collection method is an innovation in the enterprise's financial and cash management; and Alibaba's notion of an ecosystem is an innovative management system. Tecsun's constant technical innovation in products provides them with improved quality and reduced costs, along with a modest profit margin of between 15 % and 25 % that guarantees the sustainable development of the firm, but makes it less attractive for outsiders to enter this niche market.

Table 16.4 Comparison of themes on management philosophy and leadership practices between and across industries

	Themes	Finance industry	Technology industry	Real estate industry	Consumer industry
General common themes across industries	Innovation	**Strong**	Strong	Strong	Strong
	Moral and ethical principles	Strong	Strong	**Strong**	Strong
	Market focus	Strong	Strong	**Strong**	Strong
	Organisational capability	Strong	Strong	Strong	**Strong**
Frequent common themes across industries	Business sustainability	Strong	Strong	**Strong**	Weak
	Constant transformation	Strong	Strong	Moderate	**Strong**
	Humanistic management	Moderate	**Strong**	Strong	Moderate
	Dual systems	Moderate	**Strong**	Strong	Moderate
Less frequent common themes across industries	Branding	Moderate	Moderate	Moderate	**Strong**
	Risk management	**Strong**	Moderate	Strong	Weak
	Credibility and reputation	**Strong**	Moderate	Moderate	Moderate
Industry- and company-specific themes	Differential management	**Strong**	Weak	Weak	Weak
	Tolerance of mistakes	Weak	**Strong**	Moderate	Moderate
	Simplicity in management	Weak	Weak	**Strong**	Moderate

Notes:
Strong: When all the companies in the industry have this theme.
Moderate: When 2 out of 3, or 2 to 3 out of 4, of the companies in an industry have this theme.
Weak: When none or only one of the companies within an industry has this theme.
Bold text means that the theme has been deduced from analysing the original interview texts to be salient in all the companies within an industry.

All industries exhibit a strong market focus, as highlighted by leaders in the real estate industry. Similarly, organisational capability is salient in the consumer industry but is also present in other industries. While market focus is commonly referred to as an orientation towards identifying market needs and customer demand, there is variation in interpreting the content of organisational capability. Some firms refer to it as a concept for general development (Wahaha, Fosun), while other firms refer to employees' capability or abilities (China Merchants Bank), or to teamwork as an important element of overall organisational capability (Li-Ning).

A fourth common theme is moral and ethical principles. While initially this theme was salient in the real-estate industry, it became clear that it is important in all four industries. The real estate industry emphasises moral and ethical values because of the widespread corrupt social practices in the sector, but such values are also part of the corporate culture in other enterprises. Ma's demands for moral correctness among Alibaba's employees, and Zong's call for Wahaha employees to serve the big family and beyond are examples in another industry. Similarly, Ma of China Merchants Bank states that social responsibility is its main concern along with customers and employees.

Apart from the example of the leaders in the real estate industry, the theme of moral and ethical principles is always mentioned implicitly in leaders' discourse in the other industries. This principle is often taken for granted as being relevant in all industries, thus it may not be seen as a distinctive principle to maintain a competitive advantage. The irony is that keeping this focus may set these firms apart from the rest, and hence contribute to their success.

Frequent common themes across industries

The themes of business sustainability, constant transformation, a humanist approach, and dual systems (using both hardware—systems and structures, and software—culture and values) are also common across the industries though to a lesser extent than the general common themes. Business sustainability in terms of long-term survival is indicated in different forms and different languages in all the industries apart from consumer and retailing. Despite successful performances and their sustainable development with their current business models and management structure, Zong at Wahaha and Wang at Kidswant did not express any concern about this issue in their interview discourses. The management philosophy and principles follow the dominant logic of branding with innovation, organisational capability and constant transformation, which contain the underlying logic to sustain the business in the long run. The absence of the theme of business sustainability in Zong's interview is probably because of the company's strong market share and penetration, so that business sustainability is taken for granted at the present time. In the case of Wang, Kidswant is in a period of full expansion with its innovative business model, which would account for the relatively low concern about sustainability. Nonetheless, business sustainability underlies well-balanced management and business models.

Constant transformation is another frequent theme across industries. Since all enterprises have co-evolved with the economic development of China to some extent, the development of business has gone through different transformations, as described in Chap. 1 on the evolution of Chinese private enterprises. There does not appear to be a consistent pattern between industry type and the evolutionary phase of POEs—there are firms in all industries founded in different evolutionary phases. It is interesting that three enterprises were founded in 1992, the year of Deng Xiaoping's southern visit (i.e. Fosun, HC360 and Tecsun) and a further one (Vantone) was founded immediately after them, in 1993. These enterprises' leaders were called the 'generation of 1992,' who took full advantage of the take-off of economic development during this period. Kidswant was the most recent enterprise, and its business model takes advantage of the internet in managing customer relationships by capitalising on the information in its membership databases. Kidswant's parent company, Five Star Holdings, was founded in the second phase of rapid growth, and has gone through a number of corporate changes in adapting to the dynamic business environment. Despite Kidswant being in a relatively early stage of development, it has also experienced different corporate transformations and restructuring to adjust itself to develop the company's current successful business model. The only leader who did not mention a constant transformation specifically is Nie at Tecsun Homes. In his interview, Nie conveyed that Tecsun has been successful since the very start in the niche home market, and they have had no real competitors since then. Building on a management philosophy of moral and ethical principles, market focus for business sustainability, and a simple management system, Nie has built a sustainable business model of adding higher value to customers at lower cost. This provided a stable and reasonable profit margin from the outset.

All the leaders spoke of the importance of a strong corporate culture, but each interpreted corporate culture from a different angle and with different terms of emphasis. At Vanke, culture extends to customers and suppliers, since it consists of values and norms that guide behaviours. Ma of China Merchants Bank believes that when a culture is practised and takes root, rules are implemented automatically. Related to the strong emphasis on corporate cultures, a humanist management approach has been articulated by many leaders across the industries. However, it is denominated in different ways, including a family style (Wahaha, Lenovo), entrepreneurial spirit (Neusoft), co-operation (Fosun), transparency (Tecsun), teamwork (Li-Ning) or an ownership culture (HC360.com). Essentially, the humanist approach in management philosophy is to set rules for the deployment of people's talents and encourage a people-oriented decision-making process. Being human is the most crucial factor; performance is just the result of realising the abilities and potential of people (Liang of Fosun).

A third frequent theme common across industries is a dual system—the concurrent use of both structure and culture—which is closely related to maintaining balanced and sustainable development. With a strong corporate culture and a humanist approach to management, delegation, empowerment, openness, transparency, trust and many other related values are introduced into the corporations. However, this may not work appropriately if it is not supported by a strictly controlled structure and system, though the latter may or may not be salient or emphasised in the corporate culture development process. Leaders in the technology industry explicitly discussed this theme, and Wang of Kidswant, a consumer/retail industry, also developed a strong data monitoring and central control system to support the culture of strong customer relationships. Nie of Tecsun found it problematic if people were unsupervised, noting that the task of supervisors is first control and then reward. Taikang has specific procedures for risk-control and problem resolution. This dual system focus, however, is not consistently present among the companies in the financial services and consumer/retail industries.

Less frequent themes common across industries, and industry- and company-specific themes

There is no consistent expression across the companies and industries of the themes of branding, risk management, credibility and reputation. While branding is very important to firms in the consumer/retail industry, it is only moderately important in the other three industries. Risk management also received inconsistent attention among the 13 leaders. Perception of risk may reflect a cognitive style of the leader but also may be a sensitivity requirement in a specific industry. Risk management is highly salient in the financial services and real estate development industries. It is easy to understand why the theme of credibility is particularly important in the financial industry. Loss of credibility could lead to instant liquidity problem and potential bankruptcy for a consumer-oriented bank such as the CMB.

There are a few themes that are either industry- or company-specific. Differential management is important to the finance industry, tolerance of mistakes to the companies in the technology industry, and simplicity in management in the real estate industry. These three themes are not shared among the companies in the other three industries. In Spender's (1989: 6) inductive case studies on three industries in the UK, the author highlights the specific industrial knowledge base, which experienced managers in the industry take as professional common sense, to deal with specific uncertainties characteristic of that industry. Hence both general common attributes and industry-specific attributes are worthy of attention for further understanding leaderships of entrepreneurial success in industries.

A Concentric Model of Chinese Private-Firm Leadership

Through the attribute content analysis, we confirmed four personal attributes that describe these successful private-firm leaders, the four Ds; and generated a new personal attribute for Chinese private leaders: reflective thinking. Through the thematic content analysis, we identified 14 management thoughts and associated leadership practices (we use the term 'management principles' to capture this idea) with eight of them common across the 13 firms and six unique to an industry or a firm. Integrating the five personal attributes and eight of the 14 management principles, we developed a concentric model of Chinese private-firm leadership, which is shown graphically in Fig. 16.1.

At the centre of this concentric model is the personal attribute of reflective thinking. We consider this attribute to be fundamental, since it

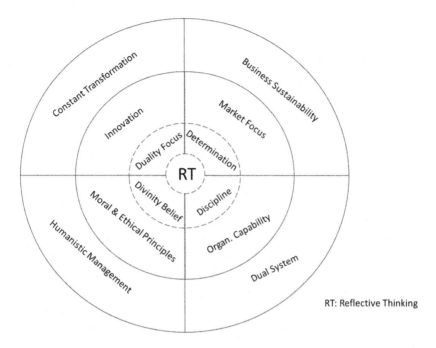

Fig. 16.1   A concentric model of Chinese private firm leadership

enables the leaders to reflect on and learn from their own personal experiences, from the observation of others' successes and failures, and reading the works of great thinkers and leaders who changed the world in their lifetimes: reflective thinkers learn from their own and others' experiences. Mintzberg (1994) considers reflective thinking to be an important managerial approach to learning. It plays a crucial role in the development of novel strategies through internalising, understanding and synthesising information.

The next circle consists of the four D attributes. These personal attributes relate to the cognitive processing of information about the firm and the environment (duality focus), priorities and decisions guided by an inner compass of integrity and compassion (divinity belief), development of systems that ensure consistency and professionalism (discipline), and the indefatigable pursuit of their dreams and aspirations (determination). These personal attributes influence management thoughts and practices.

The two outer rings capture the four general management principles (third ring), and four frequent common management principles (fourth or outer ring). Not included in this model are the six unique or less frequent common management principles of branding, risk management, credibility and reputation, differential management, tolerance of mistakes, and simplicity in management. Some of these may be terms used uniquely by a particular industry (e.g. risk and differential management in the finance industry) or by a leader (e.g. simplicity), but it is more likely they are part of the other principles in the third and fourth circles (e.g. tolerance of mistakes may be part of humanist management, and branding as part of market focus).

The four common themes suggest that Chinese private enterprises and their leaders have relied to a great extent on innovation constantly to transform themselves, to upgrade their capabilities, to adapt to the changing environment, and to sustain success over time. During this process, the determination of the leader has been fundamental for persistence and commitment to their businesses despite the low odds of success in the extremely trying conditions prevailing in the first two decades of economic reform.

There seems to be an apparent conflict between some of the management principles. For example, moral and ethical principles may not be compatible with a market focus; a commitment to ethical principles may compromise short-term market performance. However, in the long term, it earns the company a reputation as a firm with integrity. The attention to both market orientation and business sustainability, and to moral and ethical principles, is a unique combination that distinguishes these firms from others that use convenient (and perhaps less ethical) means to achieve short-term business success. The moral and ethical principles of management as well as the humanist approach to managing people at organisational level reflects the attribute of divinity belief by the leaders. Leaders with a high level of divinity belief are attentive to people's development, are humble, express gratitude, follow the Golden Rule and so on. On the other hand, organisational capability builds on a foundation of discipline, another important attribute of the leaders who emphasise responsibility, teamwork and co-operation, structure, rules, norms and systems. Organisational capability includes competences in both the technical domain (e.g. knowledge of marketing, operations, finance, etc.) and the social domain (e.g. teamwork, communication, conflict resolution, etc.). This is the dual system idea mentioned by many leaders. From these, we can see the close connection between the personal attributes of the leaders and the management principles they emphasise in leading their firms.

It is evident from this model that China is still in the stage of 'founders/leaders make firms,' because what is done at the firm level is essentially an extension of the founders' personal values and attributes. We wonder if this concentric model will still apply when these firms become more mature over time. There are two possible scenarios. One possible scenario is that the model will apply as long as the leaders of private firms continue to have a prominent influence. However, once the leadership changes, the values and operations of the firm will probably also change. Another possibility is that the influence of the leaders will be stronger when the firm becomes more mature, because the values and the systems would have taken firm root by then. Under this scenario, these private firms will evolve to enter the stage of 'firms make leaders;' that is, outstanding companies will be able to identify and select the right people to take the leadership position. Because of the deeply instilled values and structural systems embedded in the company culture, these people will become great leaders. We speculate that both scenarios are plausible predictions of future successful leaders and firms in China.

Looking to the Future: The Entrepreneurial Spirit

Nee and Opper (2012) considered the development of mutual support networks among entrepreneurs to be a major reason for their success, even though the entrepreneurs in their study have modest backgrounds, most were wage earners before they became entrepreneurs, and they were no more risk takers than the average person. Their study was a large random sample of entrepreneurs who had varying degree of success in business. Our sample is a group of highly successful entrepreneurs who are considered to be industry leaders. As a group, they demonstrate a strong entrepreneurial spirit with the capacity for reflective thinking and learning, and the quality of being visionary and inspiring. This entrepreneurial spirit also includes the attributes of determination, discipline, duality focus and divinity belief. This entrepreneurial spirit might be one of the driving factors that sustain the companies' successes and fuel the rising power of Chinese enterprises, in both domestic and global markets. Liu of Neusoft said, 'If Western multinationals' managers still retained the entrepreneurial spirit they had at their start-up in the US when they entered the Chinese emerging market, there would have been no chance for Chinese indigenous enterprises to compete, survive and grow.' This remark raises the question of whether the identified leadership attributes and management principles are unique to China. Does this entrepreneurial spirit reflect the developmental stage of a firm, or of the demands of the economic/social/political context? Would leaders of mature companies or founders of new enterprises in the developed Western context (e.g. USA or Europe) have a similarly high level of this entrepreneurial spirit in comparison with Chinese private enterprises?

Mintzberg (1994) observed that Western CEOs are often drawn into short-term operational issues at the expense of spending time on reflection and strategic planning. Perhaps one of the distinguishing attributes of successful Chinese leaders is that they take time to reflect and share their learning with their teams. Though certainly some cultural and institutional differences (e.g. Confucianism and Legalism) may account for different characteristics of leadership between Chinese private enterprises and Western corporations. A different company or industrial life-cycles may also determine management styles and practices.

Moreover, the phase of economic development in their country of origin may play a role. For example, Ramamurti (2012) asked whether significant differences found in emerging markets' multinationals are a result of their positions in different economic development cycles or caused by deep-rooted cultural idiosyncrasies? The high rate of economic development in China has provided an incredible opportunity for Chinese enterprises, but not all of them have succeeded. Based on the results of our study of 13 extraordinary private-firm leaders, we suggest that those who have the entrepreneurial spirit, embodied in the attributes of reflective thinking, divinity belief, duality focus, strong determination and extraordinary discipline, could accomplish their mission and reach their vision of entrepreneurial success. Further comparison with other types of enterprises in China such as public-sector and foreign-owned firms may be desirable to distinguish unique features from Chinese private entrepreneurs and other types.

The concentric model is derived primarily from the experiences and perspectives of the successful leaders who were interviewed. A logical question is whether this model would apply to entrepreneurs who are not as successful as those studied. We propose that leaders lacking some of the five personal attributes, or firms placing a low or no emphasis on some of the eight management principles, would have a decreased chance of entrepreneurial success. This conjecture should be tested in future research. Comparative studies using samples of private firms with different levels of business success would be necessary before we could prescribe the ideas for practice or use this model in entrepreneurial or leadership education. We could question the validity of a model based on a sample of 13 leaders in total, and three to four firms in each industry. Is this sample size from which derive a set of leadership attributes and management principles relevant to all successful private enterprises? Further, would this model apply to leaders and firms in the state sector, with different institutional environments and different performance expectations? We think some of the attributes would be equally important (e.g. discipline, duality focus), and some of the management principles may also apply (e.g. market focus, innovation, organisational capability). However, state-sector leaders generally have less freedom to introduce large-scale or fundamental changes in their government-controlled firms. We encourage future research to further develop, extend or confirm the current concentric model with additional firms in different industries, different ownership statuses, different regions, or different stages of development.

A further issue to consider is the future leadership of these firms. The challenges continue to exist on the path towards long-term sustainability. Most of these private enterprises are still in their first generation of leadership. Some of them have arranged succession plans, and some have handed over the management to their children or to professional management. But most of the leaders are still keeping an eye on the business and have not completely exited the stage of management. The continuity of the entrepreneurial spirit of these successful firms will be tested when the second or further generation of leaders takes over the helm of these private enterprises.

In conclusion, this book is devoted to understanding leadership in successful Chinese private firms. The Chinese economic reforms opened the door for private individuals to pursue business opportunities that were closed to them for the first 30 years of the current regime. Though the initial conditions were harsh, those with a strong determination were able to overcome the extremely inhospitable environment and lead their firms to success. A review of the published research on Chinese leadership revealed the attributes of discipline, duality focus and divinity belief in addition to strong determination. Through in-depth interviews and qualitative analysis, we confirmed these important personal attributes and revealed an additional one: reflective thinking. These five attributes characterise these successful entrepreneur/founders. The thoughts and perspectives of the 13 leaders provided us with a rich understanding of their management philosophies and practices. We offer a concentric model as a starting point in understanding the unique qualities of the leaders and the unique management practices of their firms. Assuming that this concentric model will stand the test of future research, it will have immense value in elevating the quality of management in private firms, which has been and will continue to be the primary engine propelling the growth of the largest economy in the world.

Appendix 16.1

Data analysis: Attribute content analysis and thematic content analysis

We carried out qualitative analysis in two parts. The first is analysis based on the four leadership attributes described in Chap. 2, identified from the published large-sample research on Chinese firms, including both private and state-owned firms. The four attributes (4 Ds) are Determination, Divinity belief, Discipline and Duality focus. The confirmatory content analysis method was adopted in coding the transcribed data, following a similar step employed by Tsui, Wang and Xin (2006b). The purpose was to confirm the presence of these four attributes and to identify potentially new attributes that had not emerged during the qualitative analysis of the published sample studies.

The second is an open coding process of the interview data with no previously established framework, in order to identify the principal elements in the interviewees' management philosophy, the development process of their thought, and those elements that might have driven the superior performance of their enterprises. The thematic content analysis method was used, following the step established by Boyatzis' (1998) data-driven coding process. The purpose of this phase of analysis was to identify the generic pattern of leadership's management philosophy and principle in managing business in China's dynamic and changing environment.

Attribute content analysis

One author of this book first gave training on the coding to two early-stage researchers with a Chinese cultural background, providing definitions of the four attributes and suggested keywords or key phrases to identify each attribute (see Table 16.2). The principal unit of analysis was the paragraph. The coding instruction consisted of the following procedure. The two coders read Chap. 2 to gain a very clear understanding of the meaning of 'the four Ds.' They then reviewed the keywords associated with each attribute. After gaining some familiarity with the definitions of the four attributes, they both read an interview from beginning to end twice to become very familiar with it. They then performed the coding, paragraph by paragraph. For each paragraph, they had to decide if its content captured any of the attributes. Sometimes, a leader might digress, but it is important to focus on the main idea and avoid being distracted by the digression. If the digression captures an attribute, then the coder can assign a second attribute. In other words, the coder can assign each paragraph up to two, but no more than two, attributes. If a new concept is warranted, it would be coded as a separate attribute. Once the coding was finished, the coding results were entered into an Excel sheet, and the results of the two coders' work were compared. Differences were discussed and resolved if possible. Finally, we calculated the proportion (percentage) of each attribute mentioned against the total number of paragraphs in the interview text.

One interview was selected for training and practice coding. After the two coders had completed the coding, one author of this book discussed each paragraph with them. After two rounds of coding, comparing, discussing the differences and recoding, the agreement between the third round of recoding was greater than 80 % on all the attributes.

After the second round of coding the first interview, a new attribute, 'reflective thinking,' was identified. The coding of the remaining 12 interviews was based on the five attributes, the four Ds plus reflective thinking.

For the other 12 interviews, the two coders carried out their coding independently. After completing the coding of three interviews, the two coders met with the researcher to discuss any ambiguous content and whether they had identified any new concepts. Most of the new concepts appeared in one interview only (e.g. paternalism) and did not appear in the others. If possible, we incorporated such unique concepts into existing attributes. For example, paternalism was integrated into divinity belief when it referred to benevolence or morality, and to discipline when it referred to authoritativeness. The agreement between the two coders for the five attributes ranged from 81 % to 94 %, indicating a high level of agreement.

Thematic content analysis

Another author of this book carried out an independent thematic content analysis based on a data-driven method (Boyatzis 1998), without bearing any previous theoretical framework in mind during the coding process. Following Table 16.1, the 13 companies and leaders were divided into four industries: banking, insurance and financial investment; technology and e-commerce; construction and real estate; and consumer goods and retailing. Codes and themes were identified, again based on the paragraph as the unit of analysis.

The coding process included three phases: the first was theme identification within each company; the second phase was to compare the identified themes across companies within the same industry. Third, the salient themes of each industry were applied to the companies in the other three industries to make a cross-industry comparison. A second co-author of this book participated in the third phase of coding to enhance reliability. An initial agreement of cross-industry theme comparison reached 78.6 %, higher than the required level of 75 % (Boyatzis 1998). Reasoning and discussion on these differences took place between the two authors, with a final agreement reached of 100 %.

References

Boyatzis, R. E. (1998). *Thematic analysis and code development: Transforming qualitative information.* Thousand Oaks, CA: Sage.

Chen, C.-C. & Lee, Y.-T. (Eds.) (2008). *Leadership and management in China: Philosophies, theories and practices.* Cambridge: Cambridge University Press.

Chen, C. C., & Chen, X. P. (2009). Negative externalities of close *guanxi* within organizations. *Asia Pacific Journal of Management, 26*(1), 37–53.

Chen, C. C., Chen, Y. R., & Xin, K. (2004). *Guanxi* practices and trust in management: A procedural justice perspective. *Organization Science, 15*(2), 200–209.

Chen, C. C., Chen, X. P., & Huang, S. (2013). Chinese *guanxi*: An integrative review and new directions for future research. *Management and Organization Review, 9*(1), 167–207.

Child, J. (2015). Cross-industry differences in the business models of export-active SMEs. Working paper, University of Birmingham, UK.

Conklin, W. (2012). *Strategies for developing higher-order thinking skills.* Huntington Beach (CA): Shell Education.

Fang, T. (2012). Yin Yang: A new perspective on Culture. *Management and Organization Review, 8*(1), 25–50.

Hu, H. (2015). Fosun seals two major European deals. Retrieved April 19, 2015, Chinadaily.com.cn. 20 March, http://www.chinadaily.com.cn/world/cn_eu/2015-03/20/content_19869332.htm

Jing, R. R., & Van de Ven, A. H. (2014). A Yin–Yang model of organizational change: The case of chengdu bus group. *Management and Organization Review, 10*(1), 29–54.

Li, X., & Liang, X. (2015). A Confucian social model of political appointments among Chinese private entrepreneurs. *Academy of Management Journal, 58*(2), 592–617.

Ma, L., & Tsui, A. S. (2015). Traditional Chinese philosophy and contemporary leadership. *The Leadership Quarterly, 26*(1), 13–24.

Mintzberg, H. (1994). The fall and rise of strategic planning. *Harvard Business Review* (January–February): 107–114.

Nee, V., & Opper, S. (2012). *Capitalism from below: Market and institutional change in China.* Cambridge, MA: Harvard University Press.

Ou, A. Y., Tsui, A. S., Kinicki, A. J., Waldman, D. A., Xiao, Z., & Song, L. J. (2014). Humble chief executive officers' connections to top management team integration and middle managers' responses. *Administrative Science Quarterly, 59*(1), 34–72.

Peng, S. Z., Xu, Y. F., & Lin, Q. X. (2009). *The great revolution of Shanzhai economy: The innovation comes from imitation.* Taipei, Taiwan: Showwe Information Co. Ltd.

Ramamurti, R. (2012). What is really different about emerging market multinationals? *Global Strategy Journal, 2*(1), 41–47.

Robinson, B.A. (2016). Using the golden rile(s) to teach religious tolerance and understanding. Ontario Consultants on Religious Tolerance, 2016-Feb-04, retrieved July 25, 2016 from http://www.religioustolerance.org/teaching%20 religious%20tolerance%20with%20the%20golden%20rule.htm

Rodgers, C. (2002). Defining reflection: Another look at John Dewey and reflective thinking. *Teachers College Record, 104*(4): 842–866.

Spender, J.-C. (1989). *Industry recipes: An enquiry into the nature and source of managerial judgement.* Oxford, UK/Cambridge, MA: Basil Blackwell.

Tsui, A. S., Wang, H., & Xin, K. R. (2006b). Organizational culture in China: An analysis of culture dimensions and culture types. *Management and Organization Review, 2*(3), 345–376.

Zhang, X., Chen, C., Liu, L. A., & Liu, X. (2008). Chinese traditions and Western theories: Influences on business leaders in China. In C.-C. Chen & Y.-T. Lee (Eds.), *Leadership and management in China: Philosophies, theories and practices.* Cambridge: Cambridge University Press.

Zhang, P. & Xu C. (2014). Long-term Trends Reshape China's Talent Landscape, HR Connect Asia Pacific, Retrieved May 30, 2015, http://www.aon.com/ apac/human-resources/thought-leadership/asia-connect/2014-vol7-issue3/ china-talent-landscape.jsp

Zhang, Y., & Zhou, Y. (2015). *The source of innovation in China: Highly innovative systems.* London: Palgrave Macmillan.

Index

Note: Page numbers with "n" denote footnotes.